FORBIDDEN FRIENDSHIPS

STUDIES IN THE HISTORY OF SEXUALITY

Judith Brown and Guido Ruggiero, *General Editors*

IMMODEST ACTS
The Life of a Lesbian Nun in Renaissance Italy
Judith Brown

THE EVOLUTION OF WOMEN'S ASYLUMS SINCE 1500
From Refuges for Ex-Prostitutes
to Shelters for Battered Women
Sherrill Cohen

AUTHORITY AND SEXUALITY IN EARLY MODERN BURGUNDY (1550–1730)
James R. Farr

SEXUALITY IN THE CONFESSIONAL
A Sacrament Profaned
Stephen Haliczer

COMMON WOMEN
Prostitution and Sexuality in Medieval England
Ruth Mazo Karras

HOMOSEXUALITY IN MODERN FRANCE
edited by Jeffrey Merrick and Bryant T. Ragan, Jr.

THE IMAGE OF MAN
The Creation of Modern Masculinity
George L. Mosse

MASCULINITY AND MALE CODES OF HONOR IN MODERN FRANCE
Robert A. Nye

FORBIDDEN FRIENDSHIPS
Homosexuality and Male Culture in Renaissance Florence
Michael Rocke

THE BOUNDARIES OF EROS
Sex Crime and Sexuality in Renaissance Venice
Guido Ruggiero

THE MYSTERIOUS DEATH OF MARY ROGERS
Sex and Culture in Nineteenth-Century New York
Amy Gilman Srebnick

Further volumes are in preparation

FORBIDDEN FRIENDSHIPS

HOMOSEXUALITY AND MALE CULTURE IN RENAISSANCE FLORENCE

Michael Rocke

OXFORD UNIVERSITY PRESS
New York Oxford

Oxford University Press

Oxford New York
Athens Auckland Bangkok Bogotá Bombay
Buenos Aires Calcutta Cape Town Dar es Salaam
Delhi Florence Hong Kong Istanbul Karachi
Kuala Lumpur Madras Madrid Melbourne
Mexico City Nairobi Paris Singapore
Taipei Tokyo Toronto Warsaw

and associated companies in
Berlin Ibadan

First published in 1996 by Oxford University Press, Inc.
198 Madison Avenue, New York, New York 10016

First issued as an Oxford University Press paperback, 1997

Library of Congress Cataloging-in-Publication Data
Rocke, Michael.
Forbidden friendships : homosexuality and male culture in
Renaissance Florence / Michael Rocke.
p. cm.—(Studies in the history of sexuality)
Originally presented as the author's thesis (Ph.D.—State
University of New York at Binghamton).
Includes bibliographical references and index.
ISBN 0-19-506975-7
ISBN 0-19-512292-5 (pbk.)
1. Homosexuality, Male—Italy—Florence—History.
2. Sodomy—Italy—Florence—History.
3. Gay men—Italy—Florence—History. 4. Renaissance—Italy—Florence.
5. Homophobia—Italy—Florence—History. I. Title. II. Series.
HQ76.3.I8F57 1996
306.76'69'0945'51—dc20 95-35068

1 3 5 7 9 8 6 4 2

Printed in the United States of America
on acid-free paper

To Richard C. Trexler

Acknowledgments

One of the pleasures of coming to the end of a long project such as this book has turned out to be is having the opportunity to express my deep appreciation to the individuals and institutions that, in various ways, made its completion possible. This work began, what seems like a lifetime ago, as a Ph.D. dissertation at the State University of New York at Binghamton. I am grateful to the members of the Department of History, both faculty and fellow graduate students, who lent their enthusiasm and support to a project that, at the time I began it, was still considered somewhat unorthodox and professionally risky. Funding for initial research in Italy was furnished by the department and by a grant from the Fulbright-Hays Commission. Additional postdoctoral support was offered through generous fellowships from the National Endowment for the Humanities and from the Harvard University Center for Italian Renaissance Studies at the Villa I Tatti. I wish to extend a special word of gratitude to Walter Kaiser, director of I Tatti, and to the marvelous group of fellows and colleagues at the center for the intellectual stimulus they provided and for their personal warmth and good humor during a memorable year of residence there. A grant from the Department of Humanities and Social Sciences of Syracuse University in Florence helped defray incidental expenses related to the book. My research was facilitated by the skilled and helpful staffs of the Archivio di Stato in Florence, and of other archives and libraries both in this and other cities. To all I am deeply grateful.

A number of friends and colleagues read all or parts of the manuscript at various stages in its preparation, and their insights, suggestions, and other forms of assistance have enriched this book in many ways. My thanks go to Susannah Baxendale, Alan Bray, Alison Brown, Stanley Chojnacki, Marc Deramaix, Mario Di Cesare, Nick Eckstein, Marcello Fantoni, Deborah Hertz, Ralph Hexter, Bill Kent, Dale Kent, Christiane Klapisch-Zuber, David Leavitt, Anthony Molho, Jonathan Nelson, Jean Quataert, Michel Rey, Thomas Roche, Dennis Romano, David Rosenthal, Sharon Strocchia, and Randolph Trumbach. Richard Boardman assisted me with the figures. I especially wish to thank Judith Brown and Guido Ruggiero, co-editors of the History of Sexuality series of Oxford University Press, for their careful readings of the manuscript and their helpful editorial and critical comments, as well as for their unflagging support. A warm circle of Florentine friends allowed me to develop an unusually intimate perspective on local culture and social relations, and among them I am particularly grateful to Riccardo Spinelli.

I took up this book at the suggestion and under the stimulating guidance of my mentor and friend, Dick Trexler. His unfailing encouragement and critical spirit, his dedication to scholarship, and his courage in the face of unexpected adversities have been a constant inspiration. As a small and inadequate token of my enduring appreciation, this book is dedicated to him.

Contents

FORBIDDEN FRIENDSHIPS

Florentine youths swimming in the Arno, as depicted in Domenico Cresti (called Passignano), *Bathers at San Niccolò* (1600). (Private collection)

Introduction: Florence and Sodomy

"In the whole world I believe there are no two sins more abominable than those that prevail among the Florentines," commented Pope Gregory XI in 1376. "The first is their usury and infidelity," he specified, alluding to the moneylending activities of international merchant-bankers that had made Florence one of the most prosperous and important cities in Europe. "The second," he continued, hedging his words with care, "is so abominable that I dare not mention it."[1] The sin the pope deftly avoided naming, using a standard euphemism for what the late medieval Church deemed the most evil and dangerous of carnal vices, was of course the "unspeakable" practice of sodomy. Although this term could denote a wide range of prohibited sexual behaviors deemed "contrary to nature"—so called because they did not lead to procreation, the sole "natural" purpose of sex according to Catholic dogma—it usually referred to sex between males.[2]

In underlining the predilection of Florentines for sodomy, Gregory was only lending the weight of papal authority to what was, in effect, a commonplace in the late Middle Ages and the Renaissance. If all of Italy was so defiled that it could be considered the "mother" of sodomy, as Bernardino of Siena complained in a sermon in the 1420s (voicing an opinion that other Europeans would hold for centuries to come), the notoriety of Florence far surpassed that of all other cities on the Italian peninsula.[3] The sexual renown of Florentine males was remarked on by both local and foreign chroniclers, condemned by preachers, deplored by concerned citizens, derided—or occasionally admired—by writers and poets. Their erotic tastes were so well known even north of the Alps that in contemporary Germany "to sodomize" was popularly dubbed *florenzen* and a "sodomite," a *Florenzer*.[4]

Florentines owed part of their widespread infamy, according to another distinguished preacher, Girolamo Savonarola, to the fact that they "talk[ed] and chatter[ed] so much about this vice"; many evidently did not consider it so evil that they avoided its very mention.[5] Echoes of their chatter resound in the exceptional number and variety of Florentine and Tuscan literary sources on homoerotic themes, with a range of moral stances. Following the illustrious precedents of Dante's *Divine Comedy*—in which sodomites, duly placed in hell, are paradoxically accorded great respect and affection (*Inferno*, cantos XV and XVI)—and Boccaccio's ambivalently witty tale in the *Decameron* (V, 10) of the sodomite Pietro di Vinciolo, in the fifteenth and sixteenth centuries the subjects of love and sex between males abound in local novelle, anecdotes, and poems, ranging from biting satires to humanistic elegies, from condemnatory religious lauds to amatory verse.[6] Sodomy also furnishes a basic key to the complex code of sexual word plays that permeate the entire genre of "burlesque" poetry and bawdy carnival songs.[7] Verses on same-sex love were apparently even set to music. Although seldom enforced, laws dating from the early fourteenth century, and reinforced in the fifteenth, made it a crime, punishable by fines, to compose or sing songs about "such a disgraceful and impious act."[8] In Florence, the sin so terrible that it was not to be pronounced could not, in fact, be kept quiet.

If many Florentines not only named the "unmentionable vice" but also commonly practiced it, this does not mean their community as a whole approved of sodomy or accepted it without misgivings. The passion for the classical world that characterized the elite culture of the Italian Renaissance did not, as has sometimes been uncritically assumed, revive some mythical Greek ethos in which sexual relations between males enjoyed widespread and unqualified tolerance. Quite the contrary. Many people, following the teachings of the Church, continued to regard sodomy as a serious and potentially destructive sin, and everywhere it remained a crime punishable by severe penalties, including death by burning. Especially in the fifteenth century, the ruling class of the Republic of Florence identified this sexual practice as one of the city's most pressing moral and social problems. To confront it, the government in 1432 created an innovative judiciary magistracy solely to pursue and prosecute sodomy. The evocatively titled Office of the Night (Ufficiali di notte) was probably the first and certainly one of the few criminal institutions with this specific competency in the history of Europe.

During its seventy-year tenure from 1432 to 1502, this magistracy, with the limited participation of other courts, carried out the most extensive and systematic persecution of homosexual activity in any premodern city. Yet in doing so the courts also brought to light a thriving and multifaceted sexual culture that was solidly integrated into the broader male world of Florence. In this small city of around only 40,000 inhabitants, every year during roughly the last four decades of the fifteenth century an average of some 400 people were implicated and 55 to 60 condemned for homosexual relations. Throughout the entire period corresponding to the duration of the Office of the Night, it can be estimated that as many as 17,000 individuals or more were incriminated at least once for sodomy, with close to 3,000 convicted.[9]

These extraordinary figures, partial though they certainly are, begin to furnish a sense of the dimensions, the vitality, and the contradictory significance of homosexuality in the sexual and social life of Florence. Sodomy was ostensibly the most dreaded and evil of sexual sins, and was among the most rigorously controlled of crimes; yet in the later fifteenth century, the majority of local males at least once during their lifetimes were officially incriminated for engaging in homosexual relations. The thriving world to which these numbers point, however, has remained obscured from historical view, virtually unexplored and uncharted. This book seeks to recover that world, to map out its social and spatial parameters, and to restore it to its legitimate place as an integral part of the society and culture of late medieval and Renaissance Florence.

Scholars have long been familiar with the prominence that contemporaries ascribed to sodomy both in Florence and throughout Italy, and few have doubted that homosexual activity there was common. Until quite recently, however, the general prejudice against homosexuality, combined with an old ideological tendency to downplay features of this society thought unseemly for the edifying portrayal of the Renaissance as the noble cradle of modern civilization, effectively inhibited its study. Professional historians usually followed Pope Gregory's pious example and avoided acknowledging the topic altogether, or at best touched on it superficially, frequently with embarrassed apologies if not open disdain. Even the respected English scholar John Addington Symonds, himself homosexual and author of a pioneering apologetic on homosexuality in Greece, succumbed to prevailing moral judgments and self-censorship in his highly regarded *Renaissance in Italy* (1875–1886). He wrote dismissively that the subject of homosexuality here "belongs rather to the science of psychopathy than to the chronicle of vulgar lusts. . . . [The Italians'] immorality was nearer that of devils than of beasts."[10] Such attitudes and rhetorical tactics helped to perpetuate the stigmatization of homosexuality as an object of historical inquiry and to ensure that it remained firmly consigned, despite the wealth of contrary evidence, to the margins of representations of Renaissance society and culture.

In recent years, these barriers have to a large extent been broken down, as the visibility and acceptance of homosexuality have grown substantially and as social historians of late medieval and early modern Italy have devoted new attention to such diverse subjects as ritual, social networks, violence, criminality, prostitution, and gender, as well as to the history of the family and of subordinate groups such as women, children, and the laboring classes. Even before research and scholarly debate on homosexuality in premodern Europe began to flourish in the late 1970s and the 1980s,[11] studies by prominent historians, such as David Herlihy's on Florentine demography and family life and Richard Trexler's on boys' confraternities and state-sponsored prostitution, were overcoming the traditional reticence and raising new questions about the importance of homosexuality in Florence.[12] Since then, a number of specific works have appeared on the subject of sodomy—above all, its practice in the leading republics of Venice and, more recently, Florence. Both of these cities mounted unprecedented efforts in the fifteenth century to police this "vice," and both uncovered thriving undergrounds of homosexual activity.[13] Only further research will show whether other cities or regions shared Venetian and Florentine preoccupations or developed similar sexual cultures. Nonetheless, these studies have opened a window onto a sexual universe the significance of which was far from marginal in several of the most dynamic urban societies of Renaissance Italy. Nowhere was this more the case than in Florence, where the "problem" of sodomy assumed exceptional dimensions and where homosexual behavior, as this book seeks to demonstrate, constituted a pervasive and integral aspect of male sexual experience, of the construction of masculine gender identity, and of forms of sociability.

Homosexuality was a deep-rooted and prominent feature of life in Florence, yet it also encountered vigorous opposition and was subjected to intensive persecution. While many Florentines may have defended sodomy as a venerable native "custom," as Bernardino of Siena despaired in a 1425 sermon, it was a custom that especially in the fifteenth century also evoked great hostility and that the government took extraordinary measures to control.[14] These endeavors to "root out" sodomy, the optimistic goal set in the founding law of the Office of the Night, failed resoundingly, for it resisted and thrived. But inevitably, the efforts of public authorities and the local community to regulate sodomy constitute a fundamental part of the story of homosexuality in Florence, not only because of their broad social impact, or because of the new light such efforts cast on attitudes toward sex and on the administration of justice, but also because they unearthed a remarkable amount of sexual activity. Consequently, the most abundant evidence on homosexual behavior derives from the city's unusually rich judiciary records.

One of the aims of this book, then, is to study the evolution, substance, and contexts of government policy toward sodomy from the early fourteenth to the mid-sixteenth century and, where feasible or most useful, to analyze how the courts operated and how legal prescriptions were enforced. In the organization of this work, public responses to sodomy constitute the main subject of parts I and III, which frame an in-depth investigation in part II of the organization of homosexual behavior and its relation to the broader male culture. Chronologically this study is loosely delimited, on one end, by the earliest extant republican laws against sodomy, from the 1320s, and, on the other, by a law of 1542, the first and apparently only edict on this sexual practice enacted after the fall of the Republic (1532) and during the two-century reign of the Medici dukes and, later, grand dukes. The long period these laws delineate allows one fully to grasp and assess, within the compact cultural and political context of the Florentine Republic, the variety and magnitude of the many changes in public policy regarding sodomy.[15]

Beyond their close association with the classic period of the Republic, the boundaries these prescriptive norms stake out, though artificial, are in some respects quite significant. In particular, they help distinguish the contours of the first wide-scale persecution of homosexual behavior in European history, carried out by Florence and other Italian cities. The statutes of the 1320s embodied and codified the increasing intolerance and hostility toward homosexual activity that came to characterize all of European society in the thirteenth and early fourteenth centuries.[16] By this time Florence, like a number of other cities in Italy, had established the most severe penalties for sodomy, including castration and death by burning.[17] With minor variations, these edicts remained the legal standard for this crime for nearly a century, until the transformation in its policing introduced with the Office of the Night in 1432. Following this innovation, sodomy for long became one of the most turbulent issues in the spectrum of Florentine criminal justice and public morality. In the 110 years between 1432 and 1542, the city's legislative councils passed no fewer than seventeen substantive reforms in the penalties prescribed for sodomy or in the institutions designated to pursue and prosecute it. At the same time, convictions proliferated to the astonishing levels noted previously. By the middle of the sixteenth century, however, in Florence, as in Venice, this sustained wave of official concern over sodomy subsided considerably. The law of 1542 in effect marked its conclusion. The harsh punishments it ordained would endure unaltered for centuries, and this immobility, together with the subsequent conspicuous decline in condemnations, indicate that sodomy was no longer the compelling issue, at least for the new ducal state, that it had been in the not very distant past.

While this broad chronological scope has served to reveal long-term shifts in the orientation of public policy toward sodomy, the seventy years of the operation of the Office of the Night, from 1432 to 1502, constitute this book's central focus. This magistracy, whose creation was the result of heated agitation during the preceding three decades for more energetic repression (examined in chapter 1), formed the institutional cornerstone of governmental efforts to police sodomy until the beginning of the sixteenth century. Its role and impact were decisive. Through a combination of intensified surveillance, rapid summary proceedings, and radical innovations in penalties, the Office of the Night transformed the control of sodomy in Florence. With this magistracy, the government abandoned the previous judiciary praxis of harsh but sporadic punishment directed mainly against violent same-sex rape or child abuse. Instead, it initiated a new regime of routine and fairly mild disciplining of mainly consensual homosexual relations, which were much more diffused. Through this institution, the local ruling class deployed a "benign," but perhaps more effective, strategy of managing sodomy, the political acumen of which was attested by the thousands of prosecutions and convictions that were its most tangible results.

The critical importance of the Office of the Night for the policing of sex in itself makes it worthy of special attention. Its organization and operations are studied in chapter 2. Yet its significance also derives from the extraordinarily rich documentation it produced, a large amount of which has survived. In general, court records, as students of sexuality in medieval and early modern Europe have commonly pointed out, have serious limitations and pose particular problems of methodology and interpretation for anyone attempting to recover the historical character and meaning of sexual behavior.[18] Generated by instruments of repression and social discipline, judiciary records by their very nature normally represent the vision of only a hegemonic social and political elite. In addition, they are often fragmentary, superficial, or inaccurate; the details they record may correspond more to a need to observe proper bureaucratic form than to a concern to describe what really happened; the individuals or behaviors they document may not be representative of the broader universe of sexual activity. Furthermore—an especially crucial drawback in this case—prosecutions for sodomy focus relentlessly on sexual acts and usually reveal little about motives or about how the participants or the society around them interpreted these actions. To varying degrees, all these points are also applicable to the records of the Office of the Night.

Despite their inevitable shortcomings, however, these records are exceptional, and this book draws heavily on them. Indeed, they probably constitute one of the richest sources in premodern Europe for the reconstruction of homosexual experience and of a single community's responses toward it, as well as for the study of its practical control at the judiciary level. The Night Officers' extant registers contain information on some 10,000 persons incriminated for homosexual activity and on their various sexual relations. The degree to which this multitude reliably represents the universe of homosexual activity is, of course, a problem that requires careful assessment. Not all were found guilty, but many who by their own admission engaged in sodomy were not convicted, and most accusations were not even pursued. It would be perilous indeed to imagine that the Night Officers' proceedings compose some kind of "census" of homosexuality in the city. Nonetheless, the sheer number of people involved enhances the likelihood that a portrayal drawn through judicious analysis will be fairly true to life.

It is not only its massiveness, but also the quality and unusual range of the evidence it yields, that makes this source so remarkable, however. Unlike most other court records of the period, these document the entire procedural course of cases that came to the Night Officers' attention, from denunciations to interrogations to sentences, permitting a systematic analysis of the officials' operations and effectiveness in enforcing the law. The records also contain an uncommon wealth of biographical data on incriminated individuals and detailed information on sexual relations, allowing one to assemble nuanced profiles of the participants and to sketch thickly textured descriptions of their sexual behavior. Finally, the Night Officers' registers are nearly unique, at least for this city, in that they conserve hundreds of the accusations that Florentines made against people they claimed engaged in sodomy. The prime interest of these denunciations lies less in the dubious veracity of informers' specific claims (though many were confirmed) than in the values and mentalities they inadvertently reveal and in the lively personal and social context they restore to the more mechanical images produced by the court. They offer a rare opportunity to grasp how common people in one late medieval city viewed and interpreted homosexual behavior—often in ways that differed from the dominant and canonical representations of church and state—in the everyday life of their community.

In determining how best to exploit the evidence in these records, I was guided by two main considerations. The first was my desire to reconstruct, as far as possible, a comprehensive panorama of homosexuality in Florence, one that would highlight the norms and conventions of sexual behavior, collective portraits of participants, and the general features of the policing of sodomy, but that would also be capable of capturing nuances and variety. This encouraged a systematic and inclusive study rather than an impressionistic one based on isolated cases, an approach, in other words, that could reveal both the ordinary and the exceptional in homosexual experience. The second consideration was more practical, having to do with the nature and organization of the records. As a summary court, the Office of the Night was designed, in effect, to expedite the prosecution of large numbers of individuals, a function the officials had to carry out especially in the century's second half, when several hundred suspects came to their attention every year. Their written proceedings reflect the rapid "processing" of people accused. Confessions were recorded by the magistracy's notaries in a fairly regular format that evidently corresponded to standard questions intended both to disclose the identity of the person's sexual partner(s) and to draw out a skeletal description of the times, places, and "mechanics" of their sexual encounters. The information noted is usually brief and straightforward; the entire account often consists of no more than a few lines of text for each partner indicated. As a consequence, despite the thousands of homosexual relations these records catalogue, they contain few personal stories, few descriptive narratives that by themselves might evoke the world of love and sex between males. A comprehensive picture, therefore, has literally to be pieced together from myriad fragments.

For these reasons, an analysis that made use of computerized technologies became almost inevitable. Although fraught with difficulties, a quantitative study of the documentation from the Night Officers' records proved to be the most efficient and fruitful means to recompose the various parts of trial proceedings, to reveal general patterns of behavior and the social composition of discrete groups, and to reconstitute the case histories of individuals over time. It did not seem necessary, however, to analyze all the available data; but while a small sample could have answered some of my questions, inconsistencies in the material increased the risk of distortion, and persons who engaged habitually in sodomy would have been harder to detect. I therefore took an intermediate course, opting for a detailed computerized analysis of all the extant procedural records during a limited period—the last twenty-four years of the Night Officers' tenure, from 1478 to 1502—combined with a more conventional study of the information from the remainder of their registers. Records survive for seventeen of these twenty-four years and document 4,062 individuals incriminated for homosexual sodomy. This group, examined from various perspectives, provides the documentary core for much of this book.

Throughout this study I have also tried to draw on other evidence that might help to verify or to cast additional light on the findings that result from the analysis of the Night Officers' documentation. The period covered by the main survey was selected in part because its early years coincide with the Florentine fiscal census, or *catasto*, of 1480, which provides information not only on the wealth of local households but also on their composition.[19] Of the 1,131 persons who were incriminated between 1478 and 1483, I have identified 183 in this census. This sample serves as a control group for questions relating to the ages of males who engaged in homosexual activity and provides additional perspectives on their relative wealth and, above all, their marital status. I have also utilized a survey of prosecutions for sodomy from 1478 to 1502 by the Eight of Watch (Otto di guardia), the city's central criminal magistracy. This tribunal played a more limited role than the Office of the Night in the policing of sodomy, but it was still quite important, functioning as a compliment to the latter's operations. The Eight's records furnish added evidence from the several hundred cases it tried, as well as a critical point of comparison with the documentation of the Night Officers. In addition to the abundant judiciary materials, wherever possible I have drawn on a wide array of less public and prescriptive sources, including sermons, the records of religious confraternities, local chronicles and histories, family journals, private letters, collections of anecdotes and witticisms, and various forms of literature and poetry. Together this unparalleled body of sources offers a wide variety of perspectives for recovering the world of homosexual experience in late medieval Florence.

Although sex between males was a common and integral feature of daily life in this city, it formed part of a universe of experience and values that differed substantially from our own. In the first place, the culture of late medieval and early modern Italy was not one in which men were clearly separated into the categories of "homosexuals" and "heterosexuals." In our own culture, it has become common to imagine sexuality largely in terms of a polar opposition between heterosexuality and homosexuality. Most people are thought to fall more or less neatly into either one category or the other, but even the alternative "bisexuality" derives its sense from its hybrid position somewhere between these two extremes. Moreover, the notion that a person's homosexuality or heterosexuality profoundly defines one's personality and identity is nowadays taken practically for granted, and these categories are accepted with little questioning as part of some timeless and natural order. Yet much research by anthropologists, historians, and social theorists over the past few decades has shown, to the contrary, that such a way of construing erotic experience and sentiment is a very recent development, and one that is closely tied to the specific evolution of the contemporary Western world. Other cultures and people in other historical periods have conceived and organized sexuality in quite different ways.[20] Italians of the Renaissance would have found current beliefs about homosexuality and heterosexuality as well as much of modern sexual experience foreign indeed, and if one is to comprehend the nature and significance of homosexual behavior in this particular historical context, the parochialism of our own notions must be recognized and these cultural differences accorded their proper due.[21] A discussion of terminology will begin to demonstrate these claims, and to illustrate how certain terms will be used in this book.

People of the Middle Ages and early modern period lacked the words to convey the precise equivalents of the current "homosexuality" as a distinct category of erotic experience or "homosexual" as a person or a sexual identity. These words were coined only in the late nineteenth century, and only filtered slowly and unevenly into popular use. The terms "sodomy" and "sodomite," which were standard in the religious and juridical language of premodern Europe for conveying same-sex relations, might however seem to work as substitutes, for in some contexts they appear to have much the same meanings. From the thirteenth century on, most theologians, following the great classificatory work of Thomas Aquinas, defined sodomy as comprehending all sexual acts between persons of the same sex, whether male with male or female with female. On the basis of the gender of the sexual partners, therefore, some religious authorities differentiated sodomy from the other carnal vices "against nature," which included intercourse with animals, masturbation, and nonreproductive coitus between the opposite sexes.[22]

As these words were employed outside the subtle field of moral theology, however, "sodomy" was not strictly synonymous with "homosexuality," nor was "sodomite" the equivalent of the noun "homosexual." The tidy scholastic categories of "unnatural" practices collapsed in secular legal and judicial contexts, and apparently in popular conceptions as well. When governments came to persecute sodomy, with growing intensity from the thirteenth century on, both "homosexual" and certain "heterosexual" acts fell indistinctly into this category of sexual crime, and in some places other varieties of vice *contra naturam* did too. Florentine laws against sodomy, for example, often specified that they applied equally to both males and females. Presumably these formulations included sexual relations between women, but in all cases the context strongly suggests that they referred instead to erotic acts deemed "contrary to nature" either between males or between males and females. The latter was in fact the only form of sex involving women that lay people occasionally denounced and the courts pursued as sodomy.[23] In other words, it was certain sexual acts alone that denoted sodomy, not (as in prevailing theological views) the gender of the persons who practiced them. Correspondingly, a sodomite was not, strictly speaking, a person who engaged in sex with members of his (or her) own biological gender; the sodomite, that is, was not a homosexual, but a person who committed the various acts defined as sodomy.

This generally being the case, when Florentines used the words "sodomy" and "sodomite" in a generic way they probably had sexual relations between males in mind, since these were by far the most common and conspicuous, and aroused the greatest public concern. These terms, then, unless otherwise qualified, will be used with this sense throughout this book. Yet despite the high visibility of male homosexual activity, people in this society had no way to distinguish verbally, either with these official designations or with other vernacular terms, a man who engaged in sex with males from one who committed precisely the same acts with women, whether occasionally or even exclusively. Generally speaking, both were simply called sodomites. In a culture such as ours, accustomed to classifying people on the primary basis of the gender of their sex partners as homosexual, bisexual, or heterosexual, this apparent lack of clarity may be surprising, if not disconcerting. Today it would hardly be doubted that such men, regardless of the specific practices they engage in, possess fundamentally divergent sexual natures and should accordingly be labeled in ways that convey that difference. Although late medieval Italians, in contrast, might well have recognized that a man's tastes or habits inclined him toward one sex or the other, or both, they evidently did not find this compelling grounds on which to organize their understanding and representation of sexuality.[24]

It is not only the absence of conceptual categories based on sexual object choice that distinguishes how people in this culture experienced and comprehended sex between males, however. As discussed in chapter 3, certain social and cultural conventions quite unlike those prevailing today governed the physical expression of homosexual acts and shaped their meanings in significant ways. The evidence shows beyond much doubt that in Florence, and probably elsewhere as well, sodomy between males normally assumed a hierarchical form that would now be called "pederasty" (though this term, too, was virtually absent from the otherwise rich local sexual lexicon). Homosexual relations, that is, were usually characterized by a disparity in the age of the two partners and by a correspondingly rigid adherence to culturally prescribed roles in sexual intercourse. Normally men over the age of eighteen took the so-called active role in sex with a passive teenage adolescent. Relations in which roles were exchanged or reversed were rare and occurred almost solely between adolescents, while sex between mature men was, with very few exceptions, unknown. These patterns situate homosexual behavior in Florence firmly within an age-graded model that had ancient roots throughout the Mediterranean world and would prevail in Europe until at least the eighteenth century, when most research indicates that new forms and conceptions of homosexuality first began to appear.[25]

Although Florentines showed little concern about distinguishing sharply between "heterosexuals" and "homosexuals," they were very alert to the oppositions in sexual roles in homosexual behavior and to the conventional links between these roles and age. These distinctions figure prominently in the formal representations of sodomy in law and trial proceedings as well as in the descriptions and vernacular terminology found in popular literature and denunciations. Violations of the expected norms evoked the indignant or harsh reactions of both courts and community. A central argument of this book is that these conventions and their proper observance mattered so greatly to Florentines because, as their own expressions and images reveal, they were tightly bound up in the culture's notions of what it meant to be male. The oppositions of age and role inherent in sodomy, as it was lived and conceived, not only helped delineate the contours of successive biological and social stages in males' lives, from adolescence to youth and adulthood, but also played a related and significant part in the fashioning of masculine gender identity, as people commonly construed the active–passive sexual roles in terms of such value-laden dichotomies as masculinity and femininity, dominance and submission, honor and shame. The "active" and usually penetrating role substantially conformed to the behaviors and ideals that were defined as virile, and consequently a man's sexual relations with a boy, when enacted within these conventions, did not call into question his status as a "normal" and masculine male. To take the "passive" role in sex with a male, however, was deemed "feminine" and dishonorable, but since this role was in effect limited to the biological period of adolescence it was only a temporary wayward turn on a boy's path to full-fledged manhood. The restriction of the "womanly" role to adolescents actually permitted *all* mature men to engage in sex with boys without jeapordizing their "manly" gender identity.

The conventions that defined sodomy and the meanings ascribed to them, therefore, represent specific ways of conceptualizing and experiencing sex between males that current sexual classifications and terminology fail to capture and convey adequately. The men and boys who are the subject of this book engaged in what today would be cast indiscriminately as "homosexuality," and on this basis they would probably be considered—and in other studies of late medieval Italy are often called—"homosexuals," or at most the more fashionable "bisexuals." One might point out that the application of such reductive labels to people in this distant society is, in the best of cases, a blind leap of faith, even more so when the evidence consists, as it frequently does, of a conviction for a single homosexual act. For how can it be assumed that this embraces the full range of someone's affective and erotic experiences? More important, these terms at once evoke sexual subjectivities that would have meant little to Florentines themselves, and collapse distinctions and obscure nuances of meaning to which they assigned vital importance. The different conceptual boundaries that delineated their sexual landscape emerge clearly in the specific way they employed "sodomite," which will be followed throughout this book. While this term, as mentioned earlier, included both a man who had sex with boys and a man who engaged in the same illicit sexual acts with women, it virtually never included their "passive" partners of either sex. Not all who engaged in homosexual activity, therefore, were considered sodomites, but only those who took the dominant, "active" role. According to this schema, men who sodomized boys and men who penetrated women had more of a common character and identity than did two males who coupled sexually, whose physical union normally embodied unbridgeable distinctions of age, sexual role, and ascribed gender values.

The social and cultural conventions outlined here also played important roles in shaping other aspects of homosexual experience that are central to the concerns of this book. Chapter 4 reassembles the social profiles of men and boys implicated in sodomy in the later fifteenth century. The composite portraits that emerge not only show that homosexual activity flourished at all levels of Florentine society, from humble textile workers and artisans to members of the great banking and commercial families that formed the local patriciate, but also reinforce the argument that it had little relationship to current notions of more or less fixed sexual categories and identities. To a considerable extent, in fact, sodomy was associated with different stages or situations in the life course of local males. David Herlihy was the first historian to suggest that the sexual debauchery—including the "abominable vice"—for which this city was infamous was related in part to local marriage patterns, especially the unusually late age of marriage for men, around thirty or thirty-one on average, and to the resulting profusion of youthful bachelors. According to fiscal censuses of 1427 and 1480, only about one of every four youths between the ages of eighteen and thirty-two was or had been married.[26] Moreover, a large proportion of Florentine men, some 12 percent of those who survived to around the age of fifty, probably never took a wife. This study demonstrates that those most frequently incriminated for sodomy were indeed adolescents and unmarried youths below marriageable age and, to a lesser degree, older bachelors. For most males, homosexual relations represented a fairly common form of sexual solace and companionship during the prolonged years of adolescence and bachelorhood before taking a wife, as the majority sooner or later probably did, even though marriage did not definitively exclude the sexual pursuit of boys. Other evidence further suggests that while vast numbers of local males engaged in sexual relations with other males, most did so only sporadically or over relatively brief periods of time. Only a small group of "habitual" sodomites, mainly older unmarried men, can be identified who pursued relations with boys throughout a considerable part of their adult lives. Men's homosexual behavior, however intense or engaging it may have been, did not constitute a permanently "deviant" condition, but was, for most, an occasional or temporary transgression that did not preclude sex with women either concurrently or during other periods of their lives.

Homosexual activity thus formed part, at one time or another and with varying significance and degrees of involvement, of the life experience of very many Florentine males of the late Middle Ages and Renaissance. Despite the pervasiveness of sodomy, however, the ethnographic account of the organization and character of homosexual behavior developed in chapter 5 suggests that this sexual underground did not constitute a separate world or a truly distinctive "subculture." Both casual sexual encounters and more durable relationships occurred or evolved in largely familiar, everyday social contexts, and were tightly insinuated into other typical forms of male sociability, from the camaraderie of gangs of youths or the bonds of work and neighborhood to relations between patrons and clients or the sodalities of kin and friendship networks. Sodomy was one of the many strands that composed the fabric of male experience, one that not only grew out of established social bonds and patterns of collective life but also contributed in creative ways to fashioning and reinforcing them.

Homosexuality was deeply integrated into that cluster of social structures, gender values, and forms of aggregation that together helped constitute male culture in Florence. It was this profound penetration of the male world that, in turn, made the regulation of sodomy there such a peculiarly volatile and problematic issue. The control of homosexual behavior as well as the ethos of same-sex relations themselves were part and parcel of the tensions that animated the social, cultural, and political ferment of one of the premier cities of the Renaissance during a period that was among the most dynamic and celebrated of its history. The changes that transformed public life in Florence—the decline of a corporative "popular" regime based on guilds and its substitution with an oligarchy of the merchant-banking elite in the late fourteenth century; the ascendancy of the Medici in the 1430s and the subsequent sixty years of their quasi-princely hegemony; the revival of republicanism in the 1490s and the holy terror of Savonarola; the restoration of the Medici in 1512; the definitive fall of the Republic in 1532 and the installation of a duchy under Medicean rule—all had significant consequences as well for the policing of sodomy. Shifts in the forms and equilibriums of power produced, almost as an inevitable consequence, a continual reelaboration of the public strategies and means for managing and containing homosexual behavior. By the same token, however, homosexuality and its control can serve as a kind of prism for illuminating the structures and exercise of power. In this way, the restoration of homosexual behavior to its proper place as an integral part of Florentine life seeks not only to throw new light on the history of sexuality in one late medieval Italian setting, but also to open fresh perspectives on the society, politics, and culture of Renaissance Florence.

PART I

1

Making Problems: Preoccupations and Controversy over Sodomy in the Early Fifteenth Century

> Those marvelous competitions of fencing, tournaments, and high jousts are no longer furiously performed for women; he who best can, now does his shows for young lads.
>
> Domenico of Prato (1389–1432?)[1]

Domenico of Prato, a notary and rather old-fashioned poet from a small town near Florence, depicted this evocative scenario of men competing fiercely for the attentions of boys in a poem he composed "in opprobrium of sodomy" probably in the 1410s or 1420s. Not content to follow the divinely ordained example of Adam and Eve, he lamented, men were abandoning "just matrimony" to pursue this "filthy infamy," and "it seems that blessed is he who most satiates himself." According to the poet, the love of men for boys was so widespread, and not only in Florence, that it no longer troubled anyone. Now more than ever before, as he put it, everyone visited the seductive lands of Sodom and Gomorrah.

Whether the erotic desires of Florentine men were undergoing the dramatic transformation Domenico of Prato imagined is hard to determine. But the preoccupations his verses manifest expressed well a current of fear and anxiety over sodomy that had been gaining force in his society since the beginning of the fifteenth century. A sense of urgency about the "abominable vice" troubled a generation of civic leaders and moralists, producing, over three decades, numerous laws against it and leading in 1432 to the creation of the Office of the Night, the special commission charged with policing sodomy.

To be sure, sodomy was not the sole moral and sexual concern of the governors of Florence in this period. The disorderly excesses of prostitution and the sacrilege of sex with nuns, among other aspects of public morality, also fell subject to tighter regulation in what amounted to a vast, if piecemeal, governmental program to reform and discipline the community's morals and behaviors. But of all the carnal sins it was sodomy, thought to flout not only the edicts of God and man but also the very laws of nature, that most came to embody the evils and uncertainties of an imperfect world and to evoke the terror of divine vengeance. Voicing such fears in a law of 1418, the government proclaimed its desire "to root out the vice of the Sodomites and Gomorrhans, contrary to nature itself, for which the anger of the omnipotent God is incited in terrible judgment not only against the sons of men, but against the country and against inanimate objects."[2] An exemplary passage from a sentence that the recently instituted Night Officers pronounced against a sodomite in 1436 catalogued the universal ills that sodomy was believed to incarnate and affirmed the safe-guarding function its repression was intended to serve. Sodomy was so evil and offended God so grievously, it was said, that God declared sodomites sinners against nature and rebels from his mercy, and damned them to the eternal flames. The diligent exercise of justice against such wicked ones, however, helped appease the divine essence and stay his wrath. "In this way," the officials sweepingly asserted, "the city and its upright citizens may be freed from all commotion, wars ended, plague abolished, enemy plots curbed, and cities turned toward good government and praiseworthy conduct."[3]

Sodomy certainly acquired a portentous rhetorical meaning in the early fifteenth century, with its control acclaimed as a sort of panacea for society's ills. Yet on close examination, the official response to this "vice" was not as coherent or resolute as such extravagant claims and the various laws against it imply. Marked by hesitation, bland or failed initiatives, and apparent divisions within the regime, the troublesome issue of how to control sodomy effectively dragged on unresolved for thirty years before the creation of the special magistracy in 1432. These discordant responses played a large role in determining the radical innovations adopted at that time, and provide a telling indicator of the problematic nature of sodomy in Florence.

Traditional Controls

The institution of the Office of the Night marked a decisive turning point in the policing of sodomy, culminating a thirty-year period of agitation and legislative measures aimed at rendering its control more incisive. Yet long before the creation of this magistracy, sodomy had been an extremely serious offense. Since at least the late thirteenth century—the century when growing hostility toward homosexual activity was being codified across Europe—sodomy had shared the legal status of murder, repeated theft, and counterfeiting as an "atrocious crime" (*enorme delictum*).[4] A study of prescriptive norms and judiciary practice regarding sodomy before the founding of the Night Officers helps to illuminate the clamor for reform and to explain the nature of the sweeping changes introduced with the new magistracy.

Before 1432 the surveillance and punishment of sodomy fell indiscriminately to the city's three main tribunals: the podestà, the capitano del popolo, and the esecutore degli ordinamenti di giustizia. According to the statutes of the podestà of 1325, both his court and that of the capitano were responsible for investigating evidence of sodomy in the city at least once every month, proceeding either ex officio—that is, on the court's own initiative—or in response to denunciations. In the latter case, informers' identities were to be kept secret, and if a conviction were handed down they were to receive a reward of half of any fine levied.[5]

Florentine law prescribed harsh punishments for sodomy and for facilitating it in any way, though penalties changed considerably over the course of the fourteenth and early fifteenth centuries. The earliest surviving legislation, the fragmentary statutes of the podestà of 1284, lacks penalties for sodomy but reveals indirectly that it was punishable at least by exile.[6] By 1325, when new statutes were redacted, penalties were severe. This code prescribed castration for a man found to have sodomized a boy; boys aged fourteen to eighteen who allowed someone to sodomize them were to be fined 100 lire, and those under fourteen fined 50 lire or flogged nude through the city.[7] The last punishment was stipulated as well for women over fourteen (presumably this refers to females sodomized by males, not to sexual relations between women). These statutes also drew a sharp distinction between the persons just mentioned and *trapassi* or *malandrini*, evidently foreign vagabonds or common criminals, who forced Florentine boys to commit sodomy with them. The latter were treated in a separate rubric seething with fiery rhetoric and images that are completely lacking in the first rubric, which seems to refer only to residents. Unlike others caught sodomizing, such foreigners found abusing local boys could be caught and beaten by people of the community without fear of penalty, tortured by the authorities and, if found guilty, burned to death.

Already by this time, the Commune had also attempted to extend its controls over the social and urban environment thought to foster sodomy. The 1325 statutes set a fine of 500 lire for pimps or intermediaries, for men who enticed boys by offering them money or gifts for sex, and even for fathers who persuaded or allowed their sons to commit sodomy. The house or building where sodomy was committed with the owner's permission, or simply his knowledge, was to be burned down. If a man was found in a garden or an edifice with a boy unrelated to him, in circumstances deemed suspicious, he could be fined 500 lire merely on the presumption of his evil intentions. This code prescribed a fine of 10 lire even for composing or singing poems or songs about sodomy, which authorities evidently feared might help popularize the practice. Following a typical medieval assumption that rich foods and sensuality went hand in hand, the statutes of the capitano (1322–1325) forbade innkeepers to serve a long list of delicacies and sweets, because they were said to attract "many boys and men" who might fall into vice and "perpetrate wicked sins that are abominable before God and men," clearly meaning sodomy. Innkeepers also had to deny entrance to *malandrini* or *trapassi* and to any boy with them; if they allowed anyone to commit sodomy in their establishment, it was to be burned to the ground.[8]

A new law in 1365 increased and made more arbitrary many of these penalties, for unknown reasons; the law's preamble cites only the usual fear of divine wrath erupting against the city.[9] Dropping the distinction between *trapassi* or *malandrini* and other offenders, this law mandated that anyone who committed sodomy, whether "active" or "passive," or who facilitated it in any way, could be burned to death. The podestà, however, retained wide discretion to apply this penalty depending on the "age, quality, and condition" of the persons involved. The one exception was for "passive" minors under the age of eighteen, who could not be executed under any circumstances; their punishment was left to the court's choice and could even be waived altogether. For a man who sodomized someone against his will or who aided a violent sexual assault, the law unconditionally prescribed death by burning, while the victim was to be absolved. Harsh penalties were also set for attempted sodomy, ranging from fines or corporal punishment to execution if the perpetrator used violence.

Moreover, the 1365 law included new measures to facilitate the identification of suspects and to encourage confessions. For example, if a boy under eighteen who had been sodomized, or a close relative, voluntarily revealed his sexual relations before he was denounced or arrested, then he was not to be punished, a strong incentive for him to implicate his partners. Traditional standards of proof were also lowered, the normal tax on accusations was abolished, and a reward was assured to informers even when the courts levied nonmonetary penalties. Finally, this law gave judges exceptionally broad authority to torture persons accused or suspected of sodomy.

The wide-ranging norms contained in the laws of the fourteenth century imply that homosexual activity was fairly common, for they suggest that male prostitution existed, that fathers sometimes promoted their sons' trysts, that innkeepers and property-owners often accommodated them, that people sang and wrote of sodomy's pleasures, and that any encounter between nonrelated men and boys could be suspect. These laws also give an impression of tight surveillance and unrelenting repression of sodomy. But a study of how the courts prosecuted sodomy, rather than of prescriptive norms, provides a different picture. Despite the seemingly broad surveillance, the harsh rhetoric and penalties, and evidence that sodomy was rather commonplace, convictions were both infrequent and limited in scope.

Although a full survey of the massive extant judiciary records is impossible, several samples point to similar conclusions. First, up through the early fifteenth century the courts, which normally pursued sodomy ex officio, handed down very few convictions. Often they condemned no one for this crime in any given year or even in several consecutive years, as at least two studies found.[10] Another survey, for the years 1352 to 1355 and 1380 to 1383, documented respectively eight and five convictions.[11] My own study of all extant court sentences from 1390 to 1410 located thirty-three persons convicted in cases involving sodomy, including ten for attempted sodomy only, and in twelve of these twenty-one years there were no condemnations at all.[12] As will be discussed later, it was in these years around the turn of the century that new concerns over sodomy appeared, and in fact half of the convictions followed calls in 1403 and 1404 for rigorous repression. Except for this brief reaction, sodomy failed to attract much attention from the courts in Florence, a situation analogous to that of fourteenth-century Venice.[13]

Second, if prosecution was infrequent, the character of the sexual activity the courts pursued was also highly circumscribed. Most often, these cases dealt with homosexual rape or other assaults, with sodomy perpetrated on young children, or with men who committed serious crimes in addition to sodomy; few individuals were condemned in this period for what might be considered, on the basis of the descriptions provided, consensual or noncoercive sexual relations alone. In sufficiently documented cases involving fifty-six persons condemned for sodomy or related crimes between 1348 and 1432, the year the Office of the Night was created, over three-quarters of the convicted were found guilty of violent attacks, child abuse, or multiple crimes. The courts levied forty-four death sentences and two of castration, while the other penalties were usually huge fines of 1,000 lire or more. Not all of these cases involved homosexual sodomy: three men had sodomized girls aged five, six, and seven, and one woman had prostituted her daughter to men for sodomy (for which she was beheaded).[14] Another seventeen cases dealt either with sodomy committed on a boy aged twelve or under, with an assault with the intent to commit sodomy, or with rape, which often resulted in severe anal injury.[15] And twenty-two men were convicted not for sodomy alone, but because they had also committed theft, assault, murder, or extortion; had attempted suicide; or had kidnapped someone for ransom and repeatedly raped him.[16]

Although the few remaining cases reportedly did not involve violence or child abuse, they usually dealt with another special class of offenders—men who engaged in sodomy with several partners or habitually over a long period. Often such a man was labeled a *publicus et famosus sodomita*, implying notoriety and a long history of sodomitical activity. For example, in 1352 Miniato di Lapo was charged with having sodomized Antonio di Salvestro "many, many times," the motive for his prosecution, but his sentence also noted that Miniato, who had fled, was known to be a "public and notorious sodomite, defiled with wicked desire and the sodomitical vice, who has practiced the vice of the sodomites for a long time in the city of Florence publicly and openly, with many, many boys."[17] In another exemplary case from 1348, Agostino di Ercole, described as "dedicated . . . to the vice against nature," first recounted his attempt to sodomize a youth in an inn, foiled by the suspicious host, who threw them out. Then he named ten others he had sodomized on various occasions. Finally Agostino admitted that he had engaged regularly in sodomy—escaping the courts' notice and certain punishment—for the previous twelve years.[18] These and similar cases suggest that a good deal of noncoercive homosexual activity probably went on in Florence "publicly and openly," as it was said, without arousing much concern among either the community or the authorities.

In the cases examined, the courts normally punished only men who took the "active" role in sex, in part because "passive" partners were so often hapless victims of violence or abuse and hence considered innocent. Yet as far as can be determined, even those who willingly let themselves be sodomized usually went unpunished, probably out of regard for their consistently young age.[19] Of the fifty-six persons convicted in these cases, only four—at least three of whom were in their teens—were sentenced for voluntary "passive" sodomy, even though numerous others were implicated in relations of an apparently noncoercive nature. Most of these cases involved unusual circumstances that may account for the convictions and harsh punishments; it is also probably no coincidence that three cases date from 1404 and 1405, in the wave of condemnations mentioned earlier after the repressive appeals of 1403 and 1404. One youth of nineteen was the companion of a married man for two years; a second, aided by three of his lovers, murdered another unwelcome suitor.[20] A third, fifteen-year-old Giovanni di Giovanni, convicted in 1365, had willingly let himself be sodomized for some time by many men, including several reputedly infamous sodomites. His sentence unusually labels Giovanni himself a "public and notorious passive sodomite," and for this reason the podestà inflicted on him an exemplary and barbaric punishment. After being paraded on an ass to the "place of justice" outside the city walls past the Franciscan basilica of Santa Croce, he was to be publicly castrated. Then, so that he would be punished "in that part of his body where he allowed himself to be known in sodomitical practice," he was to be mutilated between his thighs with a red-hot iron.[21] With this gruesome spectacle played out on the body of a mere fifteen-year-old, coming shortly after the passage of the harsh 1365 law, the authorities undoubtedly intended to terrorize other youngsters who might have been tempted to yield obligingly to men's desires.

Of all these cases, only one, from 1404, was said to involve a long and captivating affair, and in its very singularity it illustrates the sort of consensual relations that the courts in this period apparently tended to ignore. Salvestro di Niccolò Alamanni and Jacopo d'Amerigo da Verrazzano came from well-to-do and prominent families in the neighboring parishes of Santa Lucia de' Magnoli and San Niccolò. Salvestro was thirty-six years old and married with a two-year-old son when, according to his confession, he and Jacopo, probably aged seventeen, began their relationship in 1402. For the next two years, they carried on a steady affair, perhaps aided by influential friends: among the places where they had slept together were houses of the patrician families Ardinghelli and Bardi, the Peruzzi bank where Salvestro worked, and the palace of the podestà in the town of Fucecchio. Clearly enamored of his young friend, Salvestro admitted that he had given him gifts of clothing and money worth the considerable sum of 250 florins or more, and even confessed that he preferred Jacopo to his own wife.[22]

It is hard to imagine that a relationship of this length, sentiment, and relative visibility completely escaped the notice of authorities. In fact, it might only have been in response to new calls to repress sodomy in 1403 and 1404 that the esecutore finally investigated and arrested the two early in 1404. Both confessed and were penalized severely: Salvestro was fined the staggering sum of 1,500 gold florins and exiled to Genoa for six years, while Jacopo was fined 1,000 lire (roughly 250 florins) and exiled to Venice for four years, and both were interdicted from public office.[23] But tellingly, by the end of the year, in response to their appeals, the government significantly reduced Salvestro's sentence and canceled Jacopo's altogether.[24]

To summarize the characteristics of the policing of sodomy in this period, then, the courts rarely prosecuted this crime, and when they did, they proceeded on their own initiative and not on accusations. The few cases they pursued overwhelmingly involved violent acts of assault or rape, the violation of young children, sodomy committed together with other crimes, and, less frequently and often only after years of illicit sexual activity, publicly known habitual sodomites. These cases undoubtedly capture some common and frankly deplorable features of sexual and social life in late medieval Florence. Yet it is improbable that the picture that emerges from them, mainly one of reckless child abuse and of a violent criminal underground, accurately represents homosexual behavior in the city at this time. Indeed, these cases differ dramatically both in number and in character from the homosexual relations that were prosecuted from the 1430s on. Their peculiar emphases suggest that in the fourteenth and early fifteenth centuries the authorities singled out only the most brutal, morally reprehensible, or conspicuous cases of sodomy for exemplary punishment, while they willfully ignored a good deal of sodomitical activity that was more discreet or less troubling to collective sensibilities.

At least one man understood, and resisted, his being made an expiatory example by the courts' discriminatory practices. The words of Agostino di Ercole, the "dedicated sodomite" convicted in 1348 after admitting his twelve-year involvement in sodomy, are all the more extraordinary since the censorious machinery of the judiciary system so seldom allowed the voices of sodomites to filter through. According to his trial protocol, Agostino, "as a man who was and is totally inflamed by such a serious crime, said he did not believe this crime was so serious, and that if for this reason he, the guilty Agostino, should be sentenced to death, then many others were also to be considered deserving of death." At this point the censor prevailed, for before being dragged off to be burned at the stake, Agostino also said "many other detestable and unpleasant things, which are thought best to leave in silence."[25] The stifled protest of one common man who defended his homosexual relations as a relatively innocent practice shared by many others reveals some small sense of a system of values and behaviors quite at odds with official representations of sodomy.

Agitation for Reform, 1400–1432

Against this background of selective and sporadic punishment, concerns about sodomy and about how to control it more effectively emerged forcefully in the early fifteenth century. Poets in public squares and preachers from city pulpits derided and condemned the practice and demanded harsher measures against it. At the same time, the Commune adopted wide-ranging measures to intensify the repression of sodomy, to promote sexual alternatives for males, and even to screen sodomites from the governing class, before finally creating the special magistracy for sodomy in 1432.

Before examining these developments, it might well be asked whether this sudden agitation was a response to a conspicuous growth or a new visibility of sodomitical activity in Florence. Some contemporaries, such as Domenico of Prato, as quoted in the epigraph to this chapter, and Bernardino of Siena in his sermons from the 1420s, did imply that sodomy, while perhaps not new, was flourishing as never before. Moreover, although convictions for sodomy in these years remained low, they would soon soar, from one or two a year to more than fifty a year after midcentury. This might seem to indicate a corresponding increase in sodomy. In Venice, too, where new concerns about repressing sodomy were appearing in the same decades, prosecutions rose considerably. On the basis of this expansion and, in particular, of the more frequent conviction of noblemen and of what look like extended circles of males with the same homoerotic tastes, Guido Ruggiero has proposed that this new rigor was the Venetian government's response to the emergence or greater exposure in the early fifteenth century of a distinctive and socially diversified homosexual subculture.[26]

The problem of "homosexual subcultures" will be taken up at greater length at a later point (chapter 5). Here it should be said, however, that if indeed the practice of sodomy was becoming more open and assuming new and characteristic collective features, this probably did not resemble anything like the highly visible, organized subcultures of the modern world populated by a consciously distinct and coherent category of persons who today might be called "homosexuals," an anachronistic model that hardly applies to these traditional societies.[27] More to the point here, it is questionable whether any of the available evidence proves sufficiently that sodomy was increasing or assuming new traits, or that this in itself provoked the reactions of Italian civic leaders in the early fifteenth century. The pious complaints of moralists that sodomy was spreading can scarcely be taken at face value (in any case, the preacher Giordano of Rivalto had already claimed as early as 1305 that "nearly all . . . or at least the majority" of Florentine men were sodomites).[28] Such charges might have made for good polemics, but they were far from being objective observations. The explosion of prosecutions for sodomy can also be misleading. It may be tempting to deduce that more trials mean more sodomy or that changes in the character of prosecuted activity mirrored real variations in behavior. Yet the judiciary records are not so transparent. It has already been seen how selective the fourteenth-century Florentine courts were. And the huge increase in convictions in the fifteenth century, both in Venice, as Ruggiero points out, and in Florence, was so clearly the result of new, specialized institutions and more effective methods for policing sodomy as to render comparisons of the extent or the nature of this practice over the two centuries problematic at best. While laws and prosecutions can reveal something about fluctuating concerns and the administration of justice, what they can convey about the incidence of sodomy over time or about the chronology or causes of possible changes in its character is much less certain.

Indeed, it may be that the agitation over sodomy was related in only a limited or an indirect way to this sexual practice in itself. In Florence, at least, other social and political factors played a decisive role in shaping the new repressive orientation in the early fifteenth century. Florentine society in this period was undergoing a series of crises and transformations that, on the one hand, led to broad changes in the administration of justice and, on the other, induced a stronger preoccupation about regulating many aspects of public morality, especially sexuality.

Between the 1380s and the 1430s, Florence undertook a campaign of expansion that made it the region's dominant power, but also created serious fiscal strains and new challenges in governing a vast regional state. At the same time, the corporative foundations of the old medieval commune were eroding as the social base of the political class shrunk and power was increasingly concentrated in the hands of a more managerially oriented merchant oligarchy.[29] All this generated political and social demands for a more centralized and efficient system of justice and a more direct role for the local elite in the maintenance of public order.[30]

One manifestation of this process was the creation of several permanent judicial commissions to confront special problems, especially matters of public morality. These commissions were staffed by citizens rather than by the foreign dignitaries who presided over the traditional courts (podestà, capitano, and esecutore). Empowered to administer summary justice, the new magistracies helped to weaken the roles of the foreign rectors and gave the local patriciate more flexibility and influence in regulating these sensitive areas. The regime instituted citizen magistracies in these years to uncover and prosecute political conspiracies (1378),[31] to regulate prostitution and administer municipal brothels (1403),[32] to protect the inviolability and sexual purity of convents (1421),[33] to enforce the norms of public office holding (1429),[34] and, finally, to pursue and punish sodomy (Officers of the Night, 1432).[35] The policing of sodomy was only a single facet of a broad effort to manage sexuality and public morality, all part of a more concentrated and efficient program of social control.[36]

Other social concerns, interwoven with these developments, heightened a sense of urgency about controlling sodomy. In particular, the demographic catastrophes linked to recurring plague, and related insecurities about marriage, children, and family life, nourished perceptions that the nonprocreative sins "against nature" posed a threat to the very foundations of human society. The cultural resonance of this continent-wide demographic crisis may go some way toward explaining similar shifts in attitudes toward sodomy and in efforts to control it that occurred at roughly the same time in numerous Italian and European cities.[37]

In Florence and Tuscany, the effects of this crisis were especially sharp. The Black Death of 1348 swept away as many as 80,000 Florentines, two-thirds of the estimated population of 120,000 in the 1330s. The second great wave of plague in 1363 and 1364 took its highest toll among children, while the brutal "plague of the Bianchi" in 1400 claimed 12,000 lives out of a populace that had recovered to some 60,000. Serious outbreaks occurred again in 1417, 1423/1424, and 1430. The population of Florence fell to its lowest point probably in the 1410s and remained stagnant for several decades at around 40,000 inhabitants. Only after 1460 did population growth show signs of renewed vigor.[38]

To be sure, none of the laws of this period explicitly linked demographic crisis and stronger controls over sodomy, though it is suggestive that laws and public discourse on sodomy often followed close on the plague.[39] The connection, however, did not escape contemporaries such as the influential preacher Bernardino of Siena, who made it a major theme of his terrifying sermons against sodomy in Florence and Siena in the mid-1420s. As will be seen, Bernardino not only blamed sodomites for causing the plague, which he claimed was God's retribution for their sins, but also attributed local population losses to sodomites' alleged erotic apathy toward women, reluctance to marry, hatred of children, and sterile sexual practices.

High mortality and uncertainty over the future also engendered fears about the survival and stability of family lineages. Such concerns were reinforced by local marriage practices and were sometimes perceived to be related to sodomy. As noted earlier, Florentine men normally put off marriage until the average age of thirty or thirty-one, and a large proportion never took a wife. Among other social consequences, the abundance of virile young and not-so-young bachelors denied legitimate sexual outlets tended to foster an environment in which unauthorized sexual activity of all sorts flourished.[40] Such sexual "debauchery" was surely not new to Florence, but it is likely that with family lines dying out at alarming rates, it now came to be seen as more detrimental and dangerous. Again, Bernardino of Siena plainly drew out these connections, especially with regard to sodomy. He insisted that sodomy deterred young men from marrying, that bachelorhood fostered sodomy, and that most sodomites were unmarried.

Against this background of demographic instability and worry over family survival, new sensibilities toward children, marriage, and the family and new concerns for their tutelage appeared in Florence and elsewhere.[41] Since sodomy was often perceived to be associated with these issues, the growing preoccupation about regulating it was likely related to this context. The new sentiments were expressed in myriad ways. Domestic themes proliferated in Tuscan art, as artists reelaborated traditional scenes of mother and child and introduced new ones portraying family life, marriage, and childhood. Although they masked more sobering realities, these idealized images mirrored an attention to children and an interest in their upbringing and welfare that can also be found in family diaries and domestic manuals, in humanist writings on the family and in new pedagogical methods, in the founding in 1419 of the hospice for abandoned children, the Innocenti, and in the confraternities for the moral training of adolescents that sprang up in the 1410s and 1420s.[42] This solicitude toward the very young might have stiffened Florentine resolve to repress sodomy, perhaps seen as a way to control adolescent sexuality more firmly or to protect boys from the sexual lust of adult men, which all too often involved intimidation, abuse, or outright rape.

Marriage also received new impulses and support from various quarters. Against traditionally negative and misogynous views, humanists like Coluccio Salutati, Leonardo Bruni, and Francesco Barbaro began to champion a more positive outlook on marriage that stressed both its personal pleasures and its social benefits. As David Herlihy and Christiane Klapisch-Zuber suggest in their study of the Tuscan family, this humanistic campaign in favor of marriage was plainly a response and challenge to the social, moral, and sexual problems of Tuscan towns, especially sodomy.[43]

The Florentine Commune also intervened to aid and reinforce the institution of marriage. In this regard, its most notable achievement was a celebrated dowry fund created in 1425 to help families amass the money needed to dower and marry off their daughters and, initially, to provide savings for future husbands.[44] In 1421 the government even tried to make marriage a requisite for civic office for all citizens from the ages of thirty to fifty, an extraordinary measure intended to pressure men to marry, and perhaps indirectly to bar sodomites and other unmarried rakes from public life. But this heavy-handed tactic aroused a storm of protest, above all from youths and bachelors who saw their personal freedoms menaced, and the government had to withdraw the proposal.[45]

The regime's activism in regulating morality also aimed in part at safeguarding the family. When civic fathers decided in 1403 to promote prostitution in public brothels, they acted in part on the medieval truism that prostitution, however distasteful or sinful, was needed to prevent the even worse excesses of sodomy with boys or the rape of "honest" wives and daughters.[46] Sumptuary laws were also justified by appealing to conjugal ideals. As legislators affirmed in a 1433 edict, women's costly clothes and ornaments discouraged men from marrying (and, Bernardino of Siena added, drove them to sodomy), while such vanities distracted women from their duties "to bear men" and "replenish the city."[47] Even sex between laymen and nuns was now condemned by likening the fidelity these cloistered women were to show toward their spiritual husband, Christ, to the sexual loyalty required of earthly marriage.[48] Although laws and other civic discussions on sodomy did not adduce similar arguments, the sense of urgency about the "sterile sin" probably derived much of its force from this contemporary discourse on the family.

Given this political and social context, it is hardly surprising that sodomy came increasingly under attack. What is striking is how falteringly the official response to sodomy evolved, a revealing indicator of how problematic the issue was for the governors of Florence. During the early decades of the fifteenth century, appeals rang out from government chambers, public squares, and churches demanding that sodomy be brought under control. Civic leaders discussed or implemented numerous initiatives, testifying to the resolve of at least part of the governing class that something be done about the "vice." Yet the regime seemed divided and uncertain about how best to confront the problem, and was plainly unable or unwilling to undertake a campaign of harsh repression. The various measures that were adopted were repealed, undermined, or so bland that they could have had little real effect. Tellingly, sodomy was the first of the great moral issues that caught the regime's attention and initiated the wave of institutional reforms, but it was the last to find a workable solution, after three decades, and then only in the radical innovations that accompanied the creation of the Office of the Night. A review of the expedients the government took in the early fifteenth century reveals how difficult it was in Florence to effect a more thoroughgoing control of homosexual activity.

The first clear sign of official concern over sodomy and over new methods to police it appeared with novel legislative proposals in 1403. A law of April 24 specially authorized the Signoria, the city's nine-member executive body, to draw up new regulations and spend whatever sum was necessary "for the elimination and extirpation of this vice and sodomitical crime, and for its purging and its punishment."[49] Recommended measures included either the creation of a magistracy made up of citizens or the investment of a new foreign rector, to be charged with searching out and punishing sodomy. The law also stipulated that before assuming office, each new Signoria and all the foreign judges were to swear an oath "to pursue sodomites and to condemn and punish them."

These proposals aimed to intensify the repression of sodomy, and the spurt of convictions that followed suggests that they had a brief echo in the courts. Yet a surprising turn of events produced quite a different outcome, revealing apparent dissension within the regime over how or even whether to confront the problem. On April 30, just six days later, the Signoria did create a citizen magistracy, but not to police sodomy, as the original law intended. The priors subverted the task delegated to them by instituting a commission, the Officers of Decency, charged instead with overseeing the public administration of female prostitution. These officials were to establish brothels in the city, license prostitutes and pimps to work in them, regulate their activities, and adjudicate criminal cases involving the women under their supervision. Nothing in their statutes indicates they were to prosecute sodomy.[50]

The motives behind the government's sudden reversal remain obscure, and no evidence has surfaced that might help to elucidate the matter. The institutionalized encouragement and tolerance of prostitution was a common phenomenon in fifteenth-century Europe, and better management of the unruly and often violent world of prostitution was an essential part of the moralizing designs of the Florentine regime throughout the century.[51] Also, in line with the typical medieval belief that prostitution served a positive social function, civic leaders might have tacitly assumed that furnishing men with an abundant supply of professional whores with whom to satisfy their sexual desires would help to keep them away from boys and to channel their erotic impulses in more acceptable directions. Whatever the explanation, the government clearly seems to have decided to avoid confronting the original problem of sodomy directly and to abandon, or at least postpone, plans to repress the "vice" in a more thoroughgoing fashion. The control of homosexual activity evidently presented greater complexities and met with greater resistance than a more rational management of prostitution.

This unexpected move did not satisfy everyone, however, and signs of division within the regime soon surfaced. In advisory councils in January 1404, dissenters raised the issue of sodomy and the original repressive aim of the 1403 reforms. Speakers pressed the government not only to carry through with the delayed creation of the Office of Decency, but also to take decisive action against sodomy by passing a new law and urging the foreign rectors to repress the "vice" more rigorously.[52] When a proposed law stemming from these suggestions was later submitted to the councils for approval, tougher repression of sodomy indeed seemed to be its highest priority. The version passed by the Council of the Popolo on March 12, 1404, was summarized as "the Officers of Decency must make a law on the vice of sodomy and must suppress it."[53] Yet once more, those who advocated harsher controls were to be disappointed. Inexplicably, and quite unusually, the measure passed into law by the Council of the Commune the next day was considerably altered, again deflecting attention away from sodomy. This edict merely revoked the special powers granted the Signoria the previous April to coordinate the control of sodomy, and reconfirmed the authority of the Officers of Decency without once mentioning any jurisdiction over sodomy or any intention of policing it more aggressively.[54] Although the dynamics of this intricate maneuver remain obscure, the government's unwillingness to implement repressive measures evidently brought to the surface tensions and divergences over sodomy within the core of the regime.

Some of the difficulties faced by advocates of strenuous controls on sodomy can be inferred in the striking changes in the revised statutes drawn up in 1408 and 1409 and adopted in final form in 1415. Here the government implicitly admitted that the draconian penalties of the past, which no doubt motivated the narrow judiciary focus on violent or notorious acts of sodomy, had come to be seen as an obstacle to its effective and widespread control. Penalties were now considerably mitigated, with the candid reasoning that magistrates would consequently be able to enforce the law with greater care and diligence, and thus would not let sodomy go unpunished, as the text revealingly states, "out of fear of the truth."[55]

The new statute expressly forbade the exile, mutilation, or execution of sodomites for a first conviction, prescribing instead a fine of 1,000 lire, an enormous sum but clearly a more humane punishment. It also allowed judges to impose an optional flogging or other humiliation depending on the offender's age and status. Only persons condemned a second time were to be put to death. Reinforcing this more lenient approach, the statute also decreed that men convicted of sodomy for the first time could not for this reason be denied civic office or other communal honors, not even if their sexual behavior provoked "talk, scandal, uproar, or disturbances."[56]

Apparently the regime had determined that only by making penalties less cruel and by guaranteeing—up to a point—the physical safety and civic identity of sodomites could it broaden its effective control over sodomy. This pragmatic response marked a sharp departure from the past, and heralded what would come to be the typical approach to policing sodomy in Florence throughout most of the Renaissance. By assuring convicted men of their political privileges, moreover, this ruling tacitly acknowledged the presence of sodomites in civic life. Concern over what was feared to be the potentially subversive influence of sodomites in government would recur frequently in the future, as will be seen later. Such influence might in fact help explain the often ambivalent public reactions to sodomy in Florence.

Echoing the preoccupations expressed in ruling circles, an unprecedented wave of popular poetry against sodomy swept Florence in the early fifteenth century. The best known of these poems are two long satires, "La buca di Montemorello" and "Il gagno," composed probably between 1407 and 1412 by Stefano Finiguerri, known as Za.[57] On the simplest level, both deride spendthrifts and profligates seeking easy money, whether in the treasure buried in a cave on Mount Morello overlooking the city of Florence, or in the soft life on the "isle of earnings" (*gagno* or *guadagno*). But erotic double entendres pervade both poems, and on a second level both can be read as vast metaphors of sodomy. The titles themselves have obscene allusions: in contemporary Tuscan burlesque literature, *monte* was a metaphor for buttocks, while both *guadagno* and *buca* or *buco* (hole) referred to the anus.[58] There was also a tavern in Florence called the Buco, whose host, Antonio Guardi, was depicted in "Montemorello" as a sodomite and around which much of the poem's action revolves; judiciary evidence shows that in the later fifteenth century, the Buco was a common haunt of sodomites.[59] "La buca di Montemorello" describes a procession of over 200 local men, many portrayed as sodomites, who are eagerly taking their turn at descending into the treasure-filled cavern on the mount.[60] In Za's metaphor, the treasure/pleasure they seek is anal penetration.

These satires, probably recited to raucous audiences in city squares, mocked sodomites with typical Florentine wit and ambivalent morality. Yet in his third poem, "Lo studio d'Atene," Finiguerri openly decried sodomy and criticized the negligence of the courts. Reproaching a notary, who was also a prior of the Signoria, for his lascivious attraction to boys and his indifference to the law, he complained, "Oh how many of them lie there in that den [of sodomy]! But if justice had its due, the evil beast would be humbled."[61]

Other contemporary verse condemned sodomy in more straightforward terms. Probably about this time, Domenico of Prato composed his moralistic poem said to be "in opprobrium of sodomy," in which he railed against the widespread "vice" and augured terrible misfortune to those who practiced it.[62] The anonymous poem "L'Aquettino," dated between 1417 and 1425, ironically recounts several men's efforts to woo a stunning fourteen-year-old boy. But the author intended less to entertain his audience than to exhort it to greater vigilance and severity, a goal all the more significant if its author, as has been suggested, was the herald of the Signoria and, in virtue of his office, recited his poem before the assembled priors.[63] This is one telling passage:

> This is the wicked sodomy, which in its foulness offends nature and
> irritates Him who sends us on this path.
> It may well be that the world is full of that filth, but so much the more is
> it unbecoming to you [Florence], risen to such great heights.
> So without being obstinate any longer, do such that the stern law is
> observed, the one created for you, which you find ineffective:

> So that a few arrogant ones aren't the reason your loftiness is abased, but upon them may the vendetta fall.[64]

At the end of his tale, the poet again urged his listeners to join him in rooting sodomy out of the city: "I who together with you suffer this irritation humbly request your aid to throw off that which both you and I despise."[65]

Around the mid-1410s, local clergymen were also promoting a campaign against sodomy, which contributed to a new wave of governmental discussions and reform proposals. In a meeting on December 7, 1415, counselors urged the Signoria to commend the churchmen who were condemning sodomy, since, as one noted, "the city was exceedingly corrupted [by it]."[66] He advised the priors to convene the magistrates and press them to enforce the law more zealously, and to appoint a committee of citizens to propose ways of controlling sodomy more effectively. A second speaker suggested that new laws be drafted and reminded the assembly of "how abominable [these acts] are in the sight of God, and how [their suppression] will redound to the honor and reputation of the Signoria and the city."[67] The next day, another adviser, speaking, he said, for a group of twenty-one eminent citizens whose names were entered into the record, praised the motions already made and proposed that new ordinances be drawn up. To resolve the persistent problem of lax enforcement, he also recommended the appointment of a single judiciary official to ensure that the laws against sodomy were observed.[68]

It appears that the government did not at this time name a commission to review the laws or propose new ones, but it did act immediately on the final suggestion. A law was quickly approved that gave exclusive responsibility to the esecutore to enforce the laws against sodomy.[69] He was also required to proclaim publicly at least once a month that all sodomites were to abandon the city or risk punishment. The regime was thus moving toward an institutional solution that would concentrate the policing of sodomy in a single magistracy. But this effort to intensify judiciary pressure on sodomy was soon overturned, like similar attempts in the past. In less than a year, the measure was eviscerated when the esecutore's staff was reduced and his exclusive jurisdiction revoked.[70] Again, the regime betrayed a lack of determination about controlling sodomy in a more systematic fashion.

By now, this equivocation risked undermining the regime's credibility, or so an adviser implied in a meeting in 1418 when he urged the government to act so that "it will be shown to the people that the priors and the councils wish to take measures [against sodomy]."[71] Accordingly, new laws were passed in 1418 and 1419, with two general aims. The first was to exhort magistrates to repress sodomy more rigorously. At least once a month, the priors were to summon the foreign rectors and incite them, "using those efficacious words . . . which will most fervently induce [their] souls to the said effect," to enforce the ordinances and to seek out and punish sodomites diligently. To sweeten their task, the government was prepared to offer magistrates who pursued sodomites with special zeal an "honorarium" of money or of gifts bearing the city's insignia up to a value of 100 florins. Moreover, to ensure that no sodomite went unpunished through the influence of powerful friends and patrons, the priors were forbidden to interfere in trials for sodomy.[72] The obvious difficulty of enforcing the laws even raised suspicions that judges might themselves be sodomites. Thus the law of 1419 decreed that candidates for the offices of podestà, capitano, and esecutore be screened for evidence of sodomitical activity, and if any doubts arose, electors were ordered not to vote for them.[73]

The second aim of these ordinances was to thwart the potential influence of sodomites in government by filtering them out from among citizens eligible to hold office. The 1418 law ordered that when scrutinies were held to draw up electoral lists for any civic or guild office, the notary had to warn the presiding officials and accept their sworn oaths not to qualify anyone they knew or suspected was a sodomite.[74] In 1419 the same injunction was extended to those who appointed the electoral committee itself.[75] Evidently it was feared—perhaps with good reason—that politically active sodomites might constitute a sort of conspiratorial support network.[76]

Still the government must have recognized that these measures, insipid and of dubious feasibility, were inadequate to solving the problem. The law of 1418 in fact authorized the Signoria to appoint a commission of eight irreproachable citizens who, during the following year, were "to ponder and to search their souls for ways and methods by which [sodomy] might be eradicated from the city and county of Florence."[77] Evidence of this group's activities or recommendations has not surfaced, though its mention again in the law of 1419 implies that the commission was formed. According to this law, the eight had to approve the bestowal of the honorarium on magistrates who excelled in pursuing sodomy. They were also to meet once a month with the priors, their advisory bodies, and the foreign rectors to recall their duty to enforce the laws against sodomy.[78] Apparently, city leaders envisioned this group as a sort of civic morals committee that was to keep vigil over successive governments and magistrates as well as to devise new techniques for policing sodomy.

Yet again, as far as extant documentation shows, little or nothing came of these efforts. They fell victim to the same wavering and irresolution, or perhaps outright sabotage, that had frustrated similar attempts in the past to intensify the repression of sodomy. Prosecutions remained rare, and the Commune maintained intact its traditional apparatus for controlling the "vice" through the 1420s up to the creation of the Night Officers in 1432. Unfortunately, the mainly public and prescriptive character of the available sources makes it difficult to identify or better comprehend the nature of the differences over sodomy that clearly seem to have divided the regime. Whatever the reasons, Florentines' chronic inability to repress sodomy decisively set the stage for the detailed and withering critique of homosexual activity by Bernardino of Siena in the mid-1420s.

The Attack from the Pulpit: Bernardino of Siena

At the Commune's invitation, Bernardino, a Franciscan friar and one of the most charismatic and influential preachers in fifteenth-century Italy, came to Florence to preach the Lenten cycles in 1424 and 1425. In his sermons, he denounced a wide variety of local sins, but he reserved some of his most vitriolic passages and chilling threats for sodomy. He devoted three consecutive sermons in his 1424 cycle and one more in 1425 exclusively to sodomy, and he commented often on it in others. In Siena, his nearby natal city, he preached at least one full sermon on sodomy in 1425 and a second in 1427.[79] Tellingly, unlike elsewhere, not even Bernardino's moral standing and alarming warnings induced the Florentines to make any changes in the policing of sodomy.[80] Still, his sermons focused people's attention on sodomy and on those practices that he believed fostered it. Over time, his teachings might have helped mold public sentiment and dispel indifference about controlling sodomy more vigorously. Yet whatever their effects, Bernardino's sermons, a rich mixture of popular wisdom and his own acute observations but also replete with gross contradictions and caricatures, are an invaluable source of information about local sexual behaviors and attitudes in the early fifteenth century. And more often than not, the wealth of information from court records in the later part of the century corroborates his descriptive remarks.

One of Bernardino's goals was to convince his audiences of the danger sodomy ostensibly posed. He skillfully manipulated the arsenal of invective that the Church had assembled over the centuries. Everything unpredictable or calamitous in human experience he attributed to sodomy, from wars and floods to pestilence and plague. A vengeful God threatened to rain down fire on Florence as on Sodom and Gomorrah, an ominous refrain running through his sermons. Sodomy also dragged with it an endless train of other mundane sins: gambling, blasphemy of God and the saints, gluttony, frequenting taverns and other places of ill repute, lying, mistrust, deception, theft, "and a thousand curses: you see well the damage it does to your country."[81]

Such notions were traditional, of course. Bernardino struck a more sensitive and timely chord by calling attention to demographic problems. In this city wracked by plague, he insisted that there was an obvious link between its rampant sodomy and population decline: "You don't understand that this is the reason you have lost half your population over the last twenty-five years. Tuscany has the fewest people of any country in the world, solely on account of this vice."[82] He told the Sienese that they too would have more children were it not for sodomites, and contrasted their stunted growth with that of Milan, rich in marriageable girls and brimming with children.[83] Sodomites did not want offspring of their own, he claimed, thus giving up a comfort in their old age; indeed, since they hoped that no children would be born at all, they enmitized God, who for this reason sent pestilence.[84] This was not homicide but, "even more dreadful to imagine," filicide.[85] Above sodomites' heads, he told the Sienese, one could hear the ghastly cries of unborn babies urging "vendetta, vendetta, vendetta" against their sterile fathers. He recounted how he awoke one night to find every courtyard, corner, and tower in the city alive with the eerie voices of unborn children crying out "to the fire, to the fire, to the fire!"[86]

In addition to terrorizing his audiences with tales like these, Bernardino derided them with taunts about their reputation. The "stench" of sodomy, as he put it, that came from Italy and, above all, from Tuscany rose to the heavens and reeked throughout the world, giving its inhabitants the "pretty name" of sodomites. He claimed to know of a country where no Tuscan was allowed to live on account of their infamy and said that in Genoa, Tuscans were forbidden to teach school for fear they would corrupt the boys: "Oh Tuscany, what a cuckolding this is, what a disgrace for you throughout the whole world!"[87]

Bernardino's attention to social problems and local self-esteem also led him to attack Tuscan family life and child-rearing practices, issues high among local concerns, as has been seen. Here, in his view, lay the root of the problem of sodomy. However hard they may be to verify, his opinions on the causes of sodomy and its development in domestic and daily life help illuminate contemporary representations and interpretations of this practice.

According to Bernardino, parents were responsible for disposing their sons toward sodomy, whether through their bad example and lack of moral guidance, their failure to discipline them, or, worse, their encouragement. Some boys, he claimed, learned about the vice from their fathers, who were sodomites themselves (evidently not those child-hating sodomites he parodied elsewhere).[88] But most parents were simply negligent or uncaring. Although they taught their boys when little to behave properly, parents left them to their own ways when they reached puberty and began to experiment with sex, and then they excused their misdeeds by saying they were "only boys" and did not make them go to confession.[89] Parents seemed to love their horses more than their own sons, he charged, since if their horse fell into a ditch they would do everything they could to pull it out, yet they stood idly by when they saw their sons falling into sodomy. Because they did not care, parents in effect became their sons' "pimps."[90] They failed to forbid them to frequent sodomites, those "congenial, stylish, merry companions who love [their sons] so much" and corrupted them with flattery, money, and gifts.[91] Bernardino advised parents to inspect their son's stockings and hood when he returned home after an evening out to learn whether they were a gift from a suitor. Or after he was asleep, his mother should hold his coin bag to her ear and listen carefully; if the coins cried out "fire, fire, fire!" they surely came from a sodomite.[92] He reproached mothers for not demanding to know the source of the money in their sons' pouches, for in their willful ignorance they sent them straight to the house of the devil.[93] While we might find his sleuthing methods amusing, the preacher's concern about ill-earned gifts and money did reflect common practices. As will be seen, men typically bestowed gifts of money, clothes, or other items on the adolescents they courted or sodomized.[94]

Above all, as he often remarked, parents sinned by dressing their young sons too fashionably, grooming them too well, making them too attractive. For this only made them alluring targets for sodomites, if not sodomites themselves. "It's a serious crime," he taught, "to have a short doublet made for [your sons] and stockings with a tiny patch in front and another in back, so that they show a lot of flesh for the sodomites."[95] He warned Sienese parents that such attractive boys ran the risk of being taken by force and raped on the streets, a reality that was common enough and so disturbing that he urged mothers to lock their sons in the house and send only their daughters outdoors; according to him, girls were in no danger. But even if their daughters were raped, he coolly reassured them, he could "consent" to this, since it was "less evil" than sodomy perpetrated on their sons.[96]

Yet what troubled Bernardino most about boys being too "spruced up" was the danger of confusing gender distinctions. "Send [your boys] out [dressed] decently, not like girls!" he insisted. "They're the beautiful color of hyacinth, these boys of yours become girls. Shame on you, fathers and mothers! Punish them, keep them at home at night or take them with you, fathers, and don't send them out spruced up like maidens!"[97] Displaying a misogynous habit of mind typical of late medieval moralists, he thought women were especially guilty of "effeminizing" their sons through fancy dress and refined manners: "Oh silly, foolish woman, it appears you make your son look like yourself, so that to you he's quite becoming: 'Oh, isn't he the handsome lad!' and even 'Isn't he the pretty girl!' "[98] Now it is unlikely that boys actually cross-dressed, and even more improbable that their parents dressed them as girls; in hundreds of sodomy denunciations to the courts and thousands of trial proceedings I have reviewed from the fourteenth to the sixteenth century, not a trace of transvestite boys has yet come to light.[99] Bernardino's fears and criticisms were directed more against male ornament and finery than outright transvestism. Still, his comments reveal a strong association in this culture between boys' passive role in homosexual acts and feminine gender imagery, which emerges even more vividly from denunciations for sodomy.[100]

According to Bernardino, self-interest, more than vanity or negligence, sometimes led parents to consent to their sons' involvement in sodomy.

His intriguing interpretation of parental compliance situates the dynamics of this sexual practice within a vast commerce in goods and favors that was a basic feature of social and political relations in late medieval Italy. Hard to prove, his views are nonetheless suggestive. Some parents, he alleged in Siena, "permit their sons to do every disgraceful, evil, and sinful thing possible," referring to sodomy, "and the reason they allow it is to obtain civic offices or money. Mothers permit it for the money," he specified, "and fathers to gain influence with people."[101] In Florence he charged that parents accepted their sons' relations with men as long as they brought their suitors home, made them feel welcome, and secured a promise to promote their fathers' civic careers.[102] Bernardino was suggesting that sodomy functioned at times as an exchange of favors or influence, the son's sexual companionship in return for his father's political advancement or other benefits. If true—and other supporting evidence will be reviewed later—homosexual affairs could be seen as yet another strand in the ubiquitous networks of friendship and patronage that bound this society together.[103] As actors in this male prestige game, fathers might well have been pleased and proud to see their attractive boys win the attentions of other men, as the preacher indicated elsewhere.[104]

Bernardino also had much to say about men who pursued boys. Although he painted a detailed psychological portrait of sodomites designed to make them appear unstable, selfish, and dangerous,[105] his characterizations of their social traits are more original and more valuable.

Age, Bernardino thought, had a crucial bearing on sexual activity. He believed that young men were especially susceptible to sodomy and to sensuality in general, a view of youth his contemporaries widely shared. Between the ages of fourteen and twenty-five, he asserted, young males lost all sense of reason because of their sexual lust.[106] In one sermon, he sketched an outline of sexual behavior according to age groups. The *giovani*, or youths, a category that in Florentine usage included young men roughly in their twenties and thirties, would all be consumed by fire, he said, for all "unbridled and crazy young men" engaged in sodomy. Of mature and old men, however, he rather inconsistently alleged that some had never been stained by sodomy, others had practiced it only in their youth but later abandoned it, while a third group had by now grown old and obstinate in their attraction to boys, and were incorrigible or "inveterate" sodomites.[107] These patterns roughly resemble later, better-documented homosexual activity, in which youths were prominent, mature and aged men were relatively less visible, and a small number of men were implicated throughout much of their lives.[108]

As his attention to age suggests, Bernardino recognized that life stages shaped homosexual experience in important ways. Indeed, he specified the age of thirty-two or thirty-three as a crucial turning point in males' sexual lives. He believed that it was especially hard for men past this age to give up a passion for sodomy, so he urged youths to do so while still young:

"This cursed vice is rarely abandoned, especially when you have grown old in it and pass 32 years of age."[109] Again: "The devil blinds him so badly that if he passes 33 years of age, it's nearly impossible for him to reform. He can, but it's very hard to stop . . . it's nearly impossible."[110] Although perhaps derived from a patristic source,[111] and a traditional reference to the age of Christ at his death, Bernardino's insistence on the critical age of thirty-two or thirty-three might also have been related to a basic event in the life course of local men, who typically married at around this age. His typology of sexual behavior probably reflected a social reality in which many youths indulged their sexual desires in a variety of illicit ways before marrying in their early thirties.

Correspondingly, Bernardino was certain not only that marriage raised a bulwark against sodomy, a common Christian perspective, but also that most mature sodomites were not married. "Woe to those men who fail to take a wife when they are the right age and have a legitimate reason!" he thundered in Florence in 1424. "For if they don't marry they become sodomites. Make this a general rule: when you see a grown man in good health who doesn't have a wife, you can take this as an evil sign about him, especially if he hasn't chosen for spiritual reasons to live in chastity."[112] Again evidence from later in the century suggests that the preacher's remarks had some substance, for most men of all ages implicated in sodomy appear to have been unmarried.[113]

Bernardino apparently assumed that sodomites often rejected marriage not simply because they were dissolute rakes, but because they had little erotic interest in women or were rabid misogynists. "The sodomite hates women"; indeed, he "can't bear the sight of women," he claimed, arguing that it was natural and just for women to despise sodomites in return.[114] Some men were so "wrapped up" in sodomy, he asserted, "that they don't esteem a single woman, so base do they consider them."[115] Preaching on husbands' and wives' duty to love each other, he proposed that God made Eve from Adam's rib, not his head or foot, because women were to be the equal of men, a notion he thought sodomites in particular would repudiate:

> Isn't there any sodomite here who dislikes this, and says that woman isn't worth as much as man? . . . We shall speak here of the cursed sodomites, who are so blind in this wickedness of theirs that no matter how beautiful a woman may be, to him she stinks and is displeasing, nor will he ever want to yield to her beauty.[116]

Disdain of women pervaded this intensely male culture; Bernardino would have found few, if any, late medieval Tuscan men willing to admit that women were their equals. In part, the attitude he ascribed to sodomites was his society's typical misogyny exaggerated to the point of caricature. But it is significant that Bernardino also attributed some sodomites' rejection of women to their erotic disposition. Sodomites were not aroused or attracted, in his view, by even the most desirable of women. In a culture and age in which sodomy was usually not considered a condition of certain people but a sin that anyone could commit, and men were commonly thought capable of (and can be found) desiring both boys and women, still Bernardino believed that the sexual tastes of at least some sodomites focused one-dimensionally on males and more or less precluded relations with females.[117]

Yet at the same time, Bernardino knew that some sodomites married, not an unlikely proposition even for him in a society in which marriage alliances had little to do with romance or sexual tastes but were inextricably tied to families' economic and political strategies. Consistent with his views on sodomites' erotic propensities, however, he predicted unhappy consequences for such unions. To the Florentines he offered "a general rule: the greater a sodomite he is, the more he will hate his wife, as pretty as she may be," and he warned fathers not to marry off their daughters to such men.[118] He believed that a woman married to a sodomite would face constant conflict over her husband's inclinations toward boys and his faint interest in fulfilling his conjugal duties, or worse, she might be forced to submit to his "unnatural" passions, thus endangering her own soul.[119] Although he feared that the frustated wife of a sodomite could do little to change her husband's nature, he still offered advice on how she should behave toward him: when opportune, she should use "sweet words" to entice him away from his male friend; she should stop trying to seduce him by using cosmetics and wearing provocative clothes "like prostitutes wear," for she would only repel him further and drive him to boys; she should never reveal to her spouse that she was menstruous, for he would welcome this excuse to avoid having sexual relations with her and would turn instead to a boy.[120] As he once summarized, emphasizing again the threat of sodomy to family extinction,

> When young men are seized by this pestilential ruin, they are hardly ever cured, and scarcely or belatedly, if at all, do they allow themselves to be united in matrimony. If by chance they take a wife, they either abuse her or they do not love her. For this reason they do not procreate children.[121]

Nor did Bernardino ignore the implications of sodomites' presence in public life. Just as the government's attempts to disqualify them from office suggested, so too he feared that sodomites formed a potentially dangerous interest group in politics. This was one reason he insisted that bachelors be deprived of office and banished, on the grounds they were probably sodomites.[122] This also illuminates his charge that when a man was arrested for sodomy, someone—often another sodomite—usually rushed to plead his case with the court.[123] As seen earlier, he depicted sodomy almost as part of political-patronage networks, assuming that sodomites often had power and influence to use on behalf of their boyfriends' fathers. In fact, on the few occasions he alluded to sodomites' social status, he usually spoke of the wealthy or those he said were capable of serving the Republic.[124] In his comments on age groups noted previously, he claimed that some middle-aged men—that is, men who were socially established or competing for political office—justified their interest in boys by arguing that "all men of the elite [*uomini da bene*] belong to that trade,"[125] as if sodomy were a virtual status symbol.

Speaking in Florence in 1425 of the "custom" of sodomy there, he was even more explicit about the seductive links between political and sexual bonds:

> Sodomy is a custom in all of Tuscany. Go ahead, justify yourself with this excuse that it's a custom, and don't let it bother you that the sin increases with this excuse. . . . It is a custom among you men of parties, whether Guelf or Ghibelline; you will abandon it only when the devil carries you off. If someone tells you not to swear loyalty to one party or another, you won't obey on account of this custom.[126]

One cohesive element of group loyalties in factions, the preacher intriguingly suggested, was partisans' common homoerotic interests.

Bernardino's accusations have broad implications for the social and political life of Florence, habitually plagued by factionalism and party strife. However, they assume special import in light of the long power struggle within the ruling class that broke out into factional conflict in 1426 and led in 1434 to the political supremacy of the Medici family, one of the most decisive events in the history of the Republic. The Medici's astute nurturing and exploitation of an intricate web of kinship, neighborhood, and patronage relations were crucial to their ascendancy and to their later exercise of power.[127] Given Bernardino's conviction that homoerotic bonds played some role in creating and maintaining party loyalties, he was perhaps alluding subtly to sodomites who enjoyed the protection of the Medici when, preaching in Florence in 1425, he demanded, with a possible play on words, "Do justice quickly with this sin [sodomy], so that the doctors [*i medici*] don't run to cure the wicked!"[128]

There are, indeed, some suggestions that the cultural and political interests of the Medici in these years were fostering an environment in which sodomy could be discreetly, if not openly, condoned. As noted earlier, neither the Medici nor any of their known allies were among the prominent civic leaders who in 1415 attached their names and their influence to proposals to intensify repression of sodomy, an absence that may indicate their indifference or even their opposition to such an effort.[129] Perhaps more revealing, it was to Cosimo de' Medici, the great cultural patron who was soon to become head of the family and unofficial lord of the city, that the young humanist Antonio Beccadelli ("il Panormita") in 1425 dedicated his *Hermaphroditus*, a collection of sexually explicit Latin epigrams whose first book (of two) unabashedly praises love and sex between males, while the second celebrates the joys of heterosexual intercourse.[130] The work scandalized moralists across Italy, and Bernardino himself publicly burned it and effigies of its author in various cities. Later reputed a sodomite, Beccadelli lived in Florence in 1419 and 1420, when he was about twenty-five, and frequented the brilliant circle of humanists around Cosimo. By dedicating the book to Cosimo, he probably hoped to gain the eminent benefactor's patronage, perhaps not so much because he would have fully approved of its subjects or shared its sentiments as out of his appreciation of its elegant Latin form and imitation of the classics. Nonetheless, Beccadelli must have had good reason to believe that Cosimo would have found the sexual content and message of the *Hermaphroditus* inoffensive.[131]

Furthermore, as the final conflict that would secure the ascendancy of the Medici neared, one of their most devout partisans worried that their "soft" attitudes toward sodomy might have adverse political effects. This is implied by a letter in 1432 from Niccolò Tinucci to Cosimo's cousin Averardo, a key figure in the family's rise to power. Tinucci reproved Averardo for his intimacy with a Florentine condottiere, Micheletto degli Attendoli of Cotignuola, who Tinucci inferred was suspected of sexual unorthodoxy in part because poems of his circulating in Florence were considered "indecent." He warned his patron that his reputation was at stake, and urged him to reassure his fellow citizens that "the blemish does not come from the doctor [*dal medico*]," a plain allusion to the family that echoes Bernardino's phrase. Finally he came to the point, evidently referring to Micheletto's sexual behavior and hinting euphemistically at sodomy: "To tell you the truth, it is deemed far too great a shortcoming that you have spent so much time with him, and yet you are unable to say whether he is a man or a woman; I would therefore do everything possible to clarify this, and may the smoke fly wherever it will!"[132]

This was the context, then, that allowed Bernardino to depict sodomy as woven so tightly into the social, familial, and political fabric of his society. The solution, in his view, was to burn it out. He condemned the ease with which sodomites escaped punishment in Florence and Siena, due to authorities' lack of will, and demanded that the strict laws be enforced.[133] He gave examples from elsewhere, urging his audience to be equally cruel: in Verona a man convicted of sodomy was quartered and his limbs hung from the city gates; in Genoa they burned sodomites, and he advised the Sienese to do the same even if they had to execute every male in the city.[134] In Florence he recounted the gory details of the burning of a sodomite he had witnessed in Venice. There they really applied justice, he taunted: "They don't pardon the gentleman or the important citizen for sodomy, but banish irrevocably even the greatest citizens. Unlike you Florentines, who before the wound has healed have already rescinded the culprit's exile."[135] He advised that they erect a pyre on every street corner and burn fathers, mothers, and companions, all guilty of spreading sodomy.[136]

None of these directives, however, matched the power and imagination of the spectacle he orchestrated in the 1424 Lenten cycle in Florence. Between April 5 and 8 he preached three consecutive sermons on sodomy. On April 6, building up to the final entertainment planned, he told the congregation to deride sodomites by spitting whenever they heard sodomy mentioned: "If they won't change their ways otherwise, maybe they'll change when they're ridiculed. Spit hard! Maybe the water of your spit will extinguish their fire. Like this, everyone spit hard!"[137] The scribe recording the event wrote that the spittle striking the stone pavement of Santa Croce "seemed like thunder." On April 9, Bernardino gave a fourth sermon, on lust. Returning at the end to the theme of sodomy, he roused the people to fever pitch and then shouted, "To the fire! They are all sodomites! And you are in mortal sin if you try to help them!" The faithful packing the basilica then thronged outside to the great church square, where a huge pile of "vanities" had been prepared. As they reverently looked on, Bernardino set the heap ablaze, a searing warning to sodomites and to the society of which they were part.[138]

Deep divisions over sodomy were emerging in Florence in the first third of the fifteenth century, perfectly captured in the conjuncture in 1424 and 1425 of Bernardino's harsh critique and the *Hermaphroditus*'s open embracing of sodomy. Over some three decades of growing concern and strong ideological and social pressures to react against sodomy, the regime failed to implement any significant program to repress the "vice" directly and more effectively. Despite appeals from church pulpits, public squares, and government councils for decisive action, civic leaders seemed reluctant or unable to confront the issue. These contradictory responses, whose social and political contours unfortunately remain vague, and the long procrastination they produced, played an important role in shaping the unusual measures the regime finally adopted in 1432 with the institution of the Office of the Night. We now turn to a study of this magistracy, which so thoroughly altered the regulation of sodomy in Florence.

2

The Officers of the Night

> You are called Officers of the convents and sodomites, magistracies all too useful in every city and village.
>
> Anonymous informer (1461)[1]

> Be ardent about rooting out this vice, which is the cause of the ruin of our city.
>
> Anonymous informer (1496)[2]

"[The government] wishes to root out of its city the abominable vice of sodomy, called in the holy scriptures the most evil sin, and having decided that if what is written herein is done, for the most part this will be accomplished." Thus began the law resoundingly approved on April 17, 1432, with which Florence finally instituted a special magistracy to pursue and prosecute sodomy.[3] Culminating a thirty-year period of agitation for repression, on the one hand, and of contradictions, indecision, and failed expedients, on the other, the founding of the Office of the Night and the reforms introduced along with it signaled a watershed for homosexual activity and its regulation. For long prosecuted rarely and selectively, sodomy now became subject to systematic and routine control. During the next seventy years, until it was suppressed in 1502, the Office of the Night played what many Florentines deemed an indispensible role, as the informers' comments suggest, in the community's efforts to discipline the sexual behavior of its members.

The government's decision to assign the policing of sodomy to a special magistracy was quite unusual, reflecting the peculiarly problematic nature of this "vice" and its control in Florence. True, the growing recourse to citizen commissions with jurisdiction over public morals had been heading toward an institutional solution of this sort. But the repeated failure in the past to adopt similar measures for sodomy made such a choice far from inevitable. This may explain in part why the founding law of the Office of the Night included stiff penalties of 1,000 lire both for the governing priors, should they fail to implement the law, and for men who declined to accept their election to the office.[4] Furthermore, an autonomous magistracy dedicated solely to the surveillance and punishment of sodomy, as this office was conceived, had no exact precedents and remained an exception among judicial institutions in Italy and Europe. Previously only Venice possessed something roughly analogous: the *collegium sodomitorum*, a subcommittee of the city's main criminal court, the Council of Ten, which was set up in 1418 to apprehend sodomites and expedite proceedings against them before sentencing by the full tribunal.[5] In 1448 Lucca, the western rival of Florence, also founded a magistracy to police sodomy, the Officers of Decency, which appears to have been similar to its Florentine predecessor.[6] Other Italian cities had general "public morals" offices, which probably also had jurisdiction over sodomy, like the Office of Virtue created in Genoa in 1482,[7] but none besides the cities just mentioned is presently known to have had a magistracy with this single competence. That Florence had the dubious distinction of possessing such a peculiar and self-incriminating "office of the sodomites" or "of the buggers," as townspeople often called it, came eventually to weigh negatively on citizens' sense of civic pride and reputation, and this was one persuasive reason why the magistracy was abolished in 1502.[8]

The original purpose of the Office of the Night was solely to pursue and punish sodomy, which in practical terms was surely understood as sexual acts between males. Although "sodomy" normally included relations "contrary to nature" between persons of both the same and the opposite sexes, the wording of the magistracy's founding law unusually implied that it was intended only to police male homosexual activity. Unlike past injunctions against sodomy, neither this nor any other law pertaining to the office until the 1490s explicitly mentioned women.[9] And in fact, the Night Officers began to prosecute heterosexual sodomy with some frequency only as late as the 1480s and 1490s; earlier, convictions were rare and almost always involved the special case of the sexual abuse of very young girls.[10] Not long after the founding of the magistracy, in 1433 its jurisdiction was expanded to include safeguarding the inviolability and sexual purity of female convents, formerly the duty of a commission created for this purpose in 1421.[11] This involved granting licenses to men, usually workers or provisioners, to enter nunneries, and prosecuting illicit entries and sexual trafficking between laymen and nuns. In 1454 the Night Officers were also authorized to guard convents from the contaminating presence of prostitutes and other "dishonest" women in their immediate vicinity.[12] Nonetheless, the crimes of the violation of convents and of sodomy between males and females constituted only small fractions of the cases the Office of the Night prosecuted (in the last quarter of the century, respectively 1 percent and 3 percent). The Night Officers' main responsibility was and always remained the policing of sexual acts between males.

Whether the Office of the Night served as an effective deterrent to sodomy is questionable. But to judge by the sheer amount of homosexual activity it brought to light, its success, however partial, was nothing short of remarkable. Largely as a result of this magistracy, prosecutions and convictions for sodomy in fifteenth-century Florence far exceeded those in any other late medieval or early modern city on record, both in Italy and elsewhere in Europe. In the much larger city of Venice, from 1426 to 1500, roughly the same years as the Night Officers' tenure, authorities prosecuted 411 individuals, and from 1406 to 1500 convicted 268.[13] Reliable figures for most other Italian cities are lacking, but it is known that 8 men were executed for sodomy in Ferrara from 1440 to 1520; although aggregate figures are unavailable, convictions in sixteenth-century Lucca were probably rather high (43 in 1556 and 20 in 1579).[14] In Geneva only 5 persons were convicted from 1444 to 1500, 33 from 1501 to 1600, and 32 from 1601 to 1700.[15] In Palermo, under Spanish dominion, an estimated 100 men were put to death for homosexual sodomy between 1567 and 1640.[16] In Spain itself, secular courts executed between 100 and 150 men in Madrid from the 1580s to the 1650s and over 100 in Seville from 1575 to 1620; from 1570 to 1630, the Inquisition in Barcelona prosecuted 102 cases of homosexual sodomy and put 14 men to death, in Valencia tried 156 and executed 34, and in Saragossa tried 187 and executed 27.[17] In contrast, during the Night Officers' seventy-year tenure from 1432 to 1502, between 15,000 and 16,000 individuals implicated in homosexual activity came to their attention, and they probably levied over 2,400 convictions. Taking into account the sentences handed down by other magistracies, the total number of convictions for homosexual sodomy in these years approached 3,000.[18]

These remarkable figures reveal something of how widespread homosexual activity was in Florence, and offer a compelling measure both of the revolution the Office of the Night effected in the policing of sodomy and of its social impact. But they also raise doubts about the efficacy of this institution, and even about the regime's intention, to "root out" the practice entirely, as the law of 1432 stated. In fact, the Night Officers represented a new, "benevolent," and somewhat accommodating strategy of social control and discipline, aimed less at repressing homosexual activity rigorously than at containing it within tolerable bounds. How this strategy of managing sodomy was deployed in the structure, evolution, and praxis of the Office of the Night is the main subject of this chapter.

The Institution

Although no governmental discussions on the founding, form, and procedures of the Office of the Night have come to light, it was clearly conceived with a view toward remedying inadequacies in the existing judicial apparatus and effecting a broader and more efficient control of sodomy. In part, this was facilitated by the institution's structure and limited competence. Unlike the cumbersome courts of the podestà, capitano, and esecutore, presided over by foreign dignitaries with large professional, administrative, and police staffs, the Office of the Night, like the other "morals" commissions, comprised a small number of lay citizens assisted by few personnel. Their jurisdiction over limited problems—in this case, sodomy and, later, convents—rendered control of these sensitive areas more flexible and effective, while the local patriciate had a more direct hand in their regulation. In other respects, however, especially its novel penalties, the Office of the Night possessed innovative, indeed radical features that reflected the specific problem of sodomy. They had the effect of making this ostensibly most dreaded and dangerous of sexual sins appear much less menacing, little more than a common misdemeanor.

There were six Officers of the Night, elected annually. From the beginning, the Signoria and its councils closely supervised their election by drawing on a limited pool of hand-picked citizens, presumably to keep the office firmly under the regime's control.[19] Normal electoral procedures like those for other offices were conceded only in 1446.[20] The officials' staff included a notary, a treasurer, and two or three retainers who carried out executive tasks (issuing citations, making arrests) and also acted as informants.

The Night Officers had to meet certain qualifications that, in effect, ensured the dominance of the social and political elite. Five had to be members of the seven major guilds, made up mainly of substantial merchants, bankers, industrialists, and professionals, while only one represented the fourteen minor guilds of artisans and shopkeepers. Each had to be at least forty-five years old, one of the highest age requirements for any city office. Evidently this reflected a common worry in this society that the passions of younger men might sway their judgment, especially with regard to this particular sexual crime. Finally, in a notable exception to the norms for most civic offices, the Night Officers had to be married—that is, publicly committed to the lay and Christian ideal of "licit" sexuality within matrimony.[21] These qualities, as will be seen, sharply distinguished the officials from those whose sexual behavior they tried to discipline. From this perspective, the management of sodomy had strong social and generational foundations: well-established, powerful, mature or elderly men, whose age and married status were thought to make them less prone to erotic license, sat in judgment over the homosexual activity of adolescents and mainly young men and bachelors, who came from the powerless poor and artisanal classes or were the dissolute sons of the wealthy.

According to the law of 1432, the modest monthly sum of 12 florins derived from convicted sodomites' fines was to cover the salaries of all the officers and their staff plus operating expenses, including the rent of their meeting quarters, normally in guild halls.[22] But by 1444, the Night Officers were evidently collecting enough money from fines that the government raised each official's salary plus those of their notary and treasurer to a respectable 5 florins a month.[23] Account books from the mid-1450s show that in addition to basic expenses, a good deal of money was spent on candles or food–geese, ducks, capons, young goats–for celebrating various feast days.[24] The officials also took part, along with the city's other magistrates, in the annual ceremonial offering to the patron saint, John the Baptist, the city's major civic ritual event.[25] These celebrations probably helped mold a sense of unity among the officers and their staff, and also indicate that the Night Officers had a collective public identity reinforced by their participation in the city's ritual life.[26]

Empowered to exercise summary justice, the Officers of the Night, laymen with no special legal training, were not required to observe the inquisitorial procedures of the traditional courts. In this regard, one important innovation was their simplified mode of opening proceedings. They were instructed to proceed on the basis of secret denunciations, formal accusations, or by any other means, "disregarding any legal or statutory custom or principle."[27] In contrast with the professional courts, they almost never acted ex officio, or on their own initiative, which put the burden of proof on the court. Nor did they proceed on formal charges brought by an injured party (*accusatio*), which also required supporting evidence. Rather, they initiated proceedings on the basis of denunciations, usually anonymous (*tamburatio* or *notificatio secreta*, a "render of notice"), which did not require the accuser to provide proof. Dependence on secret accusations was typical of all the citizen magistracies, and their use grew substantially in the fifteenth century.[28]

To encourage the community to make accusations, the Night Officers offered informers a reward of one-fourth of the convicted sodomite's fine and guaranteed their anonymity to protect them from retribution.[29] Informers sometimes handed denunciations to an official or a retainer, but more commonly they dropped them into boxes, called *tamburi*, affixed in churches in Florence and in several provincial towns. In the second half of the century, when their locations are known, the Night Officers had *tamburi* in San Piero Scheraggio, Orsanmichele, and the cathedral in Florence, and at different times in Prato, Pistoia, Pisa, Empoli, and Arezzo. At least once a month, the boxes were opened and the denunciations they held were reviewed and copied into the office's registers.[30]

The widespread use of secret accusations made the whole community potential participants in the policing of sodomy. Of course, this system encouraged some people to indulge their morbid curiosity about other people's lives, and no doubt led to false denunciations to defame one's enemies or avenge old disputes. Anonymous charges could as easily express social and neighborhood tensions as sentiments against sodomy. For this reason, they had obvious drawbacks for the magistrates, as they do for the historian, and many were simply ignored. Still, they created an enormous pool of suspects: lists of accusations from 1452 to 1502 yield roughly 4,750 names.[31] And while the denunciations must be used with all due caution, they preserve not only important descriptive evidence but also a more or less authentic "popular" voice against sodomy whose value cannot be overstated.

As their herald warned the townspeople in their annual proclamation upon assuming office on April 23, the Night Officers also employed a number of "spies" or "secret explorers." In general, these spies were probably their retainers, who may have looked into charges before the officials proceeded but also ferreted out information and made denunciations on their own.[32] Like all informers, retainers who denounced people who were later convicted got one-fourth of the fine, a sure incentive to perform their duties ardently.

Although simplified, the Night Officers' procedure was not arbitrary. They followed guidelines set down in law; at times, they also sought the advice of professional lawyers.[33] With the required agreement of four of the officers, after a denunciation an investigation proceeded with the arrest and interrogation of one of the alleged partners.[34] While the law did not specify which, the officials almost always first questioned the "passive" partner, probably because they assumed that his young age made it easier to elicit a confession, especially with the threat and sometimes the application of torture.[35] To convict someone, they normally had to have the confession of at least one (but not both) of the partners. A conviction could also be obtained without a confession, provided they had the testimony of two eyewitnesses, one eyewitness and two people who attested to public knowledge of the fact, or four people who confirmed its public knowledge.[36] Usually, however, the Night Officers depended on the confession of only one partner and seldom heard other witnesses. Also, by law they could prosecute persons only for sexual relations they had had within the previous year. After a confession, the magistrates cited or arrested the partner(s) implicated and gave them a chance to confirm or deny the charge.

Finally, after swearing to follow the dictates of their conscience, disregarding "hatred, jealousy, love, entreaties, bribes, and any other human passion, and turning their mind and attention to God, justice, and the good government of the city," the officials voted on the sentence. Usually a simple majority sufficed to convict, but five votes were needed in cases that called for one of the maximum penalties—that is, exile, interdiction from office, or execution. In the last case, the citizen magistrates had no authority to execute the convicted man, but had instead to transfer him to one of the professional judges for the application of the sentence.[37]

The institution of the special magistracy alone ensured that sodomy would now receive unprecedented attention. The most remarkable feature of this plan to "eradicate" sodomy, however, was the radically new penalties associated with it. In fact, as the government moved to intensify the surveillance and repression of sodomy, it sharply reduced the penalties for it. This measure, more than anything else, opened the floodgates to the subsequent wave of convictions. Little attests more eloquently to the problematic nature of sodomy in Florence or to the ambivalence of efforts to control it.

The harsh penalties for sodomy in the fourteenth and early fifteenth centuries had discouraged the consistent and widespread repression of this crime, and helped determine that the courts prosecuted only the most violent or morally offensive cases. That the regime recognized the problem is clear from the attempt to resolve it in the proposed statutes of 1408 and 1409, and their definitive redaction in 1415, by introducing a fine and barring penalties of mutilation, death, exile, or loss of political rights for a first conviction. But penalties were still severe—a large fine of 1,000 lire and optional public humiliation for a first offense, and death by burning for a second. Passive partners under age eighteen were to be punished at the court's discretion.[38]

With the institution of the Night Officers, the Commune introduced new penalties and other innovations as part of its strategy of "benevolent" but more effective control. The penalty for the first conviction of an adult aged eighteen or above, whether as the active or the passive partner, now fell from 1,000 lire to 50 gold florins. This was still a very high sum—roughly what a skilled artisan in the construction trade earned in one year—but it was only one-fifth of the previous fine.[39] The 1432 law also established an extensive scale of graduated penalties for multiple convictions. An adult's second conviction brought a fine of 100 florins; his third, a fine of 200 florins plus interdiction from office for two years; his fourth, 500 florins and privation from office for life. Finally, his fifth conviction brought death by burning.[40]

Penalties prescribed for minors also diverged sharply from previous norms. For the first time in a sodomy law, adolescents between the ages of twelve and eighteen were treated as a separate category based solely on their age, regardless of their role in sexual relations. In the past, boys this age who took the active role were subject to the same penalties as adults; passives under age eighteen received special consideration, probably because they were assumed to be more or less involuntary victims. Now, however, "since youth is less capable of deceit and should be punished for crimes with lighter penalties," the law of 1432 prescribed for all minors lower and even more extended graduated fines than those for adults. They incurred a fine of 10 florins for a first conviction, 25 for a second, and 50 for a third. A fourth offense raised the penalty to 100 florins and one hour in the pillory (*gogna*). A fifth brought a fine of 200 florins and exile from the territory for one year; a sixth, a 500–florin fine and ten-year exile. If convicted a seventh time, a youth could be sentenced to death, but only if he had passed his eighteenth birthday.[41]

Importantly, the age up to which one was legally considered a minor in sodomy, eighteen, was significantly higher than the statutory age of majority in Florence for all other crimes, which was only sixteen.[42] In part, this exception probably reflected and accommodated the prevailing age configuration of sodomy, since the passive role was mainly limited to boys up through age eighteen.[43] Moreover, as will be seen, the Night Officers only briefly observed the norms on punishing minors. For most of their seventy-year tenure, they regularly absolved all adolescents aged eighteen or under, whatever their role, thereby reinforcing the notion of their sexual innocence and, in effect, tacitly sanctioning their homosexual activity.[44] This legal and practical recognition of the special status of twelve- to eighteen-year-olds perhaps reflected the growing attention in Florence to adolescents as a particular age-defined social group.[45]

Finally, two other important provisions of the 1432 law allowed for all these penalties to be reduced further or avoided altogether. First, if a person whom the magistrates arrested or cited freely confessed his alleged misdeeds, then they would reduce his fine by one-half.[46] The government in 1449 added a threat to this incentive by declaring that if accused sodomites were condemned without confessing, their names and crimes would be proclaimed in the legislative councils, an embarrassing public admonition in the city's main civic forum.[47] With these measures, the authorities hoped to encourage people to divulge the names of others with whom they had engaged in sodomy. More dependable than secret denunciations, such revelations could give officials direct, first-hand access to larger networks of homosexual activity.

The same logic even more clearly motivated the second provision, one of the most remarkable and unusual features of the new system of policing sodomy. In essence, the regime agreed to absolve sodomites who denounced themselves to the Night Officers. If a person voluntarily turned himself in before he was implicated by other means, confessed his sexual relations, and named his partners, then he was guaranteed full immunity from prosecution.[48] Sodomy was the single crime for which the judiciary system in Florence granted immunity.[49] This unique benefit for self-confessed sodomites is a telling indication of how far the regime was willing to go in order to cast its controls over sodomy more widely. When the Venetian government passed a similar measure in 1516, it was greeted with disbelief and derision.[50] Over the years, many hundreds of individuals exploited this loophole to avoid a conviction and a heavy penalty. In the 1470s and 1480s, the only period in which self-accusations were regularly noted in extant registers, an average of some forty people denounced themselves for sodomy every year.[51]

Taken together, the changes introduced with the Office of the Night could hardly have been more sweeping or, given the past clamor for repression, more unexpected. As noted earlier, an institution solely to prosecute sodomy was nearly unique in Italy. The new penalties, moreover, broke sharply with a long tradition of severe punishments for this crime.[52] Compared with the other major Italian republic, Venice, where sodomites were exiled, maimed, and burned throughout the century, the Florentine approach appears even more unusual.[53]

Despite the appearance of lenience, however, these changes should not be mistaken for a newfound tolerance of sodomy. Viewed against the backdrop of three decades of tough-sounding enactments but few concrete results, the 1432 revisions have a plain strategic and pragmatic cast. If the regime hoped to expand its effective control over sodomy, it probably had little choice but to reduce and extend penalties for it. In part, the harsh sanctions of the past apparently ran counter to community sensibilities toward nonviolent sodomitical acts, which many Florentines perhaps disapproved but regarded as not so serious as to merit cruel punishment. Evidence to be reviewed later, moreover, suggests that sodomy was common enough across the social spectrum that rigorous repression might have created unpredictable tensions in a city already torn by internal strife.[54] Instead, the regime chose a less confrontational, "benevolent" approach that was more likely to gain social consensus.[55] Considering the controversies and failed initiatives of the previous thirty years, along with evidence that citizens even of eminent families engaged in sodomy, this "benign" strategy was conceivably a compromise struck to overcome indifference or covert opposition within the governing class itself.

There were also patent financial motives behind the new institution and especially the novel fines. From the early 1420s, Florence had been undergoing a severe fiscal crisis that reached alarming proportions in the early 1430s, just when the Office of the Night was created.[56] This magistracy was clearly no solution to the city's fiscal plight, though one compelling attraction of all the self-financed citizen commissions was their minimal cost compared with that of the expensive bureaucracies of the traditional courts. More important, the pragmatic merchant-bankers who ruled Florence seem to have reasoned that if sodomy was impossible to "eradicate," they could at least raise money from those who practiced it. To some extent, the (relatively) low and graduated fines can be seen as a "tax" on sodomy instead of the retribution required by past laws, much like the taxes on prostitution or sumptuary abuses. In fact, men who denounced themselves to win immunity had to pay a small sum, 2 lire and 9 soldi, that was literally called a "tax."[57]

Certainly the fines sodomites paid could make no more than a tiny dent in the city's huge budget deficit.[58] But their payments were put to worthy civic uses, such as rebuilding convents or assisting hospitals or poor nuns, a kind of ritual cleansing and recycling of sex-offenders' money. In 1435, when Pope Eugenius IV ordered that seven convents on via San Gallo be combined into two, the government directed the Night Officers to contribute 100 florins from fines to finance the renovations; in 1440 half their fines were allotted for this purpose.[59] From 1447 on, they gave a portion of fines plus regular gifts of flour, meat, and wine to support the nuns known as the Convertite.[60] Later, convicted sodomites had to pay a tax to the foundling home of the Innocenti.[61]

Furthermore, the regime carefully kept its repressive options open. While the 1432 law limited the new penalties and benefits to those persons tried by the Night Officers, the traditional courts were directed to continue prosecuting sodomy according to the severe regulations of the past.[62] This reinforced the peculiar status and function of the Office of the Night, at the same time retaining the regime's prerogative of punishing sodomites in certain cases with harsher penalties. Later laws clarified this implicit division of labor. In 1440 the Night Officers were forbidden to prosecute persons who allowed others to use their houses for sodomy. Hereafter, this crime was reserved to the foreign rectors and the penalty prescribed was death by burning.[63] A law of 1449 prohibited the Night Officers from trying men who committed sodomy "in unusual and horrible fashion, that is, with damage to the anus" of their partners; reportedly as a result of violent assaults, several boys were gravely ill and some had died from their injuries. According to the law, the "leniency" of the Night Officers' penalties failed to deter men from perpetrating such serious crimes, and even gave them "audacity and incentive." Again, the government restricted such cases to the professional courts and, later, the Eight of Watch.[64] The same courts also had exclusive competence over acts considered sacrilegious, such as sodomy between Jews and Christians and sodomy committed in churches, and they usually gave offenders exemplary punishments.[65] These violent or especially disturbing cases, however, had always been severely punished. With the Office of the Night, the control of sodomy expanded to include much more common consensual or nonviolent homosexual relations, which for the most part local courts had long ignored.

The creation of the Office of the Night thus marked a crucial turning point in the policing of sodomy in Florence. Despite the law's stated goal of "eradicating" sodomy, this magistracy was a tacit admission of the extent of its practice and the unlikelihood of eliminating it. Reserving the option of harsh repression for sensational or especially reprehensible cases, the government instituted a more conciliatory response for more common and evidently tolerable forms of sexual relations between males. The regulation of sodomy would become less severe, on the whole, but more pervasive. The more than 15,000 males implicated for homosexual activity to the Night Officers in just seventy years are eloquent testimony to the shrewdness of this sexual politics. The problem of managing sodomy, however, was not resolved definitively in 1432. It remained a dynamic issue throughout the fifteenth and early sixteenth centuries.

Politics and Sodomy in the 1430s

The debut of the Night Officers on the Florentine stage was little short of spectacular after the inconclusive thirty-year prelude. Convictions for sodomy multiplied rapidly, striking even prominent members of the regime. Yet at the same time, the novel magistracy and the publicity it gave sodomy exposed the problematic nature of homosexual activity in Florence and highlighted a certain ambivalence that would long characterize its control.

Almost predictably, a flood of accusations overwhelmed the new magistrates. Far from satisfied, however, the government construed these charges as a malicious attempt to slander innocent men or, more alarmingly, as a concerted effort to undermine the Office of the Night. Less than three months after the office was founded, the preamble to a law of July 5, 1432, noted that "many men have been denounced who, in the opinion of the Night Officers and others, have never been known to be suspected of such vices."[66] Two possible sources of the defaming allegations were indicated. Perhaps they had been written by "perverse and wicked men, so that the lives of others will suffer dishonor," a familiar practice in these factious years.[67] Alternatively, the government suspected a crafty resistance by sodomites: that is, men who "could not openly attack such a virtuous law" were covertly trying to sabotage it "to protect their own shameful way of living." Their goal, it was feared, was that "either by means of a multitude of disgraceful and unjust denunciations and infamies, which usually have a damaging effect among the ignorant, or out of disgust over useless absolutions and inquisitions, [the new] law will be destroyed or rendered completely ineffective."[68]

Little could be done to halt the flow of ostensibly false charges, but their damage could be blunted by censoring them. Foreseeing this problem, the framers of the Night Officers' founding law had ordered that when notaries sent the required notice of aquittals to the cameral offices, they were not to record the accusations. Innocent men would thus not suffer "calumnies" because of "filthy and indecent denunciations."[69] The July law reinforced this by forbidding notaries even to notify the cameral offices of absolutions for sodomy.[70]

If these denunciations were perhaps an effort to subvert the new court, they also reflect the explosive political climate of the early 1430s. The years around the creation of the Office of the Night were decisive for the future of the Republic. Long-standing differences within the ruling class had flamed into open factional conflict after the mid-1420s, and by 1432 partisan struggle dominated the city's political life. In October 1433, the conservative regime in power banished Cosimo de' Medici, leader of the opposing "popular" party, and other members of his family. The apparent victory of the Albizzi faction was short-lived, however. In September 1434, a pro-Medicean Signoria recalled Cosimo from exile.[71] His return and the subsequent punishment or exile of many of their opponents marked the beginning of the Medici ascendancy, a position the family would maintain, with two notable interruptions, through the fall of the Republic in 1532 and beyond, under the Medicean principality, until 1737.

No evidence has emerged that directly links the founding of the Office of the Night to this struggle or to one faction or the other. Nonetheless, it appears that the control of sodomy, a sensitive problem open to abuse, became entangled to some extent in this political conflict. The purportedly false accusations in part suggest as much. But it is even more indicative that several of the Night Officers' early convictions for sodomy struck the very center of the governing class and at least one of the main factions.

Remarkably, the first person they condemned was none other than the recent Gonfalonier of Justice, the highest official of the Republic, Doffo di Nepo Spini, member of an ancient and illustrious family. There is some irony, if not political motive, to Spini's conviction, for it was under his administration in April that the Office of the Night had been founded. On May 22, 1432, fourteen-year-old Francesco di Giovanni, who worked for a barber in piazza Santa Trinita, site of the imposing Spini palace, confessed that Doffo had sodomized him in his house. Three days later, the seventy-year-old patriarch confirmed his charge. Since he confessed, he was fined the reduced sum of 25 florins.[72] Spini's conviction evidently caused a public sensation, enough to move Pagolo del Pagone to mention it in his domestic chronicle, a rare thing indeed in such sources. That he wildly exaggerated the details may suggest something of the marvel and gossip that surrounded the case: "At the time of [Doffo di] Nepo Spini the law of the sodomites was created. It so happened that the first man investigated on this account was [Doffo di] Nepo Spini. He was fined 1,000 florins, and he paid them."[73]

Spini's conviction alone points to the possibly potent mix of politics and sodomy in Florence and suggests that this "vice" attracted even the highest ranks of society. Yet charges of prominent men's involvement in or connection to homosexual activity did not end here. The boy who named Spini also inculpated another man who, unlike the former Gonfalonier, had little status, a sixty-year-old German horse trainer named Ciamberlano di Giovanni; he, too, confessed and was fined 25 florins.[74] All this would be unremarkable except for the fact that Ciamberlano's master happened to be Palla Strozzi, the wealthiest man in Florence and an eminent figure in the regime. Strozzi, moreover, took a personal interest in his employee's case, for Ciamberlano's fine was paid by his distinguished son-in-law, Giovanni Rucellai.[75]

Soon afterward, another patrician of note was implicated in sodomy. After a secret accusation, Sandro di Cristoforo, a trumpeter of the Commune, confessed that he had been sodomized by Antonio di Lionardo Dell'Antella, scion of an ancient family.[76] Like Doffo Spini, Dell'Antella had recently held high political office as a prior (May–June 1432). But in contrast with the former Gonfalonier, who simply confessed, Dell'Antella evoked the privilege of judiciary immunity for recent members of the Signoria. After hearing a defense by his brother Roberto—who, as it happens, had also just pledged surety for a man suspected of hosting sodomites in his house—and after seeking the opinion of a lawyer who decided in his favor, the officials absolved him.[77] Antonio's reprieve was short, however, for after his immunity elapsed at the end of June 1433, new officials cited him again on the same charge, and when he failed to appear they condemned him in absentia and fined him 50 florins.[78] After Dell'Antella's attempt to escape conviction was foiled, and probably with his case in mind, the Medicean-backed government in late 1434 decreed that former priors and Gonfaloniers of Justice who were accused of sodomy could no longer claim immunity.[79]

In their first year, the Night Officers convicted a few other men, but Spini, Dell'Antella, and Ciamberlano (Palla Strozzi's horse trainer) were the most conspicuous, due to their own prestige or, in the last case, to his master's standing. Yet what is especially significant about these men is their common bond as partisans or friends of the conservative, anti-Medicean faction. Palla Strozzi was a leading exponent of the aristocratic party, and was banished after the Medici returned in 1434.[80] Doffo Spini was not an active partisan, but he was linked to this faction through both kinship and neighborhood ties. He rented his house from Palla Strozzi, his neighbor, and his kinsman Bartolomeo Spini, described as a "hardcore" conservative, was stripped of office after the Medici's return.[81] Both Dell'Antella brothers were Albizzi stalwarts and staunchly opposed the Medici. Roberto was held to be a ringleader of a secret society in 1429, along with two other men exiled in 1434, and both he and Antonio were banished after Cosimo reentered the city.[82]

The conviction of these men, all connected to the same faction, hardly seems a coincidence. Was this an example of what Bernardino of Siena had alluded to a few years earlier when he said that homoerotic bonds played a role in clientage relations and party alliances in Florence? The evidence is too inconclusive to do more than raise the question, though it will later be seen how common and extensive networks among sodomites could be.[83] Recent laws had also made it clear that officeholding citizens engaged in sodomy, so it will not do to dismiss these charges as merely "political."

Still, the factious context probably had a telling role in these events. Notably, only members or friends of the Albizzi faction were condemned as sodomites, while partisans of the Medici escaped unscathed.[84] Perhaps these convictions were part of a campaign by the Medici party to discredit its enemies, an effort evidently being waged through other magistracies as well.[85] If so, the identity of the officials must have facilitated matters, for Medici supporters dominated the Office of the Night in these years.[86]

The convictions of Doffo Spini and Antonio Dell'Antella and the case that indirectly touched Palla Strozzi illustrate perhaps how the regulation of sodomy could have had political ends. Defamation was a common risk, fostered by the system itself. But such abuses should not be exaggerated. The institution of the Office of the Night expressed a genuine concern to control widespread homosexual activity.

This broader sexual politics evolved quickly, as convictions for sodomy escalated to unprecedented levels. From eight in 1432/1433, condemnations by the Night Officers climbed to eleven the following year, sixteen the next, and thirty-seven in 1435/1436. From 1432 to 1440, they convicted 109 individuals for homosexual sodomy.[87] Most were of modest means and status, mainly artisans or textile workers; few bore surnames that would indicate a higher social or political rank.

The more than thirteen convictions annually in the first eight years of the operation of the Office of the Night represented a tenfold increase compared with preceding decades. It is highly unlikely, however, that the rising condemnations reflected a sudden upsurge in homosexual activity. They tend rather to confirm the thesis that before the creation of this magistracy sodomy was seldom reported or prosecuted. What appears to have been a massive increase in sodomy was instead a product, a fiction, of the reorganized policing apparatus.

The proliferation of convictions brought sodomy even more insistently and disturbingly into public view, and this had at least two discernible effects. One was an outpouring of fear and hostility in trial rhetoric. Never before in laws or judiciary proceedings had authorities so graphically portrayed sodomy as an outrage to God that threatened to wreak havoc on their society, or so piously proclaimed their role as protectors of the community's well-being. This outburst peaked in 1435 and 1436, the same year convictions reached the highest annual number (thirty-seven) known up to that time in the city. This heightened rhetoric and the wave of condemnations coincided both with the sojourn of Pope Eugenius IV in the city, a strong incentive to repress immorality, and, perhaps more important, with the return of Cosimo de' Medici from exile and the subsequent efforts to consolidate the power and position of the Medicean party. The absence of known anti-Mediceans among men condemned at this time for sodomy suggests that the Medici were not overtly using the Office of the Night as an instrument of personal and political vendetta (they had other, more effective, ways to achieve this end). Nonetheless, the office probably was a vehicle for affirming the authority of the new regime at a time of extreme social and civic tension. The rhetoric that the repression of sodomy stayed God's wrath, pacified subversive passions, and reinforced good civic order expressed an apt political message for the Medicean regime that was seeking to impose and legitimate its rule. According to the pregnant assertion of the Night Officers in a sentence in 1436, when those men who defied the laws of God, man, and nature by committing sodomy were punished, then "the city and its upright citizens may be freed from all commotion, wars ended, plague abolished, enemy plots curbed, and cities turned toward good government and praiseworthy conduct."[88]

More concretely, the wave of convictions for sodomy after 1432 also soon elicited a conservative backlash against the alleged liberality of the new penalties. Citing the opinion of the Night Officers, a law of 1440 stated that due to the "lenience" of the penalties adopted in 1432, "many men were not restrained from committing this vice, and, what is worse, many keep and lend houses for perpetrating this abhorrent crime."[89] Accordingly, the government abolished the lowest penalties for both adults and minors and made those who lent their houses to others for sodomy punishable by death. Revealingly, this attempt to deter sodomy by making its punishment more severe quickly proved a failure, as will be seen, and was abandoned. Nonetheless, it points to a sense of unease and to possible discord within the governing class about the "benevolent" system of policing sodomy instituted with the Office of the Night.

Despite the explosion of convictions, fiery rhetoric, and increase in penalties, however, a certain pragmatism also emerged that tempered the control of sodomy and indicated future trends. A remarkable passage from a sentence against a sodomite in 1436 expressed this more sober realism. The officials candidly admitted that sodomy was widespread and that even their best efforts had failed to stem it. The conclusion they drew from this appraisal eloquently accents the difficulties local authorities had in managing sodomy:

> [The Officers of the Night] are watching with unceasing diligence so that the horrible crime of sodomy might be rooted out of the city and its territory, and they devote themselves to almost nothing else. Yet after all their labors, words, threats, and punishments against many persons, they believe that, in effect, it is nearly impossible for any good to come about, so corrupt and stained is the city. Nonetheless, they prudently reason that if despite every sort of punishment these men are still not restrained, at least some might control themselves, and perhaps those defiled by such ignominy will not do it so openly; and if out of a thousand sodomites the authorities punish even one well, all of them experience fear. Although their crimes may not be completely prevented, they may in part be contained.[90]

The pragmatism of this passage probably reveals more about Florentine reactions toward sodomy than does the rhetoric of divine retribution. While far from a policy statement, it does express a clear tendency in the regime's efforts. The very magistrates empowered to police the "vice" admitted its ubiquity and the stubborn tenacity of those who engaged in it. They were not abdicating their duty, but resolved merely to contain sodomy within acceptable limits rather than repress it consistently. Unable to thwart males' illicit passions, they reasoned that by penalizing someone occasionally to intimidate others they could at least force sodomites into clandestinity and keep their sexual behavior out of public view. Sodomy might thus be held in check even though in fact it would often go unpunished.

This realistic appraisal may help explain the sharp decline in convictions that immediately followed. From thirty-seven in 1435/1436, they fell to eight in 1436/1437, eight again the next year, and five in 1438/1439, settling at an average of thirteen a year from 1432 to 1459.[91] Trial rhetoric also lost its fervor, and not even the Dominican reformer Savonarola's terrifying campaign against sodomy at the end of the century would fully resuscitate it. Only in the early 1460s would convictions surpass the level of 1435/1436. By then, however, the prescriptive norms for regulating sodomy had undergone another significant change.

The Turning Point in the Late 1450s

After around 1460, prosecutions for sodomy increased remarkably. Between 1459 and 1502, the Night Officers' convictions for homosexual sodomy nearly quadrupled to a yearly average of 48, with some 270 other persons implicated but absolved every year. Over roughly the last four decades of the fifteenth century, these officials alone levied 2,000 convictions or more, and over 13,000 individuals were denounced to them (or denounced themselves) for homosexual activity; other courts added several hundred additional convictions and countless more incriminated.[92] These astounding numbers were surely higher than in any corresponding period in Florentine history.

The main impetus for this huge increase was, typically, another substantial cut in the penalties for sodomy in 1459. As will be seen in detail later, this decrease resulted in the lowest penalties for this practice ever known in late medieval and early modern Florence, perhaps the lowest in Italy, if not all of Europe. They remained at this historical nadir for the next thirty-five years, half the institutional life of the Office of the Night. Only the fall of the Medicean regime in 1494 and the influence wielded afterward by Savonarola and his followers would sweep away the low penalties and end this "classic" era in the regulation of sodomy. Just eight years later, in 1502, the Commune added the finishing touch when it suppressed the Office of the Night.

At the root of the reforms in the late 1450s lay a growing crisis in the Night Officers' revenues, caused by irregularities in their administration and by their tendency to hand down very few convictions. Such problems had begun to surface long before, when the government in 1440 raised the penalties implemented in 1432 with the argument that low fines only encouraged people to sodomize. The futility of this measure soon grew apparent, however, compelling its repeal. In 1446 the government restored the original penalties.[93] The justification offered reveals some of the problems that plagued Florentine attempts to control sodomy more effectively:

> It has been learned that the Night Officers have very often been accustomed to absolving crimes when they should have condemned them—yet not without the offer of money, which is ceded with no profit to the Commune. Things like this might occur as a result of the increase and doubling of the penalties that were later introduced. [The priors] do not want such errors to be committed in this magistracy with this pretext, and want the said magistracy to be administered and governed well.[94]

This explanation confirms one motive implicit in earlier reductions in penalties in 1415 and especially in 1432: harsh penalties did not deter men from engaging in sodomy, but discouraged magistrates from convicting them and, as this text implies, might well have fostered corruption.

Continuing disorders in the office's management again provoked government intervention in the late 1450s. A law intended to restore discipline was passed on April 14, 1458.[95] This law, however, had the opposite effect, for it precipitated a crisis. These developments are worth examining in detail, since they expose some important problems and tendencies in the policing of sodomy in Medicean Florence.

"Considering how abominable the cursed and detestable vice of sodomy is, how annoying it is to God, how mortifying to the soul, and how harmful to the Republic because of the evils it draws with it," as the preamble to the April 14 law reads, the government reproached the Night Officers for their lax observance of their regulations. The text mentions few specific violations, but it implies that they sometimes levied fines below those prescribed, distorted their records to mask convictions, and manipulated their finances. The law commanded the officials to follow ordained procedures to the letter, and threatened them with heavy fines should they fail to do so. Moreover, since "the penalties against sodomites are intended not only to punish those who have erred, but also to strike terror in those who might want to err," the law directed them to record with care the name, family, guild, and parish of those they convicted "so that they will be clearly recognized." Finally, the text revealed that the Night Officers had adjudicated certain cases of sodomy even though they fell outside their jurisdiction because "the sin was so grave." The government consequently annulled the sentences from the previous six months in cases in which the Officers of the Night had overstepped their authority.

These charges of wrongdoing or laxness cannot be fully verified, since records for the mid-1450s are missing, but what evidence there is tends to support them. For example, officials did not always punish recidivists as prescribed. In 1446 they fined the wool-shearer Bartolomeo di Lorenzo only 50 florins even though the record states that this was his third conviction, for which the fine ordered by law was 200 florins.[96] They also seldom convicted minors or passive partners, ignoring the law that mandated their punishment. In their first nine years, up to 1441, they convicted twenty-three active minors and sixteen passives (all minors); but in the twelve years between 1441 and 1458 for which records survive, they condemned only nine active minors and one passive (also a minor). Magistrates' waning attention to adolescents suggests that they considered their homosexual activity relatively harmless, an attitude that tacitly sanctioned it. Most important, the Night Officers were levying very few convictions. Records show that in the twenty months before the law of April 14, 1458, two separate groups of officials together condemned a mere two men.[97] Yet they did not lack suspects, for since April 1456, nearly 200 persons had been denounced for sodomy.[98]

It was above all this apathy, combined with the other violations, that compelled the government to intervene with the April 14 law and to order the magistrates "to be swift and diligent in doing their duty."[99] Remarkably, this pressure backfired. In a surprising show of passive resistance, the Night Officers responded by virtually suspending operations. The next day, they concluded one conviction, and after this they registered not a single condemnation during the following fourteen months.[100]

Faced with the officials' obstinacy, the government had to step in again. A second law of December 9, 1458,[101] referred to the collapse of the Office of the Night, noting that since the passage of the edict in April that had raised penalties "above what was usual, the said office has been virtually abandoned, for there have been almost no or very few convictions." In addition, collecting these few fines and many others that remained unpaid would be difficult "on account of the heavy fines, which for the majority are impossible to pay, since they are very poor persons" (*persone miserabiles*). This observation finally revealed the merchant mentality that had underpinned declining penalties for sodomy since the early fifteenth century.

This emerged even more clearly in the following comment on "two evils" that stemmed from the current impasse. The first and most obvious was that sodomy "went unpunished," presumably because officials hesitated to levy fines they knew could not be paid. The second was the waning support for the Convertite, "to whom those fines are in large part allotted [and] which used to give their lives great succour." The Convertite, as the nuns of Sant'Elisabetta were known, were former prostitutes or other "anomalous women" who had converted to the religious life or retired to the seclusion of the convent.[102] Since 1447 half of the fines the Night Officers collected from sodomites and convent violators had gone to subsidize these poor nuns.[103] Already by 1455, however, this aid was seriously deficient, as a law of that year acknowledged, because the Night Officers' debtors were "in large part very poor," or else they had fled or gotten dispensations relieving them of payment. The government then agreed to cancel these men's obligations if they paid just one-fourth of their fines to the nuns.[104] Early in 1458 another attempt was made to boost the nuns' resources by letting the Night Officers renegotiate the fines of all their outstanding debtors and by channeling all the money collected from them to the Convertite.[105] Yet the basic problem persisted, and now, since convictions had collapsed, the subsidies from sodomites to these nuns had virtually wasted away, with dire results. As the law of December 1458, put it, "during the past nine months or so, in which they have been without [that aid], they have nearly died of hunger, and are dying."[106] The revision of the fines for sodomy, then, came partly from the need to provide the famished Convertite with a steadier source of income. Ironically, these former whores, whom the state had once enlisted in part to entice men away from boys, now depended on men's sodomy for their very subsistence.[107]

To overcome these problems, the government proposed an unusual solution. It repealed the previous law and empowered the Night Officers to levy any fine they deemed appropriate, depending on the "quality of the person and the crime." It also recognized that of the men convicted in the past "many remain debtors, some of whom are in prison and others have fled, men who are so poor that without some indulgence they may never be able to pay their fines. Yet it is better to exact something than nothing from them, or to let them die in prison or live by begging from others."[108] With this fiscal reasoning, the government directed officials to renegotiate and reduce the fines of all their debtors. Their payment would release these men from any further obligation.

Finally, after convictions still did not increase, the regime acted to resolve the problem definitively with a third law, passed on October 23, 1459.[109] Now it drastically reduced the fines for sodomy. The official justification for this move speaks for itself: "[I]t is evident how much sodomy is presently practiced in this city, especially by artisans and the poor [*maxime pe' mechanici e poveri*], who cannot be sentenced to pay the fines ordained by the old laws."

The government accordingly lowered the penalty for an adult's first offense to 10 florins, one-fifth the previous penalty. Second and third convictions now brought fines of 25 and 50 florins, while men convicted a fourth time were to be given over to the foreign judges, presumably for harsher punishment. This law, moreover, mentioned neither minors nor persons implicated in the passive role in sodomy (who were almost always minors), a tacit ratification of officials' tendency since at least 1441 to ignore them. Hereafter, this was the general rule. Until well into the sixteenth century—with the important exception of the Savonarolan years—minors and passive partners went unpunished. What induced officials to absolve "receptive" partners in homosexual relations (like minors in general) was their young age, not a special regard for sexual passivity in itself, which on the contrary was highly scorned.[110]

Further, "since nearly all those accused . . . of practicing those vices are very poor men, who cannot be fined since they have no money, yet should not go unpunished," the Night Officers were authorized to punish the poor with imprisonment or ritual humiliation instead of fines. Such penalties, the law stressed, served both to punish offenders and to strike "fear and terror" in the hearts of others who were tempted to commit sodomy. In effect, this meant that well-to-do men who were convicted of sodomy could pay up discreetly, while poor sodomites would often be made to suffer the public spectacles of the pillory, mitering with a fool's cap, flogging, or ass-riding through streets filled with jeering and violent crowds.

That "nearly all" alleged sodomites were wretchedly poor was a convenient fiction, as an analysis of their social composition will show. For men of means, therefore, the low fines greatly reduced the financial risks of sodomy. Yet many men accused of sodomy were in fact poor artisans and laborers, and for them and their families a fine of 10 florins was still a crushing burden. Partly for this reason, the regime would continue to have to deal with humble men who could not pay their fines and with magistrates who skirted rules to accommodate them. In a law of 1474, it was revealed that the Night Officers often let convicted men go free after they paid only 1 or 2 florins of their fine, and then juggled the records to hide the maneuver. Again the government threatened to fine the officials if they disregarded regulations, but the practice continued all the same.[111] In a law of 1490, in response to a complaint by the officials, the government noted that they found it hard to enforce prescribed penalties and, indeed, often ignored them, since "the delinquents denounced to them were commonly poor, yet the fines are very high. It has gone so far that nearly everything is done arbitrarily. If they punished [men] as they should, there would be few who could pay; therefore few people would make accusations, and the crimes would practically go unpunished." Faced with the collapse of the entire policing apparatus, the government now allowed the Night Officers to punish "arbitrarily" those men who could not afford a fine yet who, "out of a certain respect," did not merit corporal punishment.[112]

The reduced fines and financing schemes thus continued and accentuated a typical two-sided response to sodomy in Florence. On the one hand, these were plainly fiscally oriented maneuvers to boost convictions and increase revenues. This pragmatism had worked in 1432, and met with even greater success now. From very few condemnations from 1456 to 1459, convictions rose immediately to thirteen in 1459/1460, mounted to fifty-five in 1461/1462, and peaked in 1472/1473, when the Night Officers convicted a total of 161 men.[113] The low fines ultimately permitted the Medicean regime to extend its controls deep within the sodomitical underground.

On the other hand, these changes were symptomatic of a certain ambivalence in the policing of sodomy noted earlier. The problems revealed in the laws underline the officials' inability, or reluctance, to punish sodomites consistently. This was explained in the only acceptable way, as a humane response to the financial plight of humble men. Nonetheless, the difficulties that authorities had encountered in applying harsh punishments in the past, and the Night Officers' rather indulgent enforcement of the laws, to be reviewed later, suggest that accommodating social attitudes to sodomy might also have played a considerable role in mitigating penalties.

Finally, it may be that more subtle political considerations also influenced the new policy. Perhaps not coincidentally, these developments came at a critical moment for the survival of the Medicean regime. In early 1458, the Medici were facing a serious challenge to their hegemony from disaffected members of the oligarchy. To block this threat, an assembly of the citizens was convened in July, under pressure from the Medici, to approve the creation of a commission (*balìa*) with extraordinary powers to reform the constitution in defense of the existing regime.[114] It was this commission that overturned the April law ordering the Night Officers to observe prescribed regulations and penalties, and authorized them instead to punish sodomites at their discretion. After the regime was again securely under Medicean influence, the fines were sharply reduced. Could these changes have been connected somehow to the political designs of the Medici?

As noted earlier, one goal and the ultimate effect of the low fines was to cast the regime's controls more widely, since they made convictions easier to gain. Yet at the same time, the reduced penalties and debt-financing schemes must have seemed like substantial concessions to sodomites and to working men and the poor, among whom the 1459 law said the "vice" was widespread. This is significant, since as part of their pattern of domestic control the Medici deftly courted the loyalty of lower-class and young men, social groups excluded from power and among whom, as the evidence shows, sodomy was common.[115] Perhaps, then, the reduction in penalties, coming at a critical juncture for the family's continuing dominance, was partly intended to attract the support of these groups.

The evidence is too circumstantial to make this any more than a tentative hypothesis. Still, it is notable that the low fines were maintained under four generations of Medici leaders, from Cosimo to his great-grandson, Piero, and it was only in this period that laws on sodomy expressed concern for the humble. Later, opponents of the Medici associated the low penalties with their "tyranny" and their style of exercising power. After Piero was expelled in 1494, the reformed regime condemned "the evil government of those who ruled in the past" when it substituted harsh corporal and capital penalties for the fines.[116] When a new generation of Medici resumed the family's dominion in 1512, they quickly reduced punishments for sodomy again and reinstated graduated fines, in part, it seems, in recognition of the crucial role youths played in restoring them to power.[117] These developments take us some way from 1458 and 1459, but they perhaps help articulate the political contours of the policing of sodomy in Medicean Florence. With the benefit of hindsight, it may not be unreasonable to see the controlled lenience toward sodomy from the 1460s through the early 1490s as one aspect of Medicean domestic policy directed in part at youths and commoners.

In any case, the reforms of 1459 introduced a new period in the management of sodomy in Florence. The impressive dimensions of homosexual activity now began to come to light with the huge increase in prosecutions. By some unexplained coincidence, the Night Officers' proceedings from 1459 on also survive with few lacunae.[118] Transcriptions of secret denunciations, notice of self-accusations, summaries of testimony, and records of both absolutions and convictions finally permit a detailed reconstruction of the praxis of policing sodomy in the late fifteenth century.

The Magistrates at Work

By now it should be clear that considerable differences often existed between prescriptive norms and practice, between laws against sodomy and their enforcement. This section focuses on the praxis of the Officers of the Night and, to a lesser extent, of the Eight of Watch, by this time the city's main criminal magistracy, to explore some of the dimensions of the control of sodomy in the late fifteenth century. The regulation of sodomy changed substantially in the 1490s, related to the death of Lorenzo de' Medici in 1492, the collapse of the Medicean regime in 1494, and the rise and fall of Savonarola. But since my intention here is to derive a general picture, the political circumstances and institutional adjustments of these years will largely be ignored. These events and their impact on the policing of sodomy will be examined at a later point.

A quantitative study of prosecutions for sodomy in the late fifteenth century furnishes a useful framework. This study covers the last twenty-four years of the operation of the Office of the Night, from November 1478, to November 1502; full proceedings survive for seventeen years.[119] In these seventeen years, 4,062 individuals implicated in homosexual sodomy came to the Night Officers' attention, many more than once. They convicted 582, some twice or more, for a total of 638 convictions, an average of 37 or 38 per year. In this period, other institutions also had jurisdiction over sodomy—the court of the podestà, the Eight of Watch, and from 1495 the Guardians of the Law—of which the most important was the Eight.[120] Knowledge of the Eight's work is limited, however, since their records, which cover nearly twenty-two years between 1478 and 1502, preserve only those cases that ended in conviction and lack the rich detail of the Night Officers' proceedings. These records permit the identification of some 364 persons implicated in homosexual sodomy, of whom the Eight sentenced 241 in 247 different convictions, on the average 11 or 12 convictions per year.[121] Between 1478 and 1502, then, Florentine courts together convicted an average of at least 50 males annually for homosexual sodomy, in addition to numerous others, males and females, for heterosexual sodomy.[122]

The character of the cases tried by the two institutions differed markedly, especially before the Eight gained full jurisdiction over sodomy in 1494. These differences confirm that the Night Officers' role was to police mainly consensual and nonviolent forms of homosexual activity, while other courts were also meant to handle cases deemed more serious. Of the Eight's 128 convictions before 1494, 39 (30 percent) involved relations in which the passive partner, always a boy (*puer*), had suffered anal injuries. As noted earlier, a law of 1449 forbade the Night Officers to proceed in such cases, though they sometimes ignored the ruling.[123] Another 13 (10 percent) dealt with sodomy involving Jews, over whom this magistracy had near-exclusive jurisdiction.[124] Finally, the Eight condemned several men who had committed sodomy or related "lascivious" acts in churches, a sacrilege over which the Night Officers had no competence.[125] In general, in keeping with its "benign" character, the Office of the Night dealt mainly with more mundane sexual activity.

An examination of the operations of the Night Officers, whose records are more comprehensive, illuminates a number of features of their "benevolent" control of sodomy. As noted earlier, they opened an investigation usually on the basis of two kinds of denunciations: anonymous accusations and self-incriminations. If they proceeded, they normally questioned the person implicated in the passive role, almost always an adolescent. Officials' responses to denunciations, their first direct intervention, reveal a good deal about their effective policing of sodomy.

In fact, the Night Officers were far from zealous, for they pursued only a small proportion of accusations. In the 1478–1502 survey, a total of 1,276 persons were implicated as the passive partner in homosexual sodomy (1,218 individuals, some more than once during the terms of different officials). Yet as far as the records show, only 466, under 37 percent, were interrogated.[126]

This disregard might be understandable when anonymous accusations were involved, since the officials could easily have doubted their motives and veracity. Of the 765 passive partners who first came to their attention through secret denunciations, they questioned only 204 (27 percent). They probably ignored some charges because their authors provided too few details to identify the persons named.[127] In other cases, they might not have acted on anonymous accusations because they believed they were false, stemming from personal enmity and a thirst for vendetta, or even from a rejected suitor—as some suspects claimed in their defense.[128] Officials in 1496, for instance, during the factious Savonarolan period, dismissed 22 accusations against members of eminent families as slanderous and inflammatory.[129] False denunciations were common enough to discourage officials from believing every secret allegation. Also, given their often tight financial constraints, the Night Officers might have tended to ignore anonymous charges to avoid having to pay the percentage of convicted sodomites' fines that the law guaranteed informers.

More revealing is their inattention to boys implicated through their partners' self-denunciations. Presumably this was the most dependable evidence on which officials had to act. Before this benefit was curtailed in 1490 and in effect abolished in 1496 (discussed later), self-denunciations were also the single most common means by which passive partners were incriminated in the 1478–1502 survey. A total of 243 first came to the officers' attention this way, while another 19 were named by both a self-accuser and an informer (in this survey, 243 persons denounced themselves for having sodomized 272 different passive partners). Self-disclosures offered a a potentially high return if the Night Officers intended to pursue sodomy aggressively. Not only could they assume that they were true, but as they knew by experience, the boys so named and later questioned often confessed to having been sodomized by numerous others, who could then be prosecuted.

Nonetheless, of the 262 passive partners first implicated through a companion's self-accusation, the Night Officers ignored the vast majority and interrogated only 51 (19 percent). To cite one of many examples, four men denounced themselves in 1478 and 1479 for having sodomized sixteen-year-old Filippo di Giovanni Benizzi, but the officials did not question him, nor did they do so after four secret allegations named him again in 1481.[130] In contrast, the few boys who were named by self-accusers and were then interrogated admitted on average to sex with 11 partners, compelling proof of the utility of the immunity clause. The case of Andrea di ser Antonio Bonsi offers a fine illustration. In 1480 a former soldier accused himself of having sodomized sixteen-year-old Andrea and two other youngsters "many times up to the present day," but officials questioned neither Andrea nor the others.[131] The following year, however, when six other men voluntarily disclosed their sexual relations with Andrea, he was arrested and confessed that he had been sodomized by 33 partners in the past year, of whom the officials convicted 24. Over the next days and months, another 7 men came forward to denounce their affairs with Andrea, two secret accusations naming him arrived, and the officials questioned him twice more, when he named 2 other partners.[132] Yet two years later, in 1483, after 2 more men denounced themselves and named Andrea as their partner, officials again chose not to interrogate him despite his past record of promiscuity.[133]

By failing to pursue most accusations of all kinds, then, the Night Officers willfully ignored an inestimable number of prosecutable homosexual relations. Why they did so is hard to determine, though some possible motives will be discussed later. A second and equally important conclusion regards the limited nature of the judiciary evidence and the extent of sodomy in this community. Despite the remarkable numbers of persons implicated whose names the records preserve, they represent only a small, visible tip of a much more pervasive world of sodomy, a world that is now lost to view but was a thriving part of Florentine life.

The promise of immunity for persons who denounced themselves was such an unusual feature of the management of sodomy in Florence that it merits closer attention. Most of the information on how this loophole worked or who utilized it pertains to the years 1469 to 1490. No self-accusations have surfaced before 1469, probably indicating that notaries did not record them in the procedural ledgers. Between 1469 and 1490, self-disclosures appear commonly in these registers, but whether all were recorded cannot be known. In 1490 a law limiting sodomites to only one self-denunciation also ordered notaries to keep a separate book, no longer extant, for self-accusers' and their partners' names; consequently, with a few exceptions, self-accusations vanish from the procedural records.[134] And they came virtually to an end in 1496 when the benefit of immunity was abolished for all but passive partners.[135] Although the records contain indirect notice of a few self-accusers after 1490 and even 1496, most of what can be learned about them comes from the 1470s and 1480s.

In the twenty-three years for which records survive from 1469 to 1502, at least 1,199 individuals either denounced themselves or were implicated as the partner of a self-accuser. Usually it was the active partner who incriminated himself, since it was he who risked conviction and punishment: as noted, the Night Officers normally absolved those implicated in the passive role, a fact that must have been widely known. Some 484 individuals thus denounced themselves and identified 664 different partners they sodomized. Although virtually exempt from conviction, 11 passive partners also accused themselves, naming 47 persons who had sodomized them.[136]

Since this benefit provided such an easy means to escape punishment, it is surprising that even more men did not take advantage of it. While motives for avoiding self-accusation must have varied, some may have felt there was a certain shame attached to a voluntary admission of sodomy, especially for patrician men who had to confess to their peers. This may explain in part why relatively few men from prominent families denounced themselves; probably for the same reason, officials in 1485 suppressed the identity of one self-accuser "whose name," they candidly admitted, "we do not want made public."[137]

The motives that led men to denounce themselves might also have varied, but the majority probably did so to avoid paying a heavy fine. Most were of humble social extraction, and for them a fine of 10 florins could mean ruin.[138] At times, however, officials treated self-accusation as a form of repentance and made these men promise they would no longer engage in sodomy. Notaries often wrote variations on the phrase "He says he repents of these things and that from now on he will not commit this sin, and he says this to avoid the penalty."[139] Cristofano di Giovanni from Lodi, who denounced himself in 1470 for having sodomized seventeen boys, explained that he turned himself in on the advice of a former Night Officer, to whom he had sworn fervently that he would never commit sodomy again ("if I ever fall again, have me burned, and don't ever have mercy on me").[140] Of course, it is hard to know whether beneath the formulaic professions of penitence lay a sincere sense of contrition. In some cases such claims clearly rang hollow. In 1470 twenty-year-old brassworker Jacopo di Lorenzo del Cietina denounced himself for having sodomized two boys, and solemnly "promised not to get involved in this sin any more in the future"; yet four years later, he incriminated himself again, and in 1476 was also named in a boy's confession (but absolved).[141] Others who made similar pledges disappear from the records, however, perhaps indicating they kept their word—or were unusually skilled at keeping their relations secret.

Others self-confessed to protect themselves because they sensed or knew they were at risk. Some might even have been alerted by friends among the officials or their staff that they or their boyfriend had been denounced. They would then hurry to incriminate themselves before the magistrates took action against them. It was probably no coincidence, for example, that the same day the Night Officers received an anonymous charge in 1482 naming sixteen-year-old Baldovino di Giovanni Baldovini, six men showed up to denounce themselves for having sodomized him.[142] Others, after learning that a boy they had sodomized had been arrested, came forward hoping, or knowing, that he had not already divulged their names. In 1480, the day after Luigi d'Agnolo Peruzzi confessed that eleven men had sodomized him, three other lovers he conveniently "forgot" to mention rushed to self-confess that they had each been carrying on with him "up to the present day."[143] Sometimes word spread among men involved with the same boy that one of the group had denounced himself, and the others hastened to follow suit.[144] Finally, a few men seem to have denounced themselves preventively, but then turned around and recanted. In 1473 the wool merchant Zanobi di Simone Folchi self-confessed that he had sodomized Lorenzo di Francesco Strozzi "many, many times" and then immediately retracted his admission, claiming he was incriminating himself only because he feared Lorenzo would accuse him "for money."[145] This example may raise questions about the veracity of self-accusations, but officials normally took their truth for granted.[146]

Men who engaged often in sodomy also made good use of the benefit conferred by self-denunciations to win impunity. Of the 484 active partners who self-confessed, 50 did so at least twice, and 13 three to five times. Tommaso di Damiano, called Lasca, accused himself at least four times between 1481 and 1487, identifying a total of eight partners.[147] One of the most notorious sodomites in late-fifteenth-century Florence, the baker Jacopo d'Andrea, called il Fornaino (the little baker), denounced himself at least five times between 1473 and 1480, admitting that he had sodomized twenty-four boys.[148] Moreover, 125 self-accusers, one of every four, named a total of at least two partners and often many more: 74 named two or three, 30 named four to six, 10 named seven to nine, and 11 named ten or more partners. In a single self-accusation in 1473, Amerigo di Niccolò d'Amerigo indicated seven boys he had sodomized, each "many times," in a series of affairs stretching back eight years.[149] In three self-denunciations between 1475 and 1487, the butcher Francesco di Bartolomeo, called Rosaino, identified thirty-four boys he had sodomized.[150]

Some sodomites thus quite consciously exploited this loophole to their own advantage. The case of Bartolomeo di Folco, called Spezialino, is illustrative. He reportedly committed sodomy frequently, and not only denounced himself afterward to the Night Officers but also collected a reward for naming his partners. Condemning this clever abuse, the Eight of Watch intervened to end it in 1488 by giving him a public flogging and banishing him for ten years.[151]

Whether the Night Officers learned of sodomitical activity through self-denunciations or anonymous accusations, they generally levied sentences only after the confession of the passive companion(s) named. Of the 466 passive partners who were questioned in the 1478–1502 survey, 387 (83 percent) admitted that they had been sodomized by at least one person, and often by many more. Virtually all those named by self-accusers, but only two-thirds of those named by informants, confessed, results that tend to confirm both the veracity of self-disclosures and the greater unreliability of secret charges. The 387 who confessed named a total among them of 2,366 partners who had sodomized them.[152]

Of course, the testimony of these boys and adolescents, perhaps easily intimidated because of their young age (most were between twelve and eighteen), was not always dependable. They were probably interrogated in the palace of the podestà in front of the instruments of torture, and some were actually tortured, rendering their confessions suspect. However, only eight youngsters later admitted that their charges against some forty-six partners were false and retracted them. Their motives for lying varied. Some said they feared being tortured or wanted to be released from prison.[153] A few claimed that someone had incited them to accuse another person unjustly.[154] Others admitted that they wanted to avenge themselves against someone who had wronged them—for instance, a former employer with whom they had argued or who had fired them without their proper pay.[155] False accusation was a serious offense, however, and could be punished severely. In 1496 a boy who lied about his employer was whipped through the city and given thirty lashes in his master's neighborhood, to restore the man's reputation with his neighbors.[156] That same year, fourteen-year-old Torrigiano di Taddeo, who admitted that he wrongly accused several of the men he claimed had sodomized him, was given twenty-five lashes and had to pay a bushel of flour, beg forgiveness of these men, and pay their prison expenses; in addition, to shame him publicly the officials had his long hair cropped short, and requisitioned a pair of his fashionable hose, half purple and half checkered, which they made him cut to pieces.[157]

Other boys tried to protect their partners, sometimes because they had been bribed or intimidated. One fourteen-year-old admitted that he left two companions unnamed when he was first questioned because they had promised him a jacket and a pair of boots.[158] Domenico di Zanobi Biliotti, a sixteen-year-old from a prominent old family, confessed in 1497 that, on his brother's advice, he had retracted his earlier charge against their influential neighbor Luigi Pitti "because they did not want to enmitize the Pitti family."[159] Before reasserting his claim, he also recanted an accusation against Francesco di Benedetto Bonsi, from another eminent family of their quarter, after Bonsi's brother paid a visit to the Biliotti house and promised to rehire the boy or to give him anything he asked.[160] No doubt other magistrates also faced problems like these, but the young age of the boys involved might have made cases of sodomy especially prone to such manipulation.

Like their rather lax responses to accusations, how the Night Officers acted on the confessions of passive partners—that is, how they sentenced the individuals they named—betrays a similar lack of rigor. Normally they convicted only persons named in such confessions, after citing them to respond to the charge or, less commonly, after arresting them. According to their records, less than 10 percent (224) of the active partners named ever testified. Of these, nearly three of every four admitted the charges against them were true. Those who denied were absolved, but revealingly, officials also absolved seventeen men who confessed.[161]

Altogether, in the 1478–1502 survey the Night Officers levied 618 convictions of persons implicated in the active role. Subtracting those who denied (62) or whose accusers recanted (46) from the total number of active partners named in confessions (2,366), their conviction rate comes to about 27 percent. This would rise to around 32 percent if cases involving minors, who were normally absolved, and clergymen, who could not be prosecuted, were also removed.[162] The number and rate of convictions for sodomy was thus far from insignificant. Nonetheless, considering the majority of denunciations the officials ignored, the large number of self-accusations, and the high proportion of active partners named in confessions who were absolved, over four of every five cases of homosexual activity revealed to the Officers of the Night eluded punishment.[163]

Correspondingly, the same was true of individuals who came to the attention of the Night Officers, even though in absolute terms the number convicted was impressive. Of the 4,062 individuals who were implicated in homosexual sodomy in the 1478–1502 survey, 582 (14.4 percent) were convicted at least once. Normally these were men aged nineteen or over who were incriminated in the active role, since officials in effect stopped convicting boys up to eighteen and passives after the late 1450s. They did condemn 20 of the 387 passives in the survey who confessed (5 percent, or under 2 percent of the total), but in most cases these were youths past the age of eighteen or younger boys prosecuted during the repressive Savonarolan years, when officials punished both passives and minors with slightly greater frequency.[164] The remaining 562 persons convicted had taken the active role in sodomy. The Night Officers condemned approximately one-third of the active partners eligible for conviction, or fewer than 1 in 5 of the total 2,906 persons incriminated in the 1478–1502 survey. Some 80 percent escaped conviction altogether.

Of these 562, the officials convicted 43 men more than once during the period of this survey: 35 twice; 5, three times; 2, four times; and 1, six times. The last is an excellent example of how the Night Officers often waived regulations. This was the same Jacopo d'Andrea, il Fornaino, who denounced himself at least five times, naming 24 adolescents he had sodomized. Between 1470 and 1487, he collected a striking record of thirteen documented convictions for sodomy, twelve by the Night Officers and one by the Eight of Watch. Not only did the former condemn him at least twelve times even though the 1459 law prescribed that sodomites convicted a fourth time be given over to one of the foreign judges, presumably to be exiled or put to death, but they also bent the principle of graduated penalties for him, and the punishments they imposed were never excessive. He received a six-month jail term once, and of his fines, five were the minimum 10 florins; five, 25 florins; and only one, 50 florins.[165]

Many other men were also incriminated repeatedly, and how the Night Officers dealt with them is consistent with the general indulgence that has so far been revealed. Some 437 individuals, 15 percent of the total, were implicated in the active role more than once in the seventeen years of this survey; 201 appear more than twice. Yet 268 (61 percent) escaped conviction. Between 1473 and 1490, Francesco di Lazzaro de' Medici, for example, was incriminated in confessions or denunciations at least eight times, yet he was always absolved; in this case, it was no doubt Francesco's connections to the virtual lord of Florence, his distant cousin and employer Lorenzo de' Medici, that protected him, but officials also "overlooked" many others.[166] The 268 who avoided conviction included 45 men who admitted involvement in sodomy by denouncing themselves at least once, but on other occasions when they could have been prosecuted the officials ignored or absolved them. And of the 169 convicted at least once, 80 percent (135) were absolved of another charge. Repeatedly implicated men were more likely than others to be convicted, but odds were that they too would go unpunished.[167]

On the whole, then, the Night Officers sentenced men in a rather lenient and often arbitrary fashion. Although over the course of their seventy-year tenure they handed down several thousand convictions, the evidence shows that they neither pursued nor punished sodomites consistently or rigorously. Their restraint probably reflects a fair degree of popular and official accommodation, if not outright tolerance, of sodomy in Florence. Within this general context, patterns of prosecution could fluctuate considerably, depending, as will be seen, on such elements as the political climate at a given time, the composition of single groups of officials, or certain social prejudices. The Night Officers' records, however, also point to other factors that contributed to their overall moderation. These shed further light on some of the problems of policing sodomy in this community.

Living and working in this small, "face-to-face" society, the Night Officers were subject to many influences that at times conditioned their responses. That they were often called on to judge men or boys of their own social class, acquaintances, friends, and even relatives, probably helped dissuade them from pursuing certain cases. Some informers feared conflicts of interest between the demands of justice and the bonds of status and kinship, as this warning in 1467 attests: "Remember the flogging you gave a poor man a few days ago, that is, not justice for the poor and mercy for the powerful. And for a relative, don't let kinship constrain you more than the honor of God."[168]

This informant's worries had some substance, for nearly two-thirds of the Night Officers or their treasurers from 1478 to 1502 had members of their lineage who were implicated in sodomy in the same years. While it is not always possible to determine exact relationships, at least one of every five probably had close family members—brothers, sons, grandsons—accused and sometimes even convicted.[169] Niccolò di Jacopo Panuzzi, a Night Officer in 1460/1461, had two sons, Jacopo and Salvi, who were among the city's most notorious sodomites, both incriminated and convicted several times from the 1460s to the 1490s.[170] Guccio di Niccolò di messer Guccio de' Nobili, member of an old aristocratic family who was an official in 1462/1463, had three brothers who were implicated many times between 1459 and 1494.[171]

Even some men who served on the magistracy evidently found it hard to resist the temptation of sex with boys. Nofri d'Antonio Lenzoni, a Night Officer in 1480/1481, was implicated with at least four boys during the 1490s; in 1495 he was convicted and fined the large sum of 150 florins.[172] Bernardo di Taddeo Lorini, an official in 1484/1485, had been named by an adolescent but absolved in 1476, and was named by another and absolved again in 1487. But when in 1496 a third boy claimed that Lorini had sodomized him, he was now—at the height of Savonarola's moralizing crusade—inclined to disclose the truth. The sixty-five-year-old patrician could not bear the disgrace of confessing in person to his peers, however, so he sent his son Taddeo to confess in his stead and to plead with the officials to act with discretion to salvage what they could of his father's honor.[173]

Beyond such intimate considerations, how the Night Officers proceeded after an accusation of sodomy might have been affected, despite their vows of impartiality, by bonds of friendship, favors or obligations toward clients or patrons, or pressures exerted by men of power and influence. That people with money, prestige, and well-placed friends could manipulate justice in their favor was nothing new in Florence, and informers commonly alerted officials to such intrigues. An accuser in 1496, for instance, warned that a wealthy man in the town of Montelupo would use his resources and the "recommendations" of important friends in Florence to ensure that his son, denounced for passive sodomy, would not be interrogated.[174] During the Savonarolan years, when the policing of sodomy was very much in the public eye, accusers alleged more than once that officials or their staff accepted bribes to dismiss cases.[175] An informant in 1467 indicated a network of eminent citizens who allegedly sponsored a brothel of boys for sodomy that was run by a blacksmith, Zanobi di Baldo, and he cautioned that these powerful notables would use their influence to shield the man from prosecution: "[A]nd worse, with his own mouth he claims he does it at the request of leading men of the regime, and he names ten or twelve of them. Two he names are knights, and at least two others are presently officials of the Dieci di balìa. . . . I think that as soon as it is known that this has been disclosed, you'll see some of those wicked ones come to his defense."[176]

Charges of malfeasance, protection, or influence-peddling were seldom proved, but a few cases of blatant corruption were uncovered which show that abuses did occur. In 1470, Cristofano di Giovanni from Lodi revealed that a friend of a friend of his, whose brother was at the time a Night Officer, having learned that Cristofano had been denounced for sodomy, got his hands on the denunciation and gave it to his friend, who in turn informed Cristofano and then ripped up the note in his presence. In return, the official's brother was now asking Cristofano for a "present" of 12 florins to guarantee that the whole affair would be hushed up and he would never be convicted. Realizing that he was being blackmailed, Cristofano sought the advice of an acquaintance, a former Night Officer, who counseled him to abstain from sodomy in the future and to protect himself by denouncing his sexual relations voluntarily. This he did, naming seventeen boys he had sodomized in the past year.[177] In 1501, Bartolomeo Del Bianco, a patrician accused by a woman of sodomizing her, enlisted the aid of one of the Officers of the Night, Mariano Brancacci, who obligingly threatened the woman with a public flogging if she did not retract her charge, and also bribed two of the other officials. When their scheming was revealed through the woman's courageous denunciation, Del Bianco was condemned and fined 200 florins; the Guardians of the Law also convicted the three Night Officers of corruption and expelled them from the office.[178]

Sometimes allegations of sodomy had sensitive political implications that moved authorities to dismiss them. When in 1500 a foreign ambassador to the city was incriminated for sodomy, the Signoria pragmatically intervened to acquit him, "considering the quality of his person and of his lord, [and] that saving him can be of some utility."[179] Acting evidently on their own initiative, two notaries connived in 1498 to get a case dropped, not only because it involved a young relative of Pandolfo Petrucci, the lord of Siena, but also because if the boy were interrogated he might have revealed his none-too-secret sexual affair with a prominent Florentine citizen. According to the case protocol,[180] ser Bartolomeo Filippi confided to ser Lorenzo Vanelli, assistant notary and chancellor of the Eight of Watch, "I have learned that the Night Officers want to arrest a Sienese who is a servant and relative of Pandolfo Petrucci of Siena. If he is disgraced like this, he might make some reprisal against one of our Florentines. What's more, I know that a notable who holds a high office has had the boy, and it would be a good thing to protect him." Vanelli, in turn, advised the attendant whom the officials had ordered to arrest the boy not to do so "because it might cause a great scandal, and you will also be doing a favor for one of the Dieci [di balìa]." As a result of these machinations, the boy went free. As the report states, the two notaries had brought "shame and dishonor" on the Officers of the Night, and they were punished accordingly. The Eight exiled ser Bartolomeo from the city for one year, and suspended ser Lorenzo from his post as their chancellor and deprived him of all municipal offices for one year.

The regulation of sodomy in Florence was thus in part bound up in considerations of political prudence and in the dynamics of kinship, clientage, and friendship, which led at times to corruption. Sodomy was probably no more susceptible to such abuses than were other illicit activities, though its apparent ubiquity, the involvement of prominent people, and perhaps its semiclandestine nature and potential for defamation might have encouraged them. But this cannot fully explain officials' relative apathy for pursuing cases that came before them. Their disregard of most accusations and the ease with which most people, especially those with influential connections, escaped conviction also reflect a climate of controlled lenience toward sodomy.

Despite the large number of alleged sodomites who eluded conviction, the Night Officers and the Eight of Watch did condemn many, and many paid dearly. The punishments imposed on sodomites varied widely, mainly because penalties were made much harsher after the Medici were expelled in 1494, but also because the two institutions operated in quite different ways. The punishments they levied in the two periods 1478 to 1494 and 1494 to 1502 are shown in Tables A.1 through A.4, along with the alternative penalties they often provided (usually a reduced fine as an incentive to pay at least something, or sometimes a substitute for a fine or for corporal punishment). A comparison of their penalties highlights again the relative indulgence of the "office of the sodomites," but also reveals the sterner approach of the Eight, yielding a more balanced and complete picture of the policing of sodomy in Florence.

In general, the penalties levied by the Night Officers tended to be much lighter than those of the Eight of Watch. Unsurprisingly, given their "benign" role, the former usually let sodomites pay for their sins in cash rather than through public humiliation or punishments like prison or exile. Overall, 90 percent of their sentences were fines (96 percent before and 82 percent after 1494). The Eight imposed fines more sparingly, in only 38 percent of their convictions (36 percent before and 40 percent after 1494). Both magistracies were flexible with monetary penalties, however. Especially before but also after 1494, both fined many men well below prescribed sums, even in the cases of repeated offenders, such as the "little baker," Jacopo d'Andrea, with his fluctuating fines. In contrast, on rare occasions they levied enormous fines, such as the penalty of 1,000 florins the Night Officers imposed in 1477 on the recidivist Simone di Giovanni del Barbigio.[181]

The Officers of the Night occasionally and the Eight of Watch regularly also sentenced men to prison, exile, public humiliation, or a combination of such penalties, and at times they added a fine as well. Both levied few prison sentences, the Night Officers only nine (1.5 percent of their total) and the Eight, twenty-seven (11.4 percent). Prison terms imposed by the Night Officers ranged from just five weeks to three years, while those of the Eight were commonly two to ten years or even life. Many other men no doubt spent some time in the Stinche, the municipal prison, before putting up a surety for their fine, while others, unable to pay their fine or secure a guarantor, probably served a term in prison instead.

The Eight, in particular, often banished sodomites: they exiled sixty-five men (27.5 percent of their sentences), while the Night Officers exiled just seven (1.1 percent). Some men were banished only from the city, others from the dominion, and still others to specific places, commonly to Sarzana and Livorno, which apparently served as virtual penal colonies. Again, the Eight usually imposed longer terms of exile than the Night Officers. Those of the latter ranged from one to two-and-a-half years, with one man expelled for life, whereas the Eight frequently banished men for periods of between two and ten years and imposed life exile on ten men.

After fines, the penalty both institutions inflicted most often on sodomites was public humiliation, either by itself or sometimes before sending men to prison or into exile. These ritual shamings were intended to affirm the power of the Commune, guarantor of order and decorum, and to deride before the populace those who offended its honor by contravening its laws (in the case of sodomites, the laws of God and nature as well).[182] The Night Officers sentenced a total of forty-two men (7 percent) to public humiliation, all but five after 1494; the Eight, sixty-seven men (28.4 percent). The most frequent penalties were a one- or two-hour stint in the pillory, or a flogging through the streets or, commonly, at the column in the Old Market. Some men were whipped through the city while riding an ass, a traditional sign of ignominy. After 1494 a few repeat offenders were branded on the forehead with the insignia of the Florentine Commune. To add to their disgrace, men who stood in the stockades or were flogged often had to wear a miter, a fool's cap, on which was sometimes painted the epithet *sodomita* or the letter *B*, perhaps for *buggerone* (bugger).[183] A chronicler's depiction of a much later shaming of sodomites in Florence, in 1703, evokes the raucous violence that probably accompanied such spectacles two centuries earlier as well: as a man and his young partner, wearing placards that publicized their crime, were driven through the city on asses, onlookers hooted and whistled, and when the two passed through the marketplace the jeering crowd pelted them with fruits and vegetables.[184]

The Eight staged especially creative spectacles to shame sodomites. Twice they ordered men to process nude, bearing a candle, to the church of the Santissima Annunziata, where they were to offer the candle to the miraculous image of the Annunciation housed there.[185] In 1484 they levied unusually harsh sentences on two Jews: they sentenced the passive partner to pay a fine of 1,000 florins and to be given fifteen *tratti di corda* (jerks of a rope tied around the neck), and fined the active partner 1,500 florins;

in addition, on a Saturday, the Jewish sabbath, both were to be whipped while riding an ass to the "place of justice" outside the walls, where the former's nose and the latter's nose and both ears were to be cut off.[186] In 1488 they ordered four men who had sodomized a ten-year-old boy to be mitered and led to the column in the Old Market, tied facing the column, and given multiple lashes on their nude buttocks, after which they were to be paraded, still naked, to the city gates and exiled.[187]

Descriptions of public humiliations are rare, but Simone Filipepi recorded a stunning account of the shaming the Eight imposed on an infamous sodomite nicknamed Pacchierotto in 1486. His portrayal so vividly brings to life this ritual aspect of policing sodomy that it is worth citing the entire passage:

> It happened that [Pacchierotto] was arrested as a sodomite; and under torture he confessed unheard of and extraordinary filth, and also a few petty thefts. Whence he was convicted, and a very large miter was placed on his head, and then he was whipped around the Piazza [of the Signoria], and when he was in front of the lion he got twelve lashes. Then he was led into the center of the New Market, and here he was given twelve more. From here he was conducted to the street of the Furriers [via tra' Pellicciai] where he had been caught several times at such ribaldry, and here he got another twelve lashes. Then he was led to the Stinche, where he was confined for life, and he was put in the prison of the sodomites, the thieves, and the blasphemers, who were all waiting gaily for him. When he arrived they made him their new captain, merrily singing together for a little fun. Since he was so well esteemed by the group, they sat him at the head of the table with another miter, bigger than before. Poor Pacchierotto was weeping because of his shame and the pain of the flogging, but seeing among those ribalds some who had their foreheads branded, some without noses or ears, some with only one arm, and others who were worse off than he, he was somewhat consoled. And thus he remained very honorably in that place for several years.[188]

The traveling spectacle of Pacchierotto's insult ritual united a number of important symbolic elements. He was humiliated first in the space and before the signs of the Commune's authority, the government square and the statue of the lion, or Marzocco, the symbol of the city (or perhaps before the caged lion nearby); then in the city's commercial district, the foundation of its civic identity and emblem of its merchant values of decorum and respectability; then in the street of the Furriers, not only the scene of his own crimes but also a well-known haunt of Florentine sodomites.[189] After asserting the municipality's sovereignty, the message was carried into the territory of the "enemy" to deride not only this sodomite but all sodomites.[190]

Finally, and quite significantly, the two magistracies condemned only a handful of men to death for homosexual sodomy: the Night Officers, three; the Eight of Watch, eight. They levied all but one of these sentences after 1494, evidence of the post-Medicean regime's harsher stance toward sodomy. Aggravated circumstances usually dictated the severity of the penalty. The three men condemned to death by the Officers of the Night were all repeat offenders; five of the men sentenced by the Eight had severely injured the boy they sodomized, and a sixth was said also to be an infamous thief. Yet only three of the eleven sentences seem to have been carried out, for the Night Officers condemned two of these men in absentia and commuted the sentence of the third to a fine, while the Eight condemned five men in absentia. In fact, despite the thousands of convictions it is certain that very few sodomites in Florence were put to death in the fifteenth and sixteenth centuries: a list, incomplete but roughly indicative, of condemned criminals accompanied to their deaths by the confraternity of Santa Maria della Croce al Tempio, or "Neri," identifies only six men between 1420 and 1500 and three men during the entire sixteenth century who were executed for sodomy.[191]

The reluctance on the part of Florentine authorities to put men to death for sodomy, especially when they were men of some status and even if they were notorious sodomites, is well illustrated by the case of Salvi di Niccolò Panuzzi, the man whose death sentence the Night Officers commuted. Panuzzi was a retail cloth merchant from a well-to-do minor guild family of the Medici neighborhood of San Lorenzo.[192] He was fairly prominent in civic life, having served in the highest municipal offices three times (as prior in 1485, ward captain in 1490, and one of the twelve Buonuomini in 1491), and on various criminal magistracies (the Office of Decency in 1473, the Eight of Watch in 1485, and as podestà in four provincial towns in the 1470s and 1480s).[193] He was also one of the city's better-known sodomites: he was incriminated several times between 1466 and the mid-1490s, and denounced himself at least once, in 1478; in 1492 the Eight fined him 300 florins, exiled him for three years, and interdicted him from office for fondling the genitals of a young cleric in the cathedral choir during a sermon.[194] Finally, in 1496, when the now sixty-three-year-old Panuzzi not only confessed to other sexual relations with youths but also admitted that he had solicited several young men to sodomize him—a rare and abhorred reversal of a mature male's sexually "dominant" and "active" role[195]—the Night Officers condemned him to be burned after being beheaded. Nonetheless, they agreed that if he paid the large sum of 300 florins they would stay his execution and commute his penalty to life imprisonment on bread and water in the ward for the insane (*la paz[z]eria*).[196] Panuzzi or his family came up with the money, which saved him not only from a beheading but also from his confinement as a madman.[197]

Clearly, levying sentences was one thing, but whether or how they were carried out was another and in some ways is more indicative of how effective the policing of sodomy was. The records provide limited information on the results of sentences, but do give a sense of the problems involved. First, nearly three-quarters (456) of the active partners convicted by the

Night Officers in the 1478–1502 survey and one-half (114) of those convicted by the Eight were in contumacy, indicating that they had fled or in any case had not responded to the officials' summons. Some absentees might eventually have paid their fines or served their sentences, but many probably did not. Moreover, as noted earlier, after levying a penalty both magistracies often offered a reduction or substitution, which usually mitigated the original punishment considerably. The Night Officers did so in 43 percent of their convictions and the Eight in 54 percent. If a person intended to pay his fine or serve his sentence, no doubt he made every possible effort to take advantage of the alternative penalty.

Finally, the Night Officers' account books for 1495 to 1502 survive,[198] and these give some indication of how many fined sodomites settled with the court. In the five years for which procedural records survive in the same period, the officials levied fines for active homosexual sodomy on 214 men and offered an optional fine to another 35 on whom they imposed nonmonetary punishments. Yet only 104 of these men (41 percent) made any payments at all. Of these, a mere 2 paid their original fine in full, while another 9 paid their alternative fine in full. The rest paid much lower sums, often just a few florins of a 50-florin fine, bearing out the repeated complaints that convicted sodomites, often poor, seldom fulfilled their financial obligations. The original or optional fines of the 104 who made payments totaled 5,465 florins, and the fines levied on all active partners in these five years amounted to a substantial 12,366 florins. But in these cases the Night Officers collected little more than 1,350 florins.[199] If the policing of sodomy potentially represented a considerable source of income for the Commune, the concrete results were disappointing.

Community Controls

The emphasis here on the city's judiciary apparatus should not obscure the community's traditional and "informal" methods for regulating sodomy. The information is limited, but evidence from judiciary or other sources shows some of the ways in which Florentines, outside the courts, sought to discourage homosexual activity or punish offenders. These could take several forms, from private reprimands of relatives and friends to collective ridicule by an entire neighborhood.

Some families probably tried to dissuade or discipline their sons or other relatives who engaged in sodomy; such efforts form the subject of several local anecdotes, or *facezie*.[200] According to an informer in 1492, when Martino Martini found his son Marco's lover in the house, "he punished [his son] severely, and took away his slippers," perhaps, as was common, a gift from his suitor.[201] Another father reportedly threw his son out of the house for having a young boyfriend.[202]

Normally parents or relatives do not appear to have instigated accusations, for understandable reasons: it was in a family's interests—both financial and in terms of their honor—that word of their son's or other family member's sexual activity not reach the Night Officers. Indeed, some families might have settled privately with men who sodomized their sons or relatives and agreed not to take legal action against them. When one boy's brother-in-law and guardian found that the doctor who employed the boy as a servant had sodomized him many times and injured his anus, he reportedly accepted 2 florins from the doctor in return for letting the case drop.[203] Such arrangements would seldom have been recorded, so perhaps they were more common than they appear.

The case in 1465 of the horse dealer Simone di Bino reveals a glimpse of the informal pressure that disapproving family members and friends might have applied, in this case to persuade Simone to leave his friend, twenty-year-old Rinaldo di Niccolò Benizzi. The informer, seemingly part of Simone's intimate circle, said that the youth Rinaldo had been interrogated several times but had not confessed, and the two continued to see each other daily. Further, Simone "has been scolded by his business partner, by his brothers-in-law, by his godparents, and by other friends, yet to no avail. Even the Captain of the Guard has spoken to him about it, threatening to arrest him if he doesn't leave the boy. But it is of no use."[204] Well aware of his relationship with Rinaldo, Simone's close-knit network of relatives, friends, and associates apparently tried to cajole and threaten him privately before turning, as the circumstances imply, to the authorities.

Some parents did come to the Night Officers for justice, either when the offense was more serious or involved very young boys, or when their own discipline was insufficient. Several fathers and one widowed mother brought accusations when their sons, in most cases under ten years of age, had been sodomized with anal injuries.[205] Another father told officials that after two of his field-workers discovered a man sodomizing his eight-year-old son, he beat the boy with a broom to make him confess before bringing him to them to take action against the man.[206] In 1495 a distraught widow in a provincial town turned to the Night Officers with an unusual request to impose their discipline on her son and the man who sodomized him, evidently because she had failed:

> Lord officials, I implore you. I am a poor widow with a son named Niccolò. Here in Gambassi there is a man named Francesco di Piero Benghi, who takes him out every evening and sodomizes him. He gives him a half-*grosso* [a coin] each time. Arrest the boy secretly. Put a little fear in him with a whipping and he'll confess everything. My name is Maria Angelica, widow of Torme di Gallo.[207]

The experiences of Guerrieri di Tribaldo de' Rossi, as told in his father's journal, illustrate the misadventures that could befall a young Florentine involved in sodomy and reveal several family and community responses.[208] Born in 1485 into an old and once illustrious magnate family now fallen into modest circumstances, Guerrieri had a troubled adolescence. At age eleven he was already gambling with other boys and began to miss school, escapades for which his irate father beat him and temporarily threw him out of the house. He was apprenticed in 1499 to a wool merchant, but his employer fired him after only eight months, as his father recorded, "because of his wickedness and because he would obey neither him, his father, nor his mother." Placed in school again, he ran away from home after ten days, staying two nights with a young friend, Francesco Della Rena, who like Guerrieri was soon after implicated in sodomy.[209] Francesco mediated with Tribaldo, who agreed to take his son back into the household and promised not to punish him. He soon placed Guerrieri in another shop, but with little optimism, as he wrote, "because we don't see much discipline in him."

In fact, around this time Guerrieri had evidently been engaging in sodomy with numerous men. After an anonymous denunciation,[210] on May 6, 1500, the Night Officers arrested the fourteen-year-old and questioned him, releasing him upon the intervention of none other than Niccolò Machiavelli, the Rossi's neighbor. Unfortunately, the register that contained his confession is missing, but his father ruefully reported that "he confessed about many" who had sodomized him. And, as Tribaldo painfully admitted, "it was a great humiliation for him throughout all of Florence, for him and for all of us [*e gran verghongnia gli fu per tutto Firenze a lui e tutti noi*]." Disgraced at home, Guerrieri also had problems in his workshop, where his master wanted to fire him because other boys were harassing and teasing him. He eventually agreed to keep him on without pay for several months. But the boy's troubles were not over. His employer changed his mind and fired him on May 23, and in his chagrin over losing his job he ran away from home again. A friend who worked in Guerrieri's shop told Tribaldo on May 26 that he had seen the boy, and that he did not want to return home because of his "fear and shame." Finally, on May 30 the same friend brought him home. Mortified as much for himself as for his son, however, Tribaldo was forced to keep Guerrieri shut up in the house "so that he is not made fun of outside [*perché non avese la baia fuori*]."

Personal accounts like this are rare, so it is hard to know whether other boys suffered similar punishments or humiliations. There is no reason to believe, however, that Guerrieri's problems or the reactions to his sexual misdeeds were unique. Although the courts seldom penalized boys who let men sodomize them, families and the community evidently had their own ways of punishing, shaming, and even ostracizing them. Not only did Guerrieri de' Rossi, for example, suffer the taunts of his peers, lose his job, and undergo family discipline, but his father was so shaken and humiliated that even he turned his back on him. Previously Tribaldo had proudly and meticulously recorded Guerrieri's school and work experiences, but after his anguished account of the boy's sodomitical escapades until the journal ended a year and a half later, he never again mentioned his wayward son, who had apparently so disappointed his paternal aspirations.[211]

Along with the family, the neighborhood community in traditional Europe, with its strong sense of shared moral obligation and vigilance over behavior to maintain local tranquillity, was a potent source of social control.[212] It is not too surprising, therefore, that whole neighborhoods acted at times in collective, informal ways to rid themselves of a sodomite or to convince a neighbor to reform. According to an informer in 1496, someone spied the parish priest of Sant'Ilario, whom local people had long suspected was a sodomite, in the church's garden with another man and a fifteen- or sixteen-year-old adolescent. When the news spread, some fifty parishioners descended on the place to chase the priest from the church.[213] Two other men, one a priest and one a layman, were also reported in the 1490s to have been driven from churches, hospitals, and other places as sodomites.[214] The efforts of neighbors to defend the peace and virtue of their streets and districts might also have included the collective writing of denunciations, as a number of them suggest.[215]

In another striking denunciation in 1468, an informer recounted how Antonio di Jacopo, a mercer at the Canto del Giglio, was twice found in compromising situations with boys in his shop, and was treated to a chorus of ridicule by his neighbors.[216] Antonio had locked himself into his shop one evening with Zanobi, a young painter with whom he had been in love for three years, according to the informant. Someone passing by saw smoke coming from the window and, assuming the shop was on fire, raised the alarm. Unable to find Antonio, neighbors began to break down the door to put out the flames. By this time the commotion had drawn about a hundred people to the shop, with others peering from their windows. When Antonio, whose inclinations were reportedly well known in his neighborhood, finally opened the door and sheepishly emerged with Zanobi, the crowd derided and scolded him as he made his way along the street. "He has also been reprimanded by the neighbors," the accuser continued, "and by those who are fond of him so that he will mend his ways and leave the evil."

Despite the public shaming, however, Antonio apparently had no intention of renouncing his pleasures. On another evening, he was closed inside his shop "in his usual way" when someone (greedy neighbors, the informer said) who had made a point of keeping an eye on him spied Antonio inside with a boy. They hung two big lanterns outside the shop to attract the neighbors. After a crowd had gathered and the windows along the street were filled with women with candles in hand, someone beat on the door of the shop. "And Antonio, unable to avoid this disgrace . . . decided to open up, and emerged to great ridicule. And he's even an old man, around 60, with three grown sons."[217]

Such traditional forms of social control within intimate circles of family and friends or wider groups of neighbors were probably fairly common. From these and other examples, it seems that the Night Officers were at times considered a last resort to be called on only when the efforts of loved ones and acquaintances had failed. Like families, neighbors might have preferred to use customary methods of rebuking and shaming wayward friends rather than to risk rupturing bonds of local solidarity by denouncing them to the authorities. When a woman in 1467 reportedly found her husband in bed with a boy and ran angrily into the street to complain to neighbor women, the informer warned officials to question these women under oath, since "otherwise they wouldn't admit it, because they are neighbors."[218] Even anonymous denunciations—which might have been less secretive than they appear—could have worked much like neighborhood gossip to encourage people to modify their behavior or to conduct their sexual affairs more discreetly. Officials' lax reactions to accusations possibly suggest, among other things, a tendency to give room to such traditional, informal modes of regulating sexual behavior.

In any case, within a context of limited acceptance, sodomy was subject to close surveillance and regulation both by customary methods and by formally constituted authorities. Although divergent attitudes abounded, many Florentines throughout the Renaissance continued to view sodomy as a transgression, both a sin and a crime, and its control was a matter of abiding concern to them. The continual elaboration of punitive norms and the thousands of convictions over the course of the fifteenth century attest strongly to this lively and enduring preoccupation. But though it was a sin and a crime, perhaps to many Florentines it was not so "abominable" or dangerous as Church doctrine and official rhetoric portrayed it.

Homosexual activity in Florence was widespread and deeply rooted, a tenacious social and sexual reality that the community's disciplinary efforts had to acknowledge and, to a certain extent, shrewdly accommodate. In concluding this chapter, it is worth recalling the pragmatic judgment expressed by the Night Officers in the sentence against a sodomite they condemned in 1436:

> If despite every sort of punishment these men are still not restrained, at least some might control themselves, and perhaps those defiled by such ignominy will not do it so openly; and if out of a thousand sodomites the authorities punish even one well, all of them experience fear. Although their crimes may not be completely prevented, they may in part be contained.[219]

With its innovative and flexible apparatus for policing sodomy, a complex mix of lenience and pervasiveness, the governors of the city were unable and probably did not really intend to "eradicate" the "vice," but they did hope to confine it within tolerable limits. The ambivalence and contradictions of managing sodomy fully reflected the problematic but integral place of homosexuality—as the following chapters will show—in Florentine male culture.

PART II

3

"He Keeps Him Like a Woman": Age and Gender in the Social Organization of Sodomy

> If you want some fun, have sex often with boys.
>
> Proverb attributed to the Florentines by Sabadino degli Arienti, *Le porretane* (ca. 1480)[1]

> And you, boy . . . look what sorry cowardice you submit to: that God made you male, and the devil makes you female.
>
> Bernardino of Siena (1425)[2]

> Antonio di Michele . . . keeps [Jacopo Ciafferi] for use as a woman. Please, lord officials, do something so that that boy is not led astray; he's only eleven years old. . . . Consider whether it is a decent thing to use males like females.
>
> Anonymous informer (1467)[3]

This chapter takes up an exploration of the nature and significance of sodomy in male culture and sexual experience in late medieval Florence by beginning with the fundamental issues of how homoerotic interactions were typically organized and how they were perceived and represented. Recent studies in both anthropology and history have shown that the social forms in which homosexual behavior occurs, and the meanings attributed to it, vary considerably across time and culture. Many studies have stressed, moreover, that it is necessary to distinguish sexual behavior from sexual identity. Simply to project current Western conceptions of homosexuality—which are dominated by the notion of a permanently deviant and distinct minority—onto same-sex erotic relations in past or other societies inevitably tends to misrepresent their historical and cultural specificity.[4]

Regarding the traditional societies of medieval and early modern Europe, the most persuasive view now holds that homosexual behavior usually occurred between an "active" adult and a "passive" adolescent, and that most males who engaged in sex with other males probably also had sexual relations with females. Only in the eighteenth century, and then, it seems, above all in northwestern Europe (England, the Netherlands, and France), did this pattern gradually begin to be replaced by a new model. After 1700 adult males are frequently found having sex with other adult males, the rigid sexual roles of the past appear to have become more fluid, homosexuality was commonly associated with effeminacy, and distinctive subcultures developed.[5] If most studies of the medieval and early modern periods acknowledge that age-structured homosexual behavior was common, however, the frequent absence of adequate information on the ages of sexual partners, or insufficient attention to them, has impeded a fuller grasp of how widespread this pattern was. In addition, the tendency to interpret the evidence in ways apparently influenced by contemporary sexual experience and categories has sometimes caused its significance to be misconstrued.[6]

The Florentine evidence, abundant in biographical detail, offers the best-documented case presently known among traditional European societies for the absolute prevalence of homosexual behavior organized around age difference and a rigid distinction in sexual roles. To summarize briefly, same-sex sodomy in Florence normally involved an adult male over the age of eighteen who took the "active," dominant role with a "passive" adolescent usually between the ages of twelve and eighteen to twenty. Even in the few exceptions, such as sex between adolescents, partners' relative age disparity usually still determined their sexual role. Reciprocal or role-trading sexual relations were rare and limited almost entirely to adolescents, while it was rarer still for adult males to take the sexually receptive role. The predominant, virtually normative, social form of homosexual behavior in Florence was thus what might be called "pederasty," though this particular term does not appear in local sources and was apparently unknown to all but a refined literary elite.[7] Age-graded homoerotic relations like this, of course, were an ancient institution in the Mediterranean region, and seem to have persisted strongly throughout this area during the medieval and early modern periods, if not longer.[8]

The evidence from Florence, however, not only underlines the continuing prevalence of this hierarchical configuration, but further suggests that the conventions governing sexual relations between males operated within a framework of cultural premises about masculinity, status, honor, and shame that, with some possible variations, was widely shared among societies around the Mediterranean basin.[9] Occasional comments in laws, trial proceedings, sermons and literature, and above all the unstudied remarks of informers reveal that Florentines commonly construed homoerotic relations in terms of life stages and gender. The highly structured form of these relations helped to distinguish boyhood from manhood and to mark out the transition from the one to the other; correspondingly, the respective sexual roles (active or passive, dominant or subordinate) were perceived according to conventionally defined gender dichotomies as manly or womanly. In the ways in which it was enacted and understood, then, homosexual sodomy in Florence was intimately bound up in notions of male status and identity, and played an important role in the cultural construction of masculinity.

Sexual Roles and Behavior

Late medieval Florentines assumed as a matter of course that sexual interactions between males were structured in an asymmetrical way according to sharply differentiated roles in intercourse, roles that were determined above all by age. Distinctions in sexual roles pervade portrayals of sodomy both in official discourse, such as trial proceedings and laws, and in vernacular denunciations. Moreover, close attention to the sexual behavior of those who engaged in sodomy, as it was revealed through denunciations and their testimony, as well as to their ages, which will be reviewed in the next section, shows how closely homoerotic relations in fact corresponded to these representations.

Laws from the fourteenth through the sixteenth century regularly distinguished between roles in sodomitical acts, which eventually became codified as "active" and "passive." However, what behaviors these terms were taken to mean was never specified, nor, with a few exceptions, did the opposing roles entail different penalties, which were determined more by age. Fourteenth-century laws characterized sexual roles in descriptive terms instead of the categories "active" and "passive," which appeared later. These early portrayals show that these were not merely distinctions of convenience, but that contrasting cultural values adhered to them. The statute of 1325, for instance, the sole Florentine law that put so much explicit emphasis on pederastic relations, stated that "any corrupt sodomite [who] will have been discovered with some boy is to be fully castrated; a boy who, on the contrary, will have consented to foul himself with such a crime [is to be fined]."[10] Someone who sodomized a boy, that is, might be morally corrupt or depraved (*pollutus*), but a boy who agreed to be sodomized dirtied or disgraced himself (*se foedare*), implying that his honor was sullied. In a 1365 law, the value judgments attached to the two roles were drawn even more sharply. Here the dominant partner was referred to neutrally as "whatever person committed the said crime with any other person," while the subordinate was belittled as "a person who might have willingly suffered the said crime to be inflicted upon him."[11] These representations exclude all sense of reciprocity; sodomy was something that one person did to another, and a stronger feeling of stigma accompanied the latter's dishonorable submission.

The expressive language of these early laws yielded for the first time in the statutes of 1408/1409 and of 1415 to the categorical terms "active" and "passive": "whoever will have voluntarily committed the crime of sodomy, whether actively or passively [*quicumque voluntarie commiserit crimen sogdomie agendo vel patiendo*]."[12] This dualistic formula occurred routinely in rulings against sodomy from this point on to at least the mid-sixteenth century. Sometimes trial summaries also identified the respective partners as either *agens* or *agente* (active), or *patiens* or *paziente* (passive). If they failed to label the partners explicitly, the role assumed by each is still easily discerned in the language of the report. But while the representation of roles became more formulaic, the values attributed to them in earlier descriptions continued to cling to them, as the popular expressions discussed later indicate.

Significantly, only laws and trial summaries, what might be considered "official" representations of sodomy, used the terms "active" and "passive" to distinguish roles. These words rarely, if ever, appear in sources closer to spoken language, such as vernacular sermons, poems and popular tales, and denunciations. Even in the descriptive language of these sources, however, distinctions in sexual roles remain basic to the representation of sodomy.

Accusations provide the best examples of the idiomatic and dualistic ways in which common people depicted sodomy. They usually distinguished sexual roles grammatically, using either the active or the passive voice. To cite only a couple of typical examples, an accuser wrote, "Alessandro d'Antonio da Filicaia sodomized [*ha sodomitato*] Piero di Salvestro, a stationer"; that is, the "active" Alessandro sodomized the "passive" Piero.[13] Another, referring to an unnamed passive partner, wrote, "a servant of messer Carlo Martelli lets himself be sodomized by many [*si fa sodomitare da molti*]."[14] Use of the active verb form to indicate the "active" partner and either of the passive forms *si fa* with the infinitive, as in this example, or *è stato sodomizzato* (has been sodomized), to denote the "passive" was common, no matter which term an informer adopted from the rich Florentine lexicon of sexual relations. Informers most often used the verb *sodomitare* (or *sodomizzare*), but they frequently employed others with much the same meaning. These include *abbracciare* (to embrace, but here with the connotation of sexual coupling), *buggerare* (to bugger), *fottere* (to fuck), *servire* (to serve or service, in a sexual sense, referring to the passive), *usare* or *adoperare* (to use or make use of someone in sodomy, or to use sodomy with someone, but sometimes employed in the same sense as *servire*), and *fare* (to do, in the sense of "doing" sodomy or even "doing" someone). Other expressions, some of which will be discussed later, are not sexually explicit but focus on relationships, indicating that accusers (unlike the courts) were often concerned not merely with overt sexual acts but also with their social and emotional contours. That lay people who denounced sexual relations between males ignored the terms "active" and "passive," did not always use "sodomy" or "sodomize," and rarely employed the phrase "sin against nature"—all of which were privileged in religious, legal, and judiciary sources—suggests that the dominant, learned culture's representations of sodomy existed alongside other popular traditions and conceptions. But in either case, the distinction between sexual roles formed a basic point of reference in Florentine portrayals of sodomy.

Yet what did sodomy and its related role differences mean in terms of sexual practices and comportment between males? No prescriptive or religious sources offer precise answers; for these we must examine closely the erotic behaviors that lay people denounced and courts prosecuted.

It should first be observed that consummation of a sexual act between two males was not the only grounds for prosecution. Laws also set penalties for unspecified actions deemed "preparatory" to committing sodomy, even if uncompleted.[15] Although authorities treated such cases inconsistently, several men were condemned, with penalties often similar to those for full-fledged sodomy, simply because they "made an attempt on the virtue" of boys with propositions, threats, or the offer of money.[16] Two men were convicted in 1480 and two others in 1499 merely for kissing a boy they wanted to seduce.[17] In 1508, a dyer was unable to carry out his intent to sodomize a fourteen-year-old boy, but was still sentenced to an hour in the pillory because he had kissed him and fondled his genitals with his "licentious hands."[18] None of these acts were labeled "sodomy," but the attention paid to them suggests that magistrates assumed they were commonly associated with sodomitical seductions.

What Florentines intended as "sodomy" somewhat broadens our understanding of the nature and perception of erotic experience between males in this culture. First, the evidence shows that sodomy did not refer exclusively to anal intercourse, as is sometimes too narrowly assumed, but also to the simulation of intercourse between the thighs and to fellatio.[19] It also offers some new perspectives on the possible dynamics of homosexual interactions in premodern Europe. In the classical Mediterranean world, according to one recent formulation, pederastic relations expressed a "generalized ethos of penetration and domination" in which differences in status and power were articulated and enacted through the phallic penetration of the body of the subordinate "passive" partner, by the dominant "active" partner.[20] Although in many respects pederasty in Florence was bound up in this same ethos and conformed to the same behavioral configuration, it also diverged from it in certain important ways.

Besides identifying partners' respective roles, the Night Officers' records often give some indication of what sexual behaviors were involved. In about 25 percent of the cases in which at least one partner confessed, notaries recorded only generically that the one had sodomized the other, with no other details. For the remaining 75 percent, they gave more but still limited information. Usually they merely specified that one person had sodomized another either ex parte post (or sometimes retro), the most common depiction, occurring in roughly 84 percent of these cases, or ex parte ante, occurring in some 12 percent. The meaning of these phrases is rather ambiguous, but one interpretation might be that they referred to the position in which one person sodomized the other, that is, from behind or facing from the front. This, at any rate, must be the appropriate reading in the remaining small minority of cases (about 4 percent) in which notaries indicated that a person had sodomized another by thrusting his penis between his partner's thighs, either ex parte post or ante.

But when these expressions were not qualified this way, they probably meant not positions, but the body parts of the subordinate partner by means of which his companion performed the act of sodomy—that is, the anus (the part in the rear) or the genitals (the part in the front). On the few occasions notaries added an explicit description, in regard to both same-sex and opposite-sex relations, they had just this sense in mind. A helpful portrayal comes from a case in which a young man sexually abused his eight-year-old servant girl. She was hospitalized for injuries she suffered both ex parte ante and ex parte post, which the notary also rendered in Italian as *guasta dalle parti dinanzi e dietro* (injured in the front and rear parts); yet she insisted to the officials that her master had approached her only from a face-to-face position and never from the rear.[21] Here the terms referred to the girl's vulva, as the report elsewhere specifies, and anus, not to postures. Similarly, in the most explicit definition of the phrase "ex parte post" yet found in a case of homosexual sodomy, the notary wrote bluntly that a boy had been sodomized "ex parte post, that is, in the ass [*in chulo*]."[22] These depictions suggest that sodomy ex parte post meant anal intercourse regardless of the positions assumed. In this most common form of sex between males and in the infrequent form of intercrural copulation, it was always the "active" partner who phallicly penetrated the body of the "passive."

Correspondingly, in the single example of homosexual relations in which a notary elucidated the meaning of sodomy ex parte ante, he referred not to anal penetration in a face-to-face position but explicitly to fellatio. In the scribe's graphic account of Lorenzo di Francesco Ubertini's confession in 1480, sixty-four-year-old Antonio di Niccolò de' Nobili sodomized Lorenzo "ex parte ante, that is, the said Lorenzo ejaculating in the mouth of the said Antonio di Niccolò."[23] Antonio thus "actively" sodomized the presumably adolescent Lorenzo by fellating him.

Now the question of which partner conceptually takes the "active" or dominant role in oral sex can be ambiguous, but here the "penetrator" was plainly the younger "passive" partner, the reverse of the pattern in anal or intercrural copulation. Somewhat surprisingly, the evidence indicates that this was in fact the norm for fellatio in Florence. In cases that overtly describe oral sex, it was usually the older partner who fellated and was thus phallicly penetrated by the younger. In another summary, a notary wrote that Antonio di Cristoforo, a sixty-year-old goldsmith, "sodomized the said Lionardo [aged fifteen], that is, because the said Antonio sucked his penis."[24] An informer depicted fellatio in similar terms: "Tommaso, called Lasca, has sodomized . . . many boys and, moreover, he has committed this vice with his own mouth"; the seventeen-year-old questioned about this charge confirmed that "he [Tommaso] sodomized him with his mouth."[25] Numerous other examples could be cited.[26] Lest these older men's interest in "receptive" oral sex be taken as an identifying or permanent trait, however, it should be noted that among those who appear several times in the records, fellatio was apparently not their exclusive or even preferred sexual activity with boys: men like Lasca and other habitual sodomites who engaged in fellatio are usually found taking the insertive role in anal intercourse.[27]

The records yield only a few exceptions to the normal pattern of fellatio in which the junior partner was the "insertee" and the senior the "inserter." In 1496 sixty-year-old Niccolò d'Antonio admitted that he had forced a nine- or ten-year-old boy begging alms to fellate him in return for a few coins.[28] In another case, a man said to be over thirty made a seventeen-year-old "suck his nature, that is, his virile member." The notary unusually described this, however, as an abnormal or inconceivable act (*enorme a[c]tum*), implying it was thought odd and especially loathsome, probably due to the role reversal.[29]

It is commonly noted that peoples of the classical Mediterranean world considered fellatio reprehensible and shunned it, and it is rarely reported in the literature on medieval or early modern sodomy in this region.[30] If the suggested interpretation of the phrase "ex parte ante" is correct, however, then this practice was well known and fairly widely employed in homoerotic interactions in Florence (it occurs, as mentioned earlier, in 12 percent of confessed relations). Moreover, except for the case just mentioned in which the usual roles were reversed, fellatio—even when it was plainly described as such—does not seem to have aroused any more hostility or criticism than anal coitus, whether on the part of accusers, magistrates, or the persons directly involved. Nonetheless, one sixteenth-century Italian source, but which is not Florentine or probably even Tuscan, implies that fellatio was sometimes considered rather strange or curious, if not more repugnant than anal sodomy. In this libertine text, which recounts the sexual escapades of a teenage male prostitute with the allusive name Sodo, fellatio appears only once among the young protagonist's many trysts with men. Relating the experience to his friend Arsiccio, Sodo admits that he was surprised and a little afraid when his partner began to fellate him forcefully, and he found it especially odd and amusing that the man wanted him to ejaculate in his mouth.[31]

The frequency and form of fellatio in Florence thus add considerable nuance to the common phallic-centered conception of homosexual behavior in the Mediterranean cultural region and to the dynamics of power and pleasure implicit in it. Again, in the classical homoerotic ethos there was no room for reciprocal desire and pleasure, at least according to the representational ideal: the dominant partner monopolized the right to phallic pleasure in the sexual encounter, while the junior partner was expected merely to allow his companion to gratify his own desires while he remained impassive, distant, without experiencing arousal or taking pleasure himself.[32] By the Renaissance, this attitude had apparently changed substantially. Florentine men who fellated boys presumably did so because they enjoyed it themselves, but also with the intent and certainty of giving sexual pleasure to their young partners. Examples of men who kissed, fondled, or masturbated boys to excite them sexually, or masturbated their companions while they were penetrating them anally, suggest perhaps that some men thought that stimulating a boy's desire would make him more receptive to their invitations, or they were solicitous that their partner also achieved full sexual satisfaction.[33] In an epigram in the *Hermaphroditus*, Beccadelli portrayed a boy about to be anally penetrated as "full of lust," implying that some boys quite willingly let themselves be sodomized to gratify their own desires.[34] By the early seventeenth century, in a famous apology for pederasty, *L'Alcibiade fanciullo a scola* (ca. 1630), the Venetian libertine priest Antonio Rocco propagated the idea that the adolescent's erotic pleasure in anal coitus (he does not mention fellatio) not only is natural and physiological but is a conscientious lover's duty to foster. The work's protagonist, the schoolteacher Filotimo, insists that boys receive exquisite pleasure from being penetrated, some more than others due to the vicinity of certain nerves in the anal canal to the genital area, and adduces the example of youths so "avid and eager" to be satisfied in this way that they go wild with desire and plead for "the administration of the cock." Their enjoyment, he argues, depends in large part on the sensitivity and skill of the "agent," and he condemns those who, "like butchers," sodomize boys with painful force and for their exclusive pleasure: "These are not lovers, but wolves; not partakers of the most exalted delights, but deadly enemies of nature and the world."[35] During the Renaissance, it appears, a new ethos of mutual enjoyment in homoerotic interactions was emerging, without yet breaking down the rigid separation of sexual roles typical of sodomy in this culture.

In any case, Florentines normally considered the active partner, whether fellator or anal penetrator, as the one who "committed" sodomy, while the passive partner, whether fellated or penetrated, "let himself be sodomized." These role distinctions, with rare exceptions, had little to do with a person's erotic preferences. As anticipated, they were determined above all by the partners' ages.

Boys and Men

Ostensibly simply a behavioral distinction, roles in homosexual relations corresponded above all to a disparity in age between partners. In Florence the "active" partner was usually an adult over the age of eighteen, while his companion was normally an adolescent between the ages of twelve and eighteen to twenty. Even when the ages of the two companions were fairly close, normally the older took the dominant role with the younger. The two intertwined and inseparable features of diverse age and fixed roles within relationships defined and structured erotic interactions between males. Adolescents perhaps had slightly more freedom to experiment and to exchange roles, and among adults there were rare exceptions to the norm, usually viewed with horror or disgust. But generally, homosexual relations in this culture were otherwise inconceivable: adult males did not have sex together. The focus of men's homoerotic desire was on what Florentines called *fanciulli*, or boys, and we would tend to call adolescents.[36]

Sexual interactions structured by age—and pederasty in particular—also seem to have been the predominant form of homosexual relations in other southern European settings besides Florence in the medieval and early modern periods, and probably in northern Europe as well, though this point has sometimes not received the emphasis it merits (perhaps because the sources often do not permit a systematic analysis of sexual partners' ages) and in at least one case has been obscured altogether.[37] Most scholars who have worked on judiciary records agree that the passive companion in same-sex sodomy was usually relatively young. For fifteenth-century Venice, one study describes the passive as frequently young, often referred to in the sources as a boy, an adolescent, or a minor (under age fourteen),[38] while another specifies their ages as usually under fifteen and most often between twelve and fourteen[39]; none of the historical literature on Venetian sodomy in this period gives any indication of the ages of active partners. Also in seventeenth-century Venice and in early modern Valencia, homosexual relations were generally structured by age and were mostly of a pederastic nature, though again a systematic correlation of ages and sexual roles is lacking.[40]

The judiciary evidence on the prevalence of relations between adult men and boys also corresponds closely to literary representations of the period. Virtually all of the contemporary novelle on homoerotic themes, from Boccaccio on, feature the love of mature youths or men for adolescents or young *garzoni*.[41] Probably the best-known apology for pederasty in early modern Italy, *L'Alcibiade fanciullo a scola*, revolves around the persistent courting of a handsome fourteen-year-old boy, Alcibiade, by his schoolmaster, Filotimo. Filotimo instructs his protégé that the proper object of male homoerotic desire is boys (*l'amor maschio è fanciullo*) and he roundly condemns men who seek out sex with other adult males as "rebels of love, men of brutish and corrupted senses."[42] Asked by Alcibiade at what age boys are best enjoyed sexually by men, he says they are ideally between the ages of nine and eighteen, "although there is no fixed rule, since some retain their boyishness longer, and others fade early, just as some full, round little boys excite you from infancy on."[43]

Determining the ages of the respective companions in sodomy is clearly of crucial importance for a social history of homosexual behavior. In this regard, Florentine sources offer an unparalleled wealth of biographical detail that attests, among other things, to the importance of age differences to the conception and practice of sodomy. For now it will suffice simply to document the age-configuration of homosexual sodomy, drawing on my survey of cases that came to the attention of the Night Officers between 1478 and 1502, supplemented by demographic sources. The figures I will refer to here regard persons incriminated for sodomy by any means, regardless of their sentence; later the differences in the ages of persons convicted, absolved, and self-accused will be distinguished more carefully. Although this material is limited to the late fifteenth century, other evidence indicates that the same hierarchical pattern persisted from the early fourteenth to at least the mid-sixteenth century.

The passive partner in homosexual relations was almost always a teenager (Tables B.1 and B.2). In the 1478–1502 survey, of the 475 persons implicated in the passive role whose age was indicated either precisely or in general terms, 90 percent (426) were eighteen or under (that is, the age group that laws on sodomy designated as minors); 10 percent (49) were nineteen or over.[44] Their recorded ages ranged from six to twenty-six (excluding a couple of unusual cases involving older men that will be discussed later). The vast majority, however, were in their teens. Nearly 84 percent were between the ages of thirteen and eighteen, and 92 percent between the ages of thirteen and twenty; a mere 3 percent were over twenty years old. Their mean age was sixteen. A small sample of 58 passive partners incriminated between 1478 and 1483 whom I located in the 1480 *catasto*, the great Florentine tax record that has detailed information on age and household composition, yields much the same results. The ages of this group ranged from ten to twenty-three; 92 percent were eighteen or under and only 8 percent were nineteen or above, while 88 percent were between the ages of thirteen and twenty, and just 1 percent over twenty. Their mean age was fifteen.

Persons implicated in the active role, in contrast, were normally over eighteen and a good deal older than their companions. Of the 777 active partners in the 1478–1502 survey whose age was indicated either specifically or in general terms, 82.5 percent (641) were aged nineteen or older, and were thus adults according to the sodomy laws; 17.5 percent (136) were minors eighteen or under, roughly the same age as their sexual companions.[45] In fact, the proportion of minors is undoubtedly exaggerated: since officials usually absolved youngsters aged eighteen and under who "actively" committed sodomy, they or their families were more likely to furnish proof of their age (witnesses to their birth, certificates of baptism, family journals) to exonerate them, and officials were more likely to cite their status as minors as the motivation for the sentence. The sample of 118 active partners implicated between 1478 and 1483 whom I identified in the 1480 *catasto* perhaps redresses this distortion. Of these, 93 percent were aged nineteen or older, and only 7 percent eighteen or younger. Persons implicated in the active role whose ages were specified in the Night Officers' records ranged from ten to eighty-three, and their mean age was twenty-seven. Ages of the *catasto* sample group ranged from thirteen to seventy, while their mean age, considerably higher, was thirty-four.[46] In the respective sources, then, an average gap of eleven to nineteen years separated the senior and junior partners in homosexual relations. The age groups into which the two partners fell were so commonly situated to either side of the legal boundary defining majority status as above the age of eighteen—that is, active adult and passive minor—that throughout this work I will often use the conventional terms "man" and "boy" to indicate the respective partners, whatever their exact ages; when possible, age will be specified in cases in which greater precision is needed.

A hierarchy of age and sexual role was thus one of the fundamental traits of the social organization of homosexual sodomy in Florence. This distinction, with its corresponding and perhaps decisive difference in physical maturity and strength, played a key role in shaping both the expression and the perception of homosexual desire and behavior in this society. It should be noted, however, that a substantial age gap and an erotic focus on adolescents were not peculiar to same-sex relations, nor did they necessarily or merely imply a desire to dominate; rather, these features were basic to this society's social structure and mentality, for Florentine men usually also married women who were, on the average, seventeen or eighteen years of age and twelve or thirteen years their junior.[47]

Beyond the aggregate statistics, some of the exceptions strengthen the rule. First, it will be useful to consider the twenty-eight cases in the 1478–1502 survey (1 percent of the confessed relations) in which persons admitted that they had engaged in reciprocal sodomy with a companion—that is, by exchanging roles. Rare though they were, such experiences might seem to challenge the hierarchical convention. But in fact nearly all such cases in which both partners' ages are known involved adolescents of roughly the same age, not two adults or companions of widely disparate ages.[48]

A good illustration of mutual sodomy among adolescents comes from the case of Antonio di Francesco, a sixteen-year-old grocer at the Canto alla Macina. Antonio confessed in 1493 that he had been sodomized by twenty different partners. With nine of these, however, he claimed to have exchanged roles, sodomizing them ex parte post as they had him, some not once but "many many times" or "25 or 30" times. Of the eight whose ages were given, two were boys (*pueri*), two were eleven, and four were thirteen.[49] Antonio may have exaggerated, for only two of the eight boys questioned confirmed his version, but three of the six youngsters who denied it admitted in turn that they had had reciprocal relations among themselves.[50] In a similar case in 1494, fourteen-year-old Carlo di Vettorio Bramanti confessed to reciprocal sodomy with three partners; the two whose ages were recorded were fourteen and fifteen.[51] These examples suggest that the usually rigid norms of sexual role-playing loosened somewhat only when young coevals were involved. Mutual penetration was restricted almost solely to the sexually ambivalent and perhaps experimental period of adolescence.

Yet even this slight flexibility in the behavioral code had its limits, to which magistrates paid special attention. For though they rarely penalized minors for sodomy, they made exceptions in all these cases and punished many of the boys involved. The Night Officers convicted Antonio and one of his confessed partners, the three boys who denied his claims but admitted their own reciprocal affairs, and two of the boys Carlo Bramanti named. They fined Antonio the high sum of 20 florins because, as his sentence revealingly states, he committed "so many evil deeds, and of such a kind, both allowing himself to be sodomized by many and sodomizing others . . . for which he should have deserved to receive even greater punishments, especially corporal," which officials waived only in consideration of his young age.[52] In their erotic exuberance, these young friends apparently violated a tacit code of sexual and social conduct whose transgression, even among boys, was thought to pose some danger.

Normally, in fact, the hierarchical pattern prevailed even among adolescents near the same age, since it was quite unusual for a boy to sodomize another who was his senior. In the 1478–1502 survey, there are 133 confessed relations that involved partners whose recorded ages ranged from ten to eighteen and who did not exchange roles (Table B.3). In 122 of these cases, the active partner was the same age or older than the passive, while a younger boy sodomized an older companion in only 11 cases. No boys under fourteen had younger active partners, perhaps because few of the latter would have reached puberty, considered age fourteen in canon law; but even among adolescents aged fifteen to eighteen, nearly nine out of ten companions who sodomized them were their age or slightly older.

The same hierarchical model applied in the few relations that involved a passive youth older than eighteen—that is, an age when his active companion could easily have been younger than he (Table B.4). Of thirty-seven confessed relations in which the passive partner was aged nineteen or older and his companion's age is known, eight cases featured a younger active with an older passive, while in twenty-nine cases the active was the same age or older than his partner. Although these figures seem to give more prominence to relations involving a junior active partner with a senior passive, there is a ready explanation that confirms the usual pattern. Two passive youths aged twenty accounted for all but one of the eight age-reversed affairs, while nine other twenty-year-olds, in contrast, were sodomized by companions who were their age or older. Even in situations that might have lent themselves to greater flexibility or an exchange of roles, then, the junior partner normally "allowed himself to be sodomized" and the senior took the dominant role.

Another facet of the hierarchical norm that linked age and sexual role is illuminated by the experiences of persons who were implicated in both roles with separate companions (that is, not reciprocal sodomy with the same partner). Such diversity was rarely reported: only sixty-two individuals (1.5 percent of the total) appeared with different companions in contrasting roles from 1478 to 1502. Like reciprocal sodomy, this too was typical of the very young, for most were adolescents or youths in their early twenties who were incriminated as both active and passive within a single year. Of the thirty-six persons among these sixty-two whose ages were recorded, twenty-four turned up in both roles only before they reached the age of twenty-one. Moreover, thirty-four of the sixty-two were implicated in different roles during a single year, and all nineteen of these whose ages are known were from thirteen to twenty-three years old. These figures tend to confirm that adolescence conferred a small degree of flexibility in the otherwise rigid system of age-structured sexual roles.

As these findings also indicate, some adolescents who "let themselves be sodomized" continued to engage in sex with other males well into or beyond their twenties. Yet in the few cases recorded, as they grew older they consistently abandoned the passive role of their boyhood to become, in turn, the active, senior partners in relations with boys. Their early passivity was not an inherent condition, nor does their prolonged involvement with males necessarily imply that they had a single, uniform "sexual orientation"; their experiences show instead that different sexual roles were considered appropriate for successive stages of life. In 1492 fourteen-year-old Piero di Lorenzo "Broda" admitted that he had been sodomized by eighteen partners; ten years later, he was implicated in the active role with two boys, and in 1504, when he was twenty-six, the Eight fined him 50 florins and banished him from the dominion for fifteen years in part because he had sodomized Bertolino di Nofri Del Forese "many times."[53] Bartolomeo di Niccolò Segni, twelve years old in 1487 when a self-accuser said he had sodomized him, was convicted three times in 1495 and 1496, at the ages of twenty and twenty-one, for sodomizing boys himself; when he was caught attempting to sodomize another in 1504, at the age of twenty-nine, he was sentenced to life imprisonment as an "inveterate sodomite."[54]

Some youths perhaps went through a transitional period in which for a time they played both roles. Such was the case of Berto di Salvi Salvolini, aged twenty in 1479 when he was first implicated in the receptive role with ten men. Between the ages of twenty-one and twenty-three, he took the active role with some partners and the passive with others, but when he later reappeared in the records, between the ages of thirty-two and thirty-five, his role was exclusively the dominant one, as he was implicated (and twice convicted) for having anally sodomized five adolescents.[55] Whether it was common for males to go through a developmental period in which their sexual roles overlapped is unclear. But all those boys whose continuing sexual interactions with males can be documented did shift from the subordinate role of adolescence to the dominant role of maturity.

Considering how widespread sodomy was in Florence, and how frequently it was reported, it is rather curious that so few adolescents who were implicated in the passive role are documented as later manifesting erotic interests in boys when they were youths or mature men. What happened to those who failed to appear again in the records is understandably hard to determine. Did they later engage in sodomy with boys but escape detection, or, after their own boyhood experiences did they abstain from homosexual activity altogether? Niccolò Machiavelli, in a quip he assigned to Castruccio Castracani, the fourteenth-century lord of Lucca, traced one possible course of a young male's sexual transition as he passed from adolescence to maturity: "Regarding someone who had been a good-looking boy and later was a handsome man, [Castracani joked that] this was too great an affront, since when young he lured husbands away from their wives, and now he lures wives away from their husbands."[56] In any case, if the judiciary sources are any guide, it appears that, just as in Machiavelli's story, being sodomized as a boy did not necessarily "initiate" or channel males into homosexual activity as adults. Similarly, most youths or older men implicated in sodomy do not seem to have had an adolescent background as men's passive partners. For those who did, their sexual receptivity to males when they were young failed to impede their successful adoption of the dominant role—whether with women or boys—expected of them as mature men.

Such a transition provides the background to a piquant tale set in Florence, the "Novella di Ridolfo fiorentino" by Francesco Maria Molza (1489–1544), who located it around the time a boy's beard developed.[57] As long as the stunning beauty of the adolescent Ridolfo was unmarred by facial hair, he was surrounded by youthful suitors. But when a fuzzy down began to appear on his cheeks, Ridolfo was left no choice but to "attempt to deflower the boyhood of those younger than he, just as had been done to him."[58] Also in the forementioned dialogue between the young prostitute Sodo and his friend Arsiccio, Sodo, now aged twenty, laments the end of his "golden age" of youth: now his facial and body hair is thick, and his former admirers ignore him.[59]

In these literary sources, this transition is ideally linked to the acquisition of the secondary characteristics of manhood, resembling the judiciary evidence that reveals the passage at around the age of eighteen to twenty. The passive, usually anally receptive role, was limited almost exclusively to adolescents up to this age, though they also seem to have had some limited role-playing flexibility denied to older men. But the number of passive partners declined sharply from the ages of eighteen to twenty as boys grew older and abandoned their subordinate position to other males. Both younger and older men who continued to "let themselves be sodomized," as will be seen, not only were the objects of ridicule but also were liable to harsh punishment.

The age of eighteen to twenty thus demarcated a critical sexual and social boundary for male adolescents in Florence. On the one side were *fanciulli*, or boys, roughly between the onset of puberty and the full growth of a beard, whose sexual subordination was considered somehow proper to their age and status even though it was highly scorned. On the other side were *giovani*, or youths, who normally avoided taking the passive role with other males and with few exceptions adopted an exclusively dominant role in sexual relations with boys.

The location of this frontier adds a new dimension to traditional late medieval conceptions of the stages of life, which often drew the line between adolescence and youth at age twenty-five or so and took no account of the distinction outlined here. For Dante the period of adolescence stretched unbroken even by puberty from birth to age twenty-five, when youth began.[60] In his *Vita civile*, Matteo Palmieri defined adolescence as extending from the age of discretion to twenty-eight, while Bernardino of Siena simply depicted the time between age fourteen, or puberty, and twenty-five as a period of undistinguished sexual license.[61]

Yet in other ways, Florentines do seem to have recognized the significance of this border for young males' sexual behavior and status. They acknowledged it in law, for while the statutory age of majority for other criminal acts was sixteen, all laws against sodomy through the mid-sixteenth century categorized as minors boys up to the age of eighteen, and an edict of 1542 raised this even further to age twenty.[62] Evidence for an appreciation of this sexual divide also comes from the local boys' confraternities, which normally enrolled adolescents between the ages of thirteen and twenty-four. By the 1440s, however, some companies began to separate in different meeting halls younger boys under age nineteen from older members aged nineteen or twenty to twenty-four, who were deemed "too old to be among boys, too young to be among mature men"; one document cites as justification for this separation the "dangers"—probably sexual dangers—of allowing the two age groups to fraternize too closely.[63] The comments of informers, to be discussed later, also show their acute awareness of the boundary this age represented.

In various ways, then, Florentine society recognized the age of eighteen to twenty as a watershed in young males' lives. Boys' abandonment of the passive role around this age, whether they continued to engage in sodomy as the dominant partner or not, marked like a symbolic and sometimes experiential rite of passage their entry into the sexual world of adult males.

Becoming a Man

Few individuals were reported to have violated this code of sexual and social comportment. When they did, accusers noticed, and the magistrates often added their part by punishing the offenders with harsh or exemplary penalties. Sexual relations between males were more or less tolerated as long as they were expressed within culturally defined and accepted conventions, but when these norms were infringed, they were regarded as deviant or dangerous. The ways Florentines perceived these transgressions lead us into the system of local gender values that was intimately connected to the cultural construction of homosexual behavior and desire and, more broadly, of masculinity.

First, informants' offhand remarks show that they considered the abandonment of a young companion who had passed his adolescent prime as perfectly normal. An informer in 1497, for example, reported that twenty-seven-year-old Attaviano di Giuliano Benintendi "kept" seventeen-year-old Antonio, called Giannetto, son of the weaver Giovanni Giannini. He claimed that Attaviano began his relationship with the boy after he broke off an affair with Antonio's elder brother, because the latter had grown too old: "Giannetto has a brother whom Attaviano used to keep; now that he's grown up [*ora che è grande*], he keeps Giannetto."[64] Another accuser told the Eight in 1510 that a man from Pistoia was defrauding his former boyfriend, the now twenty-one-year-old Jacopo del Cimeta, by demanding repayment of the money he had spent on Jacopo during their three-year affair. The older man had reportedly deserted the youth in 1507 when, as the writer put it, "Jacopo was no longer any good to use [*quando detto Jacopo non era più buono di adoperarlo*]."[65] Jacopo must have been around eighteen when his lover lost interest in him, just the age at which the number of passive partners in my survey drops off sharply. These informers took it for granted that homoerotic relations would naturally end when the boy reached this unwritten age limit.

In contrast, people remarked with scorn or at least with surprise when these expectations went unmet. One informer thought it was odd that the man he accused continued to find his young companion desirable even though the boy was now too old: "[F]or several years [Piero] has kept a certain Baccio, a doublet-maker, to sleep continually with him, and for so long that the said Baccio is grown up, yet it appears he uses him all the same."[66] Another informant in 1501 emphasized how shameful it was for overaged youngsters to take the subordinate role. Denouncing a youth nicknamed il Fanciullone ("big boy," probably derogatory), a sodomite's kept lad, the informer pointedly remarked, "by now he's grown up, which is a disgrace [*è oggimai grande, che è una vergogna*]."[67] The same sense of shame pervades another denunciation that year against a twenty-two-year-old alleged passive. This informant intriguingly observed that some men preferred slightly older companions, since youths were less likely than boys to risk the humiliation (along with a possible punishment) of confessing to their receptive role, thereby implicating their partner: "Everyone likes to fuck the older ones, because they won't tell." This young man, the accuser continued, was even more compromised because in addition to being overaged he was married: "He won't want to confess because he's grown up and has a wife. You'll have to drag it out, and with more than just a lashing, because he's ashamed."[68] A youth who continued to submit sexually to other men and "let himself be sodomized" past the proper age, these informers implied, dishonored himself and his manhood.

If youths past their boyish prime who took the passive role were an embarrassment, older men who did so provoked ridicule or even stronger censure. A joke current in late-fifteenth-century Florence derided a humiliated old man (in the person of the storyteller, the Piovano Arlotto) who complained to the Night Officers about an injury done to his "rear parts"; when the bemused officials questioned him, however, they discovered it was not a sodomitical assault that had damaged his posterior, but the old nag and rough saddle he had rented from a Pisan, from whom he now demanded reparations.[69] Jokes like this could have functioned as a form of social control, making fun of even the slightest hint of aged men being sodomized. The Florentines who denounced sodomy, however, found no humor in the sexual passivity of older men. Indeed, sentiments of disgust and outrage are nowhere more acute than in the rare denunciations that alleged such role reversals. In 1496, for example, someone reported to the Night Officers what was, in his view,

> the greatest and most indecent case that has ever been heard, such that it's a wonder the earth doesn't open up to swallow such criminals. Be informed that ser Simone from Staggia, otherwise known as ser Simone Grazzini, formerly Official of the Palace . . . maintains his man-servant [*garzone*] in his home like a woman, and vice versa he lets himself be used by the said *garzone*, whose name is Valore di Lorenzo di Valore. . . . Not content with this, over various occasions he has given more than 50 florins to a dyer who does this disgraceful thing to him, that is, the said dyer is the one who indecently does it to ser Simone. . . . This is a case that would merit a Hebrew punishment.[70]

With this singular allusion probably to the Levitical death sentence for sodomites, rare in Florence, the informer made plain his aversion for this unorthodox reversal of sexual roles. To the informer's way of thinking, ser Simone, not only an older man but, equally troubling, a public official, had broken a deeply held cultural norm that abhorred sexual receptivity in adult males.[71]

Honor and shame, of course, are social as much as personal values: the sexual passivity of mature men not only disgraced them individually but also jeopardized and vilified the virile identity of all local men. This was what worried an informer in 1494 who accused a man who allegedly enjoyed sodomy both ways: "Tedice di Giovanni Villani . . . is a great sodomite. Not only does he dedicate himself to sodomizing many different young boys, but he also constantly has it done to himself from behind. Since he's an old man and of the age that he is, it is a great disgrace to this city."[72]

Adolescents could take it "from behind" because this was seen as appropriate to their age and subordinate status, but older men who did so undermined a collective masculine identity formed around serious, mature governors that was at the center of the city's public image.[73] In this regard, the attitudes of Florentines probably differed little from those of contemporary Venetians, humiliated when their government passed a law against sodomy in 1516 that implicated adult men in the receptive sexual role. It stated that "an absurd and unheard-of thing has recently become known, which can in no way be tolerated, that several most wicked men of 30, 40, 50, 60 years and more have given themselves like prostitutes and public whores to be passives in such a dreadful excess."[74] Remarking on the law, the diarist Girolamo Priuli was shocked and mortified that "Fathers and Senators," "mature, full of wisdom, with white beards," would prostitute themselves to youths; this was "truly a wicked and abhorrent thing, never before heard of in our times, especially among old men."[75] Other Venetians were equally dismayed, above all because foreigners delighted in deriding the city's compromised masculinity.[76]

Florentine authorities backed the popular ridicule and scorn evoked by the sexual passivity of adult males with the threat of punishment. Although their practice in this as in other areas was inconsistent, officials often penalized men over eighteen who allowed others to sodomize them. Usually their punishments were harsher than those levied even for active partners, evincing the greater disapproval such violations encountered and the danger they were thought to pose. Most who were incriminated and convicted were young men. In 1497, for example, the Eight convicted twenty-two-year-old Francesco di Lorenzo from Radda, who, as his sentence reads, had "passively committed the disgraceful sodomitical vice against nature many times and very often, sometimes three or four times a day, with many different men." They condemned him to be paraded through the city to the Old Market, where he was given twenty-five lashes, and then exiled him for two years.[77] The same day they fined another twenty-two-year-old youth 50 florins and also banished him for two years for his passive role in a long affair with another man.[78] In 1506 the Eight sentenced another passive, said like his companion to be over thirty years old, to be mitered and whipped through the city, a raucous public shaming for his sexual subordination, while they simply levied a fine of 50 florins on his friend who had sodomized him.[79]

Passive sodomy among older men was not unknown, at least as some informers alleged, but it seems to have been rare. Indeed, officials sometimes dismissed accusations like this in part because they took the men's ripe age as an automatic argument against the credibility of such claims. In 1466 the Night Officers absolved Piero di Geri from Prato of a charge that he had been sodomized not only because he denied it, but also because he was "advanced in years [*oneratus annis*] and his face was covered with a beard."[80] Another older man accused in 1465 of having taken the passive role was so humiliated and distressed by this insinuation that in front of the officials he fell to his knees making the sign of the cross, and with "utmost despair" and tears flowing down his face he insisted that he had never been sodomized and that it had been many years since anyone had even propositioned him. The magistrates absolved him too because he was "advanced in years and nearly gray-bearded."[81]

The single conviction I have encountered of an older man who evidently enjoyed being penetrated anally and sought out this form of erotic pleasure involved the habitual sodomite Salvi Panuzzi, who was punished severely both for his "inveteracy" and for taking the passive sexual role. After a long history of sodomizing or fondling adolescents that stretched back at least to 1466, he was arrested in 1496, at the age of sixty-three, and admitted that he had been sodomized by a twenty-six- or twenty-seven-year-old youth; had kissed and fondled another young man with the aim of either sodomizing the youth or letting the latter sodomize him; had invited another youth for a drink with the same purpose; and had been sodomized by yet a fourth youth, aged twenty-four.[82] For these outrageous offences and his persistent involvement in sodomy, the officials condemned him to death. Significantly, however, they worried that the spectacle of his execution might publicize the old man's unorthodox sexual practices and thus disgrace the city, probably in part because Panuzzi, as noted before, was a well-known citizen active in public life: "taking care lest neither his evil ways nor the torments his sentence might involve bring shame on our entire city," they commuted his punishment to the less public penalty of a large fine and life imprisonment on bread and water in the insane ward of the local jail.[83]

The rationale behind such exemplary punishments was made explicit in a sentence in 1493 against a twenty-six-year-old wool washer who confessed that he had let many others sodomize him. Niccolò di Tommaso was convicted, as the protocol stated, "because he could be called a man, not a boy [*quia potuit vocari homo et non puer*]."[84] Acceptable in boyhood, the sexual subordination of Niccolò and the others cited here, considered no longer boys but men, violated the cultural terms of their manhood. With the constant threat of punishing passive adult males, occasionally carried out, officials reinforced expected behavioral norms and helped define more clearly the boundary between boyhood and manhood.

The longstanding abhorrence of adult male passivity was finally written into law in 1542. According to this edict, anyone convicted a second time for sodomy, even if a minor, was to be fined and sentenced to forced labor on the galleys. The sole exception regarded anyone aged twenty or above who took the passive role with another male: he was instead to be singled out for exemplary punishment and "burned publicly as a wicked and infamous man."[85]

The emphasis on the acquisition and enactment of manhood in homoerotic interactions plainly had its roots not only in the life-stage transition from boyhood to adulthood but also in related perceptions of gender differences and roles. The language of denunciations, a rich repository of contemporary values, reveals the close links between the local gender system and the behavioral conventions typical of homosexual sodomy. When Florentines denounced men and boys for engaging in sodomy and described their sexual torts, they frequently distinguished the partners in gender-laden terms. Informers commonly represented the "passive" partner—but never his "active" companion—with a variety of derogatory feminine terms and metaphors.[86] To be sodomized signified assuming temporarily the subordinate status of women, subject to the domination and power of men in a sexually and socially hierarchical society. The "active" sodomite, however, whether as penetrator or perhaps even as fellator, conformed to the dominant, virile image expected of adult males in this much as in other Mediterranean cultures past and present.[87] This helps explain the disapproval or repulsion evinced when youths or older men were sodomized by others, assuming what were considered "feminine" behaviors or postures.[88] Boys and adolescents, though, were physically and socially immature, not yet fully men. In the terms of this culture, theirs was a sexually ambiguous, subaltern state that lent itself to their equation with women. In this way, homosexual behavior embodied and in turn helped shape the broader cultural and gender values of late medieval Florence.

Informers employed numerous terms with feminine connotations or effeminizing metaphors to denigrate passive boys. One they commonly used was *bardassa* or its diminutive, *bardassuola*.[89] Nouns of feminine gender, whose etymological root is an Arabic word for "slave," they denote a boy who offers himself in the receptive sexual role to males. The following phrases show some of the ways accusers used the terms: "Sinibaldo di Giovanni Monaldi [is a] *bardassa*, and . . . more than 40 young men have buggered him";[90] "Niccolò, son of Agnolo Biffoli, is a . . . public *bardassuola*, in such a way that he's the disgrace and shame of the city";[91] "Giovanni Maria di Jacopo . . . is one of the most indecent *bardasse* in Florence, and he lets himself be sodomized by many people."[92]

Often referring to promiscuous boys and mentioned with shame and moral reproach, the *bardassa* was, in effect, a young male prostitute and not simply an ordinary boy who allowed himself to be sodomized. In *L'Alcibiade fanciullo a scola*, the handsome boy who is the reluctant object of his schoolmaster's courting asks him, "Why then are boys who yield to men's pleasures scorned and esteemed disgraceful with the opprobrious name of *bardassi*?" Filotimo reassures him that "this name of *bardassa* . . . should not be and, in effect, is not given to boys who out of affection and kindness couple graciously with civil and praiseworthy lovers. . . . The *bardassa* correctly means mercenary and venal *putto*, who sells himself as mere merchandise, almost so much per measure, and cares about nothing but his servile earnings."[93] The disparaging remarks even of this character with amatory interests in boys echo the hostile sentiments of Florentine informers, suggesting that the *bardassa* was despised for his profligacy and the shameless selling of his body. Similarly, a poem by the Florentine Francesco da Colle written probably in the 1470s or 1480s vituperates "these insatiable and gluttonous *bardasse* . . . who, to show us they're charming and handsome, go about looking for someone who will fuck them from behind." One need not use much flattery to win such boys over, the author adds; a miserly meal will do.[94]

It is worth noting that Europeans in the New World used the same term (Spanish, *bardaje*; French, *berdache*) to designate forms of "institutionalized homosexuality" they found in both hemispheres of the Americas, in which males permanently assumed women's dress and economic roles and often had special religious functions.[95] In Christian Europe, with its virulent condemnation of sodomy, *bardasse* could hardly have carried out similar authorized roles, nor does it appear that Florentine *bardasse*, or any other passive partners for that matter, cross-dressed.[96] Nonetheless, the currency of the term and the evidence from trials suggest that the *bardassa* was a recognized sexual institution in Florence, as he appears to have been in other Italian cities as well as elsewhere throughout the Mediterranean region.[97]

Given the connotation of *bardasse* as promiscuous boys who earned money from sex, it is unsurprising that accusers also compared boys who were sodomized to *puttane* (female prostitutes). One informer, for example, wrote that a young cathedral cleric named Baldassare "lets himself be buggered more than the prettiest whore in the brothel, who doesn't have as much business as he does."[98] Another claimed that "the son of Amerigo del Cagnone, a student . . . is like a whore who gets fucked by three or four in turn."[99] Here the link between boys who had sex with men and the mercenary sexuality of public women is explicit, in the figure of the prostitute who sells her body. Informers also alluded to this when they called houses or shops where boys were brought for sex "brothels," or, perhaps, when they referred to a boy as a "glutton" (*ghiotto*), a word that in contemporary burlesque poetry was associated with sodomy.[100]

The most graphic slur linking boys to a "feminine" and voracious sexuality was that of estrous female dogs. Often accusers called a boy a *cagna* (bitch) or its diminutive, *cagniuola*, or, more crudely, *cagna in gestra* (bitch in heat).[101] These examples are typical: "And from him you will have more than twenty sodomites, for he's worse than a bitch in heat";[102] "There was never a bitch with as many dogs behind her as those two [have sodomites]";[103] "Simone di Bernardo Petani is a great *bardassa*, he's just like a bitch when she's in heat, he has so many sodomites around him."[104] This image of passive boys as bitches pursued by sodomite suitors appears as early as the 1420s in the sermons of Bernardino of Siena on sodomy and continues through at least the early sixteenth century.[105]

The most common and direct way Florentines represented males who were sodomized, however, was simply as women.[106] Like bitches in heat, this too was a long-established image. In his sermons, Bernardino portrayed boys as "young maidens" or "pretty girls" overdressed and preened by their parents to attract men.[107] Representations of sodomized boys as women appeared in the early fifteenth century even in protocols of sodomy trials, some of which stated that the accused "ravished and carnally knew [his partner] like a woman [*ut feminam*]."[108]

This or similar expressions rarely occur in later sentences of the Night Officers or Eight of Watch, but informers employed it frequently with several variations. Most commonly, they said that someone kept a boy "for use as a woman [*a uso di donna*]," or sometimes "like a woman" (usually *come donna* or *come una femmina*).[109] One of the earliest extant denunciations for homosexual sodomy, in 1436, alleged that "Antonio di Dino, a clothes dealer . . . keeps for his use as a woman [*si tiene a uso di donna*] a lad named Francesco d'Orlandino di Francesco di ser Orlandino."[110] Later informers often used the same phrase, as in this example from 1495: "Piero di Giuliano Gerini, a tallow candlemaker at the Piazzuola del Re . . . keeps and has kept [Piero di Jacopo Panichi] for his use as a woman [*si tiene e ha tenuto a suo uso di donna*], that is, to sodomize him, and he's been sodomizing him for a year or more."[111] Another wrote that "Bivigliano d'Alammano de' Medici keeps Anfrione Rucellai like a woman [*si tiene come donna*]," a phrase that appears regularly.[112] We shall have occasion later to study the relationships implied by the verb *tenersi* (to keep or maintain), which often occurs alone without the phrase "like a woman" or its variants. The term clearly intended a steady, ongoing exchange of a boy's sexual favors for financial support, gifts, or other benefits from his suitor(s), similar to men maintaining a mistress or courtesan.[113]

Significantly, people often carried the simile of boys as women even further and depicted homosexual relations as marriages, calling a boy the "wife" of an older lover.[114] In such cases, informers commonly said that a man kept a boy *come sua donna* or *per moglie*, as did one who wrote, " 'el Biza' di Benedetto Vecchietti keeps Lorenzo d'Antonio Cambi as his wife [*come sua donna*], and there was never a greater disgrace in this city," or another who alleged, "Giovanni d'Antonio Attavanti, called Nannino, frequents someone named Niccolò Paffi . . . and they do every possible wickedness together, and Niccolò keeps him as his wife [*per la sua moglie*]."[115] While in Italian *donna* means either "woman" or "wife," here the context and the occasional use of the more specific *moglie* (wife) suggest the latter meaning, and in fact notaries sometimes translated *donna* into Latin as *uxor* (wife).[116] It may be that the phrases *a uso di donna* and *come donna* also were understood as meaning "as a wife" rather than the generic "as a woman." In any case, the boundary between the two senses was probably indistinct.

In some cases, accusers were perhaps simply comparing such relations metaphorically to marriages and boys to men's wives; their comments might also have been satirical. Yet sometimes informers implied a practical equivalence between homoerotic relations and male–female marriages when, for instance, they specified that a man substituted a boy for his legitimate spouse or that a boy was, in effect, a man's wife. For one of several examples, in 1496 someone charged that Francesco di ser Alberto di ser Nicco, nicknamed el Gufo ("the owl," a sodomitical reference in Florence) "publicly keeps Piero and Michelangelo, sons of Benastro the wool shearer, in place of his wife [*in luogo della donna sua*]," whom he relegated to their country home in favor of the two boys.[117] The possibility that "marriages" between males were a recognized social institution in Florence, and their place within the broader spectrum of homosexual activity, will again be considered in more detail at a later point.[118]

For the moment, it is important to stress how commonly Florentines represented "passive" partners in sodomy in roles that were ascribed in this culture to women. In popular sexual imagery, boys who "let themselves be sodomized" were symbolically demoted to the status of females, whether as *bardasse*, bitches, prostitutes, or simply women or wives, used by, maintained by, and dependent on male suitors or, in effect, "husbands." Males' assumption of the subordinate position in sexual relations signified for many people a deviation from gendered norms of behavior, the surrender of one's masculine identity and the unseemly adoption of a "feminine" role.

It should be emphasized that these gendered images and metaphors seem to have referred only to boys' receptive sexual behavior and did not imply any particular mannerisms, dress, or other characteristics that might be considered "effeminate." Even though some informers minutely described boys' dress, hair color and style, and facial and body features, no hint appears in denunciations (or interrogations) that their manner or speech betrayed any "unmanly" affectations. Nor were boys who took the passive role in sex ever said to have cross-dressed as females. Similarly, although men were attracted mostly to postpubescent, beardless adolescents, there is little evidence to suggest that feminine or androgynous physical appearance stimulated homoerotic desire any more than the ideal of well-formed, muscular bodies which young males were encouraged to develop through strenuous physical exercise in competitive games, jousting, hunting, and horseback riding.[119] Men's preference in physical types quite likely varied according to personal taste.[120] In any case, the representation of sodomized boys as females did not necessarily respond to a social reality of "effeminate" boys, nor did it imply a permanent constitutional trait. Rather, it was a powerful means for conceptually organizing same-sex relations in terms of gender and status.

The contrast between accusers' depictions of boys in "feminine" roles and their "active" partners could not be more marked. Florentines virtually never imagined the dominant partner in a homosexual interaction in feminine terms. If informers labeled them at all, they called them simply a sodomite (*sodomito*) or, less often, a bugger (*buggerone*). Once a man was dubbed literally a "bugger and cocksucker [*buggerone e poppatore*]."[121] On occasion, accusers called a man a *pippione*, which in Tuscan means "pigeon" or "foolish man," but which might also have had a more veiled sexual connotation, perhaps referring to the penis.[122] Informers used none of these terms to refer to persons who were sodomized, just as they never applied the feminine epithets with which they denigrated the latter to their active partners.[123] The "sodomite," then, adhering to popular Florentine usage, was not simply anyone who engaged in sodomy (whatever the sexual acts) but, specifically, the senior, dominant partner in the relation, and this is how the word is used throughout this work.

As this semantic distinction suggests, Florentines presumably did not view the sodomite as acting contrary to the gender ideals they associated with masculine identity. As in other traditional Mediterranean societies, his erotic attraction to boys and his intercourse with them within established cultural conventions—that is, as long as he played the dominant, "active" role as anal inserter or even fellator—failed to compromise his masculinity, and in some circumstances might even have enhanced it.[124] Although no informers went so far as to say that someone was more manly because he sodomized boys, they did not question his virility. Many Florentines might have considered sodomites sinful or wicked and decried their acts as opprobrious and vile. But the fact that they had erotic desires for another male, if they were enacted according to accepted conventions, did not constitute a problem of gender deviance.

If it was common for critics to represent homosexual interactions in gendered dichotomies, to what extent did the participants themselves interpret their actions and roles in similar terms? This is difficult to answer, since despite the vast and wide-ranging documentation on Florentine sodomy, the voices of the men and boys who practiced it are seldom, if ever, heard directly. Their testimony reflects only officials' narrow interests in behavioral details, and to the extent that their words were recorded they were filtered into the bureaucratic language of the court. Within these limitations, it can be said that no passive partner who was questioned made the embarrassing admission that he had been used "like a woman" or called other feminine names by his sexual companions, nor did any men who confessed that they had sodomized boys refer to them in feminine terms.[125] But it is hard to conclude on this basis alone that those who engaged in sodomy never ascribed such gendered meanings to their actions. Across the Mediterranean in early modern Valencia, for instance, where similar phrases about males using others or being used "like a woman" in sodomy pervaded the language of both witnesses and the courts, Rafael Carrasco found that some men called the partner they sodomized their "girl" or boasted to others that he was "his woman."[126] One can easily imagine men in Florence doing the same. Just as they nearly universally adhered to the hierarchical conventions of age and behavior that governed homoerotic interactions, so many probably implicitly or explicitly accepted as "natural" the status and gendered distinctions their culture attributed to them.[127]

In any case, as it was practiced and conceived, sodomy was woven into some basic features and notions of social organization in Florence. In its hierarchical age structure and related conceptions of life stages, sodomy helped to articulate the distinction between boyhood and manhood, to mark more clearly the boundaries between immature adolescence and the physically mature and socially dominant status of youths and adult men. In addition, in their rigid adherence to well-defined sexual roles, seen as corresponding to culturally construed gender ideals and norms, homosexual relations helped fashion and reinforce important features of "masculine" and "feminine" behavior and identity.

4

Social Profiles

We're happy youths without a care, and so that we can satisfy our desires to the full, we don't ever want to take a wife. He who isn't married can always do the bom, ba, ba.

Antonfrancesco Grazzini, "Canto di giovani che per meglio sguazzare non voglion moglie" (1559)[1]

It is evident how much sodomy is presently practiced in this city, especially by artisans and the poor.

From a law of 1459[2]

To say that sodomy was a social as much as a sexual fact in Florence is, in a sense, to state the obvious. With as many as 15,000 individuals incriminated and 2,500 convictions for homosexual acts in little more than the last forty years of the fifteenth century, sodomy was no "deviant" behavior of a distinct sexual minority but a common part of male experience that had widespread social ramifications. The significance of sodomy lies not only in these impressive numbers, however. The hierarchical configuration of pederasty, for example, with its rigid code of sexual comportment, itself embodied and expressed social divisions and rank. As David Herlihy first proposed, moreover, the very social structure of Florence, with its late age of marriage for males of around thirty or thirty-one, a large proportion of men who never married, and the resulting profusion of footloose, profligate bachelors—those merrily singing about doing the euphemistic "bom, ba, ba"—probably helped create favorable conditions in which sodomy and other unauthorized sexual activities flourished.[3] Certain social dimensions of sodomy, real or perceived, also influenced the apparatus for policing it, as in 1459 when fines were reduced in response to the alleged ubiquity of the practice among craftsmen and the poor, or again in the early sixteenth century when penalties were scaled by age to the advantage of youths.[4] As precise a definition as possible of the social composition of males incriminated for sodomy, then, should contribute to a better understanding of the nature and organization of homosexual activity and illuminate social tendencies and prejudices in its control.

To this end, the Florentine sources permit a detailed reconstruction of the collective biographical profiles of men and boys who engaged in sodomy. The survey of the Night Officers' records from 1478 to 1502 documents basic traits such as age, residence, and occupation for many of the 4,062 individuals incriminated in these years, while the sample of 183 persons implicated between 1478 and 1483 whom I located in the 1480 *catasto* (16 percent of the total 1,131 found in these years) adds information on age, marital status, and wealth. To be sure, the nature of this material poses a number of problems of methodology and interpretation; among them perhaps the hardest to resolve is the extent to which the individuals who appear in the court records are representative of the participants in homosexual activity in general. The criminal records clearly do not constitute a "census" of sodomy. As has been seen, some people were incriminated wrongly, while countless others escaped detection, problems that the Night Officers' arbitrary and rather permissive praxis in pursuing or sentencing sodomites only exacerbated.

Nonetheless, partial and problematic as they are, the traces of sodomy conserved in the judiciary records probably can yield more or less accurate indications of the social contours of homosexual activity in Florence. The quasi-administrative nature of the Office of the Night, the important facts that the Night Officers did not proceed ex officio and could convict only those men revealed through confessions (thus they did not "target" certain individuals or groups for prosecution), and the sheer number of people implicated, all likely rendered those traces that the officials uncovered fairly representative. The preserved record of the entire range of their prosecutorial activity makes it possible, moreover, to compare systematically the profiles of discrete groups: all those incriminated, self-accusers, the absolved, the convicted. This comparative approach helps to define the social outlines of homosexual activity as well as to identify possible social biases in its policing.

Young and Old

Young males in Florence, as elsewhere in Italy, were thought to be ruled by their unbridled sexual passions and social irresponsibility. In a sermon to the Florentines in 1425 on "youth and the vice of lust," for example, Bernardino of Siena claimed that sexual license ruled males from the ages of fourteen to twenty-five, causing them to lose all sense of reason.[5] "The volatile youths always pursue their desires; the appetites of youths are insatiable," a character in Leon Battista Alberti's dialogue on the family remarks.[6] In part the social and political structure of Florence, which relegated young men to a position of powerlessness, helped foster among the young a common experience, amounting to something of a distinctive youthful culture, of marginality, violence, and profligacy. Youths were denied economic autonomy under their fathers' patriarchal rule, a source of frustration and domestic strife and one reason why most youths put off the responsibilities of marriage and family until they were well into their thirties. As noted earlier, according to the *catasti* of 1427 and 1480, only about one in four men between the ages of eighteen and thirty-two was or definitely had been married.[7] Young men of the political class were also denied the exercise of most civic offices and any significant public role until they were thirty, and of major offices until the age of thirty-five, forty, or even forty-five, in part because responsible citizenship and the sexual passions of youth were thought to clash: according to Donato Giannotti, an early-sixteenth-century Florentine political theorist, "they say the *giovani* should not discuss public affairs, but pursue their sexual needs."[8] Though elders and moralists might have decried the excesses of the hot-blooded young, there was a sort of tacit acceptance, within bounds, of their sexual liberality. In a letter in 1523 to Niccolò Machiavelli, Francesco Vettori responded to his friend's concerns about his son Lodovico's intimacy with a younger boy. He recommended indulgence, and recalled their own youthful experiences:

> Since we are verging on old age, we might be severe and overly scrupulous, and we do not remember what we do as adolescents. So Lodovico has a boy with him, with whom he amuses himself, jests, takes walks, growls in his ear, goes to bed together. What then? Even in these things perhaps there is nothing bad.[9]

Without political or familial duties and encouraged by a double standard that expected young men to indulge their sexual desires and to prove, indeed flaunt, their virility, but imposed chastity on unmarried women and fidelity on wives, young males had few sexual restraints. It comes as no surprise, then, that adolescents and youths predominated in homosexual activity in Florence.

The prevalence of the young is especially striking when the ages of all those implicated in sodomy are considered together, without distinguishing by sexual role (Table B.5). Of the persons incriminated from 1478 to 1502 whose ages were recorded, 83 percent were aged thirty or under, and 94 percent were forty or under, the age, that is, to which *giovinezza*, or youth, was generally thought to extend in Florence. Men over forty made up a mere 6 percent of the total; men over fifty, only 2 percent. The mean age of all those whose precise ages were indicated was twenty-three years.[10] Corresponding figures for the sample of 176 persons implicated between 1478 and 1483 whom I located in the 1480 *catasto* and whose ages were recorded also highlight the prominence of the young, though for various reasons possibly linked to the procedure of identifying these individuals, the presence of older men here is more pronounced.[11] Boys and youths aged thirty or under make up 62 percent of this group, while those forty or under make up 81 percent. Some 19 percent were over the age of forty, and 9 percent were over fifty. While the age distribution in this sample is somewhat higher than that in the full 1478–1502 survey, adolescents and youths still prevailed, and their aggregate mean age was a young 28.4.

A rough comparison with the proportion of males the same ages in the population at large, based on figures from the 1480 *catasto*, confirms the prevalence of the young in homosexual activity. Boys and youths aged thirteen to thirty made up 51 percent of the city's male populace aged thirteen to sixty-five, compared with 82 and 61 percent in the two samples; those aged thirteen to forty in 1480 made up 71 percent, compared with 94 and 80 percent in the samples.[12] On the whole, then, sodomy in Florence was associated above all with the vital, sexually energetic, and, to some extent, culturally distinct world of adolescents and young men.

As an institutional presence, the Office of the Night must consequently have loomed large, especially in the lives of the young. Considering the number of people who came to the Night Officers' attention from 1459 to 1502 (some 350 annually), and factoring in their typical age distribution, it can be roughly estimated that by the time they reached the age of thirty, at least one of every two youths in the city of Florence had been formally implicated in sodomy to this court alone; by age forty, at least two of every three men had been incriminated. These extraordinary figures confirm once more both how common homosexual activity was there, involving at some time or another a majority of the male population, and how prevalent it was among the young. They give some substance to an informer's remark back in 1436: "And there is nearly no one in [that] neighborhood between the ages of 30 and 40 who in the past hasn't committed such mischief."[13]

The experiences of people who engaged in this "mischief" varied widely, of course, depending on their age and sexual role. These aggregate figures can now be broken down to look more closely at ages according to sexual role and, where possible, over a longer time period. Unfortunately, however, before the later fifteenth century ages were seldom or inconsistently recorded in sodomy cases, and almost not at all for active partners, making it hard to draw detailed conclusions about other periods.

The one sure generalization that can be made is that from the fourteenth century on, the passive partner was usually aged eighteen or under, as in the 1478–1502 survey; the age-structured, pederastic pattern consequently persisted from at least this time well into and probably beyond the sixteenth century.[14] The statute of 1325, the earliest extant law on sodomy, in fact mentioned only sexual relations between men and boys, though this emphasis later vanished.[15] Data on age from court records before 1432 are erratic, but all the available evidence underlines the youthfulness of receptive partners. Most were identified as a *puer* (boy), while the nine whose ages were recorded in the cases reviewed were all between ten and eighteen.[16] This age profile remains unchanged after 1432, under the Night

Officers, when age was reported more consistently. Of the seventy-seven passive partners implicated from 1432 to 1440, twenty-nine of the thirty who had precise ages given were between ten and nineteen (the other was only six), while the records identified twenty-four others either as a *puer* (5) or as a minor aged eighteen or under (19); no passive partners who were convicted were fined according to the scale prescribed for adults over age eighteen.[17] The abundant evidence on age in the 1478–1502 survey provides more detail and nuance, but, as has been seen, essentially confirms the same general picture. To recapitulate briefly, ages of passive partners in the Night Officers' records ranged from six to twenty-six (in the small *catasto* sample, from ten to twenty-three), but the vast majority (92 and 88 percent, respectively) were aged thirteen to twenty and most (78 and 68 percent) were fourteen to eighteen. Their mean age was slightly over sixteen years (fifteen in the *catasto* sample). According to this information, then, most males in Florence who "let themselves be sodomized" were between puberty and the age, around eighteen to twenty, at which the growth of a beard and the appearance of other secondary sexual traits became pronounced and they began to lose what this society considered the beauty and erotic appeal of adolescence.

Before turning to the ages of active partners, it should be stressed that these figures indicate that Florentine men seldom had sexual relations either with very young boys or with youths past the age of twenty. Young men over twenty formed only a tiny proportion of the passive partners implicated from 1478 to 1502 (3 and 1 percent of the two sample groups). Boys aged twelve or under made up only 5 percent of the full survey but 11 percent of the *catasto* group, the latter perhaps a distortion related to the small sample size. In several cases, these very young boys were sodomized not by adults but by youngsters their age or a bit older, examples probably of boyhood sexual play and experimentation.[18] In other cases, however, adult men raped or otherwise abused young boys, sometimes resulting in anal injuries.[19] It is hard to draw any general conclusions from these examples about the frequency of child sexual abuse in late medieval Florence, though it apparently was not uncommon. When such cases came to their attention, the courts usually took them seriously and punished the perpetrators severely. Yet in Florence, as in contemporary society, the sexual molestation of children, especially within households or families, might often have gone unexposed. What can be said is that cases of the abuse of very young boys were probably no more frequent than similar cases involving young girls.[20]

How old, then, were the males who played the "active," dominant role in homosexual relations in Florence? Only the detailed sources of the late fifteenth century allow this important question to be answered with some reliability. In the cases reviewed before 1432, age was not recorded for a single active partner. Specific information is still rare in the years following the founding of the Office of the Night, but the new two-tiered system that prescribed different fines for adults and for minors aged eighteen or under provides some very general indications. Of the ninety-four active partners convicted from 1432 to 1440, ten were fined as minors but eighty-four as adults over eighteen; of the latter, notaries recorded the ages of only three men, aged forty, sixty, and seventy.

With the thousands of prosecutions and better recording practices of the later fifteenth century, an age profile of active partners finally takes shape. The evidence shows clearly that youths predominated, but also that older men made up a significant minority (Table B.6). As noted earlier, the ages of active partners implicated in the 1478–1502 survey ranged from ten to eighty-three, and their mean age was just over twenty-seven. About seven of every ten, however, were adolescents or youths aged thirty or under, and nine of ten were forty or under; only 3 percent were over fifty. In the *catasto* sample group, which features a higher but perhaps distorted age distribution, the proportion of older men is considerably larger, though youths still prevail overall. Roughly 45 percent of the active partners in this sample were aged thirty or under, and 72 percent were aged forty or under. Some 28 percent were over forty, and nearly 13 percent over fifty. Their mean age was slightly more than thirty-four, seven years older than in the full 1478–1502 survey, but still situated squarely among the age group of roughly nineteen- to forty-year-olds that Florentines considered youths. In both samples, this group comprises large absolute majorities.

Above all, then, it was young men—whose profligacy, irreverence, violence, and "unbridled" erotic passions were taken for granted by their elders and by moralists—who sought out boys for sex. But homosexual activity in Florence was clearly not limited to youths. A sizable proportion of older men also had sexual relations with boys, and a number of them were in fact "habitual" sodomites with long histories of prosecutions. Earlier Bernardino of Siena, it will be recalled, also noted that some men, having grown "accustomed" to sodomy in their youth, continued to frequent boys well into their maturity. He derided such men "who had grown aged and hardened in the sin against nature," calling them "crazy old men, crazier in your old age than in your youth!"[21]

Up to this point, ages have been reviewed of persons who were generically implicated in sodomy. While the profiles of discrete groups such as self-accusers or convicted men do not necessarily provide a more accurate picture, the differences in their ages shed some light on how age might have affected certain aspects of the regulation of sodomy.

First, the ages of self-confessed sodomites furnish some useful comparisons, although due to a small sample size any conclusions must be offered cautiously. Since their ages were seldom noted in the court records, the most reliable data come from the *catasto* sample group, which includes thirty-six individuals who denounced themselves (some more than once, for a total of forty-one occurrences) between 1478 and 1483.[22] On the whole, these self-accusers, whose mean age was nearly thirty-six, were somewhat older than those implicated in other ways, who were three years younger. Their number includes four boys aged eighteen or under who denounced themselves even though they probably would have been absolved as minors. But only ten of the self-accused, or 24 percent, were between the ages of nineteen and thirty, compared with 42 percent of those otherwise implicated; twenty-seven of the men who accused themselves, or 66 percent, were over thirty, compared with 52 percent of those who did not. The most likely explanation for older men's slightly greater tendency to incriminate themselves lies in their sexual histories. Some 40 percent of the self-denounced sodomites in this sample (as compared with only 15 percent of all active partners in the 1478–1502 survey) either came repeatedly to the Night Officers' attention or confessed to sodomy with multiple partners. Both considerations suggest that men who accused themselves voluntarily tended to be habitual sodomites. The older they were, the more risks they must have incurred, thus the more commonly they denounced themselves to avoid conviction.[23]

A comparison of the ages of persons convicted and absolved reveals, moreover, that when the Night Officers pronounced their verdicts they discriminated among age groups (Table B.7). Both youths and older men over fifty suffered prejudicial treatment at their hands, while middle-aged men ran a smaller risk of conviction. Considering the full 1478–1502 survey, officials convicted 31 percent of the "active" youths aged eighteen to thirty, but only 18 percent of men aged thirty-one to forty and just 12 percent of men aged forty-one to fifty; the proportion of men over fifty who were convicted rose to 25 percent. In the *catasto* sample group, with its older age distribution, they convicted 26 percent of the young men aged eighteen to forty, a mere 6 percent of men aged forty-one to fifty, and 31 percent of men over fifty. Although these figures are more indicative than conclusive, it appears that the Night Officers adopted a sterner stance toward youths, perhaps to control their sexual activity more closely or to dissuade them while still young from growing too attached to the "vice," and equally toward older men, who at this age were probably considered "inveterate" sodomites.

Despite the attention officials dedicated to young men, however, attitudes toward their sexual behavior were still ambivalent enough that city fathers could be moved to clemency by pleas depicting sodomy as fruit of the impulsive and excitable passions of youth. In a successful petition in 1444 to have his twenty-four-year-old son's conviction for sodomizing a boy canceled, a father who must have expected to win the sympathy of council members explained, "because of his young age, he went out at night for consolation"—sexual relief is understood—and when he came upon a younger neighborhood boy he was "induced by sexual desire" to sodomize him.[24] On another occasion, the youthfulness and rashness of three young friends convicted for sodomy were adduced as compelling motives for granting them a reprieve: "The truth is that, as youths, they committed something they never would have done had they been older and pondered the nature of the thing."[25]

Bachelors and Husbands

"Woe to those men," Bernardino of Siena threatened from the pulpit of Santa Croce in 1424, "who fail to take a wife when they are the right age and have a legitimate reason! For if they don't marry they become sodomites. Make this a general rule: when you see a grown man in good health who doesn't have a wife, you can take this as an evil sign about him."[26] As this and other remarks of Bernardino suggest, he believed that young men who enjoyed sex with boys tended for this reason either to delay marriage until an unusually late age or to reject conjugal union altogether, an attitude that he sometimes coupled with sodomites' presumed misogyny or lack of sexual interest in women. Although he acknowledged that some married men also pursued boys—a fact Girolamo Savonarola noted in the 1490s as well[27]—he usually painted their marital relations as unhappy and ridden with conflict on account of their erotic inclinations or their occasional same-sex affairs.

Bernardino's attention to sodomites' marital status evidently reflected broader social concerns, and encourages us to look more closely at some of the issues his remarks raise. Were men with homoerotic interests the incorrigible bachelors (and a few cold husbands) that he portrayed? What were the relationships, if any, between their marital status and the social organization of sodomy, individuals' sexual behavior and inclinations, the nature of their relations with women, and community perceptions of and responses to sodomy?

The Florentine sources permit at least some indicative responses to these questions, beginning with whether men involved in sodomy were married or not. This was as much a social as a personal issue: it has already been hypothesized that the late age at marriage for males, and the fact that a high proportion of men never married, resulted in an abundance of bachelors who, denied what society deemed the only licit sexual outlet, turned to other sexual options to satisfy their erotic needs and desires. The prevalence of young men involved in sodomy in itself supports this theory, but it is possible now to bring more specific information to bear. Trial proceedings did not note marital status, though accusers sometimes mentioned it. The sample of men identified in the 1480 *catasto*, however, provides a fairly reliable record of the marital status in that year of 154 men between the ages of eighteen and seventy who were incriminated for homosexual relations from 1478 to 1483 (Table B.8).[28] For the moment, I shall consider this group as a whole, comparing it only with those who admitted in self-denunciations to having committed sodomy; differences between absolved and convicted men will be examined later. Together with other sources, this evidence suggests that marriage played an important but not a determinant role in shaping homosexual experience in Florence.

A strikingly high proportion of the men in this sample were, in fact, unmarried. Only 24 percent of the men who were implicated in sodomy had a wife, as compared with 51 percent of all Florentine males between the ages of eighteen and seventy in 1480.[29] Not only young men who were under the average age at marriage of around thirty or thirty-one, but most men of all ages who were incriminated for homosexual activity were single. Among every age cohort in this sample the proportion of single men was considerably higher than that of bachelors in the male populace at large. Of the fifty-eight youths aged eighteen to thirty, only three were married, and none of the twelve self-accusers this age had a wife; in contrast, 19 percent of all young men this age in 1480 were married. Among men implicated in sodomy who had passed the customary age at marriage, a higher percentage had wives (43 percent), but not nearly as high as that of males the same age in the general population (73 percent). In my sample, some 44 percent of the men in their thirties (14 of 32) and 42 percent of the self-accusers this age (5 of 12) were married, as compared with 63 percent of all men in this age bracket. Above this age, the gap in marital status between men implicated in sodomy and city men overall grows even wider. Half of the men in their forties in the sample had wives (10 of 20; 2 others were probably widowers), as did three of the seven men who denounced themselves, compared with 78 percent of all men this age. And of the men between fifty-one and seventy in my sample, only three out of eleven were married, a low rate of marriage that sharply distinguished these older men from their coevals in the population at large, 81 percent of whom were married. It appears, then, that men of all ages who were implicated in homosexual sodomy tended to be unmarried, to have delayed or forgone at least the formal bonds with women that matrimony represented. Most men who pursued sexual relations with boys were youths who had not yet reached marriageable age and older, long-term bachelors, many of whom probably never took a wife.

Should the conspicuous bachelorhood of these men lead, then, to the conclusion, seemingly favored by Bernardino, that most sodomites self-consciously avoided marriage because they had no erotic interest in females and preferred boys to women? While for some individuals this might conceivably have been the case, this interpretation is problematic, not least because none of the sources, whether demographic or judicial, reveal much about the variety of sexual experiences people might have had or about what today is often called sexual orientation or preference. Whether a man was married or not can hardly be taken as evidence of his erotic inclinations, especially in this traditional society where the notion of romantic, "companionate" marriage was very weak, and marriage was seldom a matter of individual choice but a basic facet of families' political and economic strategies.[30] In the letter cited earlier (p. 114) in which Francesco Vettori spoke indulgently, almost wistfully, about Niccolò Machiavelli's son's intimate friendship with a boy, he reminded his friend, a notorious womanizer, that "you, had you known yourself well, might never have taken a wife," and he admitted with regret that his own father, "had he known my natural inclinations and ways, would never have tied me to a wife."[31] Mere allegations of sodomy also have drawbacks as evidence of sexual tastes, for obvious reasons, but even self-denunciations or convictions reveal nothing of broader or long-term erotic interests. In this context, the very question is probably anachronistic, for it assumes, in a way influenced by modern conceptions of fixed sexual categories, that the one desire automatically excludes the other.

The social configuration of sodomy that emerges from this sample in fact undermines the notion of an exclusive "homosexual orientation" for most males who engaged in same-sex sodomy. For the majority, homosexual activity appears to have been part of distinct stages in their life course, above all adolescence and the long period of youthful bachelorhood.[32] Sooner or later, most probably married; although marriage by no means excluded concurrent sexual relations with boys, the steadily declining proportions of men incriminated for sodomy who were over the age of thirty, and especially over forty, suggest that most abandoned homoerotic affairs as they grew older, took a wife, and began a family. It is hard to trace enough individual lives to form a representative sample, but many likely followed a course of experience similar to that of Francesco di Giuliano Benintendi. Denounced at the age of twenty for passive sodomy and at twenty-two and twenty-four for sodomizing various boys, afterward he vanished from the judiciary records; in 1480, now aged thirty-five, he was married and had a son of six months.[33] Still the significant minority of older men who engaged in sexual relations with boys, including a substantial proportion of married men, cautions against deriving a rigid demographic model of homosexual activity determined solely by age and marital status.

A second possible interpretation, supported by the prevalence of bachelors among men incriminated for sodomy, is that unmarried men, lacking sexual outlets with the opposite sex, turned opportunistically to relations with boys. If women were more easily available, according to this view, most men would "naturally" prefer to have sex with them. It is true that in Florence, as in other Mediterranean societies, men's social and sexual interactions with women, especially young marriageable women, were limited. Ideally, if not always in practice, "respectable" women were secluded in their homes and closely chaperoned when outdoors, or were locked behind convent walls. Males, in contrast, were encouraged from boyhood to spurn "feminine idleness" and the "debilitating" company of females, "to be bold," as Alberti put it, "about appearing among men."[34] And the social world in which they worked, played, competed, and wove dense webs of sociable relations—schools, sports and entertainments, workshops, confraternities, markets, squares, taverns, civic life—was an intensely male domain.[35] Sex between males in a largely sex-segregated context like this could possibly be seen as a temporary adaptation to the unavailability of women, a sort of "situational bisexuality."[36]

But lack of males' sexual access to females is not in fact a convincing argument for the "cause," frequency, or nature of homosexual sodomy in late medieval Florence. In the first place, this society was far from being so rigidly sex-segregated that males had no or only very limited occasions to pursue erotic relations with the opposite sex. The city abounded with women who, by choice or misfortune, ended up serving the sexual desires of Florentine males. Under the Office of Decency, the municipality itself supplied men with prostitutes and public brothels—probably in part to channel males' passions away from homosexual activity, a resounding failure. Between 1486 and 1490, in the core of my survey, this office had as many as 150 licensed whores in its charge.[37] In addition to these "public" women, others at times sold their bodies out of economic need, contributing to a submerged but thriving market in casual prostitution outside the brothels.[38] Men of middling or affluent economic standing could also avail themselves, with little reproval, of their servant or slave women for sex. The illegitimate offspring of these unions, while sometimes reared in the father's household, formed a large share of the children abandoned to the city's overflowing foundling homes.[39] Other men, and not only those too poor to afford prostitutes or servants, simply took women by force. Judiciary records in these years document frequent cases involving men, often in gangs, who violently tore women from their homes and raped them.[40] Finally, husbands, who could presumably satisfy their sexual urges with their wives, nonetheless constituted a significant proportion of the men incriminated for sodomy with boys, 25 percent overall in the *catasto* sample and 44 percent of the men over the age of thirty.

To interpret homosexual activity in Florence as, at root, an opportunistic response to limited sexual options with women not only runs up against these objective obstacles, but also inevitably posits the homoerotic as a second-rate, socially immature, and transient substitute for presumably preferred, more responsible relations with women.[41] Some local men thought otherwise. A young patrician with a wife and child who confessed in 1404 to having carried on a long, committed relationship with a youth nearly twenty years his junior proclaimed to the court that he preferred his young friend to his legitimate spouse, while the protagonist of one of the poems in Beccadelli's *Hermaphroditus* laments that he is forced to gratify his sexual needs with women only because no boys are available.[42]

Much remains to be said about the "men-in-groups" aspect of Florentine male culture and its relationship to homosexual activity. In the sexual economy of late medieval Florence, however, males' homoerotic relations were not necessarily an exclusive alternative to sex with women, but one of several possible and probably overlapping options.

There is no reason to exclude a priori the possibility that some men's sexual tastes tended mainly or exclusively toward young males, though prosecution for sodomy is clearly no indicator of this. One or two informers mentioned that the men they denounced had solely homoerotic inclinations, but the very need to point this out implies that they found it unusual: an accuser in 1496 claimed, for instance, that "Giovanfrancesco di Brancaccio Rucellai lets himself be sodomized by Andrea di Benedetto Bonsi, and the said Andrea never touches women."[43] Men with more or less exclusive homoerotic desires—most of whom, however, were married—appear more commonly in contemporary Tuscan and other novelle. In a story by Boccaccio in the *Decameron* (V, 10), the voluptuous wife of Pietro di Vinciolo discovered after their marriage that her spouse had no sexual interest in women and preferred handsome young men; women, she angrily deduced in a play on the term *contra naturam*, went against his nature.[44] In the tale of "Ridolfo il fiorentino" by Francesco Maria Molza, the youth Ridolfo, who was long devoted solely to the pursuit of boys, eventually married, but, "thinking he might transform his love more easily this way," he chose as his wife a young woman of masculine appearance with a rather deep voice. Yet despite her mannish way he, too, could arouse no passion for his wife, and so took up instead with a good-looking boy. His interest in his spouse was kindled only when the quick-witted and determined woman offered her backside for his enjoyment—but even this did not induce him to give up his boyfriend.[45] As the authors tell it, both Pietro's and Ridolfo's marriages were merely a willful subterfuge to satisfy their families and reduce the community's suspicions, making it easier for them to continue having sex with boys. Characters and situations like this were perhaps not only the fruit of writers' creative imaginations, but could also be found in everyday life. In his history of Florence, Giovanni Cavalcanti recounted the story of Trincaglia, a sodomite who "spent all his efforts in offending nature no less than human reproduction." He adduced a different motive for the man's marriage, but the outcome was much the same as that in the novelle: "I think that greed [for a dowry] rather than a desire to abandon the indecent art of his shameful life induced him to take a wife. This attests to me that both his wife and Trincaglia sought the love of young lads."[46]

There was also a misogynous strain in some literature and sermons on sodomy which implies that men who enjoyed boys sometimes had no erotic interest in women. As noted earlier, Bernardino of Siena claimed that sodomites loathed women and found them sexually undesirable: "[N]o matter how beautiful a woman may be, to him she stinks and is displeasing, nor will he ever want to yield to her beauty."[47] The theme of male disdain for women is also prominent in the poem "In Praise of Pederasty" by Francesco Beccuti ("il Coppetta") of Perugia.[48] In a novella by Pietro Fortini of Siena, a male character contemplating a disguise muses, "Shall I make myself Florentine? No, because their vices are such that they cannot bear to look at women, who they say are their enemies; in not wanting to look at women's faces they are just like the men of Lucca."[49] The Florentine protagonist of a tale by Sabadino degli Arienti in *Le porretane* insisted to the skeptical priest who was confessing him that he had never in his life carnally known a woman but had, like all fun-loving men of his native city, regularly taken his pleasure with boys. He explained his disinterest in females by admitting that although in the abstract he did not really dislike women, to look at them nauseated him.[50]

If people acknowledged that some men preferred companions of the same sex, however, this did not lead them to differentiate such men sharply from others whose erotic desires included males but varied more widely, or from those who, whatever the sex of their partner, engaged in those acts that could be defined as "sodomy." All were called simply "sodomites," with little semantic or conceptual distinction. A man with a long history of sexual involvement with boys might at most be called an "inveterate" sodomite, but so too was a man who habitually sodomized women.[51]

In any case, there is no reason to assume that alleged or confirmed sodomites limited themselves to sex with boys (or vice versa). Such individuals were probably a distinct minority. Due to the courts' narrow interests, which focused only on people's sodomitical—mainly homosexual—acts and not on their entire sexual histories, it is hard to document other erotic experiences of persons implicated in same-sex relations. Still, there is ample evidence to suggest that in late medieval and early modern Florence, males were in general rather flexible about the biological sex of the objects of their desire. This is not to say they were blindly undiscriminating in their erotic choices, that the sex of their partners did not matter to them, or that any orifice would do in their quest for sexual pleasure. Rather, having sexual relations with a person of one sex usually did not preclude having relations, whether concurrently or at various stages in life, with a person of the other. Some scholars, if they have not simply assumed that males who had sex with other males in this period were exclusively "homosexual," have adopted the seemingly more appropriate word "bisexuality" to characterize Renaissance men's interest in both sexes.[52] But this anachronistic term is only a hybrid product of the sharply drawn contemporary categories "homosexual" and "heterosexual," which were lacking in this society, and it probably misrepresents the cultural specificity of late medieval and early modern understandings of erotic experience and sentiment.[53]

Evidence for the coexistence of various expressions of desire comes from both literary and judiciary sources. The erotic wordplays of Tuscan carnival songs and other burlesque poems, for instance, playfully celebrate both vaginal and anal intercourse without drawing too fine a moral distinction between the two.[54] In a novella by Gentile Sermini, a man who is happily married nonetheless falls in love with a boy; his lovelorn wife gets her revenge by seducing her husband's none-too-reticent boyfriend.[55] In the apocryphal addition to *La cazzaria* mentioned earlier, the teenage *bardassa* Sodo tells of his many trysts with men, but he also keeps a female prostitute; he and his whore, he recounts, often visited one of his male lovers, and together they formed a "happy threesome" with the man penetrating Sodo and Sodo penetrating his concubine.[56] Similar arrangements were alleged in some denunciations to the Night Officers.[57] More concretely, numerous men were convicted for sodomy with both males and females,[58] while others implicated in or convicted of sodomy with boys were also sentenced by the Officers of Decency for various crimes involving prostitutes, probably indicating that they frequented the brothels.[59] As an accusation from 1512 suggests, Florentines found nothing at all unusual in the fact that men might desire and have sexual intercourse with both boys and women. Denouncing two brothers of the Martelli family for petty thefts and purse-snatching, the informer casually observed that, since they and their comrades had no other source of money, "if they didn't do these things they wouldn't be able to keep their boys, *bardasse*, and whores."[60]

A vivid denunciation from 1510 illustrates how easily a man with evident experience with females could also desire a young male. Paolo di Maso Ballucci, who made the accusation, was serving guard duty one night in a village near Florence with Fruosino Laschi. After they went to bed (in the same bed), Fruosino turned the conversation to sexual matters and candidly asked his bedfellow about a girl from the village, "How many times have you done it with Lisabetta?" When Paolo responded, "I've never done it, nor have I said anything," Fruosino berated him, "You're not worth much! Go ahead, do it to her!" But Paolo admitted, "I'm not good at those things." Then Fruosino, a self-styled expert, advised his friend, "When you're in the pasture, call to her and tell her to pull a thorn from your foot, and then throw a sack over her and do it to her." Paolo still resisted, so Fruosino encouraged him to follow his own dubious example: "It's not a sin. I kept one of the girls, and I did it to her more than a hundred times. Then I put her in a convent near Florence." Perhaps hoping that these intimate revelations had stimulated Paolo's desire as they had his, Fruosino then "started to touch me and wanted to do the evil things with me," at which point the reluctant Paolo moved to another bed.[61] Besides revealing Fruosino's brutal attitudes toward women, Paolo's account shows how an early-sixteenth-century man's erotic passions could easily embrace both females and males. Even if Fruosino perhaps fabricated the story about his relations with the girl merely to establish his sexual "normality" in Paolo's eyes, and despite the latter's squeamishness, the basic point remains: there would have been no contradiction in two males who perceived each other as "regular" fellows having sexual relations together (as long, of course, as they observed the customary age- and role-bound conventions).

For Florentine males, same-sex sodomy was probably one of several socially recognized and more or less accepted erotic options, without necessitating a categorical choice of one sex over the other. Perhaps the last word on this point is best left to the worldly wise Niccolò Machiavelli. In a light-hearted letter of 1514 in which he urged his friend Francesco Vettori, then Florentine ambassador to Rome, to follow his inclinations about the company he kept and ignore the prudish admonitions of his advisers, he depicted an imaginary scenario in which Vettori banished from his house both a certain "ser Sano," a man notorious for his homosexual activity, as well as his numerous courtesans. Into this sterile, joyless environment arrives Machiavelli, worried that his friend will become ill because "it appears you don't have any fun." He warns him about the lack of opportunities for pleasure indistinctly with either sex: "Here there are no young lads, nor any women. What kind of fucking house is this?"[62]

These observations provide some broader perspectives on the rather flexible relationships between marriage or bachelorhood and homosexual activity. Nevertheless, there were some noticeable differences in sodomitical behavior and reactions to it on which both age and marital status had some bearing. One admittedly crude way of assessing some of these variations is through a study of the case histories of the men implicated in sodomy who were identified in the *catasto*, whose basic biographical information is well documented. Although this evidence has clear limitations, the record of how often a person came to the Night Officers' attention in the 1478–1502 survey, and in particular of how many partners he allegedly had, can be assumed to resemble his actual sexual conduct. The court records, of course, in no way constitute a census of sexual behavior, although given the surveillance methods of the Office of the Night someone who engaged often in sodomy was likely to find himself implicated more than once. Moreover, focusing only on the number of companions men had risks giving a distorted and partial impression, for this does not take into account the length or character of their relations or disclose much about the significance they attributed to them. These important issues will be taken up further at a later point. With these qualifications in mind, the frequency of men's reported sexual contacts simply provides one useful perspective on the social organization of sodomy in Florence.

This evidence suggests that involvement in sodomy was most casual and ephemeral among youths. In contrast, the much smaller number of older men, and especially older bachelors, demonstrated a more prolonged and committed interest in relations with boys.

In fact, to judge by the number of their alleged partners, for most men of all ages sodomy was probably a sporadic or temporary transgression that, however absorbing emotionally and erotically, implied no long-term pattern of behavior. The vast majority, some 85 percent, of all males implicated between 1478 and 1502 as the senior partners in homosexual sodomy came to the Night Officers' attention only once.[63] Among the men located in the *catasto*, repeated offenders happen to be overrepresented, forming some 36 percent of the sample. When ages are taken into account, however, differences emerge in the sexual behavior of younger and older men. Of the youths in this sample who in 1480 were aged nineteen to thirty, fifteen of forty-eight (31 percent) were implicated with more than one partner between 1478 and 1502, and eight (17 percent) had more than two reported partners.[64] Among men aged thirty-one to forty, the proportion of those who had more than one partner rises to twelve of thirty-two (38 percent), while five (16 percent) had more than two partners. The highest incidence of men with multiple partners occurs among the oldest age group. Of men over forty, thirteen of thirty-one (42 percent) had more than one partner, and fully ten (32 percent) had over two companions.

Although these differences are not overwhelming, they suggest that especially for youths, sodomy was often an incidental and transitory experience. The cohort of young men aged nineteen to thirty in 1480 passed through what was considered the profligate period of their youth and into full maturity during the years of this survey. In 1502 most would have only been in their forties. Yet despite the commonness of homosexual activity among youths overall, they had fewer sexual encounters, compared with older men, and as a group had less of a long-term investment, it might be said, in sodomy. In contrast, the older men who in 1480 were already over forty manifested during the following twenty-odd years a noticeably greater and more durable interest in boys.

The men in this sample—above all the older men—also displayed different patterns of homosexual behavior, depending not only on their age but also on whether or not they were married. The youngest group of nineteen- to thirty-year-olds can be excluded, since so few were married. Among men aged thirty-one to forty, who had passed the average age at marriage but by local standards were still considered youths, marital status seems to have had little bearing on their relative involvement in sodomy. Single and married men in this age group showed roughly similar patterns of homosexual interactions. Of the eighteen men who were still unmarried in 1480, six had multiple partners between 1478 and 1502. The most notorious of these bachelors was Jacopo d'Andrea, "the little baker" discussed earlier, who in 1480 was aged thirty-five. Between 1470 and 1487—when he was knifed to death by his young shop assistant—Jacopo denounced himself for relations with at least twenty-four different boys, was accused of sodomizing sixteen others, and was convicted a remarkable thirteen times.[65] Of the fourteen men in this age group who had wives in 1480, however, six also had relations with more than one boy. The coppersmith Jacopo di Francesco di Lionardo, aged thirty-three in 1480 with a wife and two small children, denounced himself for relations with five boys and was implicated with two others between 1482 and 1489.[66] Franceschino di Lazzaro de' Medici, who worked in the bank of his illustrious cousin Lorenzo, was forty years old in 1480, married and childless, yet between 1473 and 1490 he was named in at least one denunciation and seven boys' confessions.[67] Marriage did not automatically exclude men's erotic interest in boys, perhaps especially for the young men, who might have had some difficulty adjusting to life with their newly acquired and usually much younger wives.[68]

Among men over the age of forty, however, marriage did seem to draw a dividing line between occasional and more dedicated sodomites. Of the thirteen men this age who were married in 1480, only three were incriminated for sodomy more than once from 1478 to 1502. The three exceptions include two brothers, ser Pierozzo and Jacopo di Bartolomeo Cerbini, whose marriages evidently did little to impede their numerous relations with boys. Aged forty-eight in 1480 with a wife and five children, the notary Pierozzo was denounced in 1472 and again in 1479, the latter for sodomizing three boys; in 1474 a fifteen-year-old claimed that Pierozzo had propositioned him, kissing him and fondling his genitals, but on each occasion he was absolved. In 1483 he finally incriminated himself for having sodomized two boys "many times" during the preceding year.[69] His brother Jacopo, a mercer, was forty-nine in 1480 and had probably recently married his wife, who was only eighteen.[70] His seems to have been merely a marriage of convenience, however. As a bachelor, Papino, as he was known, had long and avidly pursued boys. He was convicted for sodomy twice in 1463, denounced but absolved in 1466, convicted again in 1473 and 1474, and suffered another grievous conviction in 1476 when the Night Officers fined him the huge sum of 486 florins.[71] After this ruinous incident, his brothers might have decided that it was time for him to marry, settle down, and stop putting the Cerbini patrimony at risk. But Jacopo's marriage failed to quell his desire for young males. In 1481 he was accused of keeping a boy "for his use as a woman" and of giving him presents of stockings and tunics, and he was denounced again in 1485, 1487, and 1497, though each time he was absolved. Finally, in 1498, at the age of sixty-seven, thirty-six years after his first known accusation, the Eight of Watch convicted him once more for sodomy, fining him 50 florins and exiling him from the state for three years.[72]

With their long records of involvement in sodomy, however, the Cerbini brothers were exceptional among men of their age and marital status. Already a minority compared with unmarried sodomites, older married men appear for the most part to have had only a sporadic interest in sex with boys.

The case histories of older single men who had relations with boys reveal quite a different pattern. While homoerotic desire respected no age limits or social condition, sodomy was likely to be more frequent and habitual among older men who probably never married. Ten of the eighteen unmarried men over the age of forty in the *catasto* sample were implicated in sodomy with more than one partner between 1478 and 1502, as compared with three of the thirteen married men this age. The notorious Salvi Panuzzi, whose record between 1466 and 1496 has already been noted, was forty-seven in 1480 and apparently a permanent bachelor;[73] his brother Jacopo, implicated twelve times and convicted twice from 1463 to 1487, had once been married and had children, but most of his recorded homosexual activity occurred when he was a widower.[74] Vieri di Oddo Altoviti, aged fifty-six and single in 1480, was implicated three times from 1480 to 1493; at the age of sixty-nine, he was reputed to have been involved for three years or more with twenty-year-old Michele di Francesco Vanacci.[75] Matteo di Gheruccio Gherucci, a fifty-five-year-old bachelor in 1480, was convicted in 1461 and 1465, absolved in 1475 even though he confessed, and convicted again in 1477; he also denounced himself in 1475, 1476, and 1481 for having sodomized a total of eleven boys.[76]

Significantly, a number of these older single men with long histories of sodomy also showed an interest in sexual practices that were unusual in the Florentine context. At least four of the ten recidivist bachelors over forty in the *catasto* sample reportedly fellated boys, an act that was much less common than anal intercourse and perhaps implied a more self-conscious notion of mutual pleasure in homoerotic interactions.[77] And when a fifth, sixty-three-year-old Salvi Panuzzi, confessed his recent sexual activities in 1496, he revealed not only that he had fondled the genitals of numerous boys and youths but that, in a socially abhorred reversal of roles, he had also invited youths to sodomize him.[78]

The length, intensity, and character of these older unmarried men's involvement in sodomy all suggest that they might have been committed to it in a way that differed from that of most Florentine men. For these men, erotic relations with boys perhaps represented a more or less conscious and long-term alternative to marriage, if not to other relations with women. And although their numbers were small in comparison with those of the many youths who engaged more sporadically in sodomy, this group of repeatedly incriminated older men, mostly unmarried, must have formed a conspicuous part of the sodomitical milieu of Florence.

Although married men who engaged in sodomy were a minority, in some ways their homosexual activity seems to have been considered more problematic than that of bachelors, possibly because of its potential for disrupting domestic life. This might be one reason why the comic treatment of homoerotic themes in novelle focuses overwhelmingly on the same-sex loves and affairs of husbands. Also in the court records, although single men were most commonly implicated in sodomy, informers seldom mentioned that the men they accused were unmarried; in contrast, accusations in which men's status as husbands was made an issue are both more frequent and more descriptive. These charges reveal an unusual glimpse of the tensions and conflicts to which conjugal life in Florence was sometimes subjected. Probably few local couples struck as felicitous a compromise as the one they knew from Boccaccio's familiar story of the sodomite Pietro di Vinciolo and his sexually frustrated wife: they shared the pleasures of her handsome young lover.[79] The experiences of those men and women whose lives are briefly illuminated in the judiciary records were much less ideal.

To judge from the reports of informants, married men's homoerotic inclinations often strained domestic relations. The wife of the cloth merchant Daniello Bruscoli was "greatly distressed," an informer said in 1492, that her husband kept an eighteen-year-old in his employ with whom he had been sexually involved for two years.[80] According to an accuser, the shoemaker Marco di Nencio (who later confessed) also kept his apprentice in his bed and "for his use as a woman. This is the truth, because Marco's wife has complained and is still complaining about it, but she's complaining more [about him] than about the others he's brought into the house."[81] Another informer reported something "incredible, yet true":

> Around the end of October 1467, mona Bindella, wife of the baker Piero di Nofri di Gimignano . . . ran out of the house very angrily, and told [three female neighbors] that she had found her husband Piero in bed with a lad named Oriente, and he was sodomizing him. It's his old evil, according to his wife, since Piero is dedicated to nothing else, and he's become poor on account of this wickedness because he spends everything he has on boys.[82]

Wives who complained about their husbands' relations with boys or tried to discourage them sometimes risked provoking their spouses' rage and physical abuse. Someone charged that a certain Maso sodomized his apprentice Salvadore in the presence of his wife, "and if his wife says anything about it, he beats her"; if they arrest the boy, "she will be very pleased and will confess everything."[83] The doctor Piermatteo de' Lanfranchi also reportedly beat his wife because of a domestic squabble over a boy with whom he was in love, Bindo d'Arnoldo de' Bardi. According to a witness who said he heard the story from the woman's sister-in-law,

> she had gotten a thrashing from master Piermatteo, because once when a young boy [Bardi] went to the doctor's house and knocked on the door, his wife refused to let him in and drove him away. Later, when the doctor returned and learned what had happened, he beat her so badly that she left home and stayed away for several days.[84]

Occasionally, it seems, conjugal relations did not withstand the stress and conflict generated at least in part over sexual differences. Some marriages reputedly broke up when a man who was accustomed to having sex with boys also wanted to have anal intercourse with his unwilling wife. According to an accuser in 1482, "Bartolomeo di Niccolò, a servant at the hospital of messer Bonifacio, sodomized a young cleric who's at this hospital . . . many times. He has a wife, but she doesn't live with him because he used her from behind."[85] Another said the wife of Benedetto Sapiti, a "very great sodomite," abandoned her husband because she refused to allow him to sodomize her.[86] Some men allegedly forced their wives to leave home so as to accommodate their relations with boys more easily. An informer in 1496 claimed that Francesco di ser Alberto had kept his wife secluded in their villa for two years, and that now "publicly, in place of his wife" he kept two sons of the wool shearer Benastro.[87] Giovanni Riccialbani reportedly drove his wife from their home so that he could keep his young male friend in the house.[88] In late medieval Florence, it seems, one font of marital discord was husbands' sexual interests in boys.

Whether or not men who engaged in sodomy were married was personally and socially relevant in another way as well, for it tended to influence their fate at the hands of the Officers of the Night. The magistrates charged with policing sodomy were much more likely to convict single men than husbands. A comparison of sentences reveals this clearly (Table B.9). Excluding absolutions for self-denunciations, the officials convicted only two of the twenty-five married men in the *catasto* sample, but twenty-four of the eighty-nine men who did not have wives. The gap between married and single men widens even farther when only those who were aged thirty-one or over—that is, above the average age of marriage—are considered. The Night Officers condemned only one of the twenty-two married men this age, but twelve of the thirty-nine unmarried men. Viewed from a different perspective, bachelors made up just over half (27 of 48) of the men over thirty whom the officials absolved, but nearly all (12 of 13) of those they convicted. Single men over thirty were over six times more likely to be convicted than their married fellows.

While marriage did not keep men from having relations with boys, the officials were apparently willing to let married men's sodomy go unpunished more often, perhaps in tacit recognition of the fulfillment of their social role as family providers and fathers of legitimate children, or to avoid giving an added motive for domestic stress. As long as they were discreet and publicly devoted to their families, married men might have been able to act on their homosexual desires with relatively little risk of a public reprimand.

Not only were single men, though, seen as more disposed toward debauchery of all sorts, but their involvement with boys, as case histories suggest, also tended to be more intense and longer-lasting than did married men's, especially as they grew older. In part, then, officials perhaps acted on a common perception, grounded in experience, that bachelors more conspicuously and avidly pursued boys. Lacking the respectable "cover" a wife and family could have provided for their homosexual relations, bachelors were also more exposed than married men. This was especially true of older men who had definitively renounced conjugal union. They failed to live up to the social ideal of marriage and legitimate fatherhood, a powerful ideological spur to the campaign against sodomy in Florence earlier in the century whose echoes probably did not die out entirely in successive decades. The Night Officers, themselves all married as required by law, were less tolerant of bachelors' homosexual activity. They tended to single out unmarried men for punishment not only for their own sexual and social nonconformity, but also as a warning to others who rejected matrimony and family life.

Provenance and Residence

One of the figures prominently associated with sodomy in early Florentine legislation was the foreigner: wayfarers or brigands called in Italian *trapassi* or *malandrini*. Indeed, the earliest extant law implied that sodomy was imported from abroad and was not a local product at all. "Infected with the contagion" of sodomy, according to the arresting imagery of the 1325 statute, these outsiders came "to the borders of the city of Florence" to "sow their wicked and abominable crimes in the good and decent seedbed" of the Arno city.[89] Townspeople who saw such men seizing, striking, threatening, or otherwise molesting local boys with the intention of sodomizing them were authorized to capture and beat them, at no penalty to themselves. Moreover, this statute reserved the punishment of death to *trapassi* and *malandrini*, while others, presumably local residents, caught sodomizing were to be castrated.

This early emphasis on non-Florentines gradually faded. In the 1365 law, the distinction between residents and others disappeared, and *trapassi* or *malandrini* were not mentioned. They resurfaced in the 1415 statutes, but this was merely a repetition of past injunctions now devoid of their original sense.[90] Later the foreign sodomite vanished from the laws, remaining only a stock figure in Florentine burlesque poetry of the fifteenth and sixteenth centuries.[91]

Whether this stress on outsiders who raped local boys ever had any basis in reality, however, is doubtful. The few trials for sodomy in the fourteenth century overwhelmingly dealt with native or resident Florentines. In the late fifteenth century, too, as far as can be determined from the available evidence, local males predominated in sodomy both in Florence and throughout the state (Table B.10).

Of all the men and boys either implicated in sodomy to the Night Officers or convicted by them between 1478 and 1502, the vast majority (89 and 90 percent, respectively) resided in the city of Florence, and most (82–83 percent of the total, or 92 percent of the city residents) were probably native-born Florentines. The remaining minority of persons resident in the city (7 percent of the total implicated or convicted) had names that indicate provenance elsewhere, but this did not necessarily signify recent immigration.[92] Nearly two-thirds of these originated from towns in present-day

Tuscany, while the rest came mainly from other regions of the Italian peninsula, especially north of the Appenines (most stemmed from what are now Lombardy and Emilia Romagna). A mere nine individuals were of non-Italian origin, including four from Germany, four from Spain, and one from France. Although comparisons are approximate, the proportion of native Florentines was probably somewhat higher among persons in this survey than among the city's population at large.[93]

Sodomy in Florence, then, was mainly indigenous, associated with men and boys of local origin and, to a lesser extent, Tuscan immigrants, while foreigners appear to have been only marginally involved. This differs sharply from the situation both in contemporary Venice and later in Valencia, where outsiders made up a conspicuous part of those convicted of sodomy.[94] The homebred character of sodomy in Florence also distinguishes it from the seemingly more cosmopolitan world of the city's brothels. Not only were the prostitutes there usually foreigners, but also, judging on the basis of judiciary records, more than half of their clients came from outside Tuscany and only one-fifth were Florentines.[95] In Florence, sodomy was not associated with a floating or poorly integrated population of marginals, immigrants, or itinerant travelers, but instead had deep local roots among the city's native sons.

The Officers of the Night did not limit their pursuit of sodomy to Florence. They had jurisdiction throughout the state, with the exception of a few communities with special juridical status.[96] To facilitate control of sodomy in the dominion, the Night Officers posted denunciation boxes at various times in the provincial centers, including Pisa, Pistoia, Empoli, Arezzo, and nearby Prato, where, despite the small populace of only a few thousand inhabitants, homosexual activity was evidently so common that officials placed two boxes there in the later fifteenth century.[97] Roughly one of every ten persons incriminated or convicted for homosexual sodomy from 1478 to 1502 lived in provincial towns and villages. San Miniato, Figline, Pistoia, Volterra, and Ponte a Rifredi each had from ten to twenty residents implicated, while thirty-five came from the village of Montelupo and fifty-two from the large port town of Pisa. The town with by far the largest number of men and boys incriminated, however, was Prato, with a total of 147 (over one-third of all those who lived in the dominion). Not only was sodomy apparently widespread in this small town, but the Night Officers' authority there was also publicly challenged: at least three times, in 1481, 1492, and again in 1500, unknown "vandals"—possibly sodomites—ripped down and demolished their *tamburi*.[98] The large number of males implicated or convicted for sodomy in these towns indicates that homosexual activity, while concentrated in the dominant city, was common throughout the entire region.

A closer look at the residence of those who lived in Florence itself shows, unsurprisingly, that they came from virtually every corner of the city. In the aggregate, no distinctive patterns of residence can be discerned. Parish residence can be identified for some 18 percent of all those implicated from 1478 to 1502, and for 36 percent of the active partners convicted (Table B.11). Among both groups, as well as among the groups of active or passive partners taken separately, the distribution by parish roughly resembles that of the city's entire population.[99] Nearly every parish, no matter how small, claimed at least a few alleged or convicted sodomites. Nearly half (47 percent) of all those implicated, however, lived in five of the city's largest parishes: San Lorenzo, Sant'Ambrogio, and San Piero Maggiore on the north side of the Arno, and San Frediano and San Felice in Piazza on the south (proportions for active and passive partners are, respectively, 46 and 51 percent). Only a slightly lower proportion of the active companions who were convicted (43 percent) came from these five parishes. Although their overall distribution differs slightly, men who denounced themselves as well as their partners also lived mostly in these parishes (respectively 55 and 59 percent, with a high concentration, for unknown reasons, of self-accused in San Lorenzo and of their partners in Sant'Ambrogio and San Felice). Together these large, peripheral parishes on the outer edges of the urban center were among what have been called the working-class ghettos of late-fifteenth-century Florence.[100] This sociogeographical perspective is supported by the analysis in the following section of the social background of males implicated in sodomy, who often but by no means exclusively came from the lower and artisanal classes. But that they lived throughout the city, in heavily working-class quarters as well as in the socially varied neighborhoods of the central district, only tends to confirm how pervasive sodomy was in Florence.

All this does not mean that where people lived was irrelevant to the nature of homosexual activity. As will be discussed in the next chapter, sexual partners often came from the same neighborhood or district, and sometimes networks of friends and acquaintances involved in sodomy had a strong neighborhood base. Among the variety of social relations into which sodomy was interwoven, a common neighborhood was one of the more significant.

Social Composition

The sheer number of persons implicated in sodomy in the later fifteenth century suggests that this sexual practice was probably familiar at all levels of the social hierarchy. Despite the broad social base that the judiciary records reveal, however, this "vice" was represented in different ways in literary and prescriptive sources. Since these representations played a powerful role in organizing perceptions of sodomy, it is worth considering them first before going on to examine the more balanced evidence from the judiciary sources.

Throughout the Middle Ages and early modern period, sodomy was commonly portrayed in literature and sermons as a vice of aristocrats and the learned, an image that still reverberates in one modern assumption that homoeroticism in the Renaissance attracted above all the refined sensibilities of humanists, neo-Platonists, and artists. The sodomites in the fifteenth and sixteenth cantos of Dante's *Inferno*, one of the earliest Tuscan literary representations of sodomy, fit the stereotype well. The first person Dante meets is his spiritual mentor, Brunetto Latini, a philosopher and secretary of the Florentine Commune. When he asks this revered man who his companions in hell were, he responds, "know that all were clerks, and great men of letters and of great fame, in the world defiled by one same sin." Among them he names the Latin grammarian Priscian, by whom early commentators believed Dante intended all grammar teachers, and Francesco d'Accorso, a well-known jurist and professor of civil law; he also refers to Andrea de' Mozzi, a member of an eminent local family and bishop of Florence from 1287 to 1295. Farther along, Dante meets three other sodomites, whom he treats with utmost respect: Guido Guerra, a member of the great feudal magnate clan, the Guidi counts; Tegghiaio Aldobrandi, a knight of the ancient Adimari family of Florence; and Jacopo Rusticucci, a knight from a more modest Florentine family.[101]

The association of sodomy with the wealthy and powerful was also a topos in the sermons and burlesque literature of the Renaissance. Preachers often blamed the idleness of the sons of the rich for their sexual license and in particular for their sodomy. When Bernardino of Siena condemned the Florentine practices that he believed led to sodomy, he was plainly addressing the affluent and politically privileged classes:

> You don't make your sons work in a shop, nor do they go to school to learn any virtues. Instead you send them out in a *giornea* [a richly appointed tunic] with their long hair and revealing hosiery, and they go around polishing the benches with their falcons and their dogs on leash; they're good for nothing but lusting with sodomites, shameful acts, indecent talk, gorging themselves with food, gambling, preening, cursing. . . . Those who are wealthy and don't need to earn a living or work in a shop should dedicate themselves to moral and political studies, they should learn to live like men, they should study rhetoric and other disciplines so that, should the country need them, they can be used in embassies and in other tasks for the republic. . . . And those who lead another life, idle and bestial, drive them from the city so that they don't corrupt others, and deprive them of public offices.[102]

As noted earlier, Bernardino also once remarked that local men justified their passion for boys by arguing that "all men of the elite [*uomini da bene*] belong to that trade."[103]

Jocular poets also found in the stereotype fertile ground for their imagination. They often contrasted the alleged attraction of the "great" to sodomy with the more "natural" sexual inclinations of common people. In a poem dedicated equivocally to a "sausage," the writer Agnolo Firenzuola claimed that "roast and rump [in the burlesque code, both metaphors for sodomy] pertain above all to the great." Later he again distinguished the sexual tastes of the rich and cultured from those of the humble, citing an alleged theological authority "who reports the traditional opinion that figs [vagina] belong to commoners, but apples and peaches [buttocks] to the great masters."[104] This view was so commonplace by the mid-sixteenth century, and not only in Florence, that someone like the sculptor Benvenuto Cellini, well known for his illicit sexual interests, could wittily turn it to his advantage to defend himself. When his archrival Baccio Bandinelli hurled the epithet "dirty sodomite" at him in front of Duke Cosimo I and his court, Cellini coolly responded,

> Oh fool, you're wrong: but would God that I knew how to practice such a noble art, since one reads that Jove used it with Ganymede in paradise, and here on earth the greatest emperors and kings in the world use it. I am a lowly and humble wretch, and neither could I nor would I know how to get involved in such an admirable thing.

The artist's clever retort provoked the riotous laughter and admiration of the duke and his courtiers.[105]

In the spurious addition to *La cazzaria*, Sodo, the former *bardassa*, draws out the political dimensions of this class-bound theme: the elite make laws to control the sexuality of those subject to them, while they themselves can enjoy the forbidden pleasures because they are above the law:

> The great impose penalties on those who fuck in the ass for no other reason than this: since it's their own profession, they don't want ruffians to use it. And the game reserved for princes, well, that's nothing other than the ass, and they won't allow all kinds of people going after it. Only the eagle, as queen of the other angels, is allowed to gaze at the sun; in the same way the ass, which resembles this planet, is allowed to gaze at princes.[106]

Nor did the authors of satirical and jocular literature spare the sodomy of the clergy, whose sexual escapades had long filled popular imagery. From prelates at the court of Rome, portrayed as a den of sodomy, to itinerant friars who took advantage of innocent youths, clergymen held a prominent place among the stock literary figures of sodomites. Monks were also protagonists of several of the amorous adventures that Sodo recounted to his friend Arsiccio.[107] Their celibacy made the clergy an easy target for such satires, fanned by a long, popular, anticlerical tradition.

In contrast to literary portrayals of wealthy, educated, or clerical sodomites, Florentine laws in the later fifteenth century presented a sharply contradictory image. According to these representations, sodomy was most common among the humble and unrefined, who had no access to the classical sources from which the Renaissance elite is often assumed to have drawn its homoerotic inspiration. As the law of 1459 pointed out, "it is evident how much sodomy is presently practiced in this city, especially by artisans and the poor."[108] This was a common refrain in the period. A 1458 law referred to convicted sodomites as "wretched" and "very poor persons," while the law of 1459 asserted elsewhere that "nearly all those accused of practicing such vices are very poor men, who cannot be punished with fines since they have no money."[109] In 1490 it was again said that men denounced for sodomy "are commonly poor."[110] As noted earlier, the poverty of these men was used to justify reductions in fines and other measures to ease the burden of payment on lower-class men.

Nonetheless, the official profession of sympathy for the poor and the humble should be accepted with a good deal of skepticism as an objective assessment of the social position of Florentine sodomites, just as should literary portrayals. Despite apparent biases, the judiciary sources provide a more balanced picture than representations in literature, sermons, or laws. Judging by this type of evidence, males who engaged in sodomy came from across the social spectrum, and it is impossible to single out particular groups as more inclined to it than others.

First, the occupations of all men and boys implicated (those convicted will be examined later) furnish some initial indications of how sodomy permeated the entire society. A trade was recorded for 63 percent of all the individuals in the 1478–1502 survey (68 percent of the active partners and 52 percent of the passive partners). The special problem of those not identified by occupation will be considered in more detail, but one explanation for the different proportions of active and passive partners here is that many of the latter might have been too young to work. Those whose work was noted came from all sectors of the diversified Florentine economy and a wide range of trades, representing some 350 different occupations.

Like the general populace, the majority were artisans and tradesmen, small retail merchants, or dependent wage-earners in the textile industries. Considered according to rough occupational categories (Table B.12), males who worked in various aspects of textile production, the major local industry, formed the largest single group (24 percent of those with occupations listed). Persons involved in the making of clothing, the productive activity with the next highest number of workers according to the 1427 *catasto*, made up the second largest group implicated in sodomy (15 percent). They were followed by individuals who worked at a broad range of other crafts or in local commerce (each 11 percent), in the provision and sale of food (10 percent), and in various services, especially barbers (6.4 percent). People who worked in these sectors together made up nearly 50 percent of all those implicated and 77 percent of those whose occupation was indicated. Smaller but still sizable groups included persons who were employed in various capacities by the government; members of the clergy; people who managed or worked in taverns and inns; doctors, apothecaries, and notaries; persons employed in construction and woodworking; individuals involved in the arts or the production of luxury items, such as goldsmiths and painters; and servants. The smallest categories were made up of teachers or students (0.6 percent) and peasants (0.2 percent). Given the information available, one can draw only the broadest of comparisons with the working population at large, but it is plain that men and boys implicated in sodomy came from a wide variety of urban economic activities and social backgrounds.[111]

Considering distinct occupations separately (Table B.13), the males in the 1478–1502 survey worked most commonly as shoemakers and hosiers (9.3 percent), weavers (5.1 percent), and clothes dealers (4.8 percent), followed by butchers and barbers (both 3.7 percent), clergymen (3.6 percent), and tailors (3.3 percent). Among the ten most frequently occurring trades were also dyers (2.9 percent), grocers (2.5 percent), and carpenters and mercers (both 2.3 percent), the total representing some 43 percent of all those with occupations recorded. There were some minor differences in the occupations of active and passive partners, which can perhaps be accounted for by little-known variations in the age structure of employment in different trades. There were probably also considerable distinctions in wealth and status among these occupations or within the same trade, depending in part on one's position in the shop hierarchy or whether or not the occupation was organized in a guild. Shoemakers and hosiers, butchers, clothes dealers, grocers, carpenters, and others in less frequently appearing trades were probably enrolled in one of the minor guilds, and thus met one of the requirements for citizenship and officeholding. While often poor or of modest means, they had a more respectable status than the majority of unincorporated and disenfranchised workers. Others—like dyers, weavers, tailors, doublet makers, and other dependents of the major guilds—were barred from guild membership and from full participation in civic life. Along with many tradesmen in the lower guilds, the men who had no corporate representation mostly fell into the poorest half of the city's laboring population.[112] While a large proportion of the males implicated in sodomy came from solid backgrounds as artisans or shopkeepers, with a fairly secure if modest economic and social standing, many certainly derived from the poor and disenfranchised, lending support to laws that portrayed men accused or convicted of sodomy as frequently impoverished and unable to pay their fines.

Before examining the evidence regarding those at the higher end of the social scale, it might be useful to pause over certain groups and reconsider some stereotypes about social categories typically thought to have been drawn to homosexual activity. One obvious candidate is the clergy. In the other roughly contemporary Mediterranean cities of Venice and Valencia, the control of clergymen's homosexual activity played a prominent part in efforts to repress sodomy, and in both places churchmen were conspicuous among those prosecuted.[113] In Florence the situation was quite different.

Of course as laymen, the Night Officers and other magistracies had no jurisdiction over the clergy. Priests, monks, and clerics did, however, appear in denunciations or as the partners of boys who confessed that they had been sodomized, and several passive partners were also identified as clerics; in theory, magistrates were supposed to refer such cases to the proper ecclesiastical courts.[114] Yet in this survey, the proportion of churchmen who were implicated in sodomy was quite small, only 2.3 percent of the total and 3.6 percent of those whose occupation was recorded (2.6 percent of all active partners and 1.5 percent of all passive partners).[115] The sexual conduct of the clergy did concern the Night Officers enough to induce them on occasion to write to local prelates, urging them—evidently with little success—to correct the laxity of the religious men (and women) under their charge, as in the following letter to the archbishop of Florence in 1470:

> Most reverend and just father . . . our magistracy is entrusted with safeguarding the convents and also with obviating, as much as possible, the horrible vice of sodomy. Wishing to fulfill a part of our duty, we have arrested several young boys who have been sodomized not only by laymen, but also by numerous priests. This was made known to the representative of your most reverend lord, yet nothing has been done about it. For this reason we are most scandalized.[116]

Undoubtedly, the repeated charges of sodomy among the clergy had a good deal of truth about them, which could perhaps be verified by a study of ecclesiastical court records.[117] But in the context of the widespread homosexual activity in Florence that involved broad sectors of society, the sexual behavior of the local clergy seems rather insignificant.

The same observation can be made for two other groups commonly thought to be associated with homosexual activity, those involved in the arts and in education. The former category, which accounts for only 2.7 percent of those with occupations, includes forty-one goldsmiths, twenty-four painters, a sculptor, a maker of books, an inlayer, a stained-glass artisan, and a dancer. Of course, the presumed "homosexuality" of some Florentine artists and its possible neo-Platonic affinities have attracted a great deal of attention, both scholarly and popular.[118] Although often interpreted in the anachronistic light of modern experience, the homoerotic inclinations (alleged or well confirmed) of Donatello,[119] Leonardo da Vinci,[120] Sandro Botticelli,[121] Michelangelo,[122] and Benvenuto Cellini[123] are by now well known. I do not intend to dwell on these individual cases, observing merely that in the broader social context of sodomy in Florence the experiences, fancied or real, of these prominent artists were probably little different from those of thousands of other, less famous men. And compared with those in other trades, the number and proportion of artists and related professionals implicated in sodomy was inconsequential. To judge on the basis of this evidence, they were no more commonly involved in homosexual activity than were butchers or shoemakers.

Persons associated with schools of various sorts, students and teachers, appear even less frequently in the Night Officers' records, a mere 0.6 percent of all those implicated between 1478 and 1502. Only eight men were identified as schoolteachers (*insegnante di abaco*, *maestro di geometria*, *insegna leggere a' fanciulli*, *magister scolarum*, and four *maestri*). A single boy was identified as an elementary student (*sta all'abaco*), but this surely misrepresents the number of schoolboys,[124] while eight were university students (one *scolaro* and seven *studenti*). While not all the teachers reportedly had sexual relations with their own students, there were enough examples to suggest that, for schoolboys, being sodomized by their masters was occasionally part of their schooling experience. In 1474, for instance, Filippo di ser Francesco from Pratovecchio, a fifteen-year-old student, confessed that he had been sodomized by a total of seventeen men, including, over the preceding four years, three of his former teachers (two of whom were priests) many times during the periods in which he studied with them.[125] Still, the scarcity of teachers among the men accused of sodomy makes one think that Bernardino of Siena was only fueling a popular prejudice when he claimed that the Genoese refused to employ Tuscan teachers in their schools for fear they would corrupt the boys, and it belies the overworked parody of the pedant-sodomite in late medieval and early modern literature.[126]

This category also includes several men or youths who were instructors in nonacademic areas: four men who taught fencing, four who taught dance, and an organist who also taught singing. In the 1490s, dancing and fencing schools came under increased surveillance as part of a renewed campaign against sodomy.[127] But here again, the few cases of alleged sodomy do not seem entirely to warrant this concern. Such places might have been more exposed because of the seductive mixing of young males of different ages, but they and their teachers and students appear to have been only a marginal presence in the overall, more pervasive context of homosexual activity in Florence.

If sodomy was prevalent among artisans, shopkeepers, and the poor, as laws claimed and the evidence on occupations confirms, it also appears no less common among those social groups that enjoyed greater wealth, privilege, and prestige, a fact that the governors of the city who formulated these laws were less willing to acknowledge. Even among the men whose occupations were recorded, there were some of higher status—like doctors, apothecaries, notaries, furriers, or textile merchants and manufacturers—who were probably enrolled in one of the major guilds, an indicator of high social and political rank.[128] Moreover, those who had no profession listed, roughly a third of all active partners and half of the passives, included many elites. In tax records, failure to declare a trade was typical of the great managerial, merchant-banking families, and quite often the absence of an occupation corresponded to a more substantial fortune.[129] This principle probably also applied in recording practices in the judiciary sources, which partly accounts for those without a given profession. The large proportion of those without a declared trade who also bore family names, another rough sign in Florence of higher social status, tends to confirm this hypothesis.[130] Only 12 percent of the active partners and 16 percent of the passives with occupations recorded also had surnames. In contrast, 40 percent of the active and 43 percent of the passive partners who had no occupation bore family names. Overall, in the 1478–1502 survey some 20 percent of the active partners (627) and 30 percent of the passive partners (364) possessed family names, proportions identical to those for men who denounced themselves as well as for their young partners.

The most persuasive evidence that sodomy was common among the elite, however, comes from a comparison of the families that made up the Florentine ruling class with the individuals implicated in sodomy. As most recently defined by Anthony Molho, the group of the city's leading families consisted of 417 lineages that were distinguished by their wealth, political power, and social prestige; these lineages represented about 34 percent of the city's population.[131] Overall, 503 individuals implicated in sodomy in the 1478–1502 survey, roughly 12 percent of the total, came from these ruling class families (313 active and 190 passive partners, respectively 11 and 16 percent of the entire category). Of these 417 dominant families, fully 214, or slightly more than half, had at least one member incriminated for homosexual relations before the Night Officers in the surviving records from 1478 to 1502. At least 14 additional lineages had a member implicated in cases prosecuted by the Eight of Watch (this number is probably low, since only those cases ending in conviction are recorded). Fifty-one lineages claimed at least one member who had denounced himself to the Night Officers or was the partner of a self-accuser (19 actives and 48 passives), while altogether 54 families had one or more members who were convicted. Also among the small group of 110 preeminent lineages identified by Molho as occupying the inner core of the elite at the pinnacle of Florentine society and politics, homosexual activity was quite common. Fully 91 of these most prestigious and powerful clans had at least one member accused of sodomy in my survey of both magistracies, by far the highest proportion among the three different status groups Molho has distinguished within the ruling class. And compared with families of low or middling status, this core group of elite *casate* contained the largest absolute numbers and percentages both of families with members who incriminated themselves or were passive partners of self-accusers (23, or 21 percent), and of families with members who were convicted (26, or 24 percent). Many of the most prominent and familiar lineages of the Florentine patriciate were well represented among the total implicated, including the Adimari (8), Alberti (5), Albizzi (8), Altoviti (10), Bardi (4), Capponi (6), Cavalcanti (8), Frescobaldi (4), Guicciardini (3), Machiavelli

(4), Medici (9), Pandolfini (4), Peruzzi (4), Pucci (6), Ridolfi (9), Rucellai (12), Soderini (5), and Strozzi (5).[132]

The group of 183 persons implicated from 1478 to 1483 whom I located in the 1480 *catasto* adds further information and examples of well-to-do individuals involved in sodomy. Although this sample helps reveal some significant social distinctions among people incriminated for sodomy, it is not representative of all those implicated. It exaggerates the proportion of persons with family names (who are easiest to identify); in fact, nearly 72 percent have surnames, compared with about 24 percent overall. The wealth and status of this sample group are also consequently greater than those, on average, of others incriminated for homosexual activity, although in terms of prosperity the individuals in the sample make up a fairly representative cross-section of Florentine society. Of the 183, 61 lived in households that declared fiscal patrimonies of at least 500 florins, placing them in the wealthiest 39 percent of the city's populace at the time of the 1480 *catasto*. Fifteen came from households with a fiscal wealth of over 1,500 florins, locating them among the richest 10 percent.[133]

A number of the wealthy individuals in this sample were repeatedly incriminated from 1478 to 1502, suggesting that the charges against them probably had some truth, even though they were seldom convicted. Antonangelo di Riccardo Macigni (1,401 florins), for example, was named twice by boys under interrogation, in 1483 and 1494, but he escaped conviction both times.[134] As a boy, Tommaso di Vettorio Landi (1,238 florins) was named as the partner of a man who denounced himself in 1470, was anonymously accused of sodomizing a boy in 1483, and was named in the confessions of two other boys in 1493 and 1496. Remarkably, even his own brother lamented to the tax officials in 1480 that Tommaso, whose whereabouts were unknown, was "very corrupt with evil behaviors," yet each time the officials absolved him.[135]

Boys from affluent families also appeared frequently before the Night Officers as passive partners of sodomites. To judge by the large number of companions some of these boys revealed, they often had a wide range of homosexual relations, commonly with men whose social status was far below their own. Clearly, sodomy in Florence did not involve merely the sexual exploitation of disadvantaged adolescents by men of substance. The following examples, not at all atypical, involve boys who came from households that were among the wealthiest in the city. In 1482, fourteen-year-old Bernardo di Luigi Portinari, whose father declared a fiscal wealth of 1,873 florins, was named twice by informers and by a man who self-confessed, a goldsmith, and when interrogated he admitted to relations with four others, including another goldsmith, a barber, a weaver, and a dyer.[136] Two orphaned brothers in a household that claimed a patrimony worth 1,990 florins, Domenico and Paolo, sons of the notary ser Manno da Lamole, each had numerous sexual partners. In 1480, nineteen-year-old Domenico admitted that he had been sodomized by seventeen men, and another named him in his self-denunciation; only four of these men had family names of note, while most were tradesmen, butchers, or grocers. That same year, five men self-confessed that they had sodomized his eighteen-year-old brother Paolo, who also admitted to relations with eighteen other men; three of his partners had well-known surnames, while the others were artisans and laborers.[137]

Among those in the survey whose families had a fiscal wealth of at least 500 florins were also ten men who denounced themselves, the surest possible evidence of their involvement in sodomy. They included some who were clearly wealthy, like Girolamo di Bartolomeo Nuti (1,029 florins),[138] ser Pierozzo Cerbini (1,135 florins),[139] Bernardo di Giovanni Martini (1,750 florins),[140] and Bonaccorso di Simone Rinuccini (1,785 florins).[141] In general, however, the evidence indicates that self-accusers were poorer than men implicated by other means. The average fortune of the latter was 556 florins, while that of men who denounced themselves was 315 florins. Unsurprisingly, stark financial considerations must have motivated many who incriminated themselves: for poorer men, a fine was a greater threat.

That so many influential Florentine families had members alleged or admitted to be involved in sodomy helps account for the ambivalence toward it that characterized official policy and action throughout much of this period. Some laws prescribed that members of the governing class who were convicted of sodomy be deprived of office, along with other punishments. Yet penalties varied widely over time, and their intent was sometimes contradictory. In order to remove an obstacle to prosecution, the regime in the early fifteenth century found it opportune to guarantee the political rights and municipal honors of sodomites who suffered only one conviction. At the same time fearing the implications of their political activity, the government in the 1410s could only resort weakly to warning electoral officials not to qualify known sodomites for office or vote for them, a practice that Bernardino of Siena was still condemning in the 1420s and that no doubt persisted long afterward.[142] The 1432 law that created the Night Officers threatened to deny civic office to convicted sodomites for a certain number of years—but, tellingly, only for their third and fourth offenses.[143] Laws from 1494 on, which will be examined in more detail in later chapters, also decreed that convicted sodomites be stripped of office, but the length of the proscription and the number of convictions allowed before it went into effect changed considerably both from law to law and, importantly, among different age groups. The constant presence of sodomites and their relatives in the councils of the Republic meant that the political problem of managing sodomy in Florence had delicate implications for the governing class itself.[144]

While men of substance and influence did not escape the attention of the law or an occasional condemnation, the shame and financial burden of a conviction for sodomy tended to fall on more humble men at the margins or outside of the political community. A comparison of the occupations of active partners either condemned or absolved provides one measure of this tendential discrimination. From 1478 to 1502, the Officers of the Night convicted some 23 percent of all those implicated whose occupation was recorded (excluding self-accusers, who were automatically absolved). But they were more likely to convict men who worked at certain trades. Of the ten most commonly occurring occupations among condemned sodomites, the officials convicted conspicuously large proportions of the wool washers (50 percent), grocers (48 percent), dyers and butchers (each 36 percent), weavers (34 percent), tailors (33 percent), bakers (28 percent), and carpenters (27 percent), but only 21 percent both of clothes dealers and of shoemakers and hosiers. Of the remaining condemned men (over half) with occupations recorded, they convicted just 17 percent.

Comparison of occupational categories reveals similar inequality (Table B.14). Of the numerically more significant groups, the Night Officers punished the largest proportions of men who worked at the provision and sale of food (30 percent), and men who labored in the textile industries, mostly poor wage-earning dependents of the major guilds (27 percent); both were sectors that involved mainly the poorest half of the populace. Fully 38 percent of all condemned sodomites worked in these two areas, but only 21 percent of the men who were absolved. Officials' more repressive action against these groups stands in greatest contrast to the lenient treatment accorded the professional category most clearly at the other end of the social spectrum—doctors, notaries, and apothecaries—of whom the Night Officers convicted only 14 percent. And of all those implicated for whom no occupation was recorded—the group that contained the largest proportion of wealthy men from more prestigious families—the officials punished a mere 10 percent. This social bias also emerges clearly in a comparison of the wealth of absolved and convicted men in the *catasto* sample. The ninety-seven active partners in this sample who were absolved lived in households of an average wealth of 662 florins, while the twenty-one who were convicted possessed an average patrimony worth only 247 florins.

To be sure, men of some economic and social standing were not entirely immune from punishment for their homosexual activity. Men with family names constituted some 20 percent of those convicted from 1478 to 1502, the same proportion of men with surnames among all active partners implicated. About 16 percent of the active partners convicted by the Eight also bore surnames. More indicative still, some 8 percent of all the men condemned by the Night Officers, and 6 percent of those condemned by the Eight, stemmed from the 417 lineages that Molho has identified as making up the Florentine ruling class. In the surviving records of both magistracies between 1478 and 1502, 56 convictions by the Night Officers and 14 by the Eight involved men from these dominant families, representing 54 different lineages. Of the 313 men from the ruling class who were implicated in the active role to the Office of the Night, 49, or nearly

16 percent, were convicted. Some of the most illustrious families, however, evidently received more lenient treatment. Of the 18 prominent patrician lineages listed earlier with multiple members incriminated to the Night Officers, only 5 of the 76 active partners (6.6 percent) were convicted, and 3 of these men came from a single clan, the Rucellai.[145] It should also be noted that the majority (three-fourths) of the convictions involving men from ruling class families dated from the final decade of this survey, a period characterized by high political tension and intense moral fervor under the influence of the reforming friar Savonarola, as will be seen in chapter 6. Throughout most of the fifteenth century, until the Medici regime began to waver and finally fell, Florentine judiciary authorities generally appear to have been cautious about embarrassing or provoking the most eminent families by condemning their men for sodomy.

Officials sometimes showed favoritism toward upper-class men in other ways as well. Occasionally when men from well-known families were incriminated, their surnames were blotted out in the records to hide their identities. In an exemplary case from 1485, now legible, Filippo d'Alessandro Machiavelli, Antonio di Piero Baronci, "el Mammaccio" de' Libri, Jacopo di Tanai de' Nerli, and messer Riniero Guicciardini were all beneficiaries of this deception, and all, unsurprisingly, were absolved.[146] In a case from 1473 involving three men of the Soderini, Capponi, and Segni families, the officials convicted them but ordered their notary to suppress their names and surnames in the sentence to be sent to the cameral office, even though they admitted on record that this contravened the law.[147] The scales of justice for sodomites were not tipped relentlessly against working men and the poor. Nonetheless, the Night Officers—themselves mostly major guildsmen, men of substance and status in the community, and often members of ancient or prominent family clans—were not free of the social prejudices of their class.

Despite an occasional conviction, moreover, the favor they generally showed men of "good" families all too often gave fellow Florentines a disturbing impression of social discrimination. Informers complained with some frequency about their leniency toward the wealthy and influential. An accuser in 1494 wrote, "Lord officials, you punish the poor but not the powerful"; another in 1461 commented ironically about the unequal burden of penalties borne by the humble: "[I]t is widely seen that the poor are the ones who maintain justice."[148] After fourteen-year-old Giovanni Falchetti confessed in 1470 that he had been sodomized by Niccolaio di Giovanni Corsini, member of an ancient and powerful lineage, the officials unanimously absolved Corsini "and declared that he had not erred"—yet some skeptic who had access to their records scribbled in the margin, "but they were lying through their teeth [*ma mentirono per la gola*]."[149] And there were some among the patriciate who defended this social injustice: according to an informant in 1496, sixteen-year-old Priore Gherardini, a "shameless *bardassa*" from an old magnate family, went about the dying mills near his house boasting haughtily that "the laws are not intended for people of his status [*le leggi non si intendono per e suoi pari*]," and threatening to kill anyone who dared offend him or his lovers.[150] No remark, however, better conveys the impression that the "officers of the sodomites" protected men of their own caste and discriminated against others than the bitter words of an informer in 1473. He accused a patrician, Gherardo Risaliti, but with little hope of justice: "You won't make a meal of this one, yet if he were some poor fellow you'd drink his blood."[151]

Sodomy in Florence was not limited to any particular social group or to a distinctive and permanent "homosexual" minority. Rather, it was part of the whole fabric of Florentine society, attracting males of all ages, matrimonial condition, and social rank. Indeed, sodomy was so widespread, and the policing apparatus for unearthing it so effective in the later fifteenth century, that in this period probably the majority of local males, at one time or another, were officially incriminated.

To a considerable extent, however, their homosexual behavior was linked to and conditioned by different stages or situations in their life course. The "passive," subordinate role was restricted mainly to the period from around puberty to the age of eighteen or twenty, a sort of unwritten boundary between boyhood and young manhood. Most adult males who engaged in sodomy were youths below the customary late age at marriage, for whom erotic relations with boys, whether casual or deeply engaging, were a more or less accepted and temporary outlet for sexual gratification, diversion, and companionship during long years of bachelorhood before they took a wife, as most, sooner or later, probably did. Although marriage was no obstacle to same-sex affairs, most men's homoerotic interests seem to have declined as they grew older, perhaps married, and began a family. Also among the dwindling proportions of older men incriminated for sodomy, a conspicuous majority was unmarried; bachelorhood was especially typical of that small number of repeatedly implicated, "inveterate" sodomites, most of whom probably never took a wife and for whom relations with boys apparently figured prominently in their erotic and affective experience throughout much of their adult lives.

If social factors like age and marital status influenced the nature of homosexual activity, they also affected its regulation. The "officers of the buggers" tended most frequently to punish youths, widely perceived as profligate rakes, and older men, who were probably considered habitual sodomites; they especially singled out unmarried men of all ages. Class bias also tainted their sentences, a reflection of this society's deep and growing social divisions but less directly connected to homosexual behavior in and of itself.

These discriminatory practices should not be overstated, and there are numerous examples to the contrary. But they do suggest that in their function of social control, the Night Officers were most inclined to punish alleged sodomites whose youth, bachelorhood, and low to middling social condition placed them toward the margins of the sociopolitical community. Older married men in respected occupations or from important families were able to engage in occasional relations with boys with less fear of judiciary consequences, and perhaps of social stigma as well. As Niccolò Machiavelli wrote in 1514 to his friend Francesco Vettori, Florentine ambassador to the papal court, advising him to relax and take his erotic pleasure wherever he willed,

> He who is deemed wise during the day will never be considered crazy at night, and he who is esteemed a respectable man [*uomo da bene*], and is worthy, whatever he does to lighten his heart and live happily renders him honor, not blame. Rather than being called a bugger or a whoremongerer, one says he is a man of broad interests, easygoing, and a good fellow.[152]

5

"Great Love and Good Brotherhood": Sodomy and Male Sociability

> *L'amore masculino* is solely a work of virtue, which joins males together in various sorts of friendship, so that out of a tender age come, at a manly age, worthier and closer friends. Gian Paolo Lomazzo, *Il libro dei sogni* (1568)[1]

In 1476, an informer denounced the carpenter Piero di Bartolomeo for his sexual relations with Bartolomeo di Jacopo, son of a grocer behind Piero's workshop near the Old Market. When interrogated, fifteen-year-old Bartolomeo confessed not only that Piero had sodomized him "many times, both day and night" in his shop, but that during the past year he had also been sodomized at various times and in different places by thirteen other men, among whom were artisans and shopkeepers, a priest, a notary, a doctor, and a man from the prominent Aldobrandini family. Little in these details sets this case apart, but what is remarkable is how the informer explained Piero's erotic interest in Bartolomeo: "This he did out of great love and good brotherhood, because they are in a confraternity together, and he did as good neighbors do."[2]

"Great love" and "good brotherhood," fraternity and neighborly ties—to this particular Florentine, the outlawed behavior of sex between males seemed a natural outgrowth of and complement to the intense bonds of affect and obligation among males in his society, bonds that were nourished in part through formal associations and neighborhood. His surprising remark recalls a triad that Florentines commonly used to evoke the web of significant ties in which their lives were bound up—"kin, friends, neighbors"—a formula that has been shown to be an important key to understanding this city's complex social and political relations.[3] Implausible as it may appear, considering the hostile source and his purpose, the informer implied that homoerotic bonds, despite their interdiction, were also woven securely into this web of sodalities.

Indeed, his keen sense of the sociable milieu within which homosexual relations were played out reveals an essential feature of the nature and organization of sodomy in Florence. Not all sexual interactions between men and boys, of course, expressed such noble values as "brotherhood" and "great love": some men bullied or raped boys, masters sexually exploited their dependents, teenage prostitution was common, and encounters were often opportunistic or furtive. Nonetheless, sodomy was inextricably enmeshed in broader forms of male association and sociability in this community, from youth-group camaraderie to neighborhood ties, from occupational solidarities to patron–client relations, from kinship bonds to networks of friends. In the intensely homosocial world of Florence, *l'amore masculino*, as Gian Paolo Lomazzo has Leonardo da Vinci assert in the epigraph, was one of the threads that helped to create and reinforce bonds between males and to fashion the texture of their collective life.

This chapter is concerned with the organization and roles of homosexual activity within Florentine male culture in the later fifteenth century: the typical times, places, and rites of sexual encounters; the variety and character of homoerotic relations; and the mutually sustaining links among sexual interactions, other types of social networks, and male sociability. Naturally the sources impose limits on what can be learned. Testimony given by boys whom the Night Officers interrogated and by men who denounced themselves furnishes much useful information, but only about the stark essentials that interested officials. With a few exceptions, their recorded testimony consists only of brief, formulaic answers to standard questions such as who their partners were; when, where, how often, and for how long a time they had engaged in sexual relations; and whether and how much the boy was paid. Denunciations, though plainly jaundiced, often add useful, unstudied observations of behavior and context. A number of important problems remain obscure, especially regarding how participants saw themselves and what meanings they ascribed to their actions. Nonetheless, these and other sources throw considerable light on homosexual experience in Florence and on the social and cultural world in which it was embedded.

In the growing literature on this subject, the illicit underworlds of sodomy in traditional European cities are often characterized as distinct "subcultures." But since this term is open to various meanings and possibly misleading anachronisms, it is advisable to consider whether or in what ways it might be applicable in this specific context.[4] If some features of these sexual undergrounds seem familiar, on the whole they were fundamentally different from the highly visible, well-organized, and articulate homosexual subcultures of the contemporary world. However, only one (though crucial) aspect of the representation of "subcultures" from the past regards how sensitively we distinguish the prevailing behavioral and conceptual "model" of homosexuality operating in a given historical situation. The medieval sodomite who had homosexual relations only with passive adolescent males (but quite probably also had sex with women) was a different type altogether from, for instance, the eighteenth-century sodomites in northern European cities who commonly sought out other adult men for sex, were often effeminate or perceived as such, and sometimes socialized in transvestite clubs; and different again from the "fairies" of late-nineteenth-century New York City.[5] They were the products of different worlds and formed different sexual cultures. Other problems arise with "subculture" itself. It is not always clear, as the term is employed in the historical literature, if it refers to a distinct group or category of persons defined by their sexual behavior, to typical patterns of sexual activity and aggregation, or even generically to all homosexual activity.

Generally, evidence of known meeting places for sexual encounters, of specialized jargon or signs of recognition, or of circles of individuals with similar erotic interests has been interpreted as indicating a discrete sodomitical (or homosexual) subculture. Patterns of clandestine activities such as these have been found in numerous premodern cities, including fifteenth-century Venice and Florence possibly earlier.[6] But the fact that the pursuit of sodomy in these places often overlapped with other practices considered debauched or "immoral"—like female prostitution, frequenting taverns, and gambling—in itself provides some grounds for being cautious about isolating sodomy into its own neat, illicit subculture. Further, this first meaning of the term almost imperceptibly shades over into another, more problematic issue—that is, whether or not individuals who used familiar haunts to find partners or formed networks of like-minded companions had, as a result, a sense of belonging to a specific group that was distinct from the rest of male society, of having a separate identity based on *sexual* difference.[7] For reasons I have already discussed, participating in sodomy even in these ways probably gave such an identity to very few persons. And even though there were known rendezvous areas and networks of individuals with common sexual tastes or practices, it is far from certain that these were the only or even the main contexts in which homosexual interactions occurred.

In Florence, at least, the nature and widespread extent of sodomy were such that the notion of a distinct and coherent "subculture" is probably at once too all-inclusive and too limiting to convey the experience adequately. The evidence from the later fifteenth century suggests that many, if not most, Florentine males engaged in homosexual activity at some point in their lives. But as this chapter will show, their same-sex erotic relations, often casual and limited to brief periods in their life course, commonly evolved in the context of typical forms of male sociability and of social bonds and networks such as youth gangs, neighborhood, work, the household, and even clientage, and less so or not at all within a well-defined sodomitical underworld. This does not exclude the possibility that within this broad spectrum of homoerotic experience, there was a more or less conspicuous "core" of activity associated in part with certain locations, but especially with notorious or habitual sodomites and with recognized circles of sodomite friends, all of which are well documented. In a few sources, in fact, from accusations and chronicles to sermons and burlesque poetry, sodomites were occasionally portrayed as constituting an *arte* (corporation) or even "sects," perhaps implying a clandestine organization and specialized skill or know-how.[8] Yet however suggestive this limited evidence may be, homosexual interactions in Florence occurred in a wide range of contexts and probably carried a variety of individual and group meanings, all of which are hard to subsume within a single, distinctive subculture.

Sodomy in this society certainly had a marked sociable character. But rather than one or even several subcultures, it is probably more appropriate (if less tidy) to imagine the collective aspects of homosexual activity as a profusion of networks—networks that varied in dimensions, cohesiveness, and purpose; that sometimes, but not always, intersected with others; that comprised individuals whose involvement in sodomy differed considerably in intensity, duration, and personal significance; and within which shared homoerotic interests were often only one link among several other social and affective bonds typical of Florentine male culture.

Encounters

In a letter in 1514 to Francesco Vettori, Niccolò Machiavelli—who had himself recently been denounced for heterosexual sodomy—humorously described a sodomitical escapade of their friend Giuliano Brancacci.[9] To tell his story, he adopted a playful metaphor, rich with sexual double meanings, of Brancacci as a birdcatcher pursuing his prey one rainy evening. (In burlesque literature, *uccello* [bird] could signify variously the penis, the anus, or an accessible boy.)[10] He mapped Brancacci's search through the alleyways around the Borgo Santi Apostoli, past the palace of the Parte Guelfa, across the New Market and into the Piazza della Signoria, the government square, where he finally came upon a "little thrush" agreeable to being kissed and having its "tail-feathers ruffled." After his successful find, he sealed his conquest, as Machiavelli put it, by thrusting his *uccello* (bird, or penis) into the *carnaiuolo* (game bag, or anus).

Besides revealing a light-hearted, ironic attitude toward sodomy that many Florentines likely shared, the great political theorist's anecdote offers a fitting introduction to sodomitical encounters in Florence. Their times and spaces were more varied than a single episode can portray, nor were all relations as casual and isolated as Brancacci's with his "little thrush." Yet from the hundreds of more or less similar experiences that the court records yield, some common elements emerge. The pursuit of sodomy had its daily and seasonal rhythms, its typical locations. And although Brancacci's story does not bring out this important point, the times and places of sodomy often coincided with those of other forms of male sociability.

The quest for sodomy in Florence had no temporal limits, but it was more intense during the early evening hours and at night, the warm spring and summer months, and evidently on feast days and Sundays.[11] Most encounters occurred after sunset, suggesting one derivation for the evocative title of the Officers of the Night; indeed, "night" was a code word for sodomy in the Tuscan burlesque tradition.[12] No time was specified for most nocturnal relations, which often involved overnight stays at partners' houses. When a precise time was noted, it was usually in the early evening between nightfall, when the workday ended, and the third or fourth hour after sunset, around curfew and the closing hour of taverns. During these twilight hours, there was a good deal of movement and socializing on the streets and in taverns, which facilitated casual sexual encounters.

Men and boys engaged in sodomy throughout the year, though relations were reported more frequently during the warm season from May to October.[13] Somewhat surprisingly, interrogations reveal no noticeable increase in sodomy during the long period of Carnival, traditionally considered a time of sexual license. Some boys specified, however, that they had been sodomized during the Carnival season, on the vigil or day of Carnival proper, and, in a few cases, even "for Carnival."[14] Some informers also linked sodomy to Carnival debauchery, as if they expected sex to be less restrained than usual in this topsy-turvy festive period. Ser Jacopo Bachelli from Prato reportedly kept a boy as his wife, and according to the accuser "he's worse now [in June] than before Carnival"; another, in May 1510, claimed that "from the month of December until now he has frequented and buggered those boys . . . especially during the past Carnival."[15] Also implying a perception that sexual profligacy was common in this season, in 1486 the Eight of Watch exiled a man they declared guilty of attempted sodomy from January 6, the feast day of Epiphany when Carnival season began in Florence, until the first day of Lent, when the raucous festivities ended.[16]

In addition to Carnival, sacred and secular feast days were thought to give occasion for indulging in carnal pleasures. Commenting on Florentine confraternities for boys in 1435, Ambrogio Traversari, general of the Camaldolan monastic order, praised them for uniting boys to hear sermons, pray, and sing on Sundays and feast days, when normally, he said, "greater license for lasciviousness is usurped."[17] The many civic and religious festivals provided times to relax from work, dress in one's finest clothes, and promenade and socialize with friends. All this apparently gave an added impetus to the pursuit of sodomy. Evidence from the judiciary records suggests that sodomy often coincided with holidays, though notaries seldom distinguished between feast days and working days. A man in 1496, for example, confessed that he had sodomized a boy for the past nine months, always on Sunday.[18] The same year, an informer alleged that Francesco Dello Scarfa "goes to visit [his boyfriend, Carlo Tosinghi] every Sunday morning and every feast day before he gets up, and joins him in bed."[19] Another in 1497 claimed that Nofri Lenzoni—the former Night

Officer convicted for sodomy—had had sex with a boy in his villa during the past summer "and on almost every feast day."[20] Many boys also confessed that they had had sex with men on a particular festival. Fourteen-year-old Lorenzo di Matteo, for example, said that two men had sodomized him on Easter day; Piero di Domenico, one of the priors' pages, admitted that a man had sodomized him on Corpus Christi, in a priest's house; Antonio di Niccolò, a sixteen-year-old carpenter, claimed that a priest had sodomized him on the feast of the city's patron saint, John the Baptist.[21] Similarly, secular events such as fairs and jousts provided opportunities for sociability and for illicit sex. Several boys confessed that they had been sodomized by men they accompanied to the annual September fair in nearby Prato, while two men self-confessed in 1473 that they together had sodomized a boy they took with them to watch a joust in Peretola, a village west of the city.[22]

The judiciary records also reveal a rough topography of sodomitical activity, including a few locations that were evidently known haunts or were feared to encourage sodomy. The places where men and boys consummated sexual relations varied widely, but fall generally into four main categories: public streets or other more or less open areas (28 percent of the locations mentioned in the 1478–1502 survey); private homes (36 percent); *botteghe*, or workshops (15 percent); and taverns (15 percent). The remainder were noted usually as "various places" or other minor locations.

The physical layout of the medieval city plus a lack of domestic privacy, more than anonymity (boys rarely said they failed to recognize their partners), encouraged sex in public places. Many men and boys sodomized in fields outside the city gates or in the extensive private or conventual gardens that ringed the congested city center out to the walls. But most open-air encounters occurred in the ancient and crowded heart of the city. The narrow, poorly lighted streets; the densely packed shops and houses, with their covered doorways, overhanging upper stories, and supporting arches; the many stables and storage sheds—all afforded secluded niches for furtive trysts. Sex in public had its risks, since watchmen patroled the streets after curfew, but surprisingly few sodomites were caught in the act by these patrols.[23]

One unusually detailed case from 1497 vividly depicts a casual encounter on the streets. Carlo di Domenico, an eighteen-year-old cap maker who admitted in several hearings that he had been sodomized by twenty-nine partners, testified that one evening he was going to dinner with three men at the Tana d'Orso, in via del Moro, when he was approached by a stranger whom he called a *travestito* ("transvestite," which likely meant not a man dressed as a woman but a man masqueraded).[24] Taking him by the hand, the *travestito* drew him away from his apparently indifferent companions—one of whom was his uncle—and asked the boy to "service" him, that is, allow the man to sodomize him. Carlo declined and went to catch up with his friends, but when he reached the tavern they were nowhere to be found. So he met the *travestito* again, and the two walked hand in hand to the western gate, the Porta al Prato, where his new acquaintance sodomized him outside the customs duties office. After they returned to the via del Moro, his partner went to get money to pay the boy, but while he was waiting Carlo was approached by another young man who also wanted to sodomize him. Despite his refusal, the newcomer, who he thought was twenty-one-year-old Sandro Buondelmonti, continued to pester him. Carlo told how he tried to lose the youth as they wandered the streets, but he persisted, yelling for all to hear that the boy had just "serviced" another out by the gate but refused to do the same for him. Exasperated, Carlo finally stopped and bartered with his insistent molester. They agreed to play a game of chance (*fare* or *giocare alle corna*), with Carlo's submission as the stakes. Carlo lost, and, as arranged, they went off toward a nearby convent, where Buondelmonti sodomized the boy in a shed.[25]

Although much of the more or less public sex like this was disseminated throughout the city, often near two partners' homes, certain neighborhoods stood out. Not coincidentally, most of these areas corresponded with other places of ill repute in the urban sexual landscape—brothels, taverns, and baths—which were located mainly in the central district. The streets and alleys close to all the major prostitution zones were frequently identified as places for sodomitical encounters: the area of the municipal brothels in the heart of the city, between the Old Market and the archbishop's palace; the Chiasso de' Buoi and the streets around the nearby public baths at San Michele Berteldi; Baldracca, the seamy area south of the town hall; and streets surrounding the Chiassolino, a tavern just east of the brothels, and the Vinegia, a tavern and brothel near San Remigio.[26] Streets around other taverns, or fields near taverns at the gates, were also common sites for sodomy. As will be seen, these establishments also frequently hosted men and boys for their sexual trysts. Much of the sodomitical activity that went on outside the taverns and brothels was probably connected to the socializing and license inside.

In the late fifteenth century, at least one street in the core of the city seems to have been particularly known as an evening haunt of sodomites where sexual contacts could be made. This was the via tra' Pellicciai, or Street of the Furriers, a short street running from the southwest corner of the Old Market south past the via Porta Rossa, some distance from the brothels on the other side of the market. In March 1482, the Eight of Watch sent a constable to this street after nightfall "to investigate and arrest such men who usually frequent this place around this hour in order to engage in the vice of sodomy."[27] That night, he apprehended a notorious sodomite, fifty-two-year-old Jacopo di Niccolò Panuzzi. According to his sentence, Panuzzi was loitering in the via tra' Pellicciai around the first hour after sunset, offering money to boys who would agree to let him sodomize them. In the twilight, he imprudently mistook the guard for a willing youth, and fondled him and used other "shameful gestures" to convey his "evil desire and shameful longing." Although Panuzzi had not committed sodomy, the constable arrested him and he was fined the large sum of 20 florins. A number of other incidents also suggest that this was a well-known place for sexual encounters; indeed, it was here that the infamous "Pacchierotto" got part of his flogging in 1486 because he was caught there "many times" engaging in sodomy.[28] The geography of illicit sex perhaps shifted in Florence as it does in modern cities, with old haunts being abandoned as police cracked down and new ones appearing in response. But the reporting and circumstances of these cases indicate that there were known areas around the city where sodomites went to meet each other or to solicit boys.[29]

Public streets were also the theater of a long-lived "courting game" associated with sodomy: hat stealing, a sort of ritual extortion for sex. Men looking for sex sometimes stole boys' hats or caps to force the boys to yield to them. This was a rite shared with female prostitutes in Florence, who also made off with males' hats to compel their victims to sleep with them.[30] The dynamics in both cases were much the same. Losing one's hat meant being sexually and publicly compromised, a disgrace that both men with prostitutes and boys with sodomites could avoid only by giving in to their "aggressors." The earliest reference to this practice known to me comes from 1440, when Antonio di Niccolò, "with the intention of . . . committing sodomy," stole Alessandro Bracini's cap from the boy's head and refused to give it back unless Alessandro agreed to sleep with him some night "for the vice of sodomy."[31] In 1469, fifteen-year-old Carlo di Guglielmo Cortigiani asserted that Piero d'Antonio Rucellai had swiped his cap one evening and threatened, "I won't ever give it back to you unless you service me." Piero promptly led Carlo into a nearby alley, anally sodomized him, and then threw his cap to the ground and ran off.[32] In confirmation of the implicit threat involved with this "playful" act, another man in 1497 was alleged to have stolen a boy's cap, and when the boy refused to let him sodomize him, he cut it to pieces.[33] No other boy in the records I have seen admitted to being the object of this little game, but an informer in 1512 implied that it was commonly linked to the nightly hunt for boys in the streets of Florence. Highlighting an exploitative dimension that must often have accompanied pederasty, the writer accused "a wicked and incorrigible man, debauched in many vices. He causes a lot of trouble at night running caps, hats, and similar things as he searches randomly through the city for boys with whom he forceably engages in acts of sodomy, especially with certain poor boys who sleep in the open."[34]

Another public, though enclosed, space that attracted enough sexual transgressions to make it an official concern was churches. The Eight of Watch had specific jurisdiction over sexual acts committed in churches, a severely punished sacrilege that may strike the modern observer as implausible but that the evidence suggests was not uncommon.[35] In 1492, for example, Salvi Panuzzi was fined 300 florins, banished for three years, and deprived of public office for having fondled a boy's genitals in the cathedral choir, while the notary ser Jacopo di Matteo Del Campana was mitered, paraded around the city, exiled for six years, and stripped of office for having sodomized a boy in the cathedral.[36] The next year, Carlo di Baldinaccio Cavalcanti entered the church of Sant'Ambrogio where numerous young clerics were gathered, and caressed and fondled the boys and offered them money, hoping to find a willing sexual partner; the Eight banished him for five years.[37] Not even the most famous of Florentine sacred monuments were immune from profanation. In a self-accusation, the infamous Jacopo d'Andrea, il Fornaino, admitted that he had brazenly sodomized a boy in Giotto's Campanile on the very day in August 1473 that the great new bell was installed, an act that in its boldness seems intended to defy the established order.[38] Men and boys committed sodomy even in Brunelleschi's famed cathedral cupola, for which a man was convicted in 1482.[39] By the middle of the next century, the situation in the Duomo had evidently deteriorated even further. In 1552 the cathedral works board had to ban public access to the cupola, as a counselor to Duke Cosimo I wrote, "in order to obviate the obscenities and wrongs that are committed daily in that sacred place." His report also specified that impious young males had been seen in the tribune of the church openly practicing "many indecencies, kissing each other and giving each other the tongue."[40]

The relative privacy and comfort of homes had obvious advantages over sex in public places, and of the four main locations for sexual encounters identified earlier, homes made up the relative majority (36 percent). This possibility, however, was limited by domestic and economic circumstances. Probably only a small minority of men, older bachelors for the most part, lived alone and had the freedom to entertain their young friends discreetly in their homes.[41] Young men usually lived with their families until and often after they married, making homosexual relations at home difficult, though evidence that will be reviewed later suggests that parents sometimes facilitated their sons' affairs with males by allowing them to sleep together under the family roof.[42] It was also probably not uncommon for two or more young friends to spend the night together in one of their homes, usually in the same bed, as was typical in medieval society, a situation that could encourage sexual play.[43] In general, however, only privileged youths could have known the luxury that Vettori described in a letter to Machiavelli, explaining why young Florentine men were so wanton. When a boy started to mature sexually, he wrote, his mother gave him a bedroom to himself on the ground floor, "with a separate entrance and every convenience, so that he can do whatever he pleases and bring home whomever he likes."[44]

Although men usually brought young companions for sex to their own homes, they often used the house of another person (in 30 percent of these cases), indicating that some people facilitated friends' illicit sexual activity. Sometimes the third parties named were men who were themselves implicated in sodomy. Lending or providing a house to others to commit sodomy was considered so serious a crime that the government in 1440 forbade the Night Officers to prosecute it, reserved jurisdiction to the foreign rectors, and made it punishable by death.[45] Rarely, if at all, did authorities pursue the men named in the 1478–1502 survey for having allowed others to use their homes for sodomy, but there were earlier prosecutions. In 1455 the capitano del popolo condemned Giovanni di Michele from Cologne, himself a sodomite, for having permitted "many, many men" to use his house for their trysts with "many different boys," while in 1458 the podestà convicted the clothes dealer and sodomite Andrea di Tommaso for having given the keys to his house over a period of two years to innumerable friends "who he knew enjoyed the crime of sodomy, so that they might more easily satisfy their wicked desire in this crime."[46]

Cases like these lend some credibility to informers' claims that homes were at times used as virtual brothels for sodomy, even though such charges were seldom pursued. An accuser in 1467 asserted that Zanobi di Baldo, a blacksmith, ran a bordello for men and boys in his home under the protection of prominent citizens, noting that "he claims he does it at the request of leading men of the regime, and he names ten or twelve of them."[47] The best depiction of an alleged "brothel of boys" comes from a denunciation in 1467 written, it was said, by concerned neighbors:

> Antonio di Geri Bartoli, who lives behind the loggia degli Agli . . . keeps a brothel of boys in his house, among whom are Lionardo di Giovanni del maestro Francesco . . . , a son of Giovanni de' Pilli, and Giuliano di Tommaso di Guccio, and many others. These boys go to this house in the evening from sunset to about the third hour, and some of them sleep there. Lorenzo, a grocer . . . is the master intermediary [who brings] these boys to this house. . . . Antonio di Salvestro Segholini, clothes dealer . . . is a companion of theirs who brings many young lads to this house. To be certain of this, send one of your servants to Antonio Segholini's shop in the evening from about sunset to the second hour. You'll see that all sorts of boys congregate here, and then they go to this house or elsewhere to do indecent things that it's up to your magistracy to punish.[48]

Other informers identified homes where males came together both to gamble and to sodomize. Someone claimed in 1512, for example, that in a house in chiasso Guazachoglie "they do nothing but gamble . . . and a lot of boys come there . . . and those youths fuck those boys."[49] In a concrete example, the Eight of Watch in 1504 banished twenty-six-year-old sodomite Piero di Lorenzo "Broda" for fifteen years because he entertained illegal gambling and "men of dishonest lives and sodomites" in his home.[50] These cases again underline the connections between male sociability and homoeroticism.

Another location where men and boys frequently had sexual relations was in workshops (*botteghe*), which made up some 15 percent of the places identified. Like residences, shops afforded some privacy, and some were conveniently furnished with sleeping areas for workers. But equally as important, the *bottega* was also a basic institution of male sociability, where young apprentices mingled with older workers, and where friends met to while away the time and perhaps to drink or gamble. An informer claimed in 1476 that a workshop in the Street of the Furriers owned by Antonio Gerini, a "shameless sodomite," was little more than a front for gambling, and that gluttonous bands of "youths, ribalds, and *bardasse*" flocked there also because the shop's back door opened onto the tavern of Sant'Andrea.[51] It seems the shops of some known sodomites were conspicuous for the crowds of boys that frequented them, leading on occasion to charges that they were in effect bordellos. Someone alleged in 1467 that Francesco di Giuliano Benintendi, a twenty-two-year-old from a celebrated family of wax sculptors, not only sodomized a boy in his shop in the via dei Servi, but "keeps a bed [there], and he makes a practice of it and encourages this business in his shop. His shop is always full of boys." A second accuser said outright that he let others sodomize in his shop.[52] The same year, an informer claimed that twenty-seven-year-old Gerino Gerini, a "great sodomite" who had already been convicted of sodomy three times, ran a "brothel" of boys in his candle shop in the Piazza del Re near the Old Market.[53] Similarly, in 1502 a boy testified that "boys often congregated" at a *casino*, or "little house," possibly meaning a storage shed, kept by a convicted sodomite in the same square, and two other boys admitted that this man had sodomized them there.[54]

Other places where youths and boys socialized in an environment that could be conducive to sodomy were dancing and fencing schools. The forces of order kept a wary eye on them. In 1494, when the surveillance of sodomy was increased under the moralizing influence of Savonarola, the Eight of Watch decreed that dancing and fencing teachers had to close their "schools and taverns" at sundown under penalty of a 10-florin fine.[55] Again in 1502, under similar circumstances, they ordered the schools closed at the ringing of the Ave Maria in the evening.[56] Little is known about these schools, but fencing classes were surely limited to males, and dancing classes might have been mainly if not solely for males, since girls from "respectable" bourgeois families probably received instruction in their homes.[57]

Only a few boys whom the Night Officers questioned from 1478 to 1502 said that they had engaged in sodomy at such schools, and always in dancing schools.[58] But there were precedents for sodomy connected to fencing schools. In 1461, after learning of suspicious activities in a house rented by three youths who taught fencing there, officials conducted an unusually thorough investigation, a sign of their concern that such schools not become a breeding ground for illicit sex. The three young men eventually admitted that they had invited several boys to their school to drink and eat with them and then had sodomized them, and all three were convicted.[59] In 1495, during the Savonarolan period, when such schools became suspect, Battista di Marzocco was accused of operating a "bordello of young boys" in his school "under the pretense of fencing." Officials declined to investigate, however, possibly because many boys from prominent families were said to be involved.[60]

If these schools were rarely used for sex, authorities must nonetheless have considered them potentially dangerous environments, where youths, boys, music, and physical exercise could interact all too seductively. Such worries might have been fueled by several examples of fencers, dancers, and musicians who were sexually involved with boys. In the 1478–1502 survey, four fencing masters (one of whom denounced himself twice) and four dancing teachers (three of whom were convicted) were implicated in sodomy. Men who taught or practiced these skills, however, might have been involved in sodomy more frequently than appears from the records, as is suggested by an informer in 1501 who claimed that a boy had been sodomized by "many musicians and dancers."[61] Most seem to have earned their livings at other trades, by which they were normally identified (locksmith, embroiderer, barber, etc.), and only taught their skills part-time.[62]

Finally, in the public sexual landscape of Florence a prominent place was held by taverns and inns, which played a central role both in male sociability and in the pursuit and practice of sodomy. Moralists, authorities, and respectable citizens had always considered the city's taverns places of disrepute, because of the diverse clientele they attracted of lower-class men and profligate youths, drifters, criminals and gamblers, prostitutes and pimps, as well as because of their sexual license, risk of crime, and drunken violence.[63] Not without reason, inns and taverns were long feared to accommodate and encourage sodomy. The 1322 statutes forbade innkeepers to serve certain culinary delicacies since, it was said, they attracted "men and boys" and fueled their desire to commit "abominable sins." Fines were set for innkeepers who entertained or sold food or drink to persons suspected of sodomy, and if they allowed anyone to commit sodomy on the premises their establishment was to be burned down.[64] In his sermons a century later, Bernardino of Siena also linked rich foods to sexual lust, and condemned the taverns and "secluded places where public brothels of boys are kept, like public prostitutes, with beds where they are put up at night when their bodies are full of wine."[65] When authorities in the 1490s tightened the control of sodomy—largely due to the influence of Savonarola, who also fulminated against the sexual promiscuity in taverns[66]—they closely regulated baths and taverns, ordering them to close early and to bar entrance to "suspect boys" and other "persons suspected of sodomy."[67] In 1528 the chronicler Giovanni Cambi approvingly noted yet another crackdown on taverns, where, he said, the young sons of wealthy Florentine citizens came to eat rich foods and fraternized with working-class youths to drink, gamble, and "corrupt young boys."[68]

Many men and boys consummated their sexual relations in rooms in nearly all of the thirty to forty taverns and inns and in the several public baths spread throughout the city.[69] In addition, many said they ate or drank together in taverns before or after having sex elsewhere, and the alleys, streets, or fields around taverns were also common sites for trysts. Most establishments appear as locations for sexual encounters only a few times, but several were mentioned often enough to suggest that they were known as places where males could indulge in sodomy with no questions asked, probably—as some claimed—with the complicity of the host. It is unlikely, however, that any taverns catered only or even mainly to sodomites and their boys or only to male clients. They likely entertained prostitutes and perhaps other lower-class women, and within them a climate of relaxed morality reigned that fostered an easy coexistence between female prostitution and male sodomy.

In fact, men and boys commonly engaged in sodomy in taverns that were part of the public brothels or were found in other infamous whoring areas. Sodomy and prostitution intersected in an atmosphere of undistinguished sexual license.[70] Of all the homosexual relations reported in inns and taverns, one in four took place in the main brothel area (in the tavern of the Chiasso, the *albergo* of the Frascato, or simply the *postribolo*, or bordello) or in taverns very near the brothels (Malvagìa, Bertucce, Porco, Fico, Chiassolino, Panico). Other taverns frequently named were also notorious for female prostitution, like the Vinegia and the Baldracca. Some evidence suggests there was even a market, linked to the brothel taverns, in teenage male prostitutes who worked on their own or for procurers. Three cooks at the Chiassolino were convicted in 1492 for pimping boys in their tavern rooms.[71] Moreover, some boys who engaged promiscuously with men in sodomy were said to frequent the brothels, especially the Frascato; they often had sex with men in the bordellos, sometimes in the same rooms where women entertained their clients.[72] Many of their numerous partners also worked in the brothels as servers, cooks, or hosts; were reported to be regular whorehouse patrons; or on some occasions were even pimps of female prostitutes.[73] That prostitution and sodomy overlapped in these places supports the thesis that men commonly trafficked with ease with both women and boys.

The two preferred taverns for sodomitical encounters, however, were not particularly known for female prostitution: the Buco, mentioned most frequently, and Sant'Andrea, which together accounted for 15 percent of tavern locations in the 1478–1502 survey. Both, along with the main brothel, the Frascato, were occasionally singled out by informers as haunts of sodomites. One claimed that a certain Agnolo di Niccolò "goes after boys in the evening at the Buco and the Frascato," and another that Filippo Baroncelli and Girolamo Gini took their friend, fourteen-year-old Francesco di Davizino degli Ammirati, every evening to the Buco and Sant'Andrea.[74]

Both taverns had some special characteristics that might help explain their attraction to males interested in sodomy. Sant'Andrea, near the church of the same name south of the Mercato Vecchio, was located just off the Street of the Furriers, the well-known sodomitical haunt, and in the 1480s there was also a dancing school in the same square run by a noted sodomite.[75] The taverner in these years, a certain Francesco, was perhaps a sodomite himself—in 1482 a boy claimed that Francesco had sodomized him in the tavern, but he was absolved; evidently he also facilitated the pursuit of sodomy in his establishment, for the Eight convicted him in 1493 for having entertained boys there after hours.[76] The Buco, situated in the alley that still bears its name just off via Lambertesca near the Ponte Vecchio, had both a linguistic and a historical connection to sodomy. Its name, literally "hole," was a none-too-subtle code word for anus in burlesque poetry. Early in the fifteenth century, Stefano Finiguerri (Za), in his poem "La Buca di Montemorello," described the taverner of the Buco as an infamous sodomite and centered much of the allusive sodomitical action in the poem around the tavern.[77] Like other taverns or inns, the Buco had rooms for lodgers that some sodomites rented for sexual encounters. According to an informer in 1494, one of three brothers who were habitual sodomites had for twelve years kept a "little room" at the Buco where he brought boys for sex.[78]

Unsurprisingly, given the licentious environment, the males who worked in or managed taverns and inns were often implicated in sodomy. Some thirty-three cooks, twenty barmen, one tavern cashier, and twenty-eight taverners or innkeepers were incriminated in the 1478–1502 survey, and fifteen were convicted at least once. From 1470 to 1494, between the ages of forty and sixty-four, Galeotto di Filippo Braccesi—the taverner at various times at the Fico, the Panico, and the Chiasso in the heart of the brothel area—denounced himself twice, was implicated with at least eight other boys, and was convicted at least four times.[79] The manager of the brothel of the Frascato, Albizzo di Jacopo, was reported in 1493 to keep a boy "as his wife," and in 1494 was convicted for sodomizing him.[80]

In taverns and inns, then, sodomites found a tolerant and hospitable environment devoted to male socializing and entertainment. The taverns were a central element of an infrastructure of known public haunts, meeting points, safe houses, and shops that provided venues for sociability and facilitated the acting out of homosexual desire.

The Character of Sodomitical Relations

The nature, dynamics, and personal significance of sexual relations between men and boys in Florence varied widely, from rape to prostitution, from casual encounters to affairs that could last for years. The age structure, rigid role divisions, gender symbolism, and often aggressive style of sodomy helped express and reinforce the domineering virility expected and encouraged especially of young males. For some men, sodomy might have meant little more than an act of sexual assault and conquest, a spontaneous transgression, a casual diversion to satisfy an occasional sexual urge. For others, homosexual relations met additional emotional needs and provided other gratifications of companionship and affection, sometimes throughout much of their adult lives.

In many ways, pederasty was an expression of the power adult men wielded over boys. The often substantial gap in partners' ages, eleven years on average, signified an obvious difference in physical strength and personal autonomy, and in many cases the two partners also differed in economic means and social rank. This difference in power was reflected in the popular epithets that cast "passive" boys in the role of women. Like women's, boys' sexual subjugation went hand in hand with their social subordination.

Unsurprisingly, the greater strength of youths or mature men and the stress on proving their manhood meant that sodomy with boys all too often involved intimidation, threats, or outright violence. Cases of rape represented only a fraction of the thousands of homosexual encounters revealed to the courts, but men bullied and assaulted boys frequently enough that this inherently domineering relation was invested with a constant threat of violence.[81] From 1478 to 1502, an average of two boys a year confessed to the Eight or the Night Officers that they had been raped or sodomized against their will, often after being threatened or beaten, and a couple said that their aggressors had forced them to have sex at knifepoint. In 1496 fifteen-year-old Jacopo d'Antonio Cambi, for example, reported that Bartolomeo di Niccolò Segni, aged twenty-one, had recently "led him to engage in those vices by means of threats and fear," and that Segni had in fact been coercing him for several years to have his way with him; in 1504 Segni himself admitted that he had harassed, beaten, and kicked another boy who refused him.[82] Young Giovanni Arrigucci put up with a man's violent subjugation and sexual abuse for several years before finally turning to the authorities for aid in 1510.[83] No doubt there were many other examples of intimidation and forced submission that never reached the courts.

Numerous boys also suffered anal injuries from sodomy, which, whether reported as such or not, must often have been the consequence of rape or forceful penetration. In just six years in the 1460s, the Night Officers alone received word, through either denunciations or confessions, of at least thirty-three sodomized boys whose anuses had been lacerated. From 1478 to 1502, an average of four boys every year, many of them very young, reported anal damages to both the Night Officers and the Eight. The unreported number was probably higher; Florentine law, unlike that of

Venice, did not require doctors and barber-surgeons, who often provided medical care for the wounded boys, to disclose anal injuries to the authorities.[84]

Sometimes such injuries were caused by gang rapes, collective acts of sexual violence perpetrated on boys—most often by youths—which appear with some frequency in the sources. In 1502 three youths, two of whom were eighteen or under, attacked another as he was walking home one night, dragged him into a nearby warehouse, and raped him.[85] In 1500 the Eight exiled two youths and put two others to death—three, including two brothers, were from patrician families—who were part of a band with a long reputation for terrorizing the countryside and gang-sodomizing many boys and women. In the one exploit recounted in detail, three of the gang kidnapped fourteen-year-old Francesco di Jacopo Del Beccuccio and raped him repeatedly and with such brutality that he was confined to bed for two months from the anal damages he sustained.[86] Seven soldiers in the service of the pope gang-raped two local boys in 1521, while in 1524 four men assaulted a boy in the bell tower of the cathedral and ruptured his anus, an act "considered the basest thing ever seen," as one letter writer commented.[87] Although men could usually find boys willing to engage in sodomy without having to resort to brute force, as evidence shows, sexual violence against young males was a common feature of life in late medieval Florence.

Men's social and economic power over boys could also lead to their sexual subjugation, as shown by many examples from the world of work, where adolescents were employed in positions of dependence as apprentices or servants. Of all the boys named in the 1478–1502 survey, only 5 percent were reportedly sodomized either by their employers (54) or by co-workers (13), but other youngsters might have been reluctant to accuse their masters, on whom their livelihood depended. In any case, there are enough examples from a wide range of situations to suggest that working boys often had to give their employers their bodies as well as their labor. In 1461 an informer recounted in minute detail how master Antonio di Cosimo from Perugia, a doctor in San Miniato, had taken into his service four boys in turn, each of whom quit for the same reason: he "buggered him every night, and wouldn't let him sleep," or "he had to have his ass medicated since the doctor hurt him," and the like. After master Antonio confirmed these charges, the officials convicted him.[88] In a self-accusation in 1472, a clothes dealer related that for two years he had regularly sodomized two boys who worked in his shop and lived in his house.[89] In 1491 the Night Officers convicted the prominent patrician Francesco di Zanobi Girolami, aged forty-eight, for having repeatedly sodomized his son's seventeen-year-old tutor.[90] Some ranking churchmen also sexually exploited their servants: in 1507 the former archiepiscopal vicar of Pistoia, messer Donato di Piermaria Bochi, admitted that he had sodomized many clerics in his service over a period of ten years.[91] The widespread use of adolescent labor coincided so closely with the structure and dynamics of pederasty that sexual abuse in such situations, if not inevitable, was a common risk.

Similarly, boys who accompanied soldiers into the field as servants or pages were also sometimes forced to satisfy their masters' sexual desires. In 1497 seventeen-year-old Lorenzo di Michele d'Antonio confessed that he had been sodomized "many, many times" by thirty-year-old Benvenuto di Fabrizio Bruscoli in Bibbona, where the two served in a military company. Lorenzo was Bruscoli's page, and it was "for this reason," the boy specified, that "he sodomized him."[92] Raffaello di Niccolò, called el Pianella, and sixteen-year-old Bartolomeo di Lionardo, called la Falsina, reported that four youths, all eighteen to twenty-two years old, had taken them along (by force, one said) when they joined the Florentine militia at Castel Peccioli, and all four had sodomized both boys several times.[93] Indeed, military outposts were recognized as environments so notorious for sodomy that this could be adduced as a motive for clemency: in 1440 the government justified canceling a convicted sodomite's fine because, among other reasons, when he committed sodomy "he was at military service and frequented soldiers, who are commonly profligate in that vice."[94]

If some boys were forced to submit to men against their wills or out of their personal dependence, others evidently accepted men's sexual advances with tolerance or willingly, and some surely solicited them. The licentiousness of Florentine boys scandalized Bernardino of Siena early in the fifteenth century, as it did many informers later. As the preacher told his congregation in Florence in 1425, "I've heard of those boys who spruce themselves up and go around boasting about their sodomites, and they make a practice of it for payment, and encourage others in the ugly sin."[95] The venomous language with which accusers berated boys who "let themselves be sodomized" and the metaphors like "bitch in heat" and "whore" also expressed their disgust over boys' "profligacy." These moral judgments aside, evidence from the judiciary records confirms that male adolescents in Florence were often extremely active sexually with men.

When questioned, in fact, most boys admitted to sexual relations with numerous partners during the previous year, sometimes as many as several dozen. That so many boys so commonly reported multiple relations suggests a good deal of complicity on their parts. Some 83 percent of the boys whom the Night Officers questioned from 1478 to 1502 admitted that they had been sodomized; the 387 who confessed named a total of 2,366 partners, to whom should be added another 130 self-accusers who named some of the same boys, yielding an average of between 6 and 7 companions each. A breakdown of these aggregate figures provides an even more telling measure of the "promiscuity" of many Florentine adolescents (Table B.15). Only 25 percent (95) said that they had had just one partner in the past year, and 35 percent (136) one or two. Fully 31 percent (118) were implicated by their own admission or by self-accusers with three to six companions, and another 30 percent (115) had between seven and twenty partners. A small but significant minority had had sex during the previous year with dozens of partners: nine boys had between twenty-one and thirty, and another eight had over thirty companions, including four who were each implicated in relations with more than fifty men.[96] Further, although two-thirds of the confessed relations consisted of a single and evidently casual encounter, in one of every five relations the two companions reportedly had sex at least six times, and in one of six cases at least ten times, "many" times, or "many, many" times.[97] Far from being merely unwilling and inert victims of men's sexual desires, it appears that many Florentine boys participated actively and voluntarily in the mutual pursuit of sodomy.

Some were essentially passive male prostitutes who regularly accepted payment for their sexual favors, boys who must have been well known around the taverns, brothels, and gambling tables or among networks of sodomites. Many cases could be cited, but one noteworthy example involved a ring of four young friends, mentioned in one anothers' interrogations, who frequented the taverns and whorehouses and who claimed among them to have had some 120 sexual companions, including many of the city's most notorious sodomites.[98] Some boys worked for a procurer, a practice that legislation from as early as 1325 attempted to repress.[99] Several informers identified men who were allegedly pimps or intermediaries for boys,[100] and the authorities convicted an occasional procurer, such as a man who took a local fifteen-year-old to Siena and prostituted him there, or the three cooks mentioned earlier who organized boys' trysts in their tavern rooms.[101]

Whether or not boys "let themselves be sodomized" to earn money, some sort of material exchange often accompanied sexual relations, with boys receiving what notaries sometimes called a "gift" for their sexual "labors." Payments or gifts were mentioned in about 20 percent of confessed relations in the 1478–1502 survey, but they were certainly more common than this (some notaries systematically failed to record this information). Payment was not obligatory, however. In another 20 percent of the cases, boys specified that they had received nothing, and a few even said they had refused a proffered gift.[102] Whether money, objects, or a service of some kind, gifts from suitors to their young friends served various functions. In many cases, they represented more than mere compensation for "services" rendered. Often signs of a man's affection or love for his young friend, they helped mediate personal bonds that went well beyond the sphere of sexual gratification.[103]

Most commonly boys said they were paid a small sum of money, usually several soldi or grossi, often repeated with each encounter. For one of many examples, in 1481 Andrea di ser Antonio Bonsi, who was named by sixteen self-accusers and in turn confessed to relations with thirty-five other men, said one of his lovers paid him 10 soldi; another, a grosso; another, 2 grossi; another, 3. Several men who had sodomized him "many" times paid 2 or 3 grossi each time, and another "always gave him something as a gift."[104] If a boy had a steady lover (or more), the money he earned could eventually add up to a tidy sum. In 1502 Cristoforo di Giovanni, a seventeen-year-old tailor, admitted that a priest had sodomized him "many, many" times and had given him "a large amount of money."[105] From the other side of an affair, numerous self-accusers, whose testimony was probably fairly reliable, told officials they gave boys with whom they had been involved for some time large sums of money and other presents.[106]

In addition to money, payment or gifts often consisted of clothing or other objects, some kind of service, food or drink, or simply the fare in the tavern or inn where the two had eaten or slept. Men who took young friends to taverns usually paid the bill, as did one of fourteen-year-old Jacopo d'Agostino's companions, who "gave him nothing as a gift, but paid dinner and the hostess" at the Buco, where the two slept together.[107] Some accepted as little as a few sweets, fruit, bread, wine, or a meal. One boy said his friend gave him nothing, but taught him how to swim—and sodomized him many times during their lessons in the Arno, an example that recalls the homoerotic atmosphere of Passignano's fascinating *Bathers at San Niccolò* reproduced on page 2.[108] Men also gave boys a wide range of objects, some of evident value. Carlo di Fruosino Cambi received "a Danish knife" from the notorious Jacopo d'Andrea, called il Fornaino; from another habitual sodomite, Tommaso d'Antonio, called Lasca, he got a crystal cup.[109] Others received such presents as a carved chessboard (valued at 1 florin), a birdcage, a bow for shooting birds, a painted Carnival mask, a silver chain, a bronze pen, a set of statuettes, a pair of sculpted portraits, and musical instruments such as a fife, a drum, and even a lute. Admirers also gave boys clothing: shoes, boots, wooden sandals, hosiery, a tooled leather belt, a belt with a leather bag, a handkerchief, shirts, doublets, cloaks, hats. Priore di Filippo Gherardini, aged sixteen, confessed that he had been sodomized numerous times in a five-month period by Luca di Matteo, a twenty-five-year-old weaver, who stretched his earnings enough to present Priore with "two hats, a pair of slippers, and a lot of money."[110] This flow of money, presents, and small favors of all sorts helped men win and maintain boys' affections and, while highlighting the inequality of the relationship, added a degree of reciprocity (to say nothing of its boost to the local economy).

Some men might have used their influence and authority to perform favors or services for their young friends that went beyond a simple gesture of appreciation and manifested a solicitous and prolonged concern for their welfare. This, at any rate, was the not unreasonable opinion of some informers, though their claims are hard to verify. One writer alleged, for example, that Antonio Landi found a job in his bank for his favorite, Lorenzo Bonsi, even though the boy "was of no service to the bank," and that for this reason Landi took Lorenzo out of the shop of Andrea del

Giocondo, "who would have done more for him had he stayed in the silk trade."[111] In 1469 Giovanni Cicciaporci, a witness in the case of doctor Piermatteo Lanfranchi, who was reportedly in love with Bindo de' Bardi, testified that he had given Bindo a job on the doctor's recommendation, and that Lanfranchi himself later removed him from the workshop.[112] A Florentine official in a provincial town reportedly promised to use his position of power on his friend's behalf. According to a seemingly well informed accuser, Simone di Francesco di ser Benozzo told the young soldier he had just slept with, "now I am happy to satisfy all your wishes, and that you will return on Monday . . . for I want you to sleep with me again. And have no doubts that as long as I am the administrator of Castrocaro, I will do every favor I can for you."[113] More concretely, the infamous Salvi Panuzzi revealed how an offer of assistance was easily linked to a proposition for sex. As he testified in 1496, he had offered a loan to a twenty-two-year-old who asked to marry his maid, with the idea either of sodomizing the youth or, unusually, of having the young man sodomize him.[114] Providing a job, extending a loan, using one's influence to favor someone—all these acts, which reportedly also involved families in the sodomy of their sons, typified the ubiquitous patron–client relations that were a basic cohesive element in this society. Homoerotic relations were by no means extraneous to this social dynamic.[115]

As many of these examples suggest, sexual interactions between males often involved more than ephemeral, furtive encounters, the casual pursuit or spontaneous gratification of erotic needs and desires. Men and boys commonly formed more stable, durable bonds that presumably furnished both partners with regular sexual pleasure as well as affection and companionship. In describing such relations, informers frequently said that a man, or at times several men together, "maintained" or "kept" a boy (the verb used was *tenersi*), occasionally adding the phrase "like a woman" or one of its variations. At a minimum, their remarks imply steady, ongoing affairs, which in some cases also involved passionate emotional engagement and substantial material commitments, at least on the part of the older partner who sustained his young friend with gifts and money. A hosier at the Canto del Giglio, for example, reportedly kept his young shop assistant "for his use as a woman," and "he sends him out so dressed up that he looks like the son of some great master, with rose-colored stockings and a purple hat."[116] A weaver nicknamed Ciapero was said to have given the fourteen-year-old boy he kept "rose-colored jackets and caps, and velvet belts" and to have done him "a thousand favors."[117] Piero di Giuliano Gerini, a thirty-four-year-old tallow candle–maker and nephew of a notorious sodomite, Gerino Gerini, allegedly kept sixteen-year-old Piero Panichi "for his use as a woman, that is, to sodomize him," in an affair that had been going on for at least a year; according to the accuser, "Piero has said with his own mouth that he's cost him more than 50 florins this year."[118]

As their testimony was recorded, no one who confessed to the Night Officers or other courts admitted in these terms that they "kept" a boy or "were kept" by an older lover. The bureaucratic mentality and language of the courts reduced the human relationship that informers depicted into quantitative terms—how many times or for how long two partners had committed sodomy, and so forth. Nonetheless, that both men and boys acknowledged that they gave or received a variety of gifts and often large sums of money, and frequently revealed long-lasting affairs, tends to corroborate accusers' remarks.

According to trial testimony, some relations were fairly durable, considering the cultural imperative for boys to abandon the passive role by the age of eighteen or twenty, as well as the constant threat of revelation. As noted earlier, in nearly one of every six confessed relations in the 1478–1502 survey, partners admitted to having had sex at least ten or "many" times with their companion. Occasionally (in just 207 cases), notaries recorded how long a boy or man said he had been sexually involved with his lover. Of these 207 relationships, 31 had been going on for between six months and a year, 52 for a full year, 15 for over a year, and 41 "continuously up to the present day," as the formula put it. Most of the longest affairs whose length was specified had lasted for three years, though some went on for four, five, or even six years.[119] In a self-denunciation in 1474, Bonifacio di Mariano di Giovanni, a mercer, revealed that he had had steady sexual relations for the past four years with three boys (two of whom were brothers), and also for "many years" with his young shop assistant, to all of whom he gave "a great deal of money and other things."[120] The erotic nature of lengthy relationships like these surely changed as boys matured into youths, when taking the receptive role became personally and socially unacceptable. But while this is hard to document, it may well be that the bonds of affection and interest cultivated over the years sometimes persisted long after sexual relations had ended, flowering into those "stronger friendships" among adult men that Lomazzo, in the epigraph to this chapter, posited as the natural outgrowth of *l'amore masculino*.

Relationships in which youths or older men "kept" boys were not always free of coercion and exploitation, however, even when the boys' protectors were said to be in love with them. In a striking charge that will be discussed at length later, an informer denounced eight boys together with those among their many lovers who showed them special attention, and in describing their relations he portrayed the seamless links among passion, material support, and intimidation. After identifying them he wrote, "Those I have listed who have fucked them are the ones who love them the most, who have kept them with the most money, who have had them guarded by boys, and who have made each one they loved swear to them, or else they would tell their fathers."[121] The full dynamics of these ties are hard to decipher from this brief and hostile portrayal. Nonetheless, it seems that the boys' lovers—young, working-class, neighborhood toughs—forced the boys to swear pacts of fidelity to them and jealously had others "guard" them. Their oaths of loyalty not only guaranteed the boys their lovers' continuing affection and support through money and gifts, but also secured them against the youths' threat to reveal the boys' compromising sexual involvement to their fathers. Implicit both in this threat and in the guard the youths kept on their boys is also a promise of protection, certainly from their fathers' rage but perhaps also from molestation or rape by other men.[122] Other mentions in denunciations of men having their young friends "guarded" also suggest this dual sense of jealousy and protection.[123] And in the competitive, sometimes violent pursuit of boys by men in Florence, some probably needed or welcomed such security. According to an informer in 1476, "a multitude of ribalds" contended for the sexual favors of thirteen-year-old Martino, "and they often come to blows over the little rascal"; in 1496 two men were allegedly wounded in a fight over Ridolfo di "Zanobone"; on the evening of San Martino in 1460, "three men nearly cut each other to pieces" in a bloody brawl over a young mason.[124]

"Guarding" a boy might also have been a euphemism for prostituting him—the Italian *protettore*, literally "protector," also denotes a pimp—as an informer implied when, denouncing a boy who "lets himself be sodomized by many people," he specified that "he is guarded by two youths, that is, they dress him."[125] Some accusers alleged that a man who kept a boy not only used him for his own pleasure, but also pimped him to others.[126]

More commonly, through the hostile tone of denunciations and the sterile language of testimony filter glimpses of relationships between men and adolescents that were marked by passion, affection, and steady companionship. Paolino, an unmarried weaver from Lucca, reportedly idolized the lad he kept, nicknamed Sdrucciolo, who worked at his side in his shop and nightly shared his bed: as the informer wrote, "It's said he sees no other god but him."[127] In an early case already noted but worth recalling, thirty-eight-year-old Salvestro Alamanni was lovingly devoted to young Jacopo da Verrazzano, whom by his own admission he preferred over his own wife and showered during their two-year affair with money and clothing worth the considerable sum of 250 florins.[128] Numerous informants noted that the men they denounced were hopelessly, head over heels in love—*guasto*, literally "broken up, addled, or spoiled"—with their young friends. According to one, Piero del Galea, called Catozzo, was deeply enamored (*è nne guasto*) of eighteen-year-old Roberto di Filippo Corbizzi, made love with him every day in his butcher shop, and slept with him often; another reported that maestro Sansonetto, a doctor in Figline, was in love with Fruosino from Vinci, for whom "he commits the greatest follies in the world."[129] Some boys themselves admitted that the men with whom they were sexually involved were passionately in love with them. The case of Giovanni di Maringo Maringhi, a painter and infamous sodomite known by the feminine nickname Mea, and his young friend Guglielmo di Domenico, called Pazzuccio, furnishes a good illustration. In 1470 Mea was denounced for keeping Pazzuccio "to use as a woman," and in 1471 another informer said that the two were constantly together in the market, in the tavern of Vinegia, and elsewhere.[130] Interrogated in 1471 and again in 1472, Guglielmo confessed that he had been sodomized by fifteen men but failed to mention Giovanni, whom he was clearly trying to protect. Only when questioned a third time did he finally admit that during the past two years and more, Mea had had sexual relations with him "a hundred or an infinite number of times, and was in love with him."[131]

It should be noted that all such representations, in judiciary as well as literary sources, portray men who are avidly in love with boys, while depictions of boys in love with older men are completely lacking. Whether this conveyed the real emotional dynamics of relations or merely reflected the conventional conception of "active," dominant lovers in pursuit of reticent, uncommitted adolescents is hard to determine. But in any case, for both lover and beloved, both the sodomite and the boy he kept, such relations must often have provided a steady source of affection and companionship, as frequent remarks of informers like these suggest: "every evening after he closes his shop they go off together"; "he often has him sleep with him in his home"; "he sleeps with him every night"; "he's always either in his [lover's] house or in his shop"; "he is constantly in his [boyfriend's] shop"; "they are always together."

Indeed, the close and apparently caring nature of many relationships between youths or older men and boys often led people to represent them as virtual marriages. Claims that a man kept a boy explicitly "as a wife" (*per moglie* or *come sua donna*) are common in accusations, and the more frequent remarks that a boy was kept "as a woman" (*come donna*) or "for use as a woman" (*a uso di donna*) probably had a similar "conjugal" sense. Many examples could be added to others already noted: the baker Nencio di Paolo "keeps as his wife" Damiano di Mariotto; Paolo Vernacci "keeps a lad in his house and sleeps with him regularly and sodomizes him as if he were his wife"; Giovanni del Funaiuolo "keeps as his wife" eighteen-year-old Francesco; and so forth.[132] The depiction that best renders the likeness to a marriage regards the hosier Niccolò di Brunetto, whose spouse of preference was allegedly his apprentice Bastiano. The Night Officers received two charges against them in 1495 and 1496, here combined: "Niccolò . . . keeps [Bastiano] as his wife in his home at his expense, and provides his clothes and stockings, and this is known to everyone. . . . He is seventeen or eighteen, a fresh-looking, handsome lad, and he works with him in his shop. I'm talking about that evil sin. . . . He keeps him in his home as his wife, and he isn't married to a woman, because his wife is this boy [*e non ha moglie, ché sua donna è costui*]."[133]

While remarks like these perhaps contained an element of sarcasm, that the collective imagination seized so readily on conjugal metaphors to describe homoerotic affairs might also suggest that they were referring to something more tangible, an acknowledged bond within the intensely homosocial male world. Did Florentine men "keep" adolescents in unions that both they and their community considered the effective equivalent of "marriages," however contrary to the dominant moral system they might have been? The evidence does not permit this question to be answered conclusively, in part because the discursive politics of the judiciary apparatus, fixed on concrete acts, seldom allowed the sexual actors themselves to interpret their own experiences for the record. Yet there are several positive indicators to consider.

First, it is not hard to see how observers as well as sodomites and boys themselves could have construed passionate or long relations between males as "marriages." Both the social architecture of Florence and the configuration of sodomy bolstered such an interpretation. Men normally delayed marriage with women until their thirties, and a large proportion never took a female spouse, while their sexual access to females outside matrimony was relatively (but by no means completely) limited. Men who were sexually involved with boys were usually bachelors, whether youths below marriageable age or older men who never married. Under these circumstances, both participants and the community at large might have perceived homoerotic relations of this sort as temporary or substitute "marriages," similar to the socially acknowledged male marriages reported in some non-European cultures with comparable social features.[134] The structure of pederasty, after all, nearly mirrored that of "legitimate" marriage, since Florentine women were wedded on the average around the age of seventeen or eighteen to men who were thirteen years their senior. And the love men sometimes showed for boys, along with the substantial material support they often gave them, conferred a sense of commitment on relationships that readily translated into conjugal imagery. When a man like the dyer Giusto di Mariotto self-confessed in 1473 that he had had sexual relations with fifteen-year-old Tomme di Sali "many many times, and in various days and places, especially in his home, because he kept Tomme with him in his home and paid for his expenses and clothing," they and others could have easily viewed their domestic and emotional arrangement as a "marriage."[135]

Further, same-sex unions not only had classical antecedents in Greece and Rome, and in the Middle Ages were given a Christian blessing in special liturgical ceremonies,[136] but also are found in the fifteenth and sixteenth centuries elsewhere in central Italy. In a poem (ca. 1485) about Giacomo della Marca (1393/1394–1476), Giovanni Battista Petrucci related that after one of Giacomo's sermons in Ascoli Piceno, in the Marches, a contrite youth confessed to him that he had been married "like a woman" to another man, and produced the ring that was the symbol of their union.[137] In Rome in 1581, Montaigne reported hearing about wedding ceremonies between Portuguese males that were conducted in the church of San Giovanni a Porta Latina and included a mass with the same rites and gospel lesson used in traditional post-Tridentine matrimonies. He noted that the locals saw this as a blatant effort to legitimize illicit sodomitical unions.[138]

Nothing so explicit has yet surfaced in the Florentine context, but the judiciary records have yielded a remarkable piece of evidence which suggests that some local males also sealed marriages in formal ceremonies resembling weddings. In this case, a man and his young friend ritually solemnized their union by swearing an oath over a Bible on an altar, and even the officials who condemned them in 1497 appear to have considered the two married. When their relationship came to light, Michele di Bruno da Prulli, a dyer, and twenty-two-year-old Carlo di Berardo d'Antonio, an apothecary, had been involved for several years. As his sentence stated, "Michele . . . had been seized by love [*captus amore*], and, as it is commonly said, in love [*innamorato*] with Carlo for many, many years," and moreover "he kept him as his wife and in place of a wife, and made him a cloak and often gave him money."[139] Drawing on his confession, Carlo's sentence noted that he "remained faithful to Michele, and at Michele's request he also swore over the holy stone on the holy gospels of God to remain faithful to Michele in this sodomitical vice."[140] They no doubt performed their ceremony in a church, for the "holy stone" specified here was an altar, over which Florentines typically sealed contracts and took oaths.[141] The account made no mention of a ring or witnesses, but their simple rite would have sufficed—had they been man and woman—to validate their union according to the precepts of the pre-Tridentine church, which required only the consent of both parties.[142] In fact, the extraordinary reference in a judiciary protocol to Carlo's status as Michele's "wife" and to his ceremonial oath of fidelity suggests that the officials recognized their action as a formally binding agreement, as a "marriage," regardless of the illicit nature of their sexual union.

How common such arrangements were among Florentine males is impossible to determine, though they were almost certainly more widespread than this one surviving episode indicates. Other boys, as mentioned earlier, swore oaths of fidelity to lovers, perhaps in similar ceremonies. Of course, this society could hardly have sanctioned same-sex "marriages," however they were perceived. Nonetheless, their existence was evidently acknowledged and to some extent tolerated, as the generally lax control of sodomy implies. Among certain social groups, especially young and unmarried males, the practice of having boy-wives or older "husbands" for sexual gratification and companionship, or for other benefits, might well have been openly approved and desired.

As the different kinds of relations examined here show, sodomy could have a variety of meanings for individuals, ranging from the subjugation of dependents to casual sexual pleasure or to deeply engaging love affairs.

An added element that bears on the significance of sodomy both for individuals and in Florentine society is the duration of males' involvement in homosexual activity. This is a problem that can be addressed only in a grossly simplified and mechanical way—that is, by determining how often and for how long persons were implicated in sodomy in the 1478–1502 survey. The judiciary sources do not constitute a "census" of sodomy. Moreover, the number of recidivists would certainly be higher if more boys had been questioned, if all records from 1478 to 1502 were extant, if the survey were extended over time, or if other magistracies' records were considered. Still, despite these problems and with all due caution, it is possible to discern in case histories some useful distinctions in patterns of sexual behavior (Table B.16).

Some aspects of this problem have already been dealt with elsewhere. Only a tiny number and proportion of boys who were implicated in the passive role appeared later as the dominant partners with other boys.[143] Also the vast majority (85 percent) of persons who appeared in the active role were incriminated only once with one partner, suggesting, if their records vaguely reflect their sexual activity, that for most males sodomy was a temporary and occasional transgression. The remaining 15 percent (437) were implicated with more than one companion or, in some cases, more than once with the same companion. Within this group it is possible, in a rough and arbitrary way, to delineate different degrees of involvement in sodomy. Some 201 men (46 percent of the recidivists and 7 percent of the total) appeared with at least three partners or over a time span of five years or more. A small group of 79 individuals (18 percent of the recidivists and 3 percent of the total) was incriminated with at least five partners or over a time span of ten years or more. The latter inevitably include some men who turn up merely by chance and lack others who likely deserve to be included. Nonetheless, these 79 long-term recidivists probably made up more or less the core group of what Florentines called "inveterate" or "infamous" sodomites in the late fifteenth century. For such men, relations with boys evidently played an important role in their erotic and affective experience for a substantial part of their lives.

Several of these notorious sodomites have been mentioned elsewhere: Jacopo d'Andrea, il Fornaino (documented from 1470 to 1487 with 40 partners, 24 self-denounced, 13 convictions); Francesco di Bartolomeo, or Rosaino (1467–1491, 43 partners, 34 self-denounced, 3 convictions); Giovanni Maringhi, il Mea (1469–1492, 16 partners, 1 self-denounced, 6 convictions); Jacopo Cerbini (1463–1498, 11 partners, 6 convictions); and Salvi and Jacopo Panuzzi (respectively, 1466–1496, 7 partners, 1 self-denounced, 2 convictions; 1463–1487, 12 partners, 3 convictions). To them could be added others like the shoemaker Antonio di Michele, il Buglione (1467–1497, 8 partners, 5 convictions); the broker Tommaso di Damiano (1476–1490, 14 partners, 8 self-denounced, 3 convictions); the butcher Bastiano Del Mazzante (1475–1481, 23 partners, 17 self-denounced, 4 convictions); and numerous others with similar records. Socially they ranged from poor textile workers to members of eminent Florentine families, though as a group they ranked slightly higher on the social scale than men who were implicated less often. Some 43 percent (34) bore surnames, compared with 20 percent of all active partners. Artisans and shopkeepers predominated, with a high number of butchers (9 of the 62 with a trade), followed by shoemakers (6), brokers (4), clothes dealers (3) and notaries (3). Given their long involvement in sodomy, these men were also considerably older than the youths who made up the majority of all men implicated. The mean age of the thirty-five men whose ages were recorded was nearly thirty-nine, compared with twenty-seven for all those in the 1478–1502 survey.[144] And based on the findings reported earlier, the great majority of these men were probably unmarried.[145]

Significantly, compared to all those implicated, a high proportion of the men in this small group either denounced themselves or were convicted for sodomy during these years—added confirmation of their notoriety. Of the 2,469 men who were implicated in the active role just once, only 6 percent (150) self-confessed and 16 percent (392) were convicted, for a total of 542 (22 percent) who either denounced themselves or were condemned. Of the 437 who were implicated more than once, 20 percent (88) self-confessed, 39 percent (170) were convicted, and 54 percent (238) either denounced themselves or suffered a conviction. The longer someone was involved in sodomy or the greater number of partners he had, the more likely he was to denounce himself and the more he risked conviction. Of the 201 men implicated with at least three partners or over five years or more, 27 percent (55) self-confessed, 45 percent (90) were convicted, and 63 percent (127) either denounced themselves or were condemned. The proportions in each category are highest for the small group of 79 "infamous" sodomites, implicated with at least 5 partners or over ten years or more: 33 percent (26) self-confessed, 51 percent (40) were convicted, and fully 68 percent (54) either denounced themselves or were condemned. Moreover, in each group a progressively higher proportion of those who were convicted was condemned more than once: 25 percent (42) of all those implicated twice or more, 32 percent (29) of those in the group of 201, and 40 percent (16) of the notorious sodomites in the group of 79. The Florentine system of regulating sodomy conceded a good deal of license to men to act on their homoerotic desires, and those who engaged only sporadically in sodomy ran relatively little risk of punishment. But those who did so repeatedly or over long periods of time were sooner or later likely to be punished, often more than once. On one occasion, in 1499, the Night Officers noted explicitly that the punishment of persistent offenders was their main task: "[I]t is up to their magistracy to punish sodomy and sodomites, especially inveterates and those who have committed the most evil vice of sodomy many times."[146]

Sexual relations between men and boys in Florence thus responded to a variety of power relations, desires, and needs, and bore a wide range of personal and social meanings. But whatever their character and personal significance, sexual bonds were often only one thread of larger webs of male association into which sodomy was woven. The next sections turn from the erotic ties between individuals to examine the social relations around them.

Family Complicity

One sign of how intricately sodomy was woven into the social fabric of Florentine life is the extent to which it implicated family groups. At first glance unlikely accomplices in sodomy, families at times provided important sources of support. As has been seen, sodomy could provoke domestic conflict, between sons and shamed fathers or between frustrated wives and sodomite husbands. But some families viewed sodomy in a more tolerant or favorable light, even going so far as to facilitate the homosexual activity of sons or brothers. Among other possible reasons for such indulgent familial responses, sodomy could serve a family in various ways: by producing material and other benefits, by creating ties through sons or siblings with other men, or even by reinforcing relations within the domestic group.

Some of the oldest evidence on sodomy in Florence directly implicates families, especially fathers, in their sons' sexual activity. Preaching in 1303, Giordano da Rivalto condemned men who encouraged their sons to accept gifts of money or clothing from male admirers, presents that we now know were common to homoerotic courtship and relations for the subsequent 200 years.[147] The earliest extant sodomy laws proscribed families' involvement in their sons' relations with other males. The statutes of 1325 set a huge fine of 500 lire for fathers who persuaded, advised, or permitted their sons to commit sodomy.[148] In the 1420s, Bernardino of Siena castigated parents who showed little concern about their sons' sodomitical activity or who "prostituted" their sons for their own interests and profits. "There are some who permit their sons to do every possible shameful, evil, and sinful thing," he charged, speaking of sodomy, "and they consent in order to obtain civic offices or money: the mothers so they may earn some money, the fathers so they may gain influence."[149] Although little evidence exists from this early period to verify such claims, the repeated allegations that families took a willful, supportive role in sons' sodomitical affairs cannot easily be dismissed.

Common Florentines in the later fifteenth century also believed that some families aided and abetted their sons' trysts and accommodated their lovers, though no evidence has emerged that the courts prosecuted parents. For informants, families' motives usually centered on some sort of exchange, with parents exploiting their sons for their own benefit. And, like Bernardino, they readily accused parents of "pimping" their teenage boys. In 1481 Cipriano, a doublet maker, was denounced twice for prostituting his son Giuliano, taking money from his lovers, and letting them use his home and workshop for sex, all with the assistance of the boy's mother.[150] Another mother, an informer charged in 1496, was guilty of "personally pimping" two of her boys to a notary's son, who kept them "publicly in place of his wife."[151]

One of the more plausible cases of parental complicity in a boy's homosexual affairs involved Andrea, son of the weaver Fioravante, who worked in Domenico Ghirlandaio's *bottega*. Implicated already in 1492,[152] in 1494 Andrea was alleged to have been sodomized many times by a painter named Gilio through the mediation of his father, who "has pimped his son to Gilio, and has taken him to sleep with Gilio and others so that they will give him money."[153] He was accused again in 1495,[154] and in 1496 yet another informer charged that his parents were still aiding and profiting from his relations with men. Andrea was reportedly being kept by three men "with the consent of his father Fioravante and of his mother mona Francesca," who let his lovers sleep with him in the house. To avoid the current harsh repression of sodomy in the Savonarolan period, "Andrea with his father and mother have gone to stay in Castel San Giovanni di Valdarno . . . out of fear, and these lovers provide for all their needs. . . . His mother is a scoundrel and his father is wicked, because they've made these three lovers use up 200 florins."[155] Not only were Andrea's parents allegedly promoting their son's affairs, but the boy's lovers had assumed the responsibility of defending and providing for the family—while protecting themselves—during this dangerous period.

Although none of these charges appears to have been proved, it should not be surprising to find some parents willing to exploit their sons' good looks and desirability for a profit, just as others did their daughters in equally squalid stories of abuse and prostitution.[156] For families in precarious economic circumstances, ambitious fathers, or poor widows with few means of sustenance, the thriving demand for boys by men who could offer material and other guarantees might have seemed an acceptable avenue to better their condition. For others, however, economic gain was perhaps bound up with or secondary to other motives. Examples some informers gave suggest that parents' compliance in their sons' sodomy sometimes grew out of or helped foster relations of dependence and clientage. Accusers hinted that homoerotic ties could have been one strand in the webs of influence brokerage that interlaced Florentine social relations.

An informer in 1496 linked a father's approval of his son's "marriage" to the benefits and patronage offered him by the boy's lover. While serving in an administrative post in Modigliana, Domenico di Francesco Boscoli of Florence was said to keep a local boy "publicly, in place of a wife," and the boy's father consented because he "receives certain favors" from Boscoli.[157] In 1470 someone alleged that Gianpiero, an apothecary in Poggibonsi, let his two sons be sodomized "so that they would be well dressed" and he himself "would be aided" by his sons' admirers.[158] Apparently, Gianpiero hoped that the sexual bonds between his sons and their lovers would flower into other kinds of beneficial relations for him. Whether his ambitions were fulfilled is unknown, but at least one of his sons, Giuliano, did maintain a long relationship with a potentially influential suitor: Orlando di Bernardo de' Malavolti, a Florentine citizen resident in Poggibonsi, denounced himself in 1473 for having sodomized the boy "many, many times . . . in the past."[159]

Another striking insinuation that a Florentine father willfully allowed his sons to engage in sodomy because of the advantages their relations could reap for the family involves the complicated case of Bernardo di Lorenzo Lorenzi, a moderately well-to-do but socially undistinguished silk merchant who lived with his and his younger brother Niccolò's family behind the church of San Felice in Piazza.[160] In their teens and early twenties, three of Bernardo's sons and one of Niccolò's were often implicated in sodomy, and though most of the charges were not investigated and none were confirmed, they can at least be considered plausible. In 1492 someone alleged that a friar in Santa Croce frequently sodomized Bernardo's eldest son, nineteen-year-old Raffaello, as well as two of his brothers, probably seventeen-year-old Lorenzo and sixteen-year-old Paolo.[161] That same year, their seventeen-year-old cousin Jacopo was denounced three times as "the greatest *bardassa* in Florence."[162] Four years later, in 1496, all four Lorenzi youths were incriminated again. Jacopo, now aged twenty-one, was accused twice of having been sodomized many times by Bernardo di Zanobi Guidotti.[163] Lorenzo, also twenty-one, was denounced for having sodomized seventeen-year-old Giovanni di Bernardo Bellacci, while Raffaello, now twenty-three, was said both to have sodomized fifteen-year-old Francesco di Giovanni Cavalcanti and to be maintained by two men, Bartolomeo Strinati and the notary ser Giovanni di Neri di Francesco.[164] Twenty-year-old Paolo was simply vilified as a *bardassuola* who "indecently and shamefully lets himself be fucked" even by four or six men at a time, "just like a bitch."[165]

In themselves, the repeated charges against the youths are impressive, however unproven they might have been. But especially significant is a remark by Paolo's accuser in 1496 that described his father, Bernardo, as openly tolerant of his family's homosexual relations, for utilitarian motives. The informer said that Bernardo had been reproached many times for his sons' sexual activity, but "he doesn't trouble himself over it. He knows all about their behavior and that of the other family members," he intriguingly explained, "*because it is useful for the family.*"[166] What benefits the Lorenzi clan gained from the youths' sodomy the informant did not specify. But that Bernardo consented to it and was mindful of its potential rewards might partly have been the fruit of his own experience, for he himself, at the age of about fourteen, had been denounced twice as the "wife" of a clothes dealer in his neighborhood.[167] As for the alleged utility of sodomy to the Lorenzi family, perhaps it derived from the identity of the companions with whom the youths were weaving friendships and relations. Unlike the Lorenzi, who while fairly wealthy had little political standing, most of the young men's sexual friends who were identified by name—Bellacci, Cavalcanti, Guidotti, Strinati, the notary Giovanni—came from families of higher status who were members of major guilds and held secure positions within the ruling regime.[168] The informer's comment, read against these circumstances, implies that through homosexual relations the Lorenzi cultivated ties with influential families or individuals in order to advance their interests, much the way Florentines nurtured and exploited more orthodox alliances and friendships.

Similar considerations seem to have motivated several men who were contending in 1460 for the affections of young Francesco di Marco Fei by flattering both him and his family with presents, favors, and courtesies of various sorts. The Fei, resident in via della Scala in the parish of Santa Lucia d'Ognissanti, were of little note in the city's economic and political life (Marco was a poor, if propertied, silk worker). Yet in the microsociety of this lower-class district, the family seems to have held—or aspired to hold—a position of some importance. Despite their humble condition, the Fei possessed two houses in via della Scala, as well as a house and several rural properties in nearby Calenzano that were nestled among lands owned by none other than Cosimo de' Medici; they gradually sold off most of their country assets to Cosimo and, later, to his son Piero.[169] These contacts with the city's dominant family may suggest that the Fei were, in some measure, Medici clients. But there is another tangible and perhaps related sign of the local status and ambitions of the Fei family: in 1460, as an informer noted, fourteen-year-old Francesco had recently presided as the *messere* of a *festa* (public banquet) he and his family gave in the square of San Paolo, not far from their home, probably indicating that he was the *signore* (lord) of a neighborhood festive brigade.[170] Such events were intended not merely to entertain but also to convey a well-publicized political message, a demonstration of a family's largesse and magnanimity and an affirmation of its (or perhaps its patron's) honor and influence.[171]

This, one imagines, is partly why the four men named in the accusation who kept Francesco—at least two of whom were notorious sodomites—were doing their utmost to ingratiate themselves with his parents. According to the informer, the butcher Dietaiuto d'Antonio, called Bugnolo, sent a present of veal to their house every Saturday;[172] twenty-nine-year-old Santi di Cenni, a grocer, supplied them with barrels of olive oil;[173] twenty-eight-year-old Alessandro di Roberto Salviati, the only man of a prominent family among the four, had stockings and doublets made for Francesco and hosted him in his house for meals;[174] the carpenter Piero di Nardo Bocchi built the stage for the boy's feast at San Paolo.[175] An informer a few months later claimed that yet another admirer had "lent" him the substantial sum of 12 florins.[176] With their gifts and professions of love, these suitors were courting both Francesco and his family to gain not only his sexual favors, perhaps, but also the good will of this up-and-coming young neighborhood *signore* and his family, all the more significant if the Fei were indeed local clients of the Medici.

Sometimes close and long-lasting relations developed between a boy's parents and their son's lover, regardless of the motives. Young Attaviano di Giuliano Benintendi, from a famed family of sculptors of wax votive statues in the via de' Servi, seems to have cultivated such a relationship with the family of the weaver Giovanni Giannini, with two of whose sons Benintendi reportedly carried on long, consecutive affairs. In January 1497, an informer charged that twenty-eight-year-old Attaviano had for "several years" kept Antonio Giannini, aged seventeen, and "he makes him stockings, doublets, berets, and shoes, and makes sure he always has money in his pouch, and he sleeps with him every night." Previously, according to the informant, Attaviano had kept the Giannini's older son, whom he abandoned for Antonio only when his brother had grown too old. Moreover, Antonio's parents "know that he keeps him and are consenting"; they provided Attaviano and Antonio with a separate bed so they could sleep undisturbed together, and welcomed the youth into their home "every evening."[177]

Attaviano Benintendi already had a record of sexual relations with boys, having been named in a boy's confession in 1492 and convicted for sodomizing another in 1494, lending some credibility to this latest allegation.[178] Two of his older brothers had also been heavily implicated in homosexual sodomy in their youth. Francesco, the eldest, was accused numerous times in the 1460s between the ages of twenty and twenty-four; Matteo, renowned for his skilled painting of votive statues, was convicted in 1476, at age twenty-four, and denounced himself in 1479 for long relations with three boys.[179] Despite these precedents, when Antonio was questioned two months after the accusation in 1497 he denied the charge, and he and Attaviano were absolved in April.[180] But this did not close the case.

In May, under new officials, Attaviano and Antonio were denounced again.[181] Claiming that previous officials had known the truth but had freed Antonio because someone had exerted pressure, the informer urged that the boy be questioned under torture. Interrogated once more, Antonio denied that he had ever been sodomized. But he now admitted that he knew Attaviano well, that the latter had shared meals with his family "many times and very often," and that he frequently slept overnight with him and his brother in their home—yet he insisted that Attaviano had never sodomized him. Finally, questioned again two days later, Antonio broke down and confessed that Attaviano had sodomized him over the past year innumerable times (*pluries et pluries et multotiens et sepe sepius et sepissime*).[182] When Attaviano ignored their summons, the officials convicted him in contumacy, with a large fine of 200 florins.[183] Even this disastrous result does not seem to have interrupted their relationship, for a year later the two were denounced again. Now, however, new officials did not proceed against them.[184]

The claims of an anonymous informer and a confession perhaps elicited under torture naturally leave much to be desired as evidence. But this case raises in a credible way the possibility that Giovanni Giannini and his wife regularly offered hospitality, meals, and shelter over several years to the suitor of not one but two of their sons. Possibly motivated or sustained by Attaviano's gifts to the boy(s) or to their parents, their relationships ended up creating bonds that verged on kinship, as the youth was accepted almost as a son-in-law into the Giannini household.

Kinship ties within the same domestic group could also play a role in fostering sodomy. It happened frequently that several members of the same family were implicated in sexual relations with other males. This does not refer to incest or the abuse of boys by brothers, fathers, or uncles, documented examples of which are rare.[185] Rather, these were siblings or fathers and sons who engaged in sodomy with males outside their family. In the 1478–1502 survey, around 100 such family groups can be identified.[186]

Long before, Bernardino of Siena had claimed that some boys learned about sodomy from their fathers, who were sodomites themselves,[187] and evidence from the judiciary records would appear to support his charge. That sodomy was often linked to life stages, with unmarried youths commonly having homosexual experiences before marrying and producing children of their own, partly accounts for the appearance over time of different generations of a single family—like the Lorenzi, for instance—before the Night Officers. In 1470 and again in 1474, when he was in his early twenties, the brassworker Jacopo di Lorenzo del Cietina self-confessed to sodomy with three boys; his seventeen- or eighteen-year-old son Domenico appeared in turn in 1496, sodomized by a man who denounced himself.[188] Other fathers and sons are found engaging in sodomy during roughly the same period. For one of numerous examples, in 1492 a boy confessed that Lorenzo, called Broda, had sodomized him; a couple of months later his fourteen-year-old son Piero admitted that eighteen men had sodomized him—the beginnings of repeated sodomitical activity for which he was eventually exiled.[189] In some cases, it appears, boys' and youths' homosexual relations might have been tolerated or accepted within their family circle in part because their own fathers had once or still had similar experiences.

Brothers were accomplices in sodomy, however, more often than fathers and sons—traces of fraternal solidarities that provided support for homosexual activity and presumably reflected back on relations within the household as well. Quite commonly, for example, two or more teenage brothers were having sex simultaneously with numerous partners, almost certainly with one anothers' knowledge and complicity. In 1475 fifteen-year-old Zanobi di Simone Panciatichi was named by three self-accusers and by four more in 1476, and when questioned he divulged the names of twenty-six other men who had sodomized him. Five self-accusers in 1476 also named his thirteen-year-old brother Giovanbattista, who then confessed that he had been sodomized by an additional twenty-two men.[190] In this as in many other cases, the same man sometimes had relations with two siblings: ten of the men the Panciatichi boys named had sodomized both brothers. Other families had several brothers who were implicated at various times and at different stages of their lives. As many as six of Francesco di Rinaldo Cavalcanti's ten sons came to the attention of the Night Officers for sodomy between 1468 and 1497.[191] The Benintendi brothers mentioned earlier—Francesco, Matteo, and Attaviano—provide another good illustration. Brothers like these probably shared reports of their sexual escapades or love affairs, and found in one another a source of mutual confidence and encouragement.

Perhaps related to this domestic complicity, the numerous fraternal groups implicated in sodomy included some of the most notorious or "inveterate" sodomites in Florence. Several have already been mentioned in other contexts: Salvi and Jacopo di Niccolò Panuzzi, for instance, or ser Pierozzo, Jacopo, and Giuliano Cerbini.[192] Other brothers had equally striking records. Mario, Paolo, and Antonio, sons of Niccolò di messer Guccio de' Nobili, were often implicated from 1459 to 1494 but usually managed to escape conviction, no doubt due to their family's antiquity and honorable name and its prominent place in the regime.[193] Two other fraternal groups of infamous sodomites, both humble families of butchers, fared less well at the hands of the authorities. Giuliano, Cosimo, Damiano, and Mariotto, sons of Taddeo (called Capretta), who lived and had a butcher shop on the square of San Sisto, were "all the same" (*tutti d'un modo*) in their passion for boys, as an informer remarked in 1494; Damiano had allegedly rented a room at the Buco for twelve years where he brought his boys for sex.[194] Between 1475 and 1504, the four brothers were named in the confessions of fifteen boys and were secretly accused on three other occasions, three denounced themselves for relations with six other boys, and the same three were convicted a total of nine times.[195] Five sons of Francesco del Mazzante, who had a butcher shop on the Ponte Vecchio, also built up an impressive record of sodomy with boys. While at least three of the brothers were implicated as early as 1467 and numerous times later with absolutions, Lorenzo was convicted in 1473; Giovanni in 1476; Jacopo in 1476, 1477, and 1479, and he also denounced himself in 1485; Bastiano was condemned three times in 1476 and again in 1479, and denounced himself in 1475, 1476, and 1480 for having sodomized seventeen other boys; Bartolomeo was convicted in 1495 and 1501.[196] With this family background, it comes of little surprise to find Jacopo's ten- or twelve-year-old son Francesco, accused in 1494 of being part of a group of promiscuous Oltrarno boys to be discussed later, confessing that he had been sodomized by six other boys.[197]

This striking involvement of families in sodomy hardly seems casual, but its significance both for individual family members and for the domestic group as a whole—apart from the often grievous financial burdens their convictions must have created—remains a question on which the judiciary records throw little light. For the most part, these were young bachelors, and a brother's passing resort to boys for sexual release and companionship, or even his more durable love for a young friend, might have been viewed within the fraternal circle with comprehension and indulgence (even more so if, as often happened, his brothers could also share the pleasures of a willing boy).[198] When unmarried men with well-defined tastes for boys were involved, the family's tolerance of their inclinations could conceivably have entered into considerations of broader familial strategies, perhaps with a view toward protecting an estate from dispersion among many heirs. By the sixteenth century, the practice of limiting the marriage of sons for this reason was common among the local patriciate.[199] And Florentines hardly had to be told that sex with boys did not lead to unwanted pregnancy, a fact of life Savonarola nonetheless adduced to explain why local parents willfully allowed their sons to engage in sodomy.[200]

The suggestion that a brother resort to "sterile" sex with boys to avoid fathering children might in fact have been at issue in a dispute between Andrea and Francesco di messer Tommaso Minerbetti on the occasion of Andrea's third marriage in 1511. Francesco opposed his brother's remarriage, and argued about it with him. Unable to convince him, Francesco moved out of the house, as Andrea recorded, "pleading that he did not want me to have any more children, and saying that he would rather I did certain other things, which for decency's sake I won't mention." Earlier Andrea had written that his brother abandoned the household "because he wanted me to do something that seemed neither licit nor decent to me, and for this reason I refused and he departed."[201] While sodomy is not mentioned explicitly, the nature of the brothers' dispute and of Andrea's objections perhaps hints at it.

If it is hard to verify the thesis of family strategies at work in sons' or brothers' sodomitical relations, surely these domestic or fraternal circles at least knew about their members' illicit sexual affairs, often accepted them, and perhaps even encouraged them.[202] Their knowledge and support furnished one important source of complicity, comprehension, and solidarity for homosexual activity, and their shared experiences might well have reinforced filial or fraternal bonds within the family itself.

Friends, Networks, Sodalities

Sexual relations were often only a single thread of a weblike network of social relations—made up not only of kinship, but also of age-cohort camaraderie, neighborhood ties, common occupation or workplace, and circles of friends and acquaintances—that could link two partners, the various companions of a single boy, or, in general, groups of men with sexual interests in boys (or vice versa). The partners individuals had and the nature of their sexual contacts were often not casual, in other words, but were associated with and influenced by other sets of relations. The multifaceted social networks through which sodomy was enacted, and which sodomy in turn helped fashion and reinforce, provided crucial sources of complicity, comradeship, and solidarity. The court records do not allow the depth and range of these relations and networks to be explored fully. But they yield many traces of their existence and their significance, both for the nature of homosexual activity and for the broader phenomenon of bonding within the male society of which sodomy was a part.[203]

On first impression—reinforced by the separate listing of boys' partners as their testimony was recorded—sodomy was a preeminently private act between two individuals. Yet on closer examination, it becomes clear that homosexual activity in Florence often had a strong collective character. To cite one obvious example, it was not uncommon for two friends or sometimes groups of three or four to sodomize a boy together; in one exceptional case from 1469, a boy reported that eight men took turns sodomizing him in a shed behind the cathedral one evening around vespers.[204] About one of every ten boys who confessed to the Night Officers from 1478 to 1502 revealed at least one such experience, apart from the gang sodomitical rapes mentioned earlier. Perhaps having sex with a boy in front of or together with a companion was an added erotic stimulus, but given the gendered and social identities attached to sexually dominating a boy, it also helped validate one's virility in the eyes of a comrade, and in the shared act created complicity and solidified friendships.

Even if a boy's partners did not sodomize him together, they were very often friends or acquaintances. In most cases in which a boy had multiple companions (and these constituted the majority, as has been seen[205]), it usually takes only a bit of reconstruction to uncover various types of social networks and affiliations among his partners, whether they entailed groups of youths, people who worked at the same trade or in the same area of the city, neighbors, coteries of friends, or a combination of such ties.

An especially revealing illustration of how homoerotic relations could be densely interwoven with and reinforce other social bonds comes from a striking case in 1494 that merits a close review. In a rich and impassioned accusation, an informer denounced a group of eight dissolute boys from "di là d'Arno"—that is, the quarter of Santo Spirito—named several of their sexual companions, and alluded to "hundreds" of others who had sodomized them. "They have done things in these holy days," he complained, no doubt referring to the apocalyptic preaching of Savonarola, "that would blacken the sun, just like when our Lord died." Although the informant gave little biographical information about the boys or their alleged lovers, he did reveal, in a remark already discussed, that they were tightly bound by ties of affection, gifts and material support, oaths of fidelity, surveillance, and intimidation: "Those I have listed who have fucked them are the ones who love them the most, who have kept them with the most money, who have had them guarded by boys, and who have made each one they loved swear to them, or else they would tell their fathers."[206]

That the eight boys were accused as a group suggests that they were friends, as other details from their interrogations confirm; in fact, several had had sex with one another.[207] Most important, they probably all lived within a few blocks of one another, in the neighborhood between the church of San Felice in Piazza, the square of Santo Spirito, and the via del Campuccio south of the square.[208] On the whole, they were quite young. Of those whose ages are known, one was between the ages of ten and twelve, three were fourteen, and one was seventeen. With one exception, all came from fairly poor or artisanal families. Two were butchers' sons, two worked for tailors, one for a mercer, and one in the silk industry.

If this was a group of mainly teenage, working-class, neighborhood friends, the relations between their partners were equally dense. Among them, the five interrogated boys named forty-four individuals who had sodomized them (in addition to those they named among the eight friends); eighteen of these were convicted. According to the informer, a number of the boys' partners were themselves close friends: Tommaso del Magrezza, who named six partners, "has sex with Brancaccio and several other youths who are his companions," and Carlo Bramanti, who named twelve partners, "has sex with Ciapero and several other of his companions." Three of the individuals named each had had relations with two different boys among the eight, again underlining the links among them. Other important similarities and ties of social affiliation also linked their sexual companions. Most were older adolescents or youths; of the thirty-eight whose ages were recorded, only two were over thirty, and three out of four were between the ages of sixteen and twenty-five. Nearly half of those with occupations recorded were textile workers, mostly weavers, and the others were mainly artisans; only two bore surnames of any note. Along with their youth and social class, the other main unifying element in the boys' circles of sexual friendships was neighborhood. Two-thirds of those whose residence was indicated (17 of 25) came from the boys' own district, in the quarter of Santo Spirito and in the vicinity of the churches of San Felice and Santo Spirito and the bordering parish of San Frediano. If their partners did not live in this area, they usually worked in neighboring shops or together in the same shop.[209] By all appearances, the boys' sexual networks were formed above all of working-class adolescents and youths who resided in their own neighborhood or, less so, whom they knew from work, and a number of them were explicitly said to be companions. This was probably a typical example of those informal, mainly youthful, male sodalities devoted to pleasure and rabble-rousing known as a *brigata* (a company or gang of friends).

The nature of the bonds among this tight-knit circle of boys and youths is worth considering anew in light of the traits and affinities this reconstruction has revealed. Here the informer, so attentive to the power relations between the youths and the boys they kept, offers some crucial keys to grasping the possible dynamics involved. More than merely gratifying the young men's sexual desires, it appears, their relations with neighborhood boys helped affirm a virile social identity, created or reinforced hierarchies, and signaled their dominion and status within the rough, emarginated community of youths and laborers in Santo Spirito. The informant depicted the main "protectors" and subjugators of the eight boys—the weaver "Ciapero," the twenty-two-year-old weaver "Cantera," the eighteen-year-old gold beater Bernardino, and others who remain only names—practically as "bosses" among the district's youth. They were the ones who could lavish the most money and gifts on their boys, they who had the charisma to make them swear oaths of loyalty to them, they who had the influence to enlist other boys to "guard" their favorites, they who had the arrogance to threaten to reveal all to the boys' fathers. Their conspicuous "possession" of boys both defined and communicated to others the relations of power within their local social group and *brigata*. For the boys themselves, their relations with the older youths were perhaps a kind of informal initiation into the local gang, through which they not only gained material benefits and a position of privilege, but also learned the masculine sexual and social roles to which they also would aspire as they grew older.[210]

But the thickly textured ties of class, youthful camaraderie, neighborhood, and erotic bonds among these boys and their companions also helped fashion a collective social identity, as another striking observation by the informer implies. Referring to the boy he called the group's "squad leader," Tommaso del Magrezza—but in the context his remark could have applied to the others as well—he noted that "every evening five or six [of his protectors] go to fetch him, and they are all armed with swords and daggers, and they take him out for fun around Florence." Entertainment, yes, but with a serious message, especially now that the policing of sodomy had suddenly become repressive under the influence of Savonarola's preaching and as the Medicean regime unraveled. By brashly displaying their *bardasse* throughout the city, it would seem, these armed young toughs flaunted their sexual conquests, perhaps challenged rival gangs, intimidated critics, and defied the authorities, thereby asserting the identity and reinforcing the solidarity of their own neighborhood group.[211]

Admittedly, the wealth of detail in this denunciation is exceptional, and it is only this descriptive quality that permits the suggestion that sodomy could both define lines of influence and power within a local social group and solidify a collective identity. Yet the basic elements of this case, especially the dense ties of age, neighborhood, and work that the boys and their partners had in common, appear in numerous other examples. In the mid-1490s, for instance, a similarly tight homoerotic network based on neighborhood and age-group affinity is found across the river in the comparable lower-class district of the parishes of San Piero Maggiore and Sant'Ambrogio.[212] That the youths who kept boys sometimes constituted gangs of neighborhood toughs whose sodomitical relations were part of the control of their "turf" was also suggested by an informer in 1502, who complained about the "indecent" sexual carryings-on of young Giovannino Petrini: he said that the neighbors could not walk the streets of their neighborhood "without being eyed and threatened" by the boy's protectors.[213] Embedded in a wide variety of social bonds, sodomy helped in turn to shape and reinforce these ties.

Like neighborhood and youth-group camaraderie, the acquaintances and friendships made through the daily contacts in and around the workplace created other compliant networks for sodomitical activity. This was related only in part to the presence in shops of young apprentices or factotums, who were sometimes sodomized by their employers or fellow workers.[214] Often it was the sociable bonds forged in the all-male environment of neighboring shops that provided both companionship and a supportive atmosphere for sodomy.

One of the best examples of sodomitical networks formed around a cluster of workshops comes from a famed landmark of Florence, the Ponte Vecchio. The appearance of the bridge, except for the elevated corridor added by Vasari in the sixteenth century, remains much the same now as it was five centuries ago, with a few dozen tiny shops crowding both sides, but its social character has changed dramatically. Now a gallery of smart jewelry and antique stores, in the fifteenth century the Ponte Vecchio was lined with the stalls and shops of butchers and grocers, a baker, mercers and textile workers, hosiers and leatherworkers, coopers, metalworkers, and other artisans. It also teemed with men and boys involved in sodomy. Between 1478 and 1502, at least fifty people who worked on the bridge were implicated in homosexual relations (40 in the active and 10 in the passive role), many more than once and over long periods of time. Seventeen were convicted at least once, and six denounced themselves. Often these men and boys had more in common than the familiarity that derived from their daily vicinity. Several worked together in the same shop or belonged to the same family. The butcher shop of the notorious Del Mazzante brothers, mentioned earlier, must have been a focal point for the sodomites on the Ponte Vecchio. Not only were all five brothers who worked together there repeatedly implicated and condemned at least once for sodomizing boys, but between 1478 and 1502 four of their employees were also incriminated and two were convicted.[215] Similarly, Antonio di Giovanni Del Massaio, proprietor of a nearby grocery at the bridge, his two sons Tommaso and Jacopo who worked with him, and an employee of theirs, Andrea di Orsino, were implicated often, denounced themselves, or were convicted.[216] Men who worked on the Ponte Vecchio, moreover, sometimes consummated their sexual relations in one anothers' shops, and often shared the same boyfriends. For just a few examples of the latter, five of them sodomized Francesco di maestro Piero (for which each was convicted), five sodomized nineteen-year-old Domenico da Lamole, and six sodomized twelve-year-old Bartolomeo di Giovanni.[217]

All the different types of relations mentioned with regard to the Ponte Vecchio—clusters of workshops of men and boys implicated in sodomy, groups who worked in the same shop, shared partners among males who worked near or with each other—could be illustrated many times over with a wide variety of examples.[218] By providing a steady source of information and gossip, an indulgent and encouraging environment, and diverse networks of comrades with similar erotic interests, the sociable bonds fashioned in and around the workplace facilitated the pursuit of sodomy.

Even lay confraternities, those "ritual brotherhoods" dedicated to spiritual exercises and charitable works, and a basic institution of male sodality and sociability, could harbor more sensuous forms of bonds and networks among their ranks.[219] A coterie of sodomites mentioned by the chronicler Simone Filipepi were brothers of an unnamed confraternity; sometime after Savonarola's death in 1498, he recorded, they congregated near the church of San Tommaso, got inebriated, and then "went off to recite the office at their company, where it was the turn of Scheggia [their ringleader] to deliver the lesson."[220] According to an informer in 1475, Piermatteo Sacchetti took a young cleric twice weekly to the meeting hall of his confraternity, San Zanobi, and sodomized him there; "it's a disgrace," he said, that Sacchetti and two of his *confratelli*, the apothecary Simone di Taddeo and Giuliano Baronci, "have made a brothel of that company, because they are the three greatest sodomites in Florence. You should build a bonfire in back of the company [hall] and put all three together on it."[221] Perhaps dubious, the Night Officers declined to pursue the charge, even though Sacchetti had been convicted of sodomy in 1463 and named again by a boy in 1466, and the same officials in 1475 convicted Baronci soon after for having sodomized another boy.[222]

Confraternities indeed recognized that their members might commit sodomy and prescribed measures to discipline them. Their statutes commonly condemned the "wicked vice," along with other activities considered harmful or immoral,[223] and brotherhoods sometimes expelled members who were found to have engaged in sodomy. The expulsion of three men from the flagellant company of San Paolo in 1469 "because they were condemned by the office of sodomy" illustrates well the tight-knit social relations within which sodomy was often practiced.[224] This case involved Francesco Tolli, a cloth trimmer who joined San Paolo in 1466; Matteo di Casino, also a trimmer who not by chance worked with Tolli in the same shop; and Pietropaolo Monti, a clothes dealer who entered the confraternity of San Paolo together with Matteo on the same day in 1468. Not only were they friends, as these ties suggest, but they were also sexually involved with same boy, fourteen-year-old Giovanni di Jacopo di Bongianni, who too worked in Tolli's and Matteo's shop. Moreover, the three *fratelli* all used Monti's store for their numerous trysts, and Matteo and Monti often sodomized the boy together.[225] Their erotic relations were evidently bound up indistinctly with their other bonds of work, friendship, and spiritual brotherhood. In this context, it is worth recalling the comment of the informer cited at the beginning of this chapter, who evoked a similarly seamless fabric of fraternity, neighborhood, and erotic love to explain the relationship he was denouncing: "This he did out of great love and good brotherhood, because they are in a confraternity together, and he did as good neighbors do."[226]

A final illustration of how erotic ties to a boy often united veritable networks of men, whatever the various social relations that joined them, comes from the sodomites who denounced themselves. Frequently two friends, but often larger groups of three, four, five, or even six men appeared before the officials together to disclose their sexual relations with a single boy, or sometimes with several boys in common. Some two of every five of the "active" self-accusers from 1469 to 1502 (175 of 446) turned up with one or more friends. To cite only a few cases, six men presented themselves together in 1478 to confess that they had sodomized the sixteen-year-old carpenter Antonio di Niccolò, and six others came forward the same day in 1482 to clear themselves for having sodomized sixteen-year-old Baldovino Baldovini.[227] In 1479 Jacopino di Filippo Torelli and Matteo di Giuliano Benintendi came together to reveal that both had sodomized the same three patrician boys, Filippo Benizzi, Inghilese Ridolfi, and Giovanni Vettori, "many times up to the present day."[228] Collective self-denunciations like these were hardly accidental. Rather, they were conscious decisions taken by groups of friends who were all involved with the same boy(s) and who felt threatened enough to turn themselves in before being accused secretly and risking conviction.

Sometimes these self-disclosures occurred in chains, as word got around the circle of a boy's partners that someone had denounced himself, or that the boy had been accused and was about to be or had already been interrogated. Then the network of friends, singly or in groups, hurried to the officials to confess voluntarily and avoid a penalty. A good illustration of this sort of chain reaction comes from a case from 1475 involving the friends and lovers of fourteen-year-old Guglielmo di Michele del Buono, who worked as a shoemaker near Orsanmichele. The exposure of this sexual network began on August 31, when five men turned themselves in together and admitted that they had each sodomized Guglielmo. The next day, four other partners of Guglielmo rushed to register their own self-accusations. The boy was questioned on September 2 and named five additional men, but he conveniently failed to tell all. Two more partners denounced themselves on September 6 and another the following day. Guglielmo was reinterrogated on September 9 and named still another partner, but six days later two more self-accusers came forward. Questioned a third time on September 19, he disclosed four more companions. Finally, on September 25, one straggler whom the boy had not yet named thought it best not to press his luck and likewise ensured his impunity by denouncing himself. After the collective self-confession of the first five men, the news clearly wound its way through the large circle of Guglielmo's twenty-five friends and acquaintances—some of whom were apparently better informed, or more fearful, than others—and a fair number managed to escape possible conviction.[229]

Enmeshed in these dense and often far-flung webs of affiliation, sodomy in Florence had a marked collective character. The extensive and multifaceted networks of association and friendships among sodomites and others sympathetic to them probably help account for the vitality of sodomy in this community and, consequently, for the difficulty of "eradicating" it. In part, such circles furnished important sources of complicity and companionship for men with similar interests in boys; as one informer in 1462 warned officials, "Act quickly, because [Fruosino] makes a practice of [sodomy], and he takes courage and is emboldened with the support of the many friends he has."[230] In addition to the copious evidence on their shared sexual experiences, glimpses of their sociable activities appear frequently in the judiciary records: dinners together in inns or homes; gatherings in workshops, homes, or taverns to drink and gamble; trips together to country houses on feast days; and so forth. In an accusation in 1471 against the notorious Giovanni Maringhi, the aforementioned Mea, who was clearly at the center of a wide network of sodomite friends, an informer observed that Mea, his comrades, and their boys "have great get-togethers in Fiesole," a town in the hills overlooking the city where Florentines then as now went to escape the summer heat or enjoy the panorama.[231] Filipepi's disparaging story of Scheggia's pranks and death also unwittingly shows that groups of sodomite friends commonly socialized together. His shop near San Tommaso, he noted, was "always filled with such ribalds." These companions—whom he called a "sect," which in Florence often implied a political faction, and in any case evokes the tight-knit character of their friendship—also congregated in the evenings under a portico behind San Tommaso to drink and pass the time, and, one imagines, to exchange information on good-looking or available boys, or the latest arrests.[232] One informant, whether consciously or not, was merely pointing out a commonplace when he claimed that the "great sodomite" Gerino Gerini and two of his friends, including another habitual sodomite, Santi di Cenni, "are all three usually companions together in this buggery."[233]

In addition to companionship, networks of friends could provide concrete forms of assistance and protection. The friendships formed through and around sodomy perhaps helped some men find jobs with others who shared their erotic interests, as the many examples of employers and their workers implicated in sodomy might suggest. They could also facilitate other economic arrangements. Santi di Cenni, for instance, rented a grocery store he owned to Lionardo Gerini, the brother of his friend and companion in sodomy, Gerino, whose candle shop was nearby.[234] Sometimes sodomites aided one another by personally guaranteeing for friends who were arrested or convicted, as Gerino Gerini and a companion did in 1479 for a certain Giovanni di Paolo from Rome, or by helping friends pay their fines, as Bastiano del Mazzante and Bernardino del Gaburro, both butchers on the Ponte Vecchio, did for another butcher convicted in 1498.[235] Sodomites who had some influence or political connections might have shielded friends from prosecution for sodomy, as several informers warned: the accuser who described the collective ridicule against the mercer and alleged sodomite Antonio di Jacopo, reported in chapter 2, urged the officials to arrest him quickly, "because as soon as he hears of this he will seek protection with his friends and those of his sons, because he's one of those who have many friends for this reason."[236]

In a society like that of Florence, where power and influence were exercised in large part through and for the benefit of family clans, friends, patrons, and clients, the existence of networks of sodomites also had potential significance for political relations. This possibility was not lost on contemporaries. Earlier in the century, that perceptive critic of Tuscan life, Bernardino of Siena, condemned those who cultivated good relations with sodomites, offered them their sons, and voted them into office with a view toward promoting their own interests or political careers; he further alleged that factions were united in part by homoerotic bonds.[237] The early-fifteenth-century regime had similar concerns, as it tried without success to filter sodomites from civic office and raised the specter of such men's occult machinations to sabotage the new Office of the Night.[238] The chronicler Giovanni Cavalcanti recounted the story of a foiled conspiracy to overthrow the government in the 1430s, conceived by three aristocratic youths who were bound together in a homoerotic union. Niccolò di Paolo Bordoni and Andrea di Segnino Baldesi, he said, "had for a long time maintained a very close companionship" with the younger Cipriano di Lipozzo Mangioni, a bond filled "with many affectionate desires, more so, perhaps, than the decency of upright living called for." When their plot was discovered and Niccolò arrested, Cipriano went to each official of the Eight of Watch to plead his friend's case, as Cavalcanti suggested, "inebriated with the love of him by whom he was loved."[239] As will be seen, networks fashioned in part around sodomy also played an important role in the opposition to Savonarola in the mid-1490s, as they would again in the return of the Medici from exile in 1512.

Whether among kinsmen or neighbors, companions at work or gangs of youths, comrades at arms or confraternal brothers, patrons or clients, or simply groups of friends, *l'amore masculino* thus wove another thread into the fabric of relations that fashioned collective male identity and experience in Florence. Sodomy was intimately connected to the intense bonding and camaraderie so characteristic of male sociability in this culture.

The links between homosexual activity and broader male social relations were so dense and intertwined that there was no truly autonomous and distinctive "sodomitical subculture," much less one based on a modern sense of essential diversity or "deviance." There was only a single male sexual culture with a prominent homoerotic character. Some men may have had a conscious preference for boys, acted on their desires for substantial periods or most of their adult lives, and formed networks of friends based at least in part on their shared sexual tastes. Yet however conspicuous they might have been, they and their sexual activities were woven indistinctly into an erotic milieu in which homosexual relations were part of the experience of many, if not most, males, to varying degrees and in a more or less occasional manner, and were commonly associated with life stages and forms of sociability, without precluding sex with females. The many interconnections between sodomy and other male bonds and networks suggest, moreover, that to single out and accentuate only their sexual aspects would be to misapprehend and deform the fundamentally social nature of same-sex love and sexual behavior in Florence. Sodomy was an integral facet of male homosocial culture.

Sexual relations between males not only were a typical product of this culture, but also contributed much to its construction. The pederastic structure of homosexual relations, the values that Florentines ascribed to them, and the ways in which they were enacted played important roles in defining life stages, in articulating status distinctions among males, and in shaping and reinforcing masculine gender identity. Deeply insinuated, moreover, into the basic sodalities and networks of relations that helped constitute men's and boys' collective experience, sodomy was in turn a dynamic factor in male social interaction and cohesiveness in late medieval Florence.

PART III

6

Politics and Sodomy in the Late Fifteenth Century: The Medici, Savonarola, and the Abolition of the Night Officers

> Good government is punishing the evil ones and getting sodomites and the wicked out of your city.
>
> Girolamo Savonarola (1496)[1]

> Thank God, now we can sodomize!
>
> Government official, after an anti-Savonarolan riot (1497)[2]

At no time in the history of the Florentine Republic were the social, political, and moral divergences over sodomy in this community more strident, or disputed more publicly, than during the last decade of the fifteenth century. The epigraphs to this chapter give some sense of the terms in which this controversy was played out. For Girolamo Savonarola, the charismatic Dominican friar who exerted a powerful, yet divisive, influence on the city, the repression of sodomy and other "vices" formed a key part of his efforts to reform public morality. After the Medici fell in 1494, his program for moral renewal became tightly wedded to the political rebirth of the Republic, and was pursued not only through harsh new laws sponsored by his supporters, but also through a massive mobilization of reformed boys and adolescents to serve as examples of purity and to police activities deemed "immoral."

Yet however wide-ranging and spectacular these efforts to suppress sodomy were, they met with only brief or partial success. Popular opposition frustrated the adoption of the friar's most rabid demands; lax enforcement limited the effects of the laws; and, remarkably, for the first time in Florence—perhaps the first time in Christian Europe—groups of men, mainly youths, are found defiantly challenging attempts to repress sodomy. The armed gangs of lower-class youths, discussed in the previous chapter, who in 1494 ostentatiously showed off their boyfriends around the city were soon followed by groups of their social betters who militantly championed their right to illicit pleasures. The relieved exclamation attributed to the government official in this chapter's epigraph expresses well the resentment that many Florentines must have borne toward Savonarola for his role in curbing their pursuit of sodomy, not merely a profligate "vice" but an integral part of local male culture.

The campaign against sodomy during the Savonarolan period is certainly one of the more significant episodes in the history of this practice in Renaissance Florence. Due mainly to the fascination that the figure of Savonarola has long exerted both on scholars and on a broader public, this campaign, in its general outlines, is also among the best known of these episodes. Yet this keen interest in the controversial friar, and the heated ideological battles that have surrounded it, have too often unduly magnified the person and influence of Savonarola, and have produced a number of inaccuracies and facile generalizations both about his own contributions and about late-fifteenth-century Florentine society. In recent decades, scholars have gone far toward presenting a more accurate and dispassionate evaluation of Savonarola's place in local politics and religion.[3] But few have systematically studied the specific case of the friar's efforts to reform sexual mores and behavior, above all sodomy, and in this area some of the older preconceptions probably still persist. Both supporters and detractors, for example, have commonly assumed that the Savonarolan years constituted the consummate repressive moment in the city's history—a proof of righteous zeal for the one part, obscurant fanaticism for the other. Contrasted with this, the era of the preceding Medicean regime, especially under Lorenzo the Magnificent, has typically been portrayed either as licentious and sexually debauched, from one partisan point of view, or tolerant and enlightened, from the other.

This chapter, which studies the regulation of sodomy roughly from the beginning of Lorenzo's informal rule in 1469 to the suppression of the Office of the Night in 1502, offers some important correctives to both views. This broad chronological frame helps to assess the significance of alternating periods of greater repression and of relaxed controls, putting the experience of the Savonarolan years in perspective as part of an ongoing and far from unique concern with the management of sodomy in the last third of the fifteenth century. In fact, during the undeniably eventful years of the friar's greatest moral and political influence, many fewer convictions for sodomy were registered than in several other periods both before and after the Savonarolan era. In terms of sheer numbers of condemnations, the most consistent and widespread repression of homosexual activity in Florence occurred, significantly, under the ostensibly liberal regime of Lorenzo de' Medici. Furthermore, restoring the regulation of sodomy in these decades to its proper historical prospect requires paying close attention not only to its chronology but also to the political, institutional, and social contexts in which it evolved. Considered in this way, the policing of sodomy in the late fifteenth century—highlighted by the alternating phases of energetic and lax control, by the striking reactions to Lorenzo's death, by the impact of and resistance to the Savonarolan reform movement, and by the abolition of the Office of the Night—reveals a close, almost symbiotic relationship with the life of the Florentine community. The regulation of sodomy responded sensitively to variations in the political, religious, and emotional climate, even to single events that articulated the course of collective life, almost as if it were a measure of the city's pulse. This synchronism, together with the conflicting public responses to sodomy, provides yet another demonstration of how deeply the "abominable vice" and its control had penetrated and were bound up in the social and cultural identity of Renaissance Florence.

The Lorenzan Age

On December 31, 1494, less than two months after the Medicean regime was overturned, the restored Republic passed the harshest law against sodomy in Florence since the early fifteenth century. Among the most striking aspects of this law, the content and context of which will be studied later, are its openly partisan tone, unique in local legislation on sodomy, and its overt condemnation of the former regime for its lax regulation of this "vice": "Considering . . . how abominable and disgraceful before both God and men is the most wicked vice of sodomy," the law's preamble stated, "and how much injustice and little fear of God there has been for some time concerning the repression and extinction of this vice because of the evil government of the past regime, [the priors wish] to reform the law as is necessary in a Christian and religious Republic."[4]

The image this law projects of Medicean Florence, and especially the brilliant age of Lorenzo the Magnificent, as a period of sexual license and tolerance is an enduring one. In part, it stems from the anti-Medicean propaganda of the Republican years, reechoed by modern historians sympathetic to the Savonarolan cause, such as Pasquale Villari, who stigmatized the Florence of Lorenzo as "an orgy of pleasures" cunningly promoted by the Medici lord himself to dull the people's senses, or Roberto Ridolfi, who branded this period as "exquisitely corrupt."[5] But a number of more substantive elements have helped nourish an impression that the Medici, and Lorenzo in particular, were rather tolerant of homosexual activity. Some suggestions of indulgence on the part of earlier generations of the family have already been noted, such as Bernardino of Siena's allusion to the protection of sodomites by the Medici and Antonio Beccadelli's dedication of the *Hermaphroditus* to Cosimo in the 1420s, along with the possible Medicean interests in reducing penalties for sodomy in 1458 and 1459.[6] Certain features of the intellectual and cultural milieu fostered by the Medici have also been thought to have reflected and favored a greater acceptance of homosexuality, especially neo-Platonism with its idealized homoerotic ethos, and both the prominence of beautiful adolescents and the revival of the male nude in art.[7]

A number of Lorenzo's closest friends and companions, moreover, are known or thought to have had homoerotic inclinations. Some of these men even turn up implicated in sodomy in court records. Luigi Pulci, author of the *Morgante* and one of Lorenzo's earliest comrades, who was branded as a sodomite in a vicious satirical exchange with Matteo Franco, was named in the confessions of three different boys in the 1470s (and absolved each time).[8] Two of them also claimed that they had been sodomized by Lorenzo's distant cousin and employee Franceschino de' Medici, who was incriminated repeatedly for sodomy in the 1470s and 1480s.[9] One of these boys, Giovanni de' Maltuzzi from Milan, also admitted to sex with others of Lorenzo's intimate circle, including one of his closest friends and a key figure in the group, Braccio di Domenico Martelli; many of his trysts allegedly took place in Martelli's stable or house.[10] The famed Angelo Poliziano—Lorenzo's household protégé, teacher to his children, and author, among other things, of anecdotes about sodomy in Florence, amorous letters to youths, and a misogynous defense of homoerotic love in his drama *Orfeo*—was implicated in sodomy in 1492 and again in 1496, the latter time by a boy who claimed that Poliziano had sodomized him not long before he died (in 1494, reportedly of a fever induced by his burning passion for a youth).[11] Such personal associations, along with the cultural context, may tempt one to conclude that the Medici unambiguously cultivated both *l'amore masculino* and tolerance of it.

This impression of indulgence under the Medici, and especially in the age of Lorenzo, however, is belied in part by the harsh reality of the policing of sodomy in these years. As discussed earlier, Medicean policy on controlling sodomy had two opposing faces: while the legal reforms of 1458 and 1459 reduced penalties for sodomy to their lowest level ever in Florence, at the same time they vastly expanded the regime's practical controls over it. Four generations of the family dominated the city between this date and 1494 when, after their exile, penalties were first increased, and under all four, a large number of sodomy convictions were registered.

Indeed, during the supposedly enlightened and debauched twenty-three-year dominion of Lorenzo (1469–1492), the Night Officers alone condemned nearly a thousand men for homosexual sodomy. In particular, the dozen years following his assumption of power witnessed the most extensive repression of sodomy in Florentine history, judging at any rate by the number of convictions. In just five years, between 1469 and 1474, the Night Officers convicted an astonishing total of 535 men, 161 in the term 1472/1473 alone (Figure 6.1).[12]

No documentation has yet surfaced to help explain this massive wave of convictions, though it was perhaps linked to an effort to consolidate the authority of young Lorenzo, only twenty years old when he took up the reins of the family's dominion in 1469. External threats menaced the re-

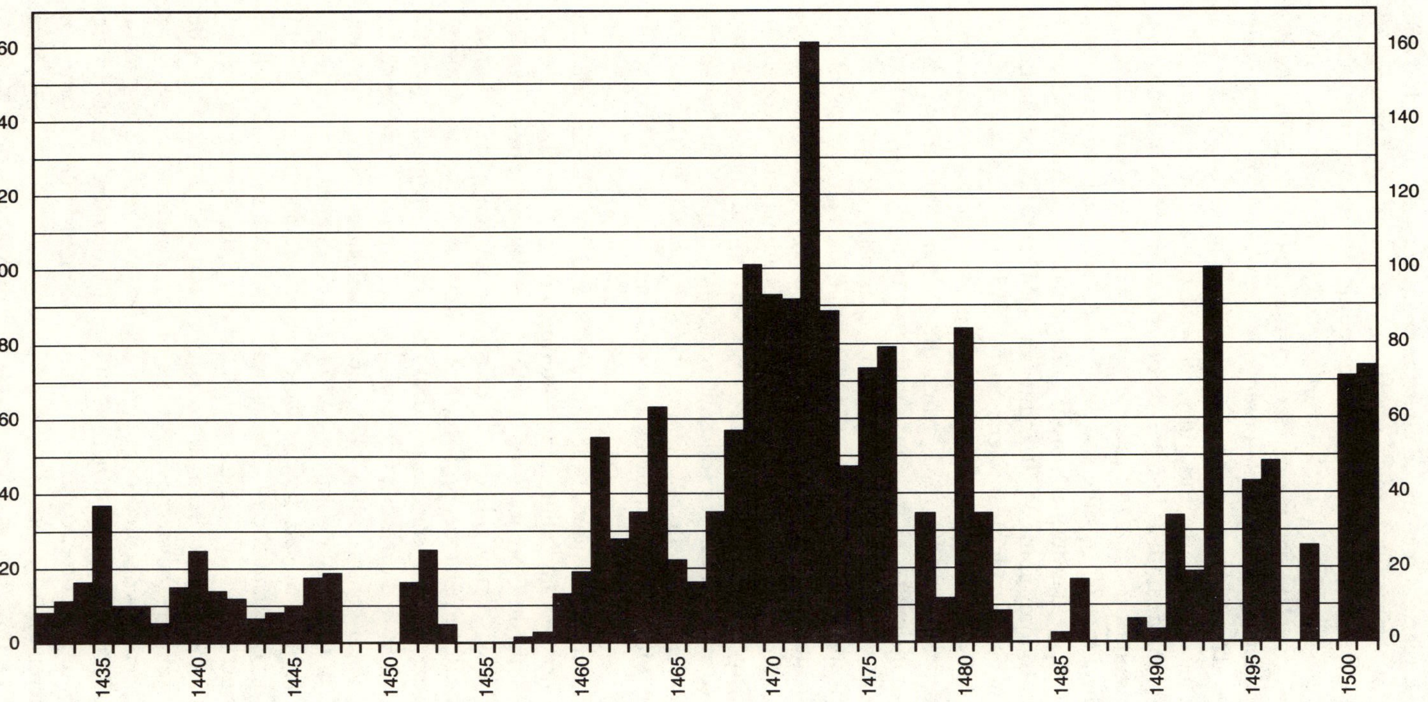

Figure 6.1. Convictions for homosexual sodomy by the Officers of the Night, 1432–1502. For the years 1432 to 1458, data cover the year beginning on April 23; for 1459 to 1472, the year beginning around July 10; for 1473 to 1502, the year beginning around November 10. The data are incomplete for the years 1440, 1451, 1453, 1457, 1458, and 1476, and are missing for the years with no convictions indicated. (*Sources*: UN 1–35; GAN 77–88)

gime in these years, as men exiled after the failed conspiracy of 1466 continued to plot against the Medici, and there were revolts in Prato (1470) and Volterra (1472) as well.[13] On the domestic front, constitutional reforms were passed in 1471 that were designed to reinforce the family's hold on the city.[14] Other measures enacted in the early 1470s limited private and public festivities, while Lorenzo himself increasingly abandoned the frivolities typical of young men his age and assumed the sober air and comportment befitting a mature ruler, all with the aim of enhancing his authority and image both at home and abroad.[15] The unprecedented, vigorous repression of sodomy in the same years was probably another means by which the Lorenzan regime sought to keep order and consolidate its rule in this delicate transitional period. Whatever the explanation, the tight regulation of sodomy in the 1470s refutes any facile equation of the Lorenzan period with unconditional tolerance toward homosexual activity.

In the 1480s, however, the judiciary situation changed significantly. After a final peak in 1480/1481, when the officials condemned eighty-four men,[16] convictions for sodomy plummeted to the lowest levels in the history of the Office of the Night. In the five years for which records survive from April 1483 to April 1492, they convicted an average of only six or seven men annually, with a conviction rate of a mere 6 percent (compared with a yearly average of 38 condemnations and a conviction rate of 27 percent in the entire 1478–1502 survey). In the same period, the Eight's condemnations for sodomy averaged eight per year (compared with 13 for the whole survey). During the last decade of Lorenzo de' Medici's life, official preoccupations about sodomy appear to have waned substantially.

If, as is commonly assumed, the humanistic and neo-Platonic ideals of the Renaissance had any influence in fostering a more "tolerant" environment for sodomy in Florence—for all, not just a favored elite—then this was realized only during this decade of relative impunity for sodomites. But again the decisive factors probably had more to do with considerations of public order and the current political climate, especially the domestic peace of the 1480s. Lorenzo's rule emerged greatly reinforced from the crisis of the Pazzi conspiracy in 1478 and the subsequent war with Pope Sixtus IV. Constitutional reforms in 1480 further tightened Medicean control of the regime, as vast powers were centralized in the new loyalist Council of Seventy and the old Republican councils lost the final shreds of their former authority.[17] The consolidation of the regime apparently encouraged a loosening of restrictions not only on sodomy but on other activities as well. The boisterous festivities of Carnival, for example, which had earlier been downgraded or suppressed, returned in full glory in the later 1480s. From this period date the first extant Florentine Carnival songs (some attributed to Lorenzo himself), many of them playfully obscene with plentiful references to sodomy.[18]

After twenty-five years of pervasive control since the reforms of 1458 and 1459, the policing of homosexual activity relaxed significantly, if not completely, during the mid-1480s to the early 1490s. This relative lenience in the last years of Lorenzo's life probably contributed to the vehemence of the reaction against sodomy after his death, under the influence of Savonarola. However, it may also have had the opposite effect of helping to root sodomy even more firmly in male culture and to lay the foundations for its eventual defense against the friar's repressive crusade. In any case, when Lorenzo de' Medici died in April 1492, this comparatively permissive climate that had briefly allowed homosexual activity to flourish came to an abrupt end.

The Coming Scourge

In a letter of April 7, 1492, one day before Lorenzo's death, twenty-five-year-old Niccolò di Braccio Guicciardini confided to his relative Piero Guicciardini, an eminent figure in the regime, that he and their whole circle of friends were terrified by the recent doom-threatening sermons of Girolamo Savonarola and other churchmen. For the past year, he reported, the prior of San Marco as well as preachers in Santa Maria Novella and the cathedral had been predicting dire consequences for the city if Florentines failed to change their ways, "especially sodomy." He then described the storm that had damaged the cathedral roof two days earlier, universally considered an evil omen, and wondered fearfully whether this was the apocalyptic sign that friar Girolamo had been prophesying. According to the nervous youth, the preachers were claiming that

> God sent this scourge so that we would repent of our sins, especially sodomy, which he wants to be done away with, and that if between now and August we don't correct ourselves these streets will run with blood . . . such that all of us are frightened, especially me. May God help us.[19]

This young man's anguished letter attests that the orchestration of terror around sodomy had made a deep impression on Florentine ruling circles long before the Medici lost their grasp on the city in November 1494. Similarly, the repression of sodomy intensified well ahead of the spectacular and better-known campaign against this and other "vices" during the period of Savonarola's greatest influence, from the collapse of the Medicean regime to the friar's own fall in April 1498.

Indeed, the tightening of controls over sodomy can be dated precisely to the very days that Lorenzo de' Medici lay on his deathbed and immediately following his demise on April 8, 1492. Significantly, among the first measures the regime took in this delicate and dangerous moment was to clamp down on the sexual liberality of the previous years. The speed with which this happened underlines how precarious and illusory was the apparent tolerance homosexual activity had enjoyed during the last decade of Lorenzo's lifetime.

This lenience had in fact begun to wear thin two years earlier. In 1490 the government curtailed the previously liberal policy on self-accusations, which many sodomites had shrewdly exploited in the past, by limiting individuals to one self-denunciation only. The same law also sought to stimulate secret accusations, which had declined sharply, by allowing the Night Officers to impose on poor men fines lower than those prescribed, thereby facilitating their payment—and consequently assuring informers of their reward, their usual motive for denouncing someone.[20] These changes had little impact on the frequency of convictions, however, which increased dramatically only after Lorenzo's death.

The regime's immediate response to Lorenzo's illness and death was to reinforce the apparatus for controlling sodomy, thus anticipating the repressive reforms after the expulsion of the Medici two and a half years later. One sign of how sodomy had come to be seen almost overnight as a threatening problem was the aggressive new role assumed in its policing by the Eight of Watch, the city's most important criminal court. Although their previous role was fairly marginal compared with that of the Night Officers, the Eight had long judged sporadic cases of sodomy involving mainly anal injuries or other serious offenses, especially as the authority of the podestà and capitano over such violations was in decline.[21] Now, at this critical moment, the Eight initiated some spectacular police actions against adolescents and sodomites and appropriated more extensive powers.

Niccolò Guicciardini's worried letter furnishes a rare private account of this magistracy's energetic intervention and of the growing climate of terror and repression. On April 3, as Lorenzo lay dying, the Eight rounded up some twenty adolescents, "all of good families," as Niccolò noted, and interrogated them about their homosexual relations; one promiscuous boy named Duccio "Mancino" implicated none other than Lorenzo's shadow, Angelo Poliziano.[22] On one of the following evenings, the Eight sent their retainers to make a sweep of the city's taverns and to detain anyone found in the company of a boy; "they arrested many," according to Guicciardini, including twenty-six-year-old Bernardino di Matteo del Gaburro, implicated several times in these years for sodomy, whom they convicted on April 6.[23] On April 5 they condemned the infamous Salvi Panuzzi, aged fifty-nine, who was caught fondling the genitals of a young cleric during a sermon in the cathedral "in sight of the most holy body of our lord Jesus Christ and in contempt of omnipotent God and the Christian religion."[24] As Niccolò revealed, the large fine of 300 florins the Eight imposed on Panuzzi struck Savonarola and others as decidedly too mild, and he and his supporters incited the magistrates to revise the sentence. Succumbing to this intimidation, the Eight arrested Salvi again on April 6, and as their retainers were conducting him to prison, the streets and squares along the route thronged with furious crowds of "people and boys" shouting, "Burn him! Burn him!"[25]

That same day, April 6, the Eight issued several decrees intended to tighten control of the urban spaces associated with sodomy. They ordered taverners to close their taverns early, two hours after sunset, and to deny entry to "suspect boys"; they also raised the reward for informers who revealed the locations of *casini*, sheds or houses used for gambling or illicit sex, and declared that men accused of sodomy or of keeping *casini* could be absolved only with the approval of all eight officials.[26] On April 11 they extended these controls to the public baths, warning their managers to keep "suspect boys" out under penalty of a fine.[27] In March 1493 the Eight again ordered taverners to close shop at the second hour after nightfall and to refuse service "to persons suspected of sodomy," while a year later they commanded them not to allow entrance to boys under the age of eighteen and imposed early closing hours on dancing and fencing schools.[28] The Eight's many convictions for sodomy after Lorenzo's death also reflect their new authority. After having convicted an average of eight persons a year for homosexual relations from the 1480s to the end of 1491, from April 1492 to February 1494 they condemned forty-four, many for cases that were not said to have involved violence or other aggravating circumstances.[29]

On their part, the Night Officers who assumed office two weeks after Lorenzo's death also for the first time ordered taverners and innkeepers to deny entrance to "any youth or boy who might commit sodomy" in their establishment.[30] In addition, they quickly moved to augment their control over sodomy in the territory by posting new denunciation boxes in Arezzo and Empoli and by replacing boxes in Pisa and Prato that must have earlier been removed.[31] In Prato this measure was contested, possibly by sodomites themselves. For no sooner had the new *tamburo* been affixed than unknown vandals destroyed it, to the Night Officers' "great dishonor," just as their box there had been torn down in 1481 and two more would be demolished in 1500.[32]

Finally, a sharp increase in denunciations to and convictions by the Night Officers manifests the changed status of sodomy after Lorenzo's death. In the year and a half from November 1489 to April 1491, they received only 4 anonymous denunciations for homosexual sodomy naming 6 individuals, and they convicted only 9 persons.[33] During the term of the last group of officials before Lorenzo died, which began on April 23, 1491—a year when Savonarola and other preachers, as Guicciardini's letter attests, were fulminating against sodomy—the number of persons denounced rose dramatically, to 133. The Night Officers, however, remained indifferent before this wave of popular and clerical antagonism: they levied only 1 conviction.[34]

Again, it was only with Lorenzo's demise, and the insecurity of the passage of power to his young son Piero, that Savonarola's threatening demands for repression began to have an effect also on the Officers of the Night. The officials who took office two weeks after his death received a flood of accusations naming 152 persons, and they condemned 32 men, the highest yearly total in over a decade.[35] And convictions continued to escalate. The officials who assumed office in April 1493, convicted 61 men, while those for 1494 condemned 59 in little more than six months, before their records break off temporarily in November.[36] The 200 convictions for homosexual sodomy levied by both the Night Officers and the Eight during Piero di Lorenzo's two-and-a-half-year dominion represent the highest number for any corresponding period since the mid-1470s—many more than during the entire final decade of his father's lifetime. Not even at the height of the Savonarolan campaign against sodomy between 1495 and 1498 would convictions reach these levels.

Repression of sodomy, therefore, intensified well before the Medici fell from power. The death of "the Magnificent," the repercussions of which extended far beyond Florentine borders, also marked a turning point in the history of sodomy in Florence. As the consensus Lorenzo had shaped within the oligarchy unraveled under Piero's inept rule, as fears of a French invasion materialized, and as Savonarola continued to sow terror over local sexual practices,[37] the regime responded in part by tightening the policing of sodomy. When the reformed Republic took up the problem after the Medici were exiled, the terrain had already been well prepared for the assault on sodomy in the coming years.

The Spirit and the Flesh: Sodomy in Savonarolan Florence

The flight of Piero de' Medici on November 9, 1494, paved the way not only for the revival of republican institutions and sentiment in Florence, but also for the implementation of the vast campaign for moral reform that Girolamo Savonarola had been preaching for years.[38] In his militant vision of Christian and civil life, good government was impossible without "clean living" (*ben vivere*). This meant above all that women and girls would dress and behave with modesty, boys would abandon their violent games and unrestrained sexual activities, prostitutes would be forced back into the brothels, taverns would be closed, and sodomy, gambling, and blasphemy would be vigorously repressed. It was largely due to Savonarola's authority that the new regime waged probably the most concentrated and effective attack on sodomy ever known in Florence.

But the attempt by the friar and his followers to impose a monastic-like rule in the city did not go uncontested. Alongside the struggle during these years over the political character of the new regime, conflict raged over the severe moral regimen that Savonarola championed. Contemporaries such as Giovanni Cambi and Francesco Guicciardini noted that the Dominican's repression of sodomy won him many enemies, who joined with others to oppose him.[39] Others portrayed youths, in particular, as the main source of this enmity. According to Lorenzo Violi, a notary who recorded many of the friar's sermons, the new morals laws greatly annoyed the "licentious youth, who previously were accustomed to engaging in every vice," while Jacopo Nardi remarked that many of those who resisted Savonarola were "sensual persons, less correct and less easily disciplined, as young men commonly are."[40]

The assault on sodomy during the Savonarolan period had two prongs. The first and more traditional approach was to reinforce the state's repressive apparatus. Jurisdiction over sodomy was extended to other courts in addition to the Night Officers, and penalties were made extremely harsh, at least by time-honored local standards.[41] The role of Savonarola and his supporters in effecting these changes was decisive, though as will be seen the friar did not have his way in all regards.

The second, more innovative, approach came directly out of the Piagnone movement[42] and was a response in part to the perceived inadequacy of traditional repressive institutions and methods. This was Savonarola's famous "reform of the *fanciulli*," a largely successful program to modify the behavior and morals of thousands of young and adolescent boys, and to install the reformed boys as guardians of the new moral order.[43] Let us first examine the new penalties and institutional changes before turning to the boys' movement and, finally, to the prosecution of sodomy during the Savonarolan years and to the conflicts it generated.

Legislative Reform

The government moved swiftly and severely against sodomy within days of the constitutional reforms, passed on December 22 and 23, 1494, that buried the old regime.[44] Just as Savonarola's authority was crucial in molding consensus around the reform of the constitution, so his intervention contributed decisively to the passage of the harsh measures against sodomy. In his celebrated political sermon of December 14 in which he threw his full support behind the proposed Great Council, the institutional cornerstone of the new Republic,[45] he also urged his all-male audience to legislate ruthlessly against sodomy:

> The Signoria must make a law against that cursed vice of sodomy, for which Florence is defamed throughout all of Italy, as you know. Perhaps you have this disgraceful reputation because you talk and chatter so much about this vice; maybe it's not so widespread in fact as it's said. I say, make a law that is without mercy, that is, that such persons be stoned and burned.[46]

Two weeks later, on December 31, 1494, the councils overwhelmingly approved the harshest law against sodomy in Florentines' living memory.[47] As seen earlier, this law was rhetorically tied to the identity of the new "Christian and religious Republic," in contrast with the ostensibly liberal policies toward sodomy of the "evil government of the past regime." Savonarola's influence probably played an important role in getting the law passed, yet the situation was no doubt more complex than that depicted by Luca Landucci, a fervent Piagnone, who wrote that this and similar laws were approved literally "on the friar's orders."[48] Piero Parenti, an important critic of the friar who was closer than the apothecary Landucci to the regime's inner circles, offered a more subtle interpretation. He cast both the constitutional reforms and the attack on immorality as part of a seamless political design; that is, eminent exponents of the ruling class realized that in order to maintain their hold on the regime they had to come to terms with Savonarola and enlist his aid in something of a quid pro quo. Their support of his calls for repression might have been part of the "agreement" Parenti mentions between these shrewd politicians and the powerful friar. But with Savonarola's intervention, some of these citizens quickly realized that he might manipulate them as they hoped to use him. According to Parenti, "They began secretly to complain that they had fallen under the power of friar Girolamo. It was one thing to govern a monastery, they said, but another to govern a city."[49]

In its specific provisions, this law was a conservative revolution that overturned the principles on which earlier sodomy laws had been based. It abolished all fines—the keystone of penalties since 1432—and prescribed only public, corporal, and capital penalties of the sort Savonarola championed, though even then it did not fully meet his brutal demands. Adults over the age of eighteen who were convicted of sodomy, whether male or female, active or passive, were to be pilloried for at least one hour and deprived of office and other communal honors until restored by a two-thirds vote of the council. If convicted a second time, he or she was to be paraded through the city's public places to the Old Market, and there branded on the forehead with the "customary public sign of fire and of the Commune"; again, males were also interdicted from office. The penalty for an adult's third offense was death by burning. The punishment of minors aged eighteen or under, male or female, active or passive, was to be left to the court's discretion, as in the old statute of 1415. This new measure thus retained the traditional age distinction in punishing sodomy as well as the principle of graduated penalties. But in doing away entirely with fines and barring convicted sodomites immediately from civic life, it overturned the foundations of Florentine sodomy laws that had been in place since the early fifteenth century.[50]

In addition, this law ratified the expanded jurisdiction over sodomy that the Eight of Watch had already usurped. The Eight and the Night Officers now had equal authority and were in theory to apply the same penalties. Revealingly, accusers still tended to favor the "officers of the sodomites," in part because their penalties were rightly seen as milder, in practice, than those of the Eight. An informer in 1496 revealed this hierarchy of authority and punishment when he warned the Night Officers that "if I hear you have done nothing about it I will inform the Eight, and this will result in greater prejudice and harm to him," a perception that was generally accurate, as a comparison of the two magistracies' penalties shows.[51] Other informers also threatened to take their cases to the Eight if the Night Officers, to whom they had first turned, failed to punish the men accused.[52] In effect, however, the new penalties and the full jurisdiction given to the Eight called into question the role and efficacy of the Office of the Night, which eventually helped undermine its autonomy and unique purpose in the city's system of managing sexual behavior. In these years, in fact, the Night Officers increasingly came to be perceived as an embarrassing liability rather than a firm bulwark against sodomy.[53]

It is impossible to document the direct effects of these changes on conviction patterns, since the records of both the Eight and the Night Officers survive only from November 1495. Nonetheless, the results must have been meager. It appears that in applying the new penalties, officials ran up against some long-standing obstacles and failed to enforce the harsh measures with rigor. During the first six months of 1495, Savonarola repeatedly condemned their laxness from the pulpit. He thundered that nothing was being done about sodomy, that Florentines were deaf to his appeals, and that God wanted them to punish sodomy or he would punish the city.[54] That the law was ineffective can also be inferred from the extant list of denunciations to the Night Officers, which shows that people were accusing few men and boys of sodomy.[55] Even in this apocalyptic and repressive climate, the disapproval of sodomy evidently did not suffice, for many Florentines, to induce them to inform on acquaintances and neighbors when no reward was forthcoming—this was the result of abolishing fines—and when citizens risked public shaming.

The community's reluctance to put sodomites to death, as Savonarola urged, is eloquently shown by the same informer who in December 1495 accused ser Simone Grazzini of the "greatest and most indecent case that has ever been heard," that is, the older man's detestable adoption of the passive sexual role: "And surely if you seek to know the truth, I don't doubt that if you had license you would make a fire of both of them. Nonetheless," he countered, "you should want to be humane and not do as much harm to them as you could."[56] Even Savonarola eventually had to admit that he had failed to win Florentines over to his grisly sense of justice. In July 1495, he condemned their stubborn refusal to burn sodomites, and in March 1496 he bluntly conceded that "if you don't want to kill them, at least drive them out of your territory."[57]

Confirmation of these difficulties soon came from the regime itself. Despite strong opposition, at the urging of the Night Officers in late June 1495 the law was revised, as the preamble to the new edict revealed, "so that these officials can put punishments into effect and can exercise their office." Predictably, the government's solution was to reintroduce a monetary fine. The Night Officers were now authorized either to fine sodomites a minimum of 50 florins for a first offense or to sentence them to the pillory; penalties for second and third offenses remained intact.[58] After this pragmatic reform, accusations began to pour into the magistracy's boxes at four times their previous rate.[59]

Conservatives surely saw this revision as a concession. Savonarola himself quickly condemned the introduction of the more flexible penalty and continued to urge authorities to burn sodomites.[60] Little time passed, in fact, before the Frateschi, the political faction supporting Savonarola, were able to make amends with two laws passed on December 18, 1495, and February 9, 1496, both under Signorie sympathetic to the friar.[61] The first law was intended to make it easier for magistrates to condemn sodomites, especially "inveterate" sodomites, to death. "From experience," it began, "it has been seen that, having tied the hands of those magistrates who are responsible [for policing sodomy], many delinquents accused to them have not been punished as their crimes would have deserved. And so that those who are inveterates in this unspeakable crime might serve as examples to others," this law authorized the Night Officers, the Eight, and now also a third magistracy, the Guardians of the Law, to punish both first and second offenders in any way they wished, even with the death penalty or any other corporal punishment.

The explicit scope of this reform was to increase the severity of penalties. Its practical effect, however, as the records show, was to allow magistrates even greater discretion to fine sodomites lightly or repeatedly. Three months after its passage, for example, the Night Officers fined four men the token sum of 2 florins each.[62] Between November 1495 and November 1497, when their proceedings are extant, they convicted six men for homosexual sodomy more than once, but sentenced only two of these according to the prescribed scale of penalties; three were fined 50 florins both times, while another, convicted three times, was fined first 50, then 100, then again 50 florins. Moreover, in the surviving records of the Savonarolan period, the Night Officers and the Eight together condemned only three sodomites to death (one for heterosexual sodomy), and they commuted two of the sentences to fines.[63] Despite the moral and judiciary rigor that Savonarola championed and the severity of the new injunctions, officials continued, as they had long done, to find ways of mitigating prescribed penalties for sodomy.

The final substantive adjustment during this period in the city's apparatus to police sodomy, in February 1496, closed the loophole of self-accusations that sodomites had exploited so fruitfully in the past to escape punishment.[64] Men who committed sodomy could no longer gain immunity by denouncing themselves, as they had been guaranteed in the Night Officers' founding law of 1432. Under the new moral order, this benefit—already weakened under Lorenzo—was surely seen as a sign of accommodation and lenience toward sodomites, hardly in keeping with the rigid new policies on the punishment of sex offenders. The immunity clause remained in effect only for passive partners up to the age of twenty, "so that in this way notice of such delinquents can be had more easily." In the past, persons of all ages who took the passive role normally went unpunished, but in the new climate, as will be seen, they ran a greater risk of being disciplined; the preservation of this safety valve for them was therefore a real incentive to confess voluntarily before they were denounced. Finally, this law also reconfirmed the exclusion of convicted sodomites from political office and from participation in the Great Council "as persons unsuited for and unworthy of the city's honors."

With these two laws, the reform of the institutional and penal apparatus for policing sodomy during the Savonarolan years reached its conclusion. A final law was passed in February 1497, under the Gonfalonier Francesco Valori, the leader of the Frateschi party, who sharply intensified repression against sodomites during his tenure.[65] This law, however, simply resolved an apparent dispute over competency by acknowledging the authority of the Guardians of the Law to prosecute sodomy, already granted in December 1495.

Contemporaries noted that the heightened repression, inspired above all by Savonarola's sermons and directives, had a visible effect on the conduct and morals of the city's residents. Piero Parenti, no friend of the Dominican, wrote around mid-1495 that "on the orders of friar Girolamo . . . all gambling was given up, and laws were made for every infamous practice. [It was] an astonishing thing that in a single stroke there was such a transformation in behavior."[66] Years later, Jacopo Nardi noted that "as a result of [the friar's] sermons, many laws were passed concerning the punishment of vices and the reformation of good morals, so that, whether out of fear of God or fear of the terrifying laws, in those days people lived in a very Christian manner in our city, compared to past times and those that followed."[67]

But in the opinion of Savonarola and his supporters, these repressive measures were evidently insufficient. More innovative solutions were needed to break Florentine males of their sexual sins and other practices contrary to the severe moral rule the friar wished to impose. Consequently, he turned his attention to boys and adolescents—that is, to precisely those *fanciulli* who were the objects of adult males' homoerotic desires and who "let themselves be sodomized" as men's receptive partners.

The Boys' Reform

From early 1496, when they burst onto the public scene, until Savonarola's downfall in April 1498, the friar's reformed boys played a key role in his program for the city's purification and salvation. Embracing boys as young as six but directed above all at adolescents aged twelve to eighteen or at most twenty, the Dominican's popular reform aimed in part to indoctrinate the riotous and undisciplined Florentine *fanciulli*—famed for their violent rock-throwing contests, desecration of corpses, and sexual license—into his ideals of upright behavior while they were still of a pliable age.[68] With their renunciation of debauchery, their self-governing companies, charitable deeds, stunning processions, and pious devotion that moved observers to tears, the transformed "innocents" were also meant to serve as living propaganda and examples to their parents and other elders.[69]

Although its overall aims were more general, the reform of the *fanciulli* had a direct impact on homosexual activity in two respects. First, one of its main goals was to end the notorious involvement of adolescents in sodomy. In the words of one Piagnone chronicler, Florentine boys were "immersed in every vice," but above all sodomy. With their splendid clothes, "shameless ornaments," and stylish long hair, "they seemed not only girls but public prostitutes, with their indecent talk and acts, especially the sodomitical vice, so that Florence was a second Sodom, certainly a horrendous thing."[70] Now that more is known about the extent of sodomy in Florence, the gender ideology that pervaded it, and the role of adolescents as the object of older males' erotic attentions, this aspect of the boys' reform takes on greater significance. In the first place, this writer's metaphorical feminization of boys—so typical of informers' comments, as has been seen—suggests that the Piagnone battle against sodomy was equally an attack on gender ambiguity. Savonarola also cultivated such fears, conjuring up a gender-ambivalent world where boys, he claimed, were like prostitutes and cows, fathers like daughters, brothers like sisters: "[T]here is no distinction between the sexes or anything else."[71] Not so with his reformed boys. They cut their hair short, donned simpler, less seductive clothing, and forsook their former "lascivious" conduct,[72] refusing to "let themselves be sodomized" and thus be turned symbolically into females.

The vast majority, moreover, of passive partners in homosexual sodomy from 1478 to 1502 ranged from the age of twelve to eighteen or twenty, with a mean age of fifteen or sixteen, precisely the age of the main corps of Savonarola's boys. The refusal of hundreds of adolescents to accept men's amorous advances sharply limited the potential pool of men's young sexual companions. To be sure, some must have spurned the friar's reforms and continued to have sex with men. But importantly, those who did so were older than in the past. During the years of Savonarola's sway, the age of passive partners rose substantially above the normal mean of sixteen to eighteen years.[73] This change probably attests to the success the reform had in removing younger boys from the sexual market.

Second, the boys' part in the friar's program to stem sodomy did not depend solely on their virtue and sexual self-restraint. They also played an organized, militant role in policing morals, backed by their spiritual leaders and with the tacit assent of the government.[74] The reformed *fanciulli* became the shock troops of Savonarola's moralizing campaign and the guardians of the new moral order. Anyone who failed to conform to his rigid prescriptions was fair target for their corrective measures—prostitutes, women and girls whose dress they found immodest, gamblers, taverners, blasphemers, and, not least, sodomites. When their movement was just getting under way, in February 1496, Savonarola himself taught his boys how to reprimand men who propositioned them for sex, beginning with individual admonition and proceeding to collective ridicule and denunciation to the authorities:

> If one of these ribalds who engages in that cursed vice speaks indecently with you in secret, the first time correct him yourselves, saying, "Ribald, you should be ashamed of yourself!" etc. The second time, several of you should give him a fraternal reprimand. The third time, all of you together should ridicule him publicly in the square, with each one shouting, "This is the ribald!" or else denounce him to the Eight.[75]

Whether they limited themselves to private reproach or resorted to threats and violence, Savonarola's teenage vigilantes spread a climate of fear and terror through the city. In intimidating bands of twenty-five to thirty, probably made up of the older youngsters, they policed the streets and taverns, and if their first polite warnings went unheeded they easily turned rough. According to the Piagnone diarist Landucci, whoever resisted the boys in their early forays went in danger of their lives, no matter how eminent they or their families were.[76] True, sometimes the young squads were insulted or even beaten up, actions that provoked fathers of the attacked boys to order the Eight to provide guards to accompany the gangs on their policing missions.[77] But usually their targets did not linger for a confrontation. As Landucci recorded, at the cry, "Here come the friar's boys!" terrified gamblers fled, and women dared not appear in public if they were not properly covered and veiled. The boys commanded such respect, he wrote, "that everyone abstained from indecent things, and especially from the unmentionable vice [sodomy]. You couldn't hear anyone even talk about such a thing, neither old men nor youths, in this holy time."[78]

The boys' companies eventually marched on city hall and petitioned the government to institutionalize their reform and their police work, "so that with your authority," as their petition was said to read, "we can persecute sodomites" and others whom they and their sponsors disapproved. This extraordinary attempt to create a teenage paralegal force failed, rejected by a regime afraid to empower adolescent gangs. Nonetheless, some citizens clearly if not openly continued to support the boys' disciplinary activities.[79]

Adolescents thus became protagonists of the campaign against sodomy by combining their own sexual purity and self-restraint with an aggressive militancy against male suitors. Not only were men largely deprived of what had once been for them a common sexual outlet, but the very boys they used to court now turned against them with taunts and violence. It was these role- and age-specific aspects of the boys' reform, as much as the increased repression, that intensified and focused the conflict over sodomy in the Savonarolan years.

The Courts, the People, and Sodomy

Let us turn now to a closer study of the prosecution of sodomy in the Savonarolan period.[80] A study of this little-known source material offers fresh perspectives not only on the regulation of illicit sex during the Savonarolan era, but also on the influence and fortunes of the Piagnone movement and on the conflicts that divided the city.[81]

It should be observed immediately, however, that in many respects the period of Savonarola's greatest influence, from the fall of the Medici in 1494 to his own demise in 1498, did not constitute the quintessential and repressive climax in the day-to-day policing of sodomy in Florence that might be imagined. In terms of institutional and penal reform and of greater public attention to sodomy, the Savonarolan years were decisive, and some distinctive features in prosecution can be identified. Yet when this period is considered against the broader perspective that the entire 1478–1502 survey offers, the campaign against sodomy in the Savonarolan era takes on less singular dimensions. It appears rather to have been simply a stage in a larger transformation in local attitudes and responses to sodomy in the late fifteenth century. This process began before the Republic's resurgence in 1494 and continued beyond Savonarola's execution in 1498 at least up to the suppression of the Night Officers in 1502. In many ways, the crucial turning point for the policing of sodomy was less the rise or fall of the reforming friar than the death of Lorenzo de' Medici.

In fact, most of the "technical" and social indicators regarding the regulation of sodomy reveal sharp differences between the period from 1478 to April 1492, on the one hand, and roughly the last decade of the operation of the Office of the Night from Lorenzo's death to its abolition in November 1502, on the other.[82] Variations can be discerned within these two periods as well, for example, in the last decade of Lorenzo's life compared with the earlier years of his dominion, or in the years of Piero's rule, the Savonarolan era proper, and the post-Savonarolan period. Both the disjunctures and the continuities need to be highlighted in order to assess the friar's sometimes exaggerated significance.

Given Savonarola's continual instigation against the "abominable vice" and the increased public attention to it, it is hardly surprising that the number of persons who were incriminated for sodomy rose sharply. Considering only those implicated to the Night Officers, whose records alone offer a fairly complete picture, 731 men and boys came to their attention from November 1495 to November 1497, an annual average of 365. This was the highest average for any period in the 1478–1502 survey, much higher than the 220 yearly during Lorenzo's lifetime, and also higher than the 298 annually in the other years from 1492 to 1502. This increase was due mainly to a flood of anonymous accusations, a measure of the sentiment against sodomy aroused by the friar's preaching, but also a symptom of the period's bitter factionalism, in which a denunciation for sodomy, whether true or false, could serve to defame a political opponent.

Despite the Dominican's hellfire preaching and all this finger-pointing, authorities were fairly restrained in their persecution of sodomites. The Night Officers, for example, interrogated only a third of the passive partners denounced to them (94 of 285) between 1495 and 1497. Under the circumstances, this was a surprisingly low rate—equal to the proportion of boys questioned during the Lorenzan period, but lower than that under the regime of Piero de' Medici (40 percent) and in the post-Savonarolan years up to 1502 (46 percent)—which seems to belie the zeal of the moralizing campaign against sodomy, at least at the judiciary level. Moreover, of the youngsters interrogated, fully 46 percent (43) denied that they had been sodomized, as compared with only 3 percent during the Lorenzan period, 10 percent under Piero, and 12 percent in the post-Savonarolan years. Perhaps another indication that false accusations abounded, this high denial rate may also suggest that in this hostile climate, especially among their peers in the companies of reformed *fanciulli*, boys were much more reluctant to admit their involvement in sodomy. Interestingly, those who confessed named on the average less than four partners each, compared with around seven partners during the Medicean regimes. This might indicate that the agitation over sodomy in this period was partially successful at discouraging the most blatant examples of teenage male prostitution and promiscuity or at effecting a real decline in homosexual activity (or possibly driving it further underground).

Although the Night Officers pursued relatively few denunciations, they did adopt a fairly repressive stance toward those implicated as sodomites in boys' confessions, technically the only grounds for conviction. From 1495 to 1497, they levied 91 convictions for homosexual sodomy, 45 a year, as compared with an annual average of 35 in the other years of the 1478–1502 survey (the Eight condemned another 20 persons annually, twice their yearly average for the rest of the survey[83]). Their conviction rate, moreover, was quite high, 46 percent (91 of 198), compared with only 17 percent (188 of 1,203) from 1478 to 1492, and with 31 percent (152 of 483) from Lorenzo's death to Piero's fall in 1494. While numerous, convictions for sodomy in the Savonarolan period were nonetheless lower than one might have expected. The 65 or so annual convictions by the Night Officers and the Eight in these years fell far short of the levels reached in certain other periods: 107 a year by the Night Officers alone between 1469 and 1474 under Lorenzo, 79 a year by the Night Officers and the Eight under Piero, and 92 a year by the two magistracies from 1500 to 1502. If the average yearly number of total convictions in the

Savonarolan period (65) was considerably higher than that between 1478 and 1492 under Lorenzo (28), it was lower than during the entire decade from Lorenzo's death through the end of 1502 (72).[84]

An analysis of the social composition of the cohort of persons incriminated and convicted for sodomy in these years reveals a number of important changes. Here again, however, the Savonarolan years proper show few distinctive features. Most of the new developments were typical of the whole decade from 1492 to 1502, and contrasted sharply with the late Lorenzan period. Among the most significant of these changes was that after Lorenzo's death the participation of youths in sodomy, always substantial, seems to have become even more prominent. The mean age of all individuals implicated to the Night Officers as the active partner in homosexual relations fell considerably, from 33.7 between 1478 and 1492, to 25.7 between 1492 and 1502. Adolescents and youths aged 30 or under accounted for 52 percent of all active partners up to 1492 (217 of 421), but fully 80 percent after 1492 (414 of 515). Ages of convicted men followed the same lines. In the earlier period, the mean age of active partners convicted by the Night Officers was 32.6, but after 1492 it fell to 25.8. Youths aged 30 or under accounted for 50 percent of the total convicted up to Lorenzo's death, but 83 percent after 1492. Ages of those implicated or convicted during the Savonarolan years did not diverge significantly from this pattern.

These figures appear to suggest, then, that toward the end of the fifteenth century, homosexual activity in Florence became identified to an even greater extent than before with adolescents and youths. But as always when using records of this sort, it is hard to determine the degree to which the apparent decline in age represents a real trend or merely greater attention to sodomy among youths. On the one hand, since the Night Officers did not act ex officio but depended solely on accusations and boys' confessions, it is unlikely that they pursued a conscious policy of persecuting the young. On the other, the prominence of incriminated and convicted youths in the century's last decade might reflect the fact that magistrates and notaries had grown more alert to the question of age and recorded it more meticulously: ages of roughly half the active partners implicated before 1492 were noted, compared with 80 percent of those after 1492. This in itself points to a new concern among the officials about age, which ended up emphasizing the attraction of Florentine youths to sodomy. In any case, whether it was new or only appeared so, the high proportion of youths incriminated for sodomy after Lorenzo's death probably helps explain why young men played such a prominent role in the opposition to Savonarola.

Another major change that characterized the last decade of the fifteenth century was the frequent punishment of minors and passive partners for the first time since the early 1440s. From 1478 to 1492, the Night Officers punished only one passive partner and three active minors (all aged 18).

But from 1492 to 1502, they condemned nineteen passives and thirty-two active minors, including several in each category as young as thirteen, fourteen, and sixteen. In the same period, the Eight also convicted at least eight young passive partners. Even when officials levied no sentence, they perhaps regularly flogged youngsters who confessed they had been sodomized, as a sentence against an eighteen-year-old active partner in 1494 suggests. He was fined 10 florins, reduced to 1 florin if he paid within eight days, or he was to be given twenty-five lashes, "as are usually given to those who commit that horrendous crime as passives."[85]

Often the penalties imposed on boys were arbitrarily lower than those levied on adults. But for passive partners over the age of eighteen, that critical legal and cultural frontier between boyhood and young manhood, punishment could be severe. In 1496 the Night Officers banished a twenty-year-old passive for five years, and in 1497 they fined another nineteen- or twenty-year-old passive the crushing sum of 200 florins.[86] Also in 1497, the Eight banished two twenty-two-year-old passives for two years, in addition to fining each 50 florins (one was given the option of receiving twenty-five lashes).[87] Such punishments reflected not only more intense repression, but also closer attention to sodomy's gender implications. The boundaries pederasty helped define between submissive boyhood and dominant manhood, between what was considered "womanly" and "manly" behavior, were being reinforced and controlled more tightly during the last years of the fifteenth century.

Perhaps related to such concerns, and certainly reflecting the growing attention to unorthodox and prohibited sexual behavior in general, a major new preoccupation with heterosexual sodomy emerged in these years.[88] During the decade 1492 to 1502, for the first time Florentines began to denounce and authorities to prosecute many cases of sodomy involving men and women. From 1478 to 1492, the Night Officers were informed of 13 cases of heterosexual sodomy and levied only 1 conviction; but after 1492, they reviewed 109 cases and handed down 37 convictions. Condemnations by the Eight for heterosexual sodomy also rose from 6 between 1478 and 1492 to 10 between 1492 and 1502. As always, it is hard to know whether this sudden and sizable appearance in the judiciary records reflected an abrupt change in behavior or, what is more likely, merely increased alertness to it. Sexual practices "against nature" must not have been unknown earlier among prostitutes, since already in 1464 the Officers of Decency had placed a pillory in the brothel area explicitly to punish whores who engaged in such acts, though in practice they rarely convicted these women for sodomy.[89] In contrast, many cases prosecuted and convicted by the Night Officers and the Eight involved prostitutes, often with multiple partners, as if some women were known and sought out for this "exotic" sexual service.[90] Prostitutes were not the only women who were allegedly sodomized, however. A wide variety of cases of heterosexual sodomy came before the courts, including men with female servants,[91] sodomitical rapes by gangs of young men,[92] and anal and oral sex between spouses, sometimes for the stated purpose of avoiding pregnancy.[93]

The social character of the policing of sodomy changed in one final significant way in the decade from 1492 to 1502, as officials after the death of Lorenzo de' Medici manifested a harsher stance toward the homosexual activity of men from ruling-class families (as identified by Anthony Molho). In absolute terms, the number of men from these dominant families who were convicted as active partners rose sharply, from fifteen by the Night Officers and two by the Eight of Watch between 1478 and 1492, to forty-one by the former and twelve by the latter between 1492 and 1502. The proportion of men from governing families among all those convicted increased only slightly, however, from 6.2 to 7.8 percent. The more punitive stance toward prominent men's sodomy emerges most clearly when one considers the judiciary fate of all men from these lineages who were implicated to the Night Officers and were eligible for conviction (that is, they were named in boys' confessions, had not denied the charge, and were not otherwise ineligible as clergymen or minors). During the Lorenzan period (1478 to 1492) officials condemned some 11.5 percent of these men from families of the ruling class (15 of 130), but after his death to 1502 they convicted nearly 42 percent (41 of 98).

It is in this context of heightened attention to the homosexual activity of males from prominent families that the single most distinctive feature of the policing of sodomy in the Savonarolan years (1495–1497) derives. During this period, when the friar's moralizing campaign became linked to the resurgence of the Republic, the number and proportion of individuals incriminated or convicted who were members of ruling-class lineages increased sharply. In all the other periods of the 1478–1502 survey, an average of between twenty-eight and thirty-two men and boys from these prominent lineages came annually to the attention of the Night Officers, but between 1495 and 1497 their number tripled to ninety every year. Men and boys from these families made up about 13 percent of all those incriminated from 1478 to Lorenzo's death in 1492, less than 11 percent during the regime of Piero de' Medici to 1494, and under 10 percent from the friar's death in 1498 to 1502, but between 1495 and 1497 they made up fully 25 percent of all those implicated. These years also stand out for the high proportion of upper-class men among people convicted. During all the other periods of this survey, men from these leading families accounted for 7 to 8 percent of the sodomites condemned by the Night Officers, but during the Savonarolan years this proportion rose substantially to nearly 18 percent (16 of 91). The combined convictions by both the Night Officers and the Eight of Watch modify these figures only slightly. Men from ruling class lineages made up 7 percent of the total convicted in the other periods of the survey (52 of 727), but 14 percent of those condemned from 1495 to 1497 (18 of 127).

This upsurge in the incrimination and conviction of individuals from prominent families of the governing class can probably be attributed, for the most part, to the political conflict and factionalism that racked the city especially after the fall of Piero de' Medici, and to the popular, anti-aristocratic elements in the Savonarolan movement.[94] Anonymous denunciations in fact account for the appearance in the records of most of these individuals, and most of them the officials simply ignored, with the result that a low proportion of only about one-third of the 114 active partners from ruling class lineages incriminated in these years were named by boys in confessions. Defamation had no political allegiance, so that followers and opponents of Savonarola as well as supporters and enemies of the Medici, even among the upper ranks of the patriciate, were denounced for sodomy.[95] No sodomites convicted in these two years, however, can be identified with certainty as partisans of any particular faction.[96] The more rigorous stance taken toward exponents of ruling families, both in these years and in the entire decade, aimed less at the highly public personalities who actually wielded political power than at an occasional notorious sodomite (such as Salvi Panuzzi) and above all at licentious upper-class youths.

Within this framework, there was a chronology of repression and popular sentiment against sodomy that provides a revealing indicator of the influence and fortunes of the Savonarolan movement between 1494 and 1498. Figure 6.2 illustrates the rhythms of the campaign against sodomy, as measured by denunciations and by the incomplete record of convictions by the Night Officers and the Eight. Overall, the most intensive repression seems to have occurred in two distinct periods. The first took place during the winter and early spring of 1495/1496, when a massive wave of accusations was followed by a high number of convictions in December, March, and April. The second and longer phase occurred in the first half of 1497, though by now denunciations had fallen off sharply. Finally, both popular sentiment against sodomy and its regulation by the courts virtually collapsed after mid-1497, as the tables began to turn on Savonarola and his supporters.

The outpouring of popular hostility against sodomy that peaked in late 1495 and early 1496 coincided roughly with the last substantive revisions in the sodomy laws in December and February, and with the organization and first public acts of Savonarola's reformed boys, including the great processions for Carnival and Palm Sunday.[97] In this first period, the friar was plainly the point of reference for many informers. For the first time in the fifteenth century, religious themes and motivations appeared frequently in denunciations, no doubt due to his influence. So great were the authority and fear Savonarola inspired that more than one informant even threatened to denounce the officials to him if they failed to act judiciously on an accusation. One writer in 1495 warned, "If you don't set this right, I'll have friar Girolamo preach and make known that you have been informed about it, for what has been told to you will be sent to him secretly in writing. So take care if you don't want to be disgraced."[98] The pious

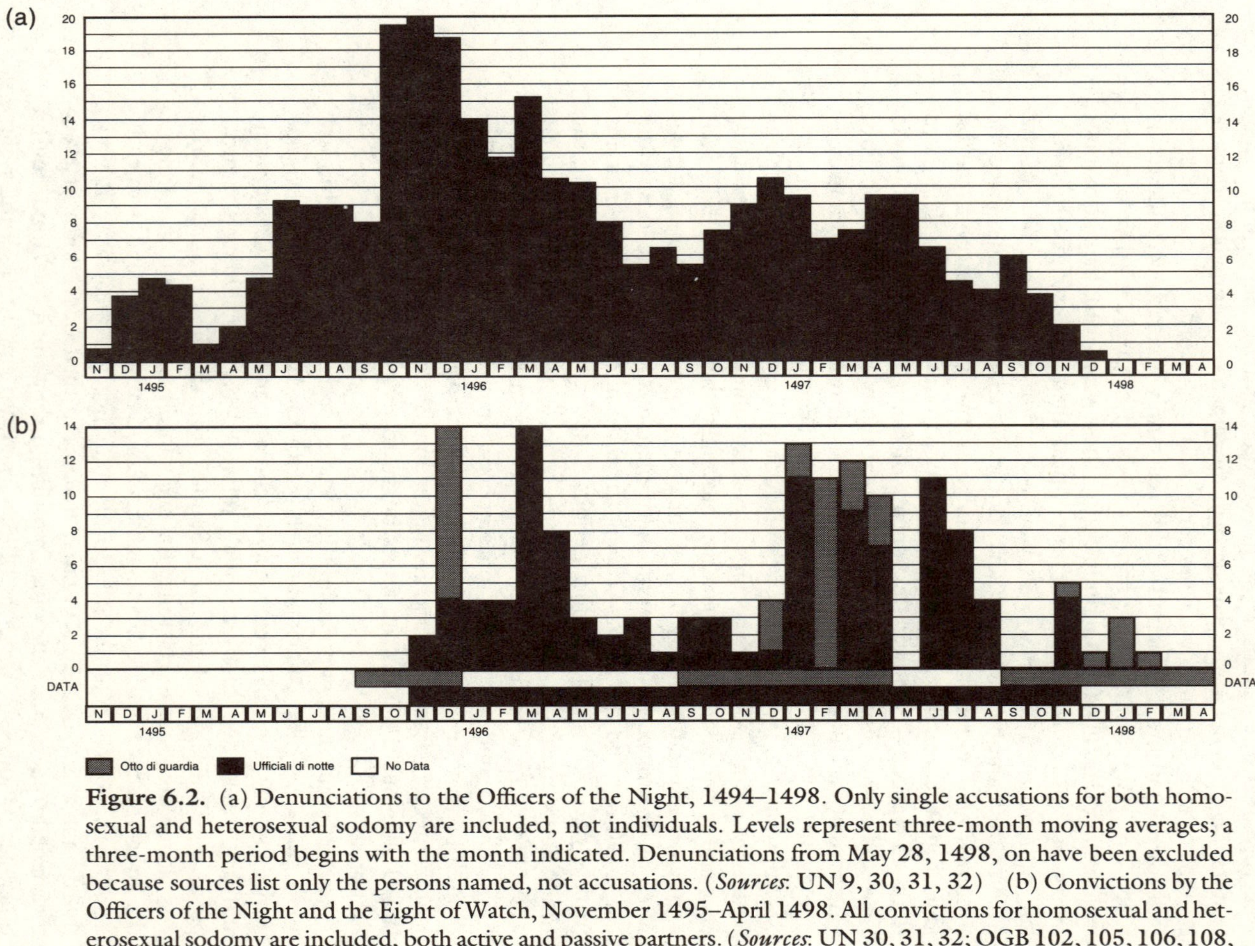

Figure 6.2. (a) Denunciations to the Officers of the Night, 1494–1498. Only single accusations for both homosexual and heterosexual sodomy are included, not individuals. Levels represent three-month moving averages; a three-month period begins with the month indicated. Denunciations from May 28, 1498, on have been excluded because sources list only the persons named, not accusations. (*Sources*: UN 9, 30, 31, 32) (b) Convictions by the Officers of the Night and the Eight of Watch, November 1495–April 1498. All convictions for homosexual and heterosexual sodomy are included, both active and passive partners. (*Sources*: UN 30, 31, 32; OGB 102, 105, 106, 108, 109)

fervor of the Piagnone movement caught up even the officials, a few of whom were known disciples of the friar. In February 1496, the Night Officers made an offering to Savonarola's boys, who for Carnival were collecting alms for the "shamed poor," and at the same time they had a devotional image of the Virgin painted for their quarters to which they prayed for guidance in their task of purging the city of sodomy.[99]

The factionalism and civil strife that plagued these years also emerged most clearly in this first intense wave of denunciations. The best example of how sodomy accusations might have been used to malign others or to create confusion comes from some twenty accusations found on March 2, 1496, against members of prominent families and important figures in the regime.[100] Their similar "defamatory" character and language suggest that they were written by the same individual or group. The accusations did not target any one faction, but named both Frateschi and adversaries of Savonarola, pro- and anti-Mediceans. To mention only a few familiar individuals among the thirty-five named, Cosimo di Bernardo Rucellai, Jacopo di Tanai de' Nerli, Piero di Gino Capponi, and Alfonso di Filippo Strozzi were all fervent opponents of both the friar and the return of the Medici.[101] Francesco di Martino Dello Scarfa, Gonfalonier of Justice when Piero de' Medici was expelled, and Luca d'Antonio degli Albizzi were important followers of Savonarola.[102] Roberto di Bernardo Nasi, son of a prominent supporter of the friar, was later "king" of a pro-Savonarolan youth group organized for a soccer match in 1497 against youths opposed to the friar, while Agostino di Girolamo Martelli, son of one of the leading Arrabbiati, was probably the "duke" of the anti-Savonarolan team.[103] Pierfilippo Pandolfini had been closely linked to Lorenzo de' Medici and belonged to the Bigi, or pro-Medicean faction, and young Lorenzo di Giovanni Tornabuoni was executed in 1497 for having plotted to restore the Medici.[104] The circumstances and nature of these accusations induced the officials to dismiss them all as "calumnious," written by "evil persons," and intended "to create discord and ignite flames in the peaceful city of Florence."[105] Other judiciary evidence, however, suggests that there was more truth to some of them than the officials were willing to admit.[106]

The second wave of intense repression, from late 1496 through mid-1497, corresponded roughly to the period in which the Frateschi party's political power and Savonarola's fame were at their height. The friar's personal credit had soared after the city miraculously escaped military disaster in November 1496. A recurrent theme in his sermons in the following months was the need to crack down severely on all vices, especially sodomy.[107] Moreover, Piagnoni dominated the Signoria for January and February 1497, when sodomy convictions rose sharply. The Gonfalonier of Justice for this term was Francesco Valori, the Frateschi party's belligerent leader. Under his tenure, the government also passed part of the reformed boys' program, regarding sumptuary regulations for boys under age fourteen, and ratified the authority of the Guardians of the Law over sodomy.[108]

There were important differences in the two periods of repression, however, that suggest a weakening in the position of the Piagnoni and in the antisodomy campaign, despite such appearances of strength. As Figure 6.2 shows, denunciations declined steadily throughout 1496. Although they rose again during this second phase, they never reached their previous heights, perhaps indicating that popular sentiment against sodomy had already abated. In addition, the ominous presence of Savonarola in earlier accusations now vanished. After May 1496, informers never mentioned him again. Finally, the astute comments of Piero Parenti, by now an open critic of the Savonarolan party, suggest that Valori's government was exploiting the crackdown on sodomy for crass political motives. During his tenure, he noted,

> gambling and sodomy were strictly prohibited, and thus we dedicated ourselves to living uprightly. It was considered, however, that those things were done more for ceremony than in truth, in order to appear good and also to be good, as long as friar Girolamo's party ruled and claimed that it, not other parties, was the sole author of good.[109]

A few pages later, Parenti referred again to the sharpened repression, branding it a flagrant bid to reinforce the Savonarolan faction:

> Other of our citizens who had fallen into the vice of sodomy were condemned and deprived of office for a time. Thus [the government] began to react with severity, in order to restrain men and keep them under religion, so that the friar's party might gain force and increase as much as possible.[110]

For Parenti, the Frateschi campaign against sodomy had become little more than a propaganda tool in the hands of crafty politicians who manipulated it for their own ends.

Although accusations and convictions remained fairly high up to mid-1497, by summer's end the repression of sodomy had virtually collapsed. Both denunciations and condemnations by the Night Officers and the Eight fell off sharply in August and never recovered while Savonarola was alive. By now, the position of the friar and his party was deteriorating. Young men had finally mounted a spirited resistance, aided by their entry into the Great Council in January 1497, when a law reduced the minimum age requirement from twenty-nine to twenty-four; a Piagnone chronicler lamented that this opened the Council's doors to "uncivil" youths who sided with the Arrabbiati against the Frateschi.[111] This opposition was led by a dissolute company of patrician youths known as the Compagnacci, whose main goal was to bring down the stern friar.[112] A pivotal victory was scored when young men staged a wild riot during Savonarola's Ascension Day sermon in the cathedral on May 4. According to chroniclers, this revolt sparked the resurgence of all those activities that had earlier been suppressed: the brothels and other taverns reopened, men gambled in public, and, it was said, sodomized with renewed zeal. Several scandalized sources reported that after the "tumult" in the cathedral, no less than an eminent official of the Republic gratefully remarked, "Thank God, now we can sodomize!"[113] The strength of the friar's adversaries and youths' disruptions and flamboyant involvement in forbidden pleasures were only reinforced when Pope Alexander VI's excommunication of Savonarola was proclaimed in the city in mid-June.[114]

The deathblow to the antisodomy campaign, however, was the bitterly contested execution on August 17, 1497, of five leading citizens charged with conspiring to restore Piero de' Medici to power.[115] The ruthless role Valori and other Piagnoni played in obtaining their harsh sentence weighed heavily against the Savonarolan party and, consequently, against its programs. From this date until mid-November, when their procedural records break off, the Night Officers convicted only one man for sodomy. The Eight, whose records are extant from September on, convicted no one in September and October, six between November and February, and none at all from then until June 1498. Denunciations tell the same revealing story: from August 17, 1497, to the end of their term in November, the Night Officers received only sixteen accusations; from then until after Savonarola's execution on May 23, 1498, nearly seven months, they found only a single denunciation in their boxes.[116] Well before the friar's downfall, then, both the authorities and the Florentine people appear to have lost interest in the cause against sodomy. For a time at least, boys and men were able to indulge in their illicit pleasures with virtual impunity.

Resistance

Savonarola's crusade against sodomy and other activities undoubtedly won him the enmity of sodomites. In response, some actively contributed to bringing about his ruin. Piagnoni chroniclers in particular gave a certain prominence to sodomites in the opposition to the friar. Giovanni Cambi, for example, recorded that among the people three things were said to account for Savonarola's downfall and execution: he prophesied the renewal of the Church against Rome and its evil prelates; he preached against the tyranny of the Medici in Florence; and he condemned vices, "especially gambling and sodomy, and [said] sodomites should be burned. So that all the people and the corrupt clergy were incited against him, and for this he was killed."[117] Unsurprisingly, Savonarola's supporters painted sodomites' and others' rebelliousness as a devilish battle of "depraved" and "lascivious" men against the humble, innocent servant of God. Putting aside this Manichaean moral judgment, perhaps we can find in their resistance to Savonarola's campaign against them evidence of sodomites' organization, group cohesiveness, and even self-conscious vindication of the legitimacy of sodomy.

Organized aggression against Savonarola and the Piagnoni came above all from the aristocratic youth company known as the Compagnacci. According to the chronicler Bartolomeo Cerretani, the group's core was formed by ten older youths known as the *vecchi* (elders) plus ten younger men, all from eminent families, with a following of several hundred other youths. To defy the friar's censure of worldly pleasures, they staged lavish, ostentatious banquets that caught the awed notice of the entire city. Adopting more direct action, they disrupted his sermons, harried his followers, and tormented his troops of boys by insulting them and attacking their processions.[118] While no one explicitly described these youths as sodomites, they were almost universally cast as dissolute young bravos who chafed under Savonarola's sexual and other restraints. Men implicated in sodomy in these years were also overwhelmingly young, so sodomites and the Compagnacci had a solid generational affinity as well as a convergence of interests in relaxing moral restrictions.

It should come as no suprise, then, if the youth brigade had sodomites in its ranks. Indeed, some of the leading Compagnacci were implicated in sodomy, though such evidence plainly needs to be weighed with caution. Their ringleader, Doffo d'Agnolo Spini, was named in a boy's confession in 1494 and denounced in 1495—that is, well before the band first appears in the sources. In 1499 the Frateschi tried unsuccessfully to get revenge on Spini and the Compagnacci by accusing him of sodomy with Tommaso Antinori's son.[119] The notorious "ser Ceccone" (Francesco di ser Barone Baroni), organizer of a celebrated Compagnacci banquet, had been jailed in Siena for sodomy as an adolescent (1465), and in 1494 was named in a boy's confession to the Night Officers.[120] Duccio Adimari, another member of the group, Jacopo di Tanai de' Nerli, and Alfonso Strozzi, who both took part in the assault on San Marco in April 1498 but were not precisely identified as Compagnacci, and others were also implicated in sodomy.[121] The infamous sodomite Pacchierotto, whose public shaming was discussed earlier, was "much favored by the Compagnacci," according to Filipepi, and was deemed (by the "whiners," no doubt) "one of the most shameful men in Florence because he derided and berated the life of friar Girolamo."[122]

Other alleged sodomites not known as Compagnacci also played an active part in the campaign to destroy Savonarola. Filipepi reported that a butcher named Giovanni di Brunetto commissioned an anti-Savonarolan libel from an Augustinian preacher and dedicated the work to his boyfriend, Carlo Federici.[123] Among the flood of songs and poems composed against the friar was a "very indecent" one by Pierandrea da Verrazzano, who reportedly attempted to sodomize a boy in 1496. The work was dedicated to Piero Soderini, future Gonfalonier of Justice for life, who was also denounced for sodomy in 1496 in the group of ostensibly "defamatory" accusations discussed earlier.[124]

Active in causing his downfall, sodomites must have reveled when Savonarola met his end on the government square on May 23, 1498. An eyewitness, the Piagnone Jacopo Nardi, recorded that during his execution a "certain ribald," almost surely a sodomite, shouted insults at the hanged friar's corpse, crying that now "the one who wanted to burn him was himself being put to the flames." Before the surprised executioner could react, the man grabbed a torch and lit the bonfire that would consume Savonarola and his two companions, thus taking out his and many other sodomites' revenge on the friar who had demanded their death or exile.[125]

The friar's death unleashed an orgy of jokes and mockery against him and his followers, including the circulation of obscene pictures of him in compromising poses with young novices.[126] According to Filipepi, after Savonarola's death the sodomites who frequented their comrade Scheggia's shop near the Old Market harrassed and derided his disciples who chanced along the street. When merchants displayed their wares for the feast of the Baptist in June, in front of his shop Scheggia placed a large live owl—a metaphor for a phallus or a *bardassa*[127]—dressed as a Dominican monk with a candle over its head and an ironic sign that bore one of Savonarola's favorite themes: "This is the true light."[128]

With the fall of Savonarola, sodomites and youths vindicated their claims to the pleasures denied them and repressed under the friar's harsh moral regime. A wave of license swept the city, provoking more than one pious Piagnone to describe these times as a hell on earth.[129] The few accusations and convictions in the years after the friar's death seem to confirm that men and boys were again able to sodomize with little fear of revelation and penalty.

But this period of sexual license was short-lived. By 1500 convictions for sodomy began to rise sharply, as will be seen later. And while young men and sodomites had won a victory with Savonarola's fall, they failed to secure it immediately by forcing changes in the laws. The repressive measures against sodomy instituted during the Savonarolan period remained intact after his death. Fines were still very high, corporal and capital penalties were now easier to apply, and in addition to the Night Officers the major Florentine tribunals now had jurisdiction over sodomy. Many changes in the policing of sodomy lay ahead—including the abolition of the "office of the sodomites"—but Florence would never again return to the fairly permissive system of the late Medicean period, with its low fines and allowances made for self-denouncers. The campaign against sodomy after Lorenzo de' Medici's death left a lasting mark both on homosexual activity and on efforts to regulate it.

The Suppression of the Office of the Night

On December 29, 1502, as part of a general restructuring of the judiciary system, the government abruptly abolished the Office of the Night. Its duties passed to the Eight of Watch and the Guardians of the Law, both of which had held full jurisdiction over sodomy respectively since 1494 and 1495.[130]

In a certain sense, the "office of the sodomites" had already become redundant with the extension of these other institutions' authority over sodomy and the leveling of distinctions in penalties. It lost its special purpose within the local judiciary and cultural system of regulating the vast field of mainly nonviolent, consensual homosexual relations. In addition, recent scandals—notaries conniving in 1498 to cover up a case, the destruction for the third time of the *tamburi* in Prato in 1500, an official in 1501 who suborned a witness and corrupted his colleagues to protect a friend—had stained the office's image and perhaps compromised its operation.[131] But it would be wrong to see the suppression of the Office of the Night merely as part of the regime's institutional housecleaning, or as an effort to end scandals and corruption, to which no local office was immune, or again as an indication that the magistracy had lost its effectiveness.

In fact, after a brief lull following Savonarola's downfall, near the end of 1500 convictions for sodomy again rose sharply, reaching levels much higher even than during the years of the friar's sway. From November 1500 to November 1502, the Night Officers levied 151 convictions for homosexual sodomy alone (145 active partners and 6 passives); the Eight, in 1501 and 1502, levied 42 convictions (34 actives and 8 passives).[132] This expansion coincided with a period of struggle within the regime over the extent of power that the republican Great Council or the traditional oligarchy would control. It was this crisis that led in 1502 to the transformation of the highest executive office, the Gonfalonier of Justice, from a two-month tenure into a lifetime appointment, filled by Piero Soderini.[133] Political confrontation probably provided much of the impetus for the intensified repression. In late 1502, the government sought to reinforce the judiciary campaign with spiritual reform when it called the preacher Giles of Viterbo to Florence, as Parenti observed, "to keep this city better disposed toward good morals." He reported that as a result of Giles's efforts—but surely due to the increased repression as well—"every vice of gambling and swearing and others declined greatly in our city."[134] Apparently, the Night Officers' role in policing sodomy had not yet been exhausted.

Why, then, did the regime decide to do away with the "office of the sodomites"? Above all, it appears that Florentines had come to consider the Office of the Night an embarrassment, an open and humiliating admission that the city had a particular problem with sodomy. Whether this discomfort was new or not is hard to determine, but sources around the turn of the century were at least more willing to express it. The law that suppressed the magistracy referred evasively to this sense of unease when it stated that the government's motive was "to remove a certain burden that is understood to ensue to the city regarding the [Office of the

Night]."[135] This reticence masked what other contemporaries, as will be seen, voiced openly: the Office of the Night had become a disgrace to the city and to the collective image the regime wanted to project.

A sense of shame and unease about this magistracy had probably been spreading among the citizenry for some years. It is striking, for instance, that even Savonarola, despite his constant demands to repress sodomy, never mentioned the Night Officers in his sermons. When he called for "justice" for this "vice," he referred only to the Eight of Watch, as if to call less attention to the "office of the sodomites." Moreover, at the time of Savonarola's greatest influence, a common citizen who shared an ideological position close to his offered the first known opinion on record that the Night Officers were an embarrassing liability to the city. In a tract published in February 1497, during the crackdown on sodomy under Francesco Valori, the mercer Domenico Cecchi put forth his plan, among other reforms, to rid the city of sodomy.[136] With unusual candor, Cecchi indicated the damage the city's image suffered, not so much on account of sodomy itself, but because of the magistracy delegated to police it. "Before all else," he urged the government, "for the honor of the city abolish the Officers of the Night, so that it cannot be said, 'Florence has a magistracy over sodomites.' For those who hate the city believe that we do nothing else here [but sodomize], and it gives us a bad reputation."[137]

Cecchi's sensitivity to such negative publicity informed his entire proposal. At a time when convicted sodomites were commonly mitered or pilloried, he discouraged this riotous ritual shaming, presumably on the grounds that it gave sodomy and sodomites too much exposure. "It is not good," he argued, "to have to stir up the people every day" for the event. Instead, he advocated an original scale of penalties for multiple offenses. His plan, which included progressive prison terms and the confiscation of property, also called for partial (and nonpublic) castration for a second conviction—"this is the real punishment," he said, "to castigate that member that commits the sin," and he pointedly noted that this would still allow the man to reproduce—and then full castration for a third conviction. Finally, for fourth-time offenders, Cecchi recommended not the publicly imposed death sentence but, significantly, lifetime seclusion "as a lunatic" in the prison ward for the insane.[138]

This shopkeeper's paradoxical proposal to do away with the compromising Office of the Night in order to rid the city of sodomy probably had little direct influence on the ruling circle's decision five years later to abolish the magistracy. But Cecchi's plan nevertheless expressed a sense of distress about an institution that evidently disturbed other Florentines as well around the turn of the century. While the government could only admit discreetly that the magistracy placed "a certain burden" on Florence, Piero Parenti's explanation pierced this veil of reticence and exposed the true nature of this "burden"—that is, the disgrace citizens felt they suffered on account of their unusual court. "The Office of the Night, which had jurisdiction over sodomites, was abolished," Parenti admitted, "because of the city's shame."[139]

Seventy years after its founding, the very magistracy created to "eradicate" sodomy had become, for Florentines and perhaps for others, a humiliating sign of the ubiquity of the practice. With their relatively indulgent regulations and lax enforcement, the Night Officers were probably never seriously intended to root out sodomy completely, but rather to contain it within acceptable bounds. The result of this strategy was that thousands of males were convicted and many thousands more implicated for their homosexual relations. Not even an effective deterrent, then, the Office of the Night only drew attention to the tenacity with which sodomy survived and flourished in Florence.

The suppression of the embarrassing magistracy brought to a close a significant chapter in Florentine efforts to police sodomy, and in particular male homosexual activity. Sodomy remained a serious crime, of course, and its control was a matter of ongoing public concern. After the Office of the Night was abolished, the Guardians of the Law and the Eight of Watch continued to prosecute the "vice" and to punish many people for it. Yet it is unlikely that convictions ever again reached the consistently high levels maintained through much of the fifteenth century under the Night Officers. The Guardians' records no longer survive, but a survey of those of the Eight from 1503 to 1514 shows that they convicted an average of seventeen men annually for homosexual sodomy and three men or women for heterosexual sodomy.[140] Frequent revisions in penalties in the first half of the sixteenth century also indicate that sodomy remained a dynamic social problem.

With the elimination of the Office of the Night, however, sodomy lost its symbolic status as an illicit sexual behavior that required extraordinary institutional attention. It was now reintegrated into the broader spectrum of criminality controlled and punished by the city's central judiciary organs. Although from all indications homosexual activity continued to be a vital part of Florentine sexual and social life, the city's reputation, at least in the hopes of the local oligarchy, would be less compromised by the existence of a telltale "office of the sodomites."

Epilogue: Change and Continuity in the Policing of Sodomy in the Sixteenth Century

In the decades following the suppression of the Office of the Night, the regulation of sodomy underwent several changes that attest to its continuing importance during the twilight of the Florentine Republic and the early Medicean principate. Following a precedent set in the late fifteenth century, reforms in the laws against sodomy followed swiftly after political upheavals—notably the fall of the "popular" regime and the restoration of the Medici in 1512; the second exile of the Medici in 1527 and the brief Republican revival; and, at a slightly greater distance, the installation of the Medicean duchy in 1532. As each new regime redrew the city's political configuration, it also reorganized the management of sodomy. Yet this was not the only sign of how closely the "abominable vice" was tied to the sociopolitical dynamics of the Florentine community. The growing rigidity of the political and social hierarchy was reflected in laws against sodomy, which for the first time set different penalties for citizens and mere subjects. Also for the first time, late Republican laws prescribed varying penalties for different age groups, with youths receiving preferential treatment. Evidently, the latter changes were made in recognition of youths' prominence in sodomitical activity as well as their new political visibility, both of which perhaps had their roots in the experiences and conflicts of the 1490s.

Unfortunately, judiciary records of the early sixteenth century shed little light on these developments. With the abolition of the Office of the Night, this unequaled source of information on the nature and social features of sodomy, community attitudes, and enforcement of the laws also vanished. The records of the Guardians of the Law survive only from 1532, while those of the Eight of Watch, with the exceptions of accusations for a few years and of occasional absolutions, preserve only convictions and generally lack the detail that distinguished the Night Officers' records. These limitations do not permit a reconstruction and analysis of the rich social and sexual texture of homosexual activity in the first half of the sixteenth century comparable to that which was possible for the fifteenth century. Nonetheless, the prescriptive sources themselves, along with observations by chroniclers and by the few informers, suggest ways in which adjustments in the policing of sodomy were connected to broader changes in Florentine public and private life, to an emerging political identity of the *giovani* (youth), and to mutations in the ruling regime in the transition from the Republic to the principate.

In the early sixteenth century, the visibility of youths in sodomy, always high, grew even more prominent, in line with Florentines' conviction that the disorderly and wanton behavior of young men now knew no bounds.[1] Informers for the first time began to identify the *giovani* (youths aged roughly 18 to between 35 and 40) collectively as the generational group typically associated with sodomy and other bawdy activities. An eloquent example comes from an accusation written in 1510, possibly by an anguished father who feared the shame he might bring down on his own house but felt compelled by despair to denounce the corruption of his son. He begged the Eight to punish Masina di mona Appollonia, "ravenous wolf of all the Florentine youth," who operated a *casino*/brothel in her house "for the dregs of all the ribalds of this city, misleaders of the poor youth, whom they bring here not only for sodomy but for gambling and things so shameful they can't easily be named." Alluding perhaps to his son, the informer said he was "marked and shamefully entangled, on account of my intimate affairs," and admitted that he would gladly keep quiet "if I weren't obligated to those things that I am forced to love like my own self."[2] A second accusation castigated the same woman as the "ruin of many youths, for besides spending everything they have, they learn to be dissolute and wicked."[3] Another informer denounced youths in the nearby village of Impruneta who hung about at night under the porticoes, vandalizing things and boasting about their sexual endowment and prowess.[4] Identifying a *casino* where gambling and sodomy occurred, yet another accuser in 1512 specified that youths (*garzoni*) frequented the place and had sex there with boys (*fanciulli*).[5] The chronicler Giovanni Cambi also emphasized the promiscuity of youths in these years. He interpreted a blizzard that ruined crops in 1511 as a warning from heaven because the city had failed to administer justice and to restrain the "wickedness of young men," who went about armed at night causing brawls and even murdering people "on account of sodomy and prostitutes."[6] Again in 1527, he condemned licentious patrician and working-class youths who met in taverns to feast, drink, gamble, and sodomize.[7]

Nothing better justifies the prominent role in sodomy ascribed to youths than the remarkable defense of convicted sodomites by a band of young aristocrats during a daring raid on city hall that helped overturn the Republican regime in 1512. On August 31, with Spanish and Medicean troops at the city gates, some thirty young partisans of the Medici led by twenty-three-year-old Antonfrancesco degli Albizzi invaded the government palace and forced the Gonfalonier Piero Soderini to resign. According to Cambi, the youths then stormed into the chambers of the bewildered priors—who were "like a fly without a head," as he put it—and demanded that they revoke the sentences of all those who had been exiled or deprived of office for sodomy.[8]

The young men's incredible request temporarily went unmet, as the priors, whose tenure ended the same evening, declined responsibility. It was soon honored by the youths' patrons, however. The next day, Giuliano de' Medici, son of Lorenzo the Magnificent, entered the city accompanied by Antonfrancesco degli Albizzi, and youths formed a conspicuous part of his retinue around the city in the following days and in his palace coup on September 16. A commission was created to reform the state, and on September 24 it authorized five citizens, among them Albizzi, to reinstate anyone exiled or convicted for any reason, including, Cambi specified, "those who were reprimanded for sodomy."[9]

These youths' concerted action to obtain pardons for their comrades convicted of sodomy succeeded, no doubt due in part to their support of the young Medicean leaders. Indeed, one person whose sentence they probably intended to overturn was the adolescent Giovanni di Giovanni di Pierfrancesco de' Medici, later known as Giovanni delle Bande Nere, famed condottiere and father of the second Medici duke of Florence, Cosimo I. The Soderini government had banished Giovanni in 1511 for his involvement in the sodomitical rape of a sixteen-year-old boy of the Neretti family.[10]

With such a prologue, it was only a matter of time before the laws against sodomy still in force since the Savonarolan years were reformed. On January 24, 1514, in the very first action taken by the newly created legislative councils of the restored Medicean regime, a law was passed that substantially mitigated the harsh penalties for sodomy of the "popular" regime.[11] It reduced the initial penalty for some offenders, reinstated graduated fines, made corporal punishment optional instead of obligatory, and, at the end of the scale, replaced the death penalty in most cases with exile or loss of office-holding privileges. This edict's chief innovation, however, was to set penalties not only according to repeated offenses, as in the past, but also according to age and eligibility for office. Two progressive scales of penalties were created, one for youths aged eighteen to twenty-five, beginning with a reduced fine of 30 florins, and the other for men over twenty-five, beginning with a fine of 60 florins (the law did not mention minors). Within each age category, moreover, both the sanctions and the number of convictions allowed before incurring the harshest penalty varied according to political status; the scale of possible convictions was more limited for sodomites ineligible for civic office and more generous for citizens.[12]

With another law just six years later, in 1520, however, the government revised and generally moderated penalties once again, reasoning that those who engaged in sodomy "are persons of different conditions, and the crimes are committed in different ways and have various importance, so that some should be punished with more severe penalties, and others with lighter penalties than those ordained in the last law of January [1514]."[13] The prejudicial provisions against men ineligible for office were attenuated considerably, and penalties for all—except for citizen youths under twenty-five, who had been most favored in the 1514 law—were lightened even further. Whatever their political qualifications, however, youths who committed sodomy maintained their special legal status. They continued to be fined at the lower scale; also with this law, the death sentence was limited to men over the age of twenty-five for their third conviction, while youths aged twenty-five or under were at most to be exiled or jailed for life or, if eligible to hold office, deprived of this privilege.[14]

The laws against sodomy promulgated by the Medicean regime certainly suggest a more lenient stance toward its control than that of the "popular" government installed in 1494. At the same time, the distinctions in age and citizen status inscribed in these laws both reflected and helped to articulate some important sociopolitical features of the new regime. That qualifications for citizenship for the first time determined penalties for sodomy mirrored and probably served to reinforce the increasingly hierarchical character of social and civic life in Florence, now on the road toward the Medicean principate.[15] Equally striking is the favored treatment given to youths. These edicts acknowledged and to some extent accommodated young men's special affinity for sodomy. As the evidence from the late fifteenth century suggests, occasional sodomy was especially widespread among just this cohort of young men who were not yet of customary marriageable age and, if citizens, still too young to assume significant political responsibilities. It was these youths under twenty-five who were accorded greater license to sodomize. But when young men reached the age at which they would probably take a wife and start a family and, if eligible, begin to hold civic office, or when their sodomy was no longer simply a youthful foible but perhaps assumed a more habitual slant, they would be punished harshly. The lenient provisions for the young likely responded to political interests as well. Their timing and character suggest that they might have been a gesture of recognition for the loyalty that youths had shown the Medici in helping restore the family to power, loyalty that the Medici in turn assiduously courted.[16]

Importantly, the combination of favoritism toward youths and their apparent prominence in sodomy seems to have elicited generational tensions over homosexuality. These conflicts are nicely illustrated in an anecdote told by the art historian and critic Giorgio Vasari. In 1515 the winner of the horse race, or *palio*, for the feast of the Baptist was a horse owned by the flamboyant Sienese painter Giovanbattista Bazzi, known as Sodoma for his overt erotic interests in young males. Following custom, after the race boys and youths trooped through the city shouting the victor's name: "Sodoma! Sodoma!" Vasari noted that the cries of "such a filthy name" scandalized certain "old notables" (*vecchi uomini da bene*), who in turn stirred up a violent mob against Sodoma and his horse.[17] Although age discrimination had tinged the control of sodomy in the past—witness the high proportion of young men convicted in the late fifteenth century—this is the first time known to me that a Florentine source explicitly located one font of opposition to sodomy among the *vecchi*.[18]

Within the limits posed by extant records, a study of how legal norms were enforced during the Medicean restoration might add important detail to the general picture provided by the laws. Lacking this, contemporary reports furnish some rough indications. Despite the more lenient regulations, violent or highly offensive acts of sodomy still provoked harsh reactions, now as in the past. In 1520 a married artisan who sodomized his own son had his flesh torn with pincers and was then burned to death; in 1521, after a captain and six soldiers in the service of a papal condottiere gang-raped two local boys, archbishop Giulio de' Medici had the captain arrested (his friends fled) and hanged from a window of the Bargello.[19]

In general, however, sodomy in this period appears to have aroused little concern. A comment by Giovambattista Busini in a letter to Benedetto Varchi neatly contrasted Medicean attitudes toward sodomy with those of the brief anti-Medicean Republic between 1527 and 1530. Busini recounted that "during the time of the Medici, when not much attention was paid to [sodomy]," Piero di Giovanni Altoviti, a wealthy aristocrat, was tried twice "as a bugger" (*per buggerone*), but got off by paying money. Then in 1529, "during the time of the people," he sodomized and injured a serving woman, and according to the statutes he was to be burned to death. Now his wealth and the pressure of powerful relatives were of no avail. The magistrates paid deference to his status only by having him hanged and burned inside the open door of the Bargello, the judiciary palace, instead of executing him publicly.[20]

The second exile of the Medici in 1527, and the short-lived resurrection of the Republic (1527–1530), did in fact bring swiftly in their wake a harsh reaction against sodomy. Just as in 1494 when the previous Medicean government fell, the new regime took quick action against the "nefarious and detestable vice" with a law passed on June 16, 1527, one month after the Medici left the city.[21] As in the earlier edict inspired by Savonarola, republican and religious rhetoric pervaded this new law. The first duty of every republic, its preamble stated, was to ensure upright and just government by repressing all vices, "especially those that are the most potent and principal cause of the city's ruin." According to the holy scriptures, it was said, sodomy was the act that most provoked the divine majesty's wrath, and consequently was the main reason nations were destroyed. The new regime, therefore, intent on "reducing the entire dominion to an upright and holy way of life," determined to intensify the repression of sodomy in the interests of the "common good."

The penalties this law prescribed were considerably harsher than those under the Medici. At the same time, this ruling not only preserved but also further articulated some of the social distinctions of previous laws, especially regarding youths. Most important, it created a third age category, of twenty-five- to thirty-year-olds, for men eligible for office, while for ineligible men it extended the benefits for youths to include all eighteen- to thirty-year-olds. Although penalties for both youths and men over thirty were raised, the young continued to enjoy a privileged legal status with respect to older men, whose punishments were much harsher.[22] The legal space young men had won was thus confirmed and even expanded—again an acknowledgment of how common sodomy was among them, and perhaps also a sign of recognition of the crucial role youths played in bringing about the Republican revolution and would continue to exercise in its defense.[23]

A final provision of the 1527 law suggests that sodomy was also becoming linked, at least in the eyes of Florentine governors, to new intellectual and religious currents that threatened to subvert both the spiritual and the social order. During the 1520s, the Protestant revolt against Rome had spread, and lawmakers were concerned that this challenge to Catholicism, to which local youths were apparently quite attracted,[24] might mix with the seductive appeal of illicit sex, a fear likely fueled by the growing allure of libertine thought.[25] The present age, as they stated in this law, was characterized by "indecent and shameful practices and discussions," especially disputes "about the faith and sacred things," which were often derided and held in contempt. Moreover, young men and women were incited to do evil by malicious persons and "by dishonest and libidinous discussions, requests, and temptations, especially about sodomy." "Disorders, excesses, and very grievous sins" resulted that dishonored God and endangered both the public and the private interest. To stifle such loose talk and occasions to sin, this edict authorized the Guardians of the Law to punish anyone considered guilty of these discussions and incitements with a fine of 5 florins or any other fitting corporal punishment.[26]

Not long after the fall of the Last Republic in 1530, and the definitive abolition of republican institutions with the installation of the Medicean duchy in 1532, penalties for sodomy underwent yet another revision. The tortuous history of Florentine legislative efforts to police sodomy during the late Middle Ages and the Renaissance drew to an end with a law of July 8, 1542, promulgated by the second duke of Florence, Cosimo I de' Medici (ruled 1537–1564).[27] In some ways this harsh law, the most severe since the Savonarolan period, also appears to signify the end of a certain social, political, and cultural environment in which sodomy had long flourished.

It was perhaps a sign of changing sensibilities that for the first time in Florence, natural calamities—an earthquake in the Mugello valley north of the city and lightning bolts that damaged the cathedral cupola and the government palace—directly inspired a law against sodomy. People feared that these prodigies were portents of great ruin and flocked to the miraculous image of the Annunciation in the Servite basilica to make votive offerings. In response, as the contemporary historian Bernardo Segni observed, "Duke Cosimo, extremely frightened, put himself in God's hands and, supported by the clergy, created two very severe laws, one against blasphemy and the other against sodomy, imposing very harsh penalties on delinquents, even death."[28]

This repressive edict was one of numerous judiciary reforms undertaken by the young Medici duke to consolidate the new princely state.[29] Reflecting Cosimo's absolutist pretensions, it also introduced a new notion in Florence of sodomy as a personal affront to the monarch. According to the law's preamble, sodomy was a "great offense" against God as well as a dishonor to mankind, but it especially offended and dishonored the prince, who was "appointed to the care, government and rule of the people." Sodomy had to be extinguished "so that in his city and dominion people will live in fear of his immense Majesty and with proper decency, as is expected in civil life."[30] The message was evidently not lost on Florentines. The diarist Antonio da Sangallo reported in 1543 on the arrests and imprisonment of a group of leading courtiers and Medici partisans on account, it was rumored, of sodomy, "the abominable vice, with which the city was infested as never before." According to Sangallo, this was the background against which many Florentines, "as persons who were always insatiable," were beginning to hope and agitate for "some kind of ruin against the Duke, who was gradually becoming more strict with his subjects."[31]

This law differed considerably from earlier Florentine measures to regulate sodomy, both in the harsh penalties it prescribed and in other features. While distinctions between citizens and subjects were partly maintained, the age classes for adults and their corresponding penalties that had favored youths were now abolished. This change possibly signaled a new generational outlook in Medicean domestic politics—which had traditionally sought to foster the support of youths—especially since young men had abandoned the Medici in their spirited defense of the Last Republic.[32] This edict instead returned to the simpler penal distinction of the distant past between minors and adults, though it extended the age of majority to twenty instead of eighteen. It also prescribed severe penalties, differentiated by sexual role, for minors, who had been virtually ignored in law and in judiciary practice for a century (with the exception of the 1490s).[33]

Another significant novelty was the singling out for exemplary punishment of adult men who took the passive role in sexual relations with men. For a second conviction, all active partners, regardless of age or status, plus passive partners up to the age of twenty, were to be fined 100 scudi and sentenced to forced labor on the galleys for life. The one exception was for a man aged twenty or above who let someone sodomize him, a practice that the fifteenth-century sources indicate was both rare and deemed highly disgraceful. Found guilty a second time, the "passive" adult was to be "burned publicly as a wicked and infamous man . . . for his own punishment and as an example to others." For all others, death was mandated only for a third offense.[34] For the first time in the city's history, this edict encoded Florentine repugnance against men who violated the long-standing cultural taboo on adult sexual passivity, thereby compromising their own and their society's masculinity.

Another unprecedented feature of this law was the attention it paid to the nature and extent of an individual's involvement in sodomy. Against those who had committed sodomy more than once with the same or different partners, the edict ordered judges to levy harsher penalties at their discretion, even up to the death sentence, depending on "the quality of the persons, the length of time they have persevered in this vice, the number of those with whom they have committed this error, and the habit they have made of it."[35] Previously the number of partners and the frequency of sexual encounters had had no apparent effect on either sentences or penalties, though magistrates tended, somewhat inconsistently, to levy harsher penalties on "inveterate" sodomites who came frequently to their attention.[36] Among other things, fifteenth-century officials' lack of concern with such details had permitted a sexual culture to flourish in which teenage prostitution and promiscuity were common and men could act on their homoerotic desires repeatedly and over long periods of their lives. This new measure, however, drew a sharper distinction between those whose involvement in sodomy was fleeting or casual and those, more culpable and subject to greater stigma, whose illicit erotic activity was more intense or habitual.

In many respects, therefore, the harsh provisions of the 1542 law seem to delineate a hardening of attitudes toward sodomy and a repressive turn in measures to police it. But this law also had contradictory effects that again underline the persistent difficulty and ambiguities of managing sodomy in Florence. Segni reported that at first the laws on sodomy and blasphemy were enforced "with no little rigor." Even figures like the aristocrat Pandolfo Pucci, whose father, Roberto, was a cardinal, and the faithful Medicean Giovanni Bandini, both of whom openly and "shamelessly" engaged in sodomy, landed in prison.[37] An English visitor to Florence, William Thomas, attested to the effects of this heightened repression, observing that "where they have been much burdened with sodomy in time past, I cannot perceive there is any such thing now."[38] But Segni also noted that "within a short time [these laws] lost all their authority, not so much because of the negligence of the Duke, but because of the negligence of other magistrates and ministers of justice."[39] A review of judiciary records for the central decades of the sixteenth century has found, in fact, that while condemnations for sodomy burgeoned in the 1540s, they dropped off sharply in the 1550s.[40] From this point on, convictions remained fairly insignificant in number (though not in the severity of punishments) well into the seventeenth century.[41] Despite changing conditions and a brief flurry of repression, then, Florentine authorities apparently continued to treat sodomy, for the most part, with the relative indulgence that had often characterized the past.

The eighteenth-century historian of the Medicean principate, Riguccio Galluzzi, perhaps pinpointed one reason why magistrates eventually hesitated to enforce the draconian penalties against men and boys who engaged in sodomy. Drawing on unidentified sources, he noted that after the law's passage, citizens "of quality" were arrested, and the courts even began to investigate acts allegedly committed before the publication of the law. The response to this increased terror, he claimed, was a mass exodus of fearful citizens and artisans who fled the city, producing a drain on resources and skills so considerable that it was "not without prejudice to the crafts and to commerce."[42] If the historian's comment was near the mark, then sodomy was evidently still widespread enough in Florence that its harsh repression could have a negative impact on the local economy.

Sensitive as always to the intricate web of material and social factors in which sodomy was bound up, and well aware of the difficulty and potential consequences of excavating too deeply into the pervasive practice, authorities apparently preferred to relax their vigilance. They tacitly allowed men, or at least some men, to sodomize in the greater interests of the "common good."

Appendix A
Penalties Levied

Table A.1. Penalties Levied by the Officers of the Night, 1478–1494

Penalties	*Alternatives*
Fines (343)	
3 fl (1)	None (1)
1F (1)	None (1)
4F (1)	Prison 4 mo (1)
5F (18)	None (13); 1 sack fl (5)
10F (280)	None (114); 2 fl (1), 3 fl (3), 16 fl (1); 3 grossi to 1F (68); 1F or 25 lashes (4); 1.5F–4F (15); 5F (2); pillory 1 h (1); prison: 6–15 d (47), 1 mo (22), 2–4 mo (2)
15F (12)	None (2); 2F–5F (2); 10F or prison 1 mo (5); prison 6 d to 1 mo (3)
19.5F (1)	Prison (length illegible) (1)
20F (5)	None (1); 6F–10F (4)
25F (21)	None (12); 4F–5F (2); 10F–15F (6); prison 1 yr (1)
50F (3)	None (1); 10F (1); 25F (1)
Public Humiliation (4)	
20 lashes (1)	None (1)
25 lashes (1)	None (1)
2 h pillory (1)	None (1)
2 h pillory, mitered (1)	None (1)
Prison (8)	
5 wk (1)	3F (1)
2 mo (1)	10F (1)
2 mo 3 wk (1)	None (1)
4 mo (1)	25F (1)
6 mo (2)	None (1); 10F (1)
1 yr (1)	None (1)
1 yr + 10F (1)	None (1)
Public Humiliation and Prison (1)	
50 lashes + prison 3 yr (1)	Prison 1 yr + 10F (1)

Note: £, lire; F, florin(s); fl, bushel(s) of flour; h, hour(s); d, day(s); wk, week(s); mo, month(s); yr, year(s). Numbers in parentheses refer to the number of people sentenced (active partners only).

Table A.2. Penalties Levied by the Eight of Watch, 1478–1494

Penalties	*Alternatives*
Fines (46)	
12 fl + 4£ (1)	None (1)
14 fl + 66 gallons wine (1)	None (1)
1F–4F (13)	None (10); 2F–6 ducats (3)
5F + 4 fl (1)	None (1)
6F–10F (9)	None (3); 3F–5F (6)
12F–20F (6)[a]	None (4); 10F (1); 10F + 6 fl (1)
25F (1)	6F (1)
30F (2)	15F (1); 30 fl (1)
50F (3)	None (1); 20F + 10F for dowry of boy's sister (1); 25F or prison 5 yr (1)
60F (2)	30F (2)
300£ (1)	100£ (1)
100F (1)	20F (1)
200F (2)	None (1); 50F + 36 fl (1)
800£ (1)	200£ (1)
1000£ (1)	400£ + 36 fl (1)
500F (1)[b]	100F (1)
Public Humiliation (7)	
Pillory 1 h, mitered, whipped (1)	None (1)
6 rope blows (1)	12 fl (1)
10–12 lashes (3)	None (3)
25 lashes (2)	30F–50F (2)
Public Humiliation and Fine (5)	
Offering nude to Annunziata + 2F (1)	None (1)
4 tratti di corda, offering nude to Annunziata, 10F (1)	None (1)
4 tratti di corda, 40 lashes, 15F (1)	None (1)
Pillory 2 hours, 25F (1)	10F (1)
Whipped riding ass, nose and ears cut off, and 1500F (1)	200F and 1500£ (1)
Prison (13)	
1 mo (1)	None (1)
3 mo (1)	5F and 5 lashes (1)
6 mo (3)	None (1); 10F + 10 lashes (2)
2 yr (5)	10F (2); 20F, or 10F in 6 d (2); 30F, or 15F in 6 d (1)
4 yr (1)	80F, or 40F in 11 (1)
5 yr (1)	10F (1)
Life (1)	50F in 1 wk (1)
Public Humiliation and Prison (11)	
Mitered, 10 lashes on bare buttocks, prison 10 yr (1)	None (1)
2 rope blows, prison 6 mo (1)	10F (for prison only) (1)
25 lashes, prison 2 yr (1)	10F (1)
25 lashes, prison life (1)	None (1)
4 tratti di corda, prison 2 yr (1)	10F (for prison only) (1)
4 tratti di corda, 25 lashes, prison 3 yr (1)	10F (for prison only) (1)
4 tratti di corda, prison life (1)	50F, 300£, deprived of office 5 yr (1)
50 lashes, prison 10 yr (1)	30F, exile 1 yr (1)
50 lashes, prison life (1)	None (1)

Penalties	*Alternatives*
Mitered and whipped while riding ass, prison 5 yr (1)	400£ and prison 3 yr (1)
Mitered and whipped through streets, prison indef. (1)	None (1)
Exile (26)	
During Carnival (1)	None (1)
2 mo (1)	None (1)
8 mo (1)	None (1)
1 yr (5)	None (4); 6F (1)
2 yr (4)	None (3); 60£ (1)
3 yr (6)	None (1); 15F (3); 60£ (1); 25F, or 6F in 8 d (1)
4 yr (1)	None (1)
5 yr (2)	None (2)
6 yr (1)	None (1)
10 yr (4)	None (3); 40F (1)
Public Humiliation and Exile (13)	
3 rope blows, exile 10 yr (1)	None (1)
20 lashes, exile 10 yr (1)	None (1)
25 lashes + exile 1 yr (1); 4 yr (1); 5 yr (1); 10 yr (1)	None (4)
30 lashes, exile 3 yr (1)	10F (1)
Mitered, 25 lashes, exile 5 yr (1)	None (1)
Mitered, 10 lashes on bare buttocks, exile 1 yr (3)	None (3)
Mitered and whipped, 12 lashes on bare buttocks, exile 6 yr (1)	None (1)
Mitered and whipped riding ass, nose cut off, exile life (1)	None (1)
Fine and Exile (4)	
10F, exile 1 yr (1)	None (1)
10F, exile 2 yr (1)	5F (for fine only) (1)
20F, exile 5 yr (1)	10F (for fine only) (1)
100F, exile 20 yr (1)	None (1)
Fine, Ban from Office, Exile (1)	
300F, exile 3 yr, deprived of office indef. (1)	None (1)
Public Humiliation, Ban from Office, Exile (1)	
Mitered, exile 6 yr, deprived of office indef. (1)	25F (for mitering only) (1)
Execution (1)	
By burning (1)	50F (1)

Note: £, lire; F, florin(s); fl, bushel(s) of flour; h, hour(s); d, day(s); wk, week(s); mo, month(s); yr, year(s). Numbers in parentheses refer to the number of people sentenced (active partners only).

[a]One man, fined 12F, also had to pay fines of 40F for each of an unspecified number of his passive partners.

[b]A collective fine levied against a large group of Jews, one of whom was charged with sodomy.

Table A.3. Penalties Levied by the Officers of the Night, 1495–1502

Penalties	*Alternatives*
Fines (213)	
2F (4)	None (2); 1F (2)
8F (1)	None (1)
25F (1)	7F (1)
50F (193)	None (182); pillory 1 hr (9); 25F (1); absolved if gives proof of minor age (1)
100F (8)	None (2); 50F (6)
200F (6)	50F (6)
Public Humiliation (36)	
Pillory	
1 h (15)	50F (15)
1 h, mitered (6)	50F (6)
1 h + 50F (1)	Pillory 1 h (for fine only) (1)
2 h (2)	None (1); 75F (1)
2 h, mitered (1)	50F
Mitered and whipped (7)	10F (5); 25F (1); 50F (1)
Mitered and branded (4)	None (4)
Exile (6)	
1 yr (1)	None (1)
2 yr (3)	None (1); 20F (1); 50F (1)
30 mo (2)	20F (1); 50F (1)
Public Humiliation and Exile (1)	
Pillory 1 h, mitered, + life exile (1)	None (1)
Execution (3)	
By beheading (1)	300F and life prison (1)
By burning (2)	None (2)
Unknown (3)	

Note: £, lire; F, florin(s); fl, bushel(s) of flour; h, hour(s); d, day(s); wk, week(s); mo, month(s); yr, year(s). Numbers in parentheses refer to the number of people sentenced (active partners only).

Table A.4. Penalties Levied by the Eight of Watch, 1495–1502

Penalties	*Alternatives*
Fines (43)	
24 fl (2)	None (2)
60£ (2)	Certain amounts of bread (2)
20F (2)	10F (2)
30F (1)	15F (1)
50F (27)	None (18); 36F (1); 20F (1); pillory 1 hr (7)
100F (6)	50F (5); 50F + 16fl (1)
150F (1)	75F + 24 fl (1)
200F (2)	50F (1); 80F (1)
Public Humiliation (19)	
Pillory 1 h (16)	None (3); 20F (1); 50F (12)
Pillory 1 h, mitered (1)	50F (1)
Pillory 2 h (1)	50F (1)
Mitered, whipped to Mercato Vecchio, branded (1)	None (1)
Public Humiliation and Fine (3)	
Pillory 1 h, 100F, 16 fl (1)	50F (1)
Pillory 2 h, 100F (1)	50F (for fine only) (1)
Pillory 1 h, mitered, 40£ to boy's father (1)	50F, + 40£ to boy's father (1)
Prison (1)	
10 yr (1)	None (1)
Public Humiliation and Prison (2)	
Pillory 1 h, prison 2 yr (1)	50F (1)
Pillory 2 h, prison 2 yr (1)	None (1)
Exile (26)	
1 yr (3)	50F (3)
2 yr (1)	40£ (1)
3 yr (3)	None (1); appear next day (2)
4 yr (1)	25F (1)
5 yr (5)	None (1); 50F (4)
8 yr (1)	100F (1)
10 yr (3)	None (2); 50F (1)
Life (9)	None (3); 50F (2); 50F + 16 fl (4)
Public Humiliation and Exile (6)	
Pillory 1 hr + exile 1 yr (1); 2 yr (1)	50F (for exile only) (2)
Pillory 1 hr, branded, exile 2 yr (1)	None (1)
Mitered and whipped, exile 1 yr (1)	None (1)
Mitered and whipped while riding ass, branded, exile 5 yr (1)	None (1)
Mitered and whipped, branded, exile 10 yr (1)	50F after 5 yr exile (1)
Fine and Exile (1)	
50F, exile 3 yr (1)	Pillory 1 h (for fine only) (1)
Execution (7)	
By beheading (2)	None (2)
By burning (5)	None (3); appear in 4 days (2)

Note: £, lire; F, florin(s); fl, bushel(s) of flour; h, hour(s); d, day(s); wk, week(s); mo, month(s); yr, year(s). Numbers in parentheses refer to the number of people sentenced (active partners only).

Appendix B
Statistical Tables

Table B.1. Ages of Partners in Homosexual Sodomy, 1478–1502[a]

	Passives				*Actives*			
	Office of the Night		*Catasto*		*Office of the Night*		*Catasto*	
Age	*No.*	*%*	*No.*	*%*	*No.*	*%*	*No.*	*%*
≤18	426[b]	89.7	66	91.7	136[c]	17.5	11	7.0
19≥	49[d]	10.3	6	8.3	641	82.5	146	93.0
Total	475	100.0	72	100.0	777	100.0	157	100.0

[a]In both samples, ages were computed and recorded for each year an individual appeared in the judiciary records (e.g., in the Catasto column the age given is not necessarily the age recorded in 1480).
[b]Includes forty-one individuals identified only as *puer* (boy) and eight as aged eighteen or under.
[c]Includes forty-six individuals with no precise age recorded but who were absolved as minors aged eighteen or under, plus three identified as *puer* or *fanciullo* (boy).
[d]Includes one person designated as a *giovane* (youth).
Sources: UN 19–35; Catasto (1480).

Table B.2. Ages of Partners in the Passive Role, 1478–1502[a]

Age	*Office of the Night*	*Catasto*	*Age*	*Office of the Night*	*Catasto*
6	2	0	17	78	5
7	0	0	18	50	6
8	5	0	19	17	4
9	1	0	20	18	1
10	7	2	21	4	0
11	1	0	22	4	0
12	6	6	23	1	1
13	23	9	24	1	0
14	46	13	25	1	0
15	76	15	26	2	0
16	82	10			

[a]See Table B.1, note a. Here I have excluded the one confirmed example of an older man who took the passive role, Salvi Panuzzi. His exceptional case and similar allegations are discussed in chapter 3.
Sources: UN 19–35; Catasto (1480).

Table B.3. Ages in Relations Involving Two Minors Aged Eighteen or Under, 1478–1502

Age of Passive	*Partner Younger*	*Partner Same Age or Older*
10	0	11
11	0	4
12	0	0
13	0	12
14	0	16
15	3	24
16	3	30
17	3	21
18	2	4

Source: UN 19–35.

Table B.4. Ages in Relations Involving a Passive Partner Aged Nineteen or Older, 1478–1502

Age of Passive	*Partner Younger*	*Partner Same Age or Older*
19	0	6
20	7	10
21	1	7
22	0	2
23	0	1
24	0	3

Source: UN 19–35.

Table B.5. Aggregate Ages of Males Implicated in Sodomy, 1478–1502[a]

	Office of the Night[b]		*Catasto*	
Age	*No.*	*%*	*No.*	*%*
≤18	562	44.9	77	33.6
19–30	476	38.0	65	28.4
31–40	138	11.0	43	18.8
41–50	51	4.1	24	10.5
51–60	17	1.4	11	4.8
≥61	8	0.6	9	3.9
Total	1,252	100.0	229	100.0

[a]See Table B.1, note a.
[b]See Table B.1, notes b–d.
Sources: UN 19–35; Catasto (1480).

Table B.6. Ages of Partners in the Active Role, 1478–1502[a]

	Office of the Night		*Catasto*		*Self-accusers*	
Age	*No.*	*%*	*No.*	*%*	*No.*	*%*
≤18	136[b]	17.5	11	7.0	4	9.8
19–30	427	55.0	59	37.6	10	24.3
31–40	138	17.8	43	27.4	14	34.1
41–50	51	6.6	24	15.3	6	14.6
51–60	17	2.2	11	7.0	3	7.3
≥61	8	1.0	9	5.7	4	9.8
Total	777	100.1	157	100.0	41	99.9

[a]See Table B.1, note a.
[b]See Table B.1, note c.
Sources: UN 19–35; Catasto (1480).

Table B.7. Ages of Active Partners Convicted and Absolved, 1478–1502[a]

	Office of the Night, 1478–1502				
	Convicted		*Absolved*		
Age	*No.*	*%*	*No.*	*%*	*% of Cohort Convicted*
18–30	149	80.6	329	65.5	31.2
31–40	24	12.9	110	21.9	17.9
41–50	6	3.2	45	9.0	11.8
51–60	4	2.2	12	2.4	25.0
≥61	2	1.1	6	1.2	25.0
Total	185	100.0	502	100.0	26.9
	Catasto, 1478–1483				
	Convicted		*Absolved*		
Age	*No.*	*%*	*No.*	*%*	*% of Cohort Convicted*
18–30	13	50.0	40	46.0	24.5
31–40	8	30.8	21	24.1	27.6
41–50	1	3.8	17	19.5	5.9
51–60	3	11.5	5	5.7	37.5
≥61	1	3.8	4	4.6	25.0
Total	26	99.9	90	99.9	22.4

[a]Ages were computed and recorded for each appearance of a given individual.
Sources: UN 19–35; Catasto (1480).

Table B.8. Marital Status of Men Implicated in Sodomy, 1478–1483[a]

	Full Sample (Catasto)			*Self-accusers*			*All Males*[b]
Age	*Married*	*Total*	*%*	*Married*	*Total*	*%*	*%*
18–30	3	58	5.2	0	12	0.0	18.5
31–40	14	32	43.7	5	12	41.7	62.9
41–50	10	20[c]	50.0	3	7	42.9	77.6
51–70	3	11	27.3	1	4	25.0	80.9
Unknown[d]	0	3	0.0				
Total	30	124	24.2	9	35	25.7	51.4

[a]Figures reflect marital status only in 1480, the year of the *catasto*, and may not accurately indicate individuals' marital status when they appeared in the judiciary records between 1478 and 1483.

[b]Percentages, based on the 1480 *catasto*, are adapted from Molho, *Marriage Alliance*, Appendix 4, 413–15.

[c]Includes two men who were probably widowers.

[d]Includes active partners only. Other evidence from their tax returns suggests that all three were mature, unmarried adults; one was probably in his thirties and another in his early forties.

Sources: UN 19–22; Catasto (1480).

Table B.9. Marital Status and Sentence of Men Implicated in Sodomy, 1478–1483[a]

	Married				
	Convicted		*Absolved*		
Age	*No.*	*%*	*No.*	*%*	*% of Cohort Convicted*
18–30	1	50.0	2	8.7	33.3
31–40	1	50.0	9	39.1	10.0
41–50	0	0.0	10	43.5	0.0
51–70	0	0.0	2	8.7	0.0
Unknown[b]	0	0.0	0	0.0	0.0
Total	2	100.0	23	100.0	8.0

	Unmarried				
	Convicted		*Absolved*		
Age	*No.*	*%*	*No.*	*%*	*% of Cohort Convicted*
18–30	12	50.0	38	58.5	24.0
31–40	7	29.2	12	18.4	36.8
41–50	1	4.2	6	9.2	14.3
51–70	4	16.7	6	9.2	40.0
Unknown[b]	0	0.0	3	4.6	0.0
Total	24	99.9	65	99.9	27.0

[a]Marital status refers only to 1480, while figures refer to all cases in which persons appeared from 1478 to 1483. Absolutions for self-accusations are excluded. I have also excluded two absolved men aged forty-six and sixty whose marital status was unclear.

[b]See Table B.8, note d.

Sources: UN 19–22; Catasto (1480).

Table B.10. Residence and Provenance of Males Implicated in Sodomy and of Active Partners Convicted, 1478–1502

	All Implicated[a]	*Active Partner Convicted*[b]
Florence	Total 3,644 (89.7%)	550 (89.0%)
Presumed natives	3,364 (82.8%)	508 (82.2%)
Origin elsewhere	280 (6.9%)	42 (6.8%)
Tuscany (182)		
Transappenine Italy (62)		
Central and South Italy (8)		
Italians, region unidentified (19)		
Ultramontanes (9)		
Territory	Total 418 (10.3%)	68 (11.1%)
Prato (147)		
Pisa (52)		
Montelupo (35)		
San Miniato al Tedesco (18)		
Figline (14)		
Pistoia (12)		
Ponte a Rifredi (12)		
Volterra (11)		
Others[c] (117)		
Total	4,062 (100%)	618 (100%)

[a]Numbers refer to individuals.
[b]Numbers refer to convictions, not individuals.
[c]Eight or fewer in each locality.
Source: UN 19–35.

Table B.11. Residence in Florence of Males Implicated in Sodomy and of Active Partners Convicted, 1478–1502[a]

	Individuals Implicated							
	Total		*Passives*		*Actives*		*Actives Convicted*	
Parish	*No.*	*%*	*No.*	*%*	*No.*	*%*	*No.*	*%*
S. Lorenzo	116	16.1	33	15.6	83	16.3	26	11.7
S. Piero Maggiore	65	9.0	27	12.7	38	7.5	18	8.1
S. Ambrogio	62	8.6	18	8.5	44	8.7	25	11.3
S. Frediano	60	8.3	19	9.0	41	8.1	14	6.3
S. Felice in Piazza	36	5.0	11	5.2	25	4.9	13	5.9
S. Niccolò	33	4.6	11	5.2	22	4.3	12	5.4
S. Maria Novella	31	4.3	—	—	25	4.9	8	3.6
S. Lucia Ognissanti	25	3.5	7	3.3	18	3.5	9	4.1
S. Paolo	24	3.3	—	—	19	3.7	10	4.5
S. Maria in Verzaia	20	2.8	—	—	—	—	9	4.1
S. Felicità	—	—	10	4.7	—	—	—	—
S. Pancrazio	—	—	9	4.2	—	—	—	—
S. Piero Gattolino	—	—	9	4.2	—	—	—	—
S. Maria Maggiore	—	—	—	—	17	3.3	—	—
Others	248	34.4	58	27.4	176	34.6	77	34.8
Total	720	99.9	212	100.0	508	99.8	221	99.8

[a]Only the leading ten parishes in each category are indicated separately. Figures in the columns "Total," "Passives," and "Actives" refer to individuals, while figures in the final column refer to sentences.
Source: UN 19–35.

Table B.12. Professional Categories of Males Implicated in Sodomy, 1478–1502[a]

	Individuals Implicated						*Self-accusers and Partners*			
	Total		*Active*		*Passive*		*Active*		*Passive*	
Category	*No.*	*%*	*No.*	*%*	*No.*	*%*	*No.*	*%*	*No.*	*%*
Textiles	619	15.0	476	16.4	143	11.7	35	14.4	24	8.8
Clothing	407	9.9	282	9.7	125	10.3	24	9.9	24	8.8
Local trades	277	6.7	217	7.5	60	4.9	22	9.1	14	5.1
Local commerce	270	6.5	187	6.4	83	6.8	6	2.5	20	7.4
Food	260	6.3	222	7.6	38	3.1	31	12.8	7	2.6
Local services[b]	167	4.0	103	3.5	64	5.3	8	3.3	5	1.8
Commune	95	2.3	89	3.1	6	0.5	7	2.9	1	0.4
Clergy	94	2.3	75	2.6	19	1.6	0	0.0	2	0.7
Taverns, inns	82	2.0	78	2.7	4	0.3	8	3.3	0	0.0
Professionals, spices[c]	76	1.8	54	1.9	22	1.8	3	1.2	4	1.5
Construction[d]	75	1.8	62	2.1	13	1.1	4	1.6	3	1.1
Arts	71	1.7	55	1.9	16	1.3	5	2.1	0	0.0
Domestic service	66	1.6	39	1.3	27	2.2	2	0.8	2	0.7
Education	25	0.6	18	0.6	7	0.6	2	0.8	1	0.4
Agriculture	12	0.3	9	0.3	3	0.2	0	0.0	1	0.4
Unidentified	14	0.3	12	0.4	2	0.2	0	0.0	0	0.0
Undeclared	1,514	36.7	928	31.9	586	48.1	86	35.4	164	60.3
Total	4,124	99.8	2,906	99.9	1,218	100.0	243	100.1	272	100.0

[a]Persons who appear in both active and passive roles in the survey are counted twice, once in each category.
[b]Barber, laborer, factotum, stablehand, gravedigger, etc.
[c]Doctor, notary, and apothecary.
[d]Includes woodworking.
Source: UN 19–35.

Table B.13. Most Common Occupations of Males Implicated in Sodomy, 1478–1502[a]

Occupation	*No.*	*%*
Hosier and shoemaker	241	9.2
Weaver	134	5.1
Clothes dealer	125	4.8
Butcher	97	3.7
Barber	95	3.6
Clergy	94	3.6
Tailor	85	3.3
Dyer	73	2.8
Grocer	62	2.4
Carpenter	61	2.3
Mercer	61	2.3
Other	1,482	56.8
Total	2,610	99.9

[a]Persons who appear in both active and passive roles in the survey are counted twice, once in each category.
Source: UN 19–35.

Table B.14. Professional Categories of Active Partners Convicted and Absolved, 1478–1502[a]

	Convicted		*Absolved*		
Category	*No.*	*%*	*No.*	*%*	*% of Category Convicted*
Textiles	147	23.8	404	14.0	26.7
Food	86	13.9	197	6.8	30.4
Clothing	56	9.1	261	9.0	17.7
Local trades	49	7.9	179	6.2	21.5
Local commerce	43	7.0	196	6.8	18.2
Local services	17	2.8	88	3.0	18.0
Commune	20	3.2	77	2.7	20.2
Construction	16	2.6	53	1.8	23.2
Taverns, inns	15	2.4	63	2.2	19.2
Professionals, spices	11	1.8	67	2.3	14.1
Domestic service	11	1.8	38	1.3	22.4
Arts	9	1.5	49	1.7	15.5
Agriculture	3	0.5	6	0.2	33.3
Education	5	0.8	13	0.4	27.8
Clergy	0	0.0	84	2.9	0.0
Unidentified	1	0.2	9	0.3	10.0
Undeclared	129	20.9	1,105	38.2	10.5
Total	618	100.2	2,889	99.8	17.6

[a]Figures in this table refer to sentences, not individuals. Absolutions as a result of self-denunciation have been excluded.
Source: UN 19–35.

Table B.15. Number of Reported Companions of Passive Partners Who Confessed, 1478–1502[a]

Number of Partners	*Number of Passives*	*%*	*Total Partners Implicated*
1	95	24.6	95
2	41	10.6	82
3–6	118	30.8	523
7–10	62	15.8	499
11–20	53	13.7	746
21–30	9	2.3	225
>30	8	2.1	326
Total	386	99.9	2,496

[a]Where applicable, figures include companions identified through self-accusations whose name did not appear in their passive partner's confession. Passive partners who were named in self-accusations but were not interrogated have been excluded from the calculations. One boy who confessed has also been eliminated, because the exact number of his partners is unknown.
Source: UN 19–35.

Table B.16. Self-Accusations and Convictions of Active Partners According to Frequency of Incrimination, 1478–1502[a]

		Self-accused		*Convicted*		*Convicted or Self-accused*	
Group[b]	*Number Incriminated*	*No.*	*%*	*No.*	*%*	*No.*	*%*
I	2,469	150	6.1	392	15.9	542	22.0
II	437	88	20.1	169	38.7	238	54.5
III	201	55	27.4	90	44.8	127	63.2
IV	79	26	32.9	40	50.6	54	68.4

[a]Absolute values in all columns refer to individuals. Percentages are of the number incriminated in the relevant group.
[b]Group I: incriminated once with a single partner; Group II: incriminated more than once or with multiple partners; Group III: incriminated with at least three partners or over five years or more; Group IV: incriminated with at least five partners or over ten years or more.
Source: UN 19–35.

Notes

Abbreviations

CP	Consulte e pratiche
CPDA	Capitano del popolo e difensore delle arti
EOG	Esecutore degli ordinamenti di giustizia
GAN	Giudice degli appelli e nullità
LF	Libri fabarum
MC Catasto	Monte comune o delle graticole, Copie del Catasto
MR	Miscellanea repubblicana
OGBR	Otto di guardia e balìa, Repubblica
Pod.	Podestà
PR	Provvisioni, Registri
Statuta 1415	*Statuta populi et communis florentiae publica auctoritate collecta castigata et praeposita anno salutis MCCCCXV.* 3 vols. (Fribourg, 1778–1783)
Statuti	Statuti del Comune di Firenze
Statuti 1322	R. Caggese, ed., *Statuti della repubblica fiorentina.* Vol. 1: *Statuto del capitano del popolo degli anni 1322–1325* (Florence, 1910)
Statuti 1325	R. Caggese, ed., *Statuti della repubblica fiorentina.* Vol. 2: *Statuto del podestà dell'anno 1325* (Florence, 1921)
Tratte	Tratte poi Segreteria delle tratte
UN	Ufficiali di notte e conservatori dei monasteri
UO	Ufficiali dell'onestà

The Italian sermons of Bernardino da Siena are cited as *Prediche* with the city and year in which they were delivered:

Florence, 1424	*Le prediche volgari.* Ed. C. Cannarozzi. 2 vols. (Pistoia, 1934)
Florence, 1425	*Le prediche volgari.* Ed. C. Cannarozzi. 3 vols. (Florence, 1940)
Siena, 1425	*Le prediche volgari.* Ed. C. Cannarozzi. 2 vols. (Florence, 1958)
Siena, 1427	*Le prediche volgari.* Ed. P. Bargellini (Milan, 1936)
Opera omnia	*S. Bernardini Senensis ordinis fratrum minorum opera omnia.* 9 vols. (Florence, 1950–1965)

Sermons of Girolamo Savonarola:

Aggeo	*Prediche sopra Aggeo, con il Trattato circa il reggimento e governo della città di Firenze.* Ed. L. Firpo (Rome, 1965)
Amos	*Prediche sopra Amos e Zaccaria.* Ed. P. Ghiglieri. 3 vols. (Rome, 1971–1972)
Ezechiele	*Prediche sopra Ezechiele.* Ed. R. Ridolfi. 2 vols. (Rome, 1955)
Giobbe	*Prediche sopra Giobbe.* Ed. R. Ridolfi. 2 vols. (Rome, 1957)
Salmi	*Prediche sopra i Salmi.* Ed. V. Romano. 2 vols. (Rome, 1969)
Ruth	*Prediche sopra Ruth e Michea.* Ed. V. Romano. 2 vols. (Rome, 1962)

All archival references are to the Archivio di Stato of Florence unless otherwise indicated. I have omitted the conventional "folio" in archival references, giving simply the folio number. The spelling of names when they appear in the text has been standardized. When quoting archival materials the original spellings have been retained but modern accents and punctuation have been added. Since the Florentine calendar began on March 25, dates between January 1 and March 24 are given in the notes only in both the Florentine and the common style; March 1, 1450/1451 indicates March 1, 1450, in the Florentine calendar and March 1, 1451, in the modern calendar. Dates in the text follow the common style.

So as not to burden the notes excessively, I have omitted the date in references to the proceedings of the Ufficiali di notte, the Otto di guardia, and the Giudice degli appelli e nullità, unless the specific date is for some reason significant. In order to furnish readers with a general indication of the date, here I list the years roughly corresponding to the volumes cited.

Ufficiali di notte (volume 1, April to April; volumes 4–16, July to July; volumes 17–35, November to November): 1 (1432–1433); 4 (1459–1460); 5 (1460–1461); 8 (1461–1462); 11 (1465–1466); 12 (1467–1468); 13 (1468–1469); 14 (1469–1470); 15 (1470–1471); 16 (1472–1473); 17 (1473–1474); 18 (1) (1474–1475); 18 (2) (1475–1476); 19 (1 and 2) (1478–1479); 19 (3) (1479–1480); 20 (1480–1481); 21 (1481–1482); 22 (1482–1483); 23 (1485–1486); 24 (1486–1487); 25 (1489–1490); 26 (1490–1491); 27 (1491–1492); 28 (1492–1493); 29 (1493–1494); 30 (1495–1496); 31 and 32 (1496–1497); 33 (1498–1499); 34 (1500–1501); 35 (1501–1502).

Otto di guardia: 54 (Nov. 1479–Feb. 1480); 55–56 (1480); 58–59 (1481); 61 (1482); 67–68 (1484); 69 (1484–1485); 70–71 (1485); 72 (1485–1486); 74 (1486); 77 (1487); 78 (1487–1488); 79–80 (1488); 82 (1489); 87 (1490–1491); 91–92 (1492); 93 (1492–1493); 94 (1493); 97 (1494); 105 (1496); 106 (1497); 109–110 (1498); 115 (1499); 117 (1500); 119, 121 (1501); 123 (1502); 128, 130 (1504); 134, 136 (1506); 141 (1508); 146, 146 bis, 147 (1510); 152, 152 bis (1512).

Giudice degli appelli e nullità: 77 (1429–1434); 79 (1434–1437); 80 (1438–1440); 82 (1446–1448); 85 (1460–1463); 86 (1464–1472); 88 (1475–1477).

Introduction

1. A. Segre, "I dispacci di Cristoforo da Piacenza, procuratore mantovano alla corte pontificale," *Archivio storico italiano*, 5th ser., 43 (1909): 85 (letter of Jan. 1). The Pope's comment was by no means disinterested, as the papacy and the city of Florence were currently at war. See R. Trexler, *The Spiritual Power: Republican Florence under Interdict* (Leiden, 1974), esp. 38.

2. The meaning of the term "sodomy" is discussed more fully later.

3. Bernardino da Siena, *Prediche* (Siena, 1427), 899.

4. Cited, along with other comments on the reputation of Florence, in R. Davidsohn, *Storia di Firenze* (Berlin, 1896–1927; Florence, 1956–1968), 7:612. Additional remarks are reported throughout this book. Two other sources deserve to be mentioned here because of the unusually approving attitudes they share and the cultural prestige of their subjects or authors. One of the protagonists of a little-known dialogue on "masculine love," written in the 1560s by the Lombard art critic and theorist Gian Paolo Lomazzo, is none other than the Florentine Leonardo da Vinci; his interlocutor pries him about his sexual relations with his young favorite, Salai, asking him euphemistically, "Did you play the game from behind, which the Florentines love so much?" (*Il libro dei sogni*, in *Scritti sulle arti*, ed. R. P. Ciardi [Florence, 1973], 1:104). The humanist Antonio Beccadelli (il Panormita), in his graphic and controversial *Hermaphroditus* (ca. 1425), minced no words in identifying the erotic tastes of the men of Tuscany, though he shifted the anatomical focus: "You're a Tuscan," he noted of one character, "and Tuscans like cock" (*L'Ermafrodito*, ed. with Italian translation by R. Gagliardi [Milan, 1980], 67). For an earlier edition, with a blander Italian translation, see *L'Ermafrodito*, ed. J. Tognelli (Rome, 1968). The context and dedication of this work are discussed in chapter 1.

5. Girolamo Savonarola, *Aggeo*, 220.

6. Much of this literature will be cited elsewhere in this work. In addition, a number of vituperative poems on sodomy as well as of homoerotic amorous poems appear in A. Lanza, ed., *Lirici toscani del '400* (Rome, 1973–1975). Several fifteenth-century manuscript versions of a spiritual laud entitled "Che fa' tu soddomito," are preserved in the Biblioteca Nazionale Centrale, Florence, Fondo nazionale, II.IX.140 (1458), II.VII.4, and II.IX.58. I am currently preparing a translated anthology of sources on homosexuality mostly from late medieval and early modern Tuscany which includes a representative selection of this literature. For a recent study of sodomy in the *Divine Comedy*, see J. Pequigney, "Sodomy in Dante's *Inferno* and *Purgatorio*," *Representations* 36 (1991): 22–42.

7. See the remarkable work of J. Toscan, *Le Carnaval du langage: Le lexique érotique des poètes de l'équivoque de Burchiello à Marino (XVe–XVIIe siècles)* (Lille, 1981); also G. Ferroni, "Il doppio senso erotico nei canti carnascialeschi fiorentini," *Sigma* 11 (1978): 233–50. Alan K. Smith explores the political dimensions of a poem in the "equivocal" tradition by Burchiello, in "Fraudomy: Reading Sexuality and Politics in Burchiello," in *Queering the Renaissance*, ed. J. Goldberg (Durham, N.C., 1994), 84–106.

8. *Statuti 1325*, 219; *Statuta 1415*, 322. The only conviction I know of for this offense comes from as late as 1556, when two men were exiled from the city for one year for singing "la cantilena dishonesta della Sodoma"; Otto di Guardia, Principato, Suppliche 2232, 295, 298. I thank Donald Weinstein for this reference.

9. The structure and operations of the Office of the Night are analyzed in chapter 2.

10. J. A. Symonds, *Renaissance in Italy* (London, 1875–1886, 1904–1908), 1: 374. For censorious comments of other historians of the early twentieth century intent on portraying homosexuality as a sign of moral decadence, a social disgrace, or even a "pathological perversion," see L. Pastor, *Geschichte der Päpste seit dem Ausgang des Mittelalters* (Freiburg im Breisgau, 1901–1933), 3:101; W. Heywood, *The "Ensamples" of Fra Filippo: A Study of Medieval Siena* (Siena, 1901), 195; Davidsohn, *Storia di Firenze*, 7:611; N. Tamassia, *La famiglia italiana nei secoli decimoquinto e decimosesto* (Naples, 1910; reprint, Rome, 1971), 75.

11. Historical works in this rapidly growing field include W. Monter, "La sodomie à l'époque moderne en Suisse romande," *Annales, E.S.C.* 29 (1974): 1023–33, published in a revised English version as "Sodomy and Heresy in Early Modern Switzerland," in *Historical Perspectives on Homosexuality*, ed. S. J. Licata and R. P. Petersen (New York, 1981), 41–55; R. Trumbach, "London's Sodomites: Homosexual Behavior and Western Culture in the 18th Century," *Journal of Social History* 11 (1977): 1–33; M. Goodich, *The Unmentionable Vice: Homosexuality in the Later Medieval Period* (Santa Barbara, Calif., 1979); J. Boswell, *Christianity, Social Tolerance, and Homosexuality: Gay People in Western Europe from the Beginning of the Christian Era to the Fourteenth Century* (Chicago, 1980); A. Bray, *Homosexuality in Renaissance England* (London, 1982); M. Rey, "Police et sodomie à Paris au XVIIIe siècle: Du péché au désordre," *Revue d'histoire moderne et contemporaine* 29 (1982): 113–24; R. Trumbach, "Sodomitical Subcultures, Sodomitical Roles, and the Gender Revolution of the Eighteenth Century: The Recent Historiography," *Eighteenth Century Life* 9, n.s., 3 (1985): 109–21; R. Carrasco, *Inquisición y represión sexual en Valencia: Historia de los sodomitos (1565–1785)* (Barcelona, 1985); J. M. Saslow, *Ganymede in the Renaissance: Homosexuality in Art and Society* (New Haven, 1986); D. Greenberg, *The Construction of Homosexuality* (Chicago, 1988), 242–346; K. Gerard and G. Hekma, eds., *The Pursuit of Sodomy: Male Homosexuality in Renaissance and Enlightenment Europe* (New York, 1989), also published as a special number of the *Journal of Homosexuality* 16, nos. 1, 2 (1988); J. M. Saslow, "Homosexuality in the Renaissance: Behavior, Identity, and Artistic Expression," in *Hidden from History: Reclaiming the Gay and Lesbian Past*, ed. M. B. Duberman, M. Vicinus, and G. Chauncey, Jr. (New York, 1989), 90–105. Studies of homosexuality specifically in Italy are cited later.

12. Herlihy hypothesizes that homosexual behavior in Florence might have been related in part to Tuscan marriage patterns, particularly the unusually late age at marriage for males; "Vieillir à Florence au Quattrocento," *Annales, E.S.C.* 24 (1969): 1346–49; "Some Psychological and Social Roots of Violence in the Tuscan Cities," in *Violence and Civil Disorder in Italian Cities, 1200–1500*, ed. L. Martines (Berkeley, 1972), 145–47; D. Herlihy and C. Klapisch-Zuber, *Les Toscans et leurs familles: Une étude du catasto florentin de 1427* (Paris, 1978), 414, 583–84. See more on this argument later in the Introduction and in chapter 4. Richard Trexler argues that both adolescent confraternities and institutionalized prostitution represented indirect responses by civic leaders in the early fifteenth century to what they perceived as the threat of homosexuality in "Ritual in Florence: Adolescence and Salvation in the Renaissance," in *The Pursuit of Holiness in Late Medieval and Renaissance Religion*, ed. C. Trinkaus and H. Oberman (Leiden, 1974), 235–36;

Public Life in Renaissance Florence (New York, 1980), 378–82; "La Prostitution florentine au XVe siècle: Patronages et clientèles," *Annales, E.S.C.* 36 (1981): 983–84, 1003–1006.

13. For Venice the most important study is G. Ruggiero, *The Boundaries of Eros: Sex Crime and Sexuality in Renaissance Venice* (New York, 1985), 109–45; see also E. Pavan, "Police des moeurs, société et politique à Venise à la fin du Moyen Age," *Revue historique* 264 (1980): esp. 266–88; G. Scarabello, "Devianza sessuale ed interventi di giustizia a Venezia nella prima metà del XVI secolo," in *Tiziano e Venezia*, Atti del Convegno Internazionale di Studi, Venezia 1977 (Vicenza, 1980), 75–84; P. Labalme, "Sodomy and Venetian Justice in the Renaissance," *Legal History Review* 52 (1984): 217–54; G. Martini, *Il "vitio nefando" nella Venezia del Seicento: Aspetti sociali e repressione di giustizia* (Rome, 1988). For an area highly influenced by Venice, see also B. Krekić, "Abominandum Crimen: Punishment of Homosexuals in Renaissance Dubrovnik," *Viator: Medieval and Renaissance Studies* 18 (1987): 337–45. On sodomy in Florence and Tuscany, see M. Rocke, "Il controllo dell'omosessualità a Firenze nel XV secolo: Gli Ufficiali di Notte," *Quaderni storici* 66 (1987): 701–23; Rocke, "Sodomites in Fifteenth-Century Tuscany: The Views of Bernardino of Siena," in *Pursuit of Sodomy*, ed. Gerard and Hekma, 7–31; Rocke, "Il fanciullo e il sodomita: Pederastia, cultura maschile e vita civile nella Firenze del Quattrocento," in *Infanzie: Funzioni di un gruppo liminale dal mondo classico all'Età moderna*, Laboratorio di storia, vol. 6, ed. O. Niccoli (Florence, 1993), 210–230; L. Marcello, "Società maschile e sodomia: Dal declino della 'polis' al Principato," *Archivio storico italiano* 150 (1992): 115–38. For a comparative study of sodomy in Venice and Florence that draws heavily on previously published work, see R. Canosa, *Storia di una grande paura: La sodomia a Firenze e a Venezia nel Quattrocento* (Milan, 1991). On the relationship between male homoeroticism and neo-Platonic ideals of love see G. Dall'Orto, " 'Socratic Love' as a Disguise for Same-Sex Love in the Italian Renaissance," in *Pursuit of Sodomy*, ed. Gerard and Hekma, 33–65. Judith Brown studies the rarely documented case of sexual relations between women in *Immodest Acts: The Life of a Lesbian Nun in Renaissance Italy* (New York, 1986). R. Sherr reconstructs a single detailed case of homosexual relations in Loreto in "A Canon, a Choirboy, and Homosexuality in Late Sixteenth-Century Italy: A Case Study," *Journal of Homosexuality* 21, no. 3 (1991): 1–22.

14. For Bernardino's comment see chapter 1, 42.

15. Transcriptions of the unpublished sodomy laws of the Florentine Republic are in M. Rocke, "Male Homosexuality and its Regulation in Late-Medieval Florence" (Ph.D. diss., State University of New York at Binghamton, 1990), 567–684.

16. Boswell, *Christianity*, 269–332; Goodich, *Unmentionable Vice*, 51–88.

17. Goodich reviews the legal status of sodomy in various Italian cities in *Unmentionable Vice*, 79–85, and in "Sodomy in Medieval Secular Law," *Journal of Homosexuality* 1 (1976): 295–302. Additional comparative information is found in J. Kohler, *Das Strafrecht der Italienischen Statuten* (Mannheim, 1897), 527–31; G. Dahm, *Das Strafrecht Italiens im ausgehenden Mittelalter* (Berlin and Leipzig, 1931), 442–43. The early Florentine laws are discussed later in chapter 1.

18. See the relevant remarks, for example, by Bray, *Homosexuality*, 38–42, and by Ruggiero, *Boundaries*, 4–5.

19. For a discussion of the 1480 tax assessment, see A. Molho, *Marriage Alliance in Late Medieval Florence* (Cambridge, Mass., 1994), 361–64.

20. Works that have been particularly influential in charting changes in the social organization of sexuality in Western culture and the evolution of the modern "homosexual" include M. Foucault, *Histoire de la sexualité* (Paris, 1976–1984), esp. vol. 1; R. Trumbach, "London's Sodomites," and "Gender and the Homosexual Role in Modern Western Culture: The 18th and 19th Centuries Compared," in *Homosexuality, Which Homosexuality?* (Amsterdam and London, 1989), 149–69; K. Plummer, ed., *The Making of the Modern Homosexual* (London, 1981); J. Weeks, *Sex, Politics and Society: The Regulation of Sexuality Since 1800* (London and New York, 1981); Greenberg, *Construction.* Most recently, George Chauncey has demonstrated persuasively that the homosexual-heterosexual dichotomy became the dominant sexual regime in American culture only in the first half of the twentieth century; *Gay New York: Gender, Urban Culture, and the Making of the Gay Male World, 1890–1940* (New York, 1994). For anthropological studies that emphasize the different social arrangements and conceptualizations of homosexual behavior in non-Western cultures see G. W. Herdt, *Guardians of the Flutes: Idioms of Masculinity* (New York, 1981); G. W. Herdt, ed., *Ritualized Homosexuality in Melanesia* (Berkeley, 1984); E. Blackwood, ed., *The Many Faces of Homosexuality: Anthropological Approaches to Homosexual Behavior* (New York, 1986).

21. See especially G. W. Herdt, "Representations of Homosexuality: An Essay on Cultural Ontology and Historical Comparison," *Journal of the History of Sexuality* 1 (1991): 481–504, 603–32.

22. Boswell traces the development of medieval theological opinions on homosexual behavior, and offers a penetrating critique of those of Thomas Aquinas, in *Christianity*, 200–206, 303–32. In his own *Summa theologica*, Antonino Pierozzi, archbishop of Florence from 1446 to 1459, closely followed the Thomist definition of the sins against nature; *Sancti Antonini summa theologica* (Graz, 1959), tit. quintus, cap. IV, par. 2 (2:667–68).

23. In the thousands of Florentine sodomy cases I have reviewed from a period of nearly two centuries, I have found not a single case of sexual relations between women (on which see Brown, *Immodest Acts*). In *Construction*, 306n.27, Greenberg cites a 1424 case of what he describes as lesbian relations between two Florentine brothel prostitutes, brought to his attention by Gene Brucker. But this case in fact deals with a woman who prostituted both her daughter and daughter-in-law to males, the former for purposes of sodomy; EOG 2045, 15r (Dec. 12, 1424).

24. See more on this point in chapter 4.

25. See chapter 3, 87–88.

26. For the relevant figures from 1427 and the general argument, see Herlihy, "Vieillir," 1346–49, and "Some Psychological and Social Roots," 145–47; Herlihy and Klapisch-Zuber, *Les Toscans*, 400–404, 414, 583–84. For 1480 see Molho, *Marriage Alliance*, 218–21 and Appendix 4. The proportion of eighteen- to thirty-two-year-olds who were or had been married actually declined from over 26 percent in 1427 to slightly more than 22 percent in 1480 while the proportion of definitive bachelors increased somewhat. Jean-Louis Flandrin also suggests that homosexuality in premodern Europe might have been linked to the late age at marriage for males in "Mariage tardif et vie sexuelle: Discussions et hypothèses de recherche," *Annales, E.S.C.* 27 (1972): 1351–78.

Chapter 1

1. A. Lanza, ed., *Lirici toscani del '400* (Rome, 1973–1975), 1:570–71.

2. PR 108, 2v (Apr. 15).

3. GAN 79 (2), 57r (Feb. 15, 1435/1436).

4. G. Rondini, ed., *I più antichi frammenti del costituto fiorentino* (Florence, 1882), 56 (from the statutes of the podestà of 1284). On the increasing intolerance toward sodomy in this period, see M. Goodich, *The Unmentionable Vice: Homosexuality in the Later Medieval Period* (Santa Barbara, Calif., 1979), 51–88; J. Boswell, *Christianity, Social Tolerance, and Homosexuality: Gay People in Western Europe from the Beginning of the Christian Era to the Fourteenth Century* (Chicago, 1980), 269–332.

5. *Statuti 1325*, 219–20. On laws against sodomy and its prosecution in the fourteenth century see U. Dorini, *Il diritto penale e la delinquenza a Firenze nel secolo XIV* (Lucca, [1923]), 71–76; R. Davidsohn, *Storia di Firenze* (Berlin, 1896–1927; Florence 1956–1968), 7:614. The most comprehensive study of the administration of criminal justice in Florence is A. Zorzi, *L'amministrazione della giustizia penale nella Repubblica fiorentina: Aspetti e problemi* (Florence, 1988). See also the special issue of *Ricerche storiche* 18, no. 3 (1988), on "Istituzioni giudiziarie e aspetti della criminalità nella Firenze tardomedievale"; L. I. Sterns, *The Criminal Law System of Medieval and Renaissance Florence* (Baltimore, 1994). Other recent studies for the fourteenth century include H. Manikowska, "Polizia e servizi d'ordine a Firenze nella seconda metà del XIV secolo," *Ricerche storiche* 16 (1986): 17–38; A. Zorzi, "Contrôle social, ordre public et répression judiciaire à Florence à l'époque communale: Éléments et problèmes," *Annales, E.S.C.* 45 (1990): 1169–88. Older but still useful studies for this period, in addition to the work by Dorini cited earlier, are Davidsohn, *Storia di Firenze*, 5:479–639; J. Kohler and G. Degli Azzi, *Das florentiner Strafrecht des XIV Jahrhunderts* (Mannheim and Leipzig, 1909).

6. Rondini, ed., *I più antichi frammenti*, 56. Not directed against sodomy per se, this law simply posted a reward for denouncing or capturing infamous thieves or persons banished for other serious crimes, including sodomy, who had illegally reentered Florentine territory.

7. *Statuti 1325*, 218–20. This is the only law between 1300 and 1550 that focused exclusively on man-boy relations in sodomy. Unlike later laws, it failed to mention males over the age of eighteen who took the "passive" role, probably not because this was condoned but because it was (or was assumed to be) so rare as to be unworthy of notice. Moreover, its wording (*quod quicumque soddomita pollutus cum aliquo puero inventus fuerit*) seems to refer only to men caught in the act, though it is unlikely the courts interpreted it this way.

8. *Statuti 1322*, 243–44.

9. PR 52, 128r (Apr. 3).

10. S. Cohn, Jr., *The Laboring Classes in Renaissance Florence* (New York, 1980), 275–80, Appendices H.1 (1344–1345) and H.2 (1374–1375), where no cases of sodomy are recorded (despite Cohn's assertion on page 196 that there were cases of homosexual rape prosecuted in the two samples). In a personal communication, Gene Brucker informed me that his surveys for 1344–1346, 1360–1361, and 1390–1391, yielded no prosecutions for sodomy. I wish to thank Brucker for sharing these findings and his extensive notes on other sodomy cases with me.

11. Dorini, *Il diritto penale*, 71–72.

12. My sources were seventy-four "books of sentences" of the podestà, capitano, and esecutore from 1390 through 1410. I found no absolutions for sodomy. The figures reported here may be slightly low, since some 25 percent of the relevant volumes were damaged in the flood of 1966 and cannot now be consulted, and some surviving volumes are incomplete. The thirty-three individuals include six noted by Gene Brucker in volumes now unavailable for consultation.

13. See G. Ruggiero, *The Boundaries of Eros: Sex Crime and Sexuality in Renaissance Venice* (New York, 1985), 127–28, Table 6; E. Pavan, "Police des moeurs, société et politique à Venise à la fin du Moyen Age," *Revue Historique* 264 (1980): 266.

14. Respectively, Pod. 4592, 26v (June 20, 1428); EOG 1288, 53v (Aug. 12, 1396); Pod. 640, 39r (Nov. 6, 1350); EOG 2045, 15r (Dec. 12, 1424).

15. For example, in 1352 two men assaulted three young sons of Boccaccio Brunelleschi with the intention of raping them, but were driven off. Both men, described as habitual sodomites, were sentenced to death by burning; Pod. 826, 351r (Sept. 22), 354r (Oct. 1). For a 1429 case of a man who gagged and raped a ten-year-old boy, severely lacerating his anus, for which the man was burned at the stake, see G. Brucker, *The Society of Renaissance Florence: A Documentary Study* (New York, 1971), 205–206.

16. In 1352 seven men kidnapped a citizen and held him for ransom for a month, and six of the gang raped him repeatedly. They were sentenced (five in absentia) to be dragged by an ass through the city, then burned to death; Pod. 873, 31r (Oct. 31). In 1404 five men, rebuffed by a boy they desired, attacked and tried to rape him, but he escaped with the aid of two customs officers; that night the five men assaulted the officers, injuring one and killing the other. All five, in absentia, were fined enormous sums, their property was confiscated, and they were sentenced to be beheaded; Pod. 4003, 31r (Nov. 10). In 1409 a notary charged with theft, simony, corruption and extortion while in office, and sodomy with four youths was beheaded; CPDA 2374, 29v (June 27).

17. Pod. 826, 141v (Oct. 4). Miniato was sentenced to death in absentia.

18. Pod. 279, 96r (May 15). See further later. I thank Halina Manikowska for this reference.

19. Ages were seldom or imprecisely recorded in the records of this period, but available information indicates that passive partners were normally adolescents or "teenagers." See chapters 3 and 4 for detailed discussions.

20. Respectively, EOG 1520, 2v (Feb. 9, 1403/1404), fined 1,000 lire and exiled to Venice for four years; Pod. 4003, 24r (Feb. 23, 1404/1405), sentenced in contumacy to be beheaded.

21. Pod. 1656, 45r (May 7, 1365). Part of Giovanni's sentence, describing his sexual activity, is published in Kohler and Degli Azzi, *Das florentiner Strafrecht*, 109–12; the editors, however, omitted his brutal punishment.

22. EOG 1520, 2v (Feb. 14, 1403/1404). Biographical information on Alamanni comes from Catasto 64, 194v–195r (1427). He seems to have reconciled with his wife, for a second son was born around 1406 and a third around 1408.

23. EOG 1520, 3r (Feb. 14, 1403/1404).

24. Salvestro's petition for clemency is in PR 93, 137r (Nov. 27, 1404), 163r (Dec. 19); that of Jacopo, brought by his father, is in ibid, 96v (Oct. 9, 1404).

25. Pod. 279, 97rv (May 15).

26. Ruggiero, *Boundaries*, 127–38. See also P. Labalme, "Sodomy and Venetian

Justice in the Renaissance," *Legal History Review* 52 (1984): 222–25; Pavan, "Police," 266–68.

27. See my comments in the Introduction. Ruggiero's casual use in chapter 6 in *Boundaries* of the term "homosexual" as a noun or adjective referring to persons may give rise to misunderstanding about the nature of the "subculture" he describes and about the conceptual model of the "sodomite" that lies behind his analysis. Though he astutely suggests elsewhere (chapter 7) that homosexual behavior in Renaissance Venice might have been particularly associated with the prolonged period of adolescence and bachelorhood, implying a a model different from the one which "homosexual" typically evokes, this is not readily apparent in his discussion of sodomy in the preceding chapter. See Randolph Trumbach's comments on the anachronistic application of modern models to sexual experience before 1700, including a critique of Ruggiero, in "Gender and the Homosexual Role in Modern Western Culture: The 18th and 19th Centuries Compared," in *Homosexuality, Which Homosexuality?* (Amsterdam and London, 1989), 161–64; the reviews of *The Boundaries of Eros* by Trumbach and Alan Bray in *The Pursuit of Sodomy: Male Homosexuality in Renaissance and Enlightenment Europe*, ed. K. Gerard and G. Hekma (New York, 1989), 506–10, 499–505. On the sodomitical milieu of Florence, and whether it is useful to represent it as a distinctive subculture, see chapter 5.

28. *Prediche inedite del beato Giordano da Rivalto dell'Ordine de' predicatori, recitate in Firenze dal 1302 al 1305*, ed. E. Narducci (Bologna, 1867), 449.

29. On these developments see M. Becker, *Florence in Transition* (Baltimore, 1967, 1968); P. Herde, "Politische Verhaltensweisen der Florentiner Oligarchie, 1382–1402," in *Geschichte und Verfassungsgefüge: Frankfurter Festgabe für Walter Schlessinger*, Frankfurter Historische Abhandlungen, Vol. 5 (Wiesbaden, 1973), 156–249; A. Molho, "Politics and the Ruling Class in Early Renaissance Florence," *Nuova rivista storica* 52 (1968): 401–20; Molho, *Florentine Public Finances in the Early Renaissance, 1400–1433* (Cambridge, Mass., 1971); R. Witt, "Florentine Politics and the Ruling Class, 1382–1407," *Journal of Medieval and Renaissance Studies* 6 (1976): 243–67; G. Brucker, *The Civic World of Early Renaissance Florence* (Princeton, 1977); J. M. Najemy, *Corporatism and Consensus in Florentine Electoral Politics, 1280–1400* (Chapel Hill, 1982). For a general overview of Florentine political institutions and processes in the early fifteenth century, see G. Guidi, *Il governo della città-repubblica di Firenze del primo Quattrocento* (Florence, 1981).

30. On the transformations in the Florentine judicial system see Zorzi, *L'amministrazione*, 1–63; see also L. Martines, *Lawyers and Statecraft in Renaissance Florence* (Princeton, 1968), 130–45; M. Becker, "Changing Patterns of Violence and Justice in Fourteenth- and Fifteenth-Century Florence," *Comparative Studies in Society and History* 18 (1976): 281–96; S. Cohn, Jr., *Laboring Classes*, 179–203; Cohn, "Criminality and the State in Renaissance Florence, 1344–1466," *Journal of Social History* 14 (1981): 211–33.

31. The Otto di guardia, created after the defeat of the workers' uprising known as the Ciompi Revolt. The Otto eventually became the city's main criminal tribunal. See G. Antonelli, "La magistratura degli Otto di guardia a Firenze," *Archivio storico italiano* 92 (1954): 3–39; Becker, "Changing Patterns"; Zorzi, *L'amministrazione*," 42–45.

32. The Ufficiali dell'onestà (Officers of Decency). See R. Trexler, "La Prostitution florentine au XVe siècle: Patronages et clientèles," *Annales, E.S.C.* 36 (1981):

983–1015; M. S. Mazzi, *Prostitute e lenoni nella Firenze del Quattrocento* (Milan, 1991), esp. 200–31. See also the discussion later.

33. The Conservatori dell'onestà dei monasteri; PR 111, 45r (June 25, 1421). This office's duties passed to the Ufficiali di notte in 1433 (see chapter 2). On the sociology and functions of convents in Florence, see R. Trexler, "Le Célibat à la fin du Moyen Age: Les religieuses à Florence," *Annales, E.S.C.* 27 (1972): 1329–50. On sex with nuns in Venice, see G. Ruggiero, "Sessualità e sacrilegio," *Studi storici* 22 (1981): 751–65; Ruggiero, *Boundaries*, 70–88.

34. The Conservatori di legge. See A. Zorzi, "I fiorentini e gli uffici pubblici nel primo Quattrocento: Concorrenza, abusi, illegalità," *Quaderni storici* 66 (1987): 725–51; Zorzi, *L'amministrazione*, 62–63.

35. See M. Rocke, "Il controllo dell'omosessualità a Firenze nel XV secolo: Gli Ufficiali di Notte," *Quaderni storici* 66 (1987): 702–704, and chapter 2; cf. Zorzi, *L'amministrazione*, 57–61.

36. For a discussion of the moral reforms promoted by the regime in the early fifteenth century, see Mazzi, *Prostitute*, 141–81; also Zorzi, *L'amministrazione*, 56–63. On the policing of sexual behavior in the Florentine territorial state in the same period, M. S. Mazzi, "Cronache di periferia dello Stato fiorentino: Reati contro la morale nel primo Quattrocento," *Studi storici* 27 (1986): 609–35.

37. See J. Rossiaud, *La prostituzione nel medioevo* (Bari, 1984), 111–33, on new approaches and attitudes toward sexuality in the period 1390–1440.

38. D. Herlihy and C. Klapisch-Zuber, *Les Toscans et leurs familles: Une étude du catasto florentin du 1427* (Paris, 1978), 165–88; A. Carmichael, *Plague and the Poor in Renaissance Florence* (Cambridge, 1986).

39. Although no causal relationship can be proved, nearly every Florentine law against sodomy in this period—those of 1365, 1403, 1418 and 1419, and 1432—as well as Bernardino of Siena's sermons against sodomy in 1424 and 1425, came during or shortly after outbreaks of plague (1363, 1400, 1417 and 1418, 1423 and 1424, 1430).

40. Herlihy and Klapisch-Zuber, *Les Toscans*, 204–209, 393–419; D. Herlihy, "Vieillir à Florence au Quattrocentro," *Annales, E.S.C.* 24 (1969): 1346–49.

41. In general, see Herlihy and Klapisch-Zuber, *Les Toscans*, 523–613, with additional bibliography.

42. On attitudes toward children see generally ibid., 552–84; C. Klapisch-Zuber, "L'Enfance en Toscane au dèbut du XVe siècle," *Annales de démographie historique* (1973): 99–122; J. B. Ross, "The Middle-Class Child in Urban Italy, Fourteenth to Early Sixteenth Century," in *The History of Childhood*, ed. L. de Mause (New York, 1974), 183–228; R. Goldthwaite, "The Florentine Palace as Domestic Architecture," *American Historical Review* 77 (1972): 1009–11; O. Niccoli, "Compagnie di bambini nell'Italia del Rinascimento," *Rivista storica italiana* 101 (1989): 346–74; Niccoli, *Il seme della violenza: Putti, fanciulli e mammoli nell'Italia tra Cinque e Seicento* (Rome and Bari, 1995); Niccoli, ed., *Infanzie: Funzioni di un gruppo liminale dal mondo classico all'Età moderno*, Laboratorio di Storia, vol. 6 (Florence, 1993). On the Commune's provisions for abandoned children, R. Trexler, "The Foundlings of Florence, 1395–1495," *History of Childhood Quarterly* 1 (1973–1974): 259–84; P. Gavitt, *Charity and Children in Renaissance Florence: The Ospedale degli Innocenti, 1410–1536* (Ann Arbor, 1990). For the history of boys' confraternities in Florence, which Trexler argues were seen as a partial response to adolescent homosexuality, see "Ritual in Florence: Adolescence and

Salvation in the Renaissance," in *The Pursuit of Holiness in Late Medieval and Renaissance Religion*, ed. C. Trinkaus and H. Oberman (Leiden, 1974), esp. 234–48, and Trexler, *Public Life in Renaissance Florence* (New York, 1980), 368–87.

43. Herlihy and Klapisch-Zuber, *Les Toscans*, 586–88. It is worth stressing the role of leading humanists in the growing campaign against sodomy, since it is often assumed that humanists' passion for antiquity contributed univocally to an acceptance of homoeroticism among the Italian elite.

44. See A. Molho, *Marriage Alliance in Late Medieval Florence* (Cambridge, Mass., 1994); also J. Kirshner, "Pursuing Honor While Avoiding Sin: The *Monte delle doti* of Florence," *Studi senesi* 87 (1977): 175–256; A. Molho and J. Kirshner, "The Dowry Fund and the Marriage Market in Early *Quattrocento* Florence," *Journal of Modern History* 50 (1978): 403–38; Molho and Kirshner, "Il monte delle doti a Firenze dalla sua fondazione nel 1425 alla metà del sedicesimo secolo: Abbozzo di una ricerca," *Ricerche storiche* 10 (1980): 21–47; A. Molho, "Investimenti nel Monte delle doti di Firenze: Un'analisi sociale e geografica," *Quaderni storici* 61 (1986): 147–70.

45. The original proposal has not survived, but it is summarized in the *priorista* of Paolo Pietrobuoni (Biblioteca Nazionale Centrale, Florence, Conventi Soppressi C.4.895, 105r) and in the *ricordi* of Pagolo del Pagone (Biblioteca Riccardiana, Florence, Fondo Moreniano, ms. 301, 50v–51r). Advanced by the Signoria and colleges, the proposal was approved only by the Council of the Popolo, where it carried against the highest number of nays for measures voted that day; LF 52v, 125v (Dec. 9, 1421). There is no evidence it was submitted to the Council of the Commune, implying the government dropped it. In fact the proposal met with bitter opposition, as records of an advisory meeting of December 11, 1421, reveal: "Many are complaining," a speaker reported, "and saying that they would not be free as their elders were," suggesting a generational conflict; CP 44, 152v. Del Pagone also noted that the proposal provoked a "huge debate in the city." That this was an indirect measure against sodomites is implied by the insistence of Bernardino of Siena that all unmarried men were sodomites and should be driven from office; *Prediche* (Florence, 1424), 2:47.

46. Belief in the deterrent function of prostitution was widespread in the Middle Ages. Giordano of Rivalto (or of Pisa), for example, preached in Florence in 1306 that if the admittedly "great evil" of prostitution were suppressed, the much worse evils of sodomy and adultery would increase; *Quaresimale fiorentino 1305–1306*, ed. Carlo del Corno (Florence, 1974), 210. In laws from the Tuscan cities of Lucca and Siena, combatting sodomy was the motive given for promoting and protecting prostitution; see S. Bongi, ed., *Inventario del R. Archivio di Stato di Lucca* (Lucca, 1872–1888), 1:213–14; T. Compton, "Sodomy and Civic Doom," *Vector* 11, no. 11 (1975): 57. Trexler stresses the role of municipal prostitution as a perceived deterrent to homosexuality in Florence in "La Prostitution," esp. 983–84. Mazzi also acknowledges this as one of the government's possible motives; *Prostitute*, 157.

47. Brucker, *Society*, 180–81. See also PR 153, 241v (Feb. 9, 1462/1463), where sumptuary controls are justified as a spur to marriage in Pisa. For Bernardino's claims, see *Opera omnia*, 2:83; *Prediche* (Florence, 1424), 2:141; (Siena, 1427), 853.

48. Brucker, *Society*, 206–7, from a case prosecuted by the Night Officers in 1435.

49. PR 92, 9r (Apr. 24, 1403). The summaries of the law in the voting register

also clearly stress its intent to repress sodomy; LF 47, 138r (Apr. 20), 140r (Apr. 24).

50. UO 1, 3r–7v (Apr. 30, 1403). This deliberation does not appear in the corpus of municipal law, the *provvisioni*, perhaps because it was an executive decree issued in virtue of the extraordinary authority (*balìa*) granted to the Signora on April 24. In the source just cited, the April 30 deliberation is incorporated with a copy of the April 24 law on sodomy, and these two measures appear the same way, in successive rubrics, in the statutes redacted in 1408/1409 (*Statuti* 23, 85r) and in 1415 (*Statuta 1415*, 3:41 ff.). These linkages seem to confirm an ideological connection between the two measures, yet they were clearly distinct, and the difference is important for the interpretation of the government's actions and aims. On this unusual and intricate turn of events see Rocke, "Il controllo," 704 and n. 19, and Mazzi, *Prostitute*, 149–59. On the Officers of Decency see Mazzi, 200–31; Trexler, "La Prostitution." The distinction between the two moments of the government's action escaped Trexler's attention (984), an oversight that reinforced his narrow interpretation of this magistracy as serving mainly to combat male homosexuality as part of a broader effort to stimulate population growth. The limits of this perspective are underlined by Mazzi in *Prostitute*, 158, and in "Il mondo della prostituzione nella Firenze tardo medievale," *Ricerche storiche* 14 (1984): 344–45.

51. See Mazzi, *Prostitute*, 141–231, and "Il mondo della prostituzione"; also Trexler, "La Prostitution." On institutionalized prostitution in Venice, Pavan, "Police," 241–66. For a general study of prostitution in early modern Italy, see R. Canosa and I. Colonnello, *Storia della prostituzione in Italia dal Quattrocento alla fine del Settecento* (Rome, 1989). For southern France, see Rossiaud, *La prostituzione*; L. Otis, *Prostitution in Medieval Society: The History of an Urban Institution in Languedoc* (Chicago, 1985).

52. CP 37, 14v (Jan. 7, 1403/1404) and again on 16v (Jan. 8). I thank Gene Brucker for this reference. Mazzi convincingly argues that the Office of Decency was not fully operational until 1415; *Prostitute*, 200–210.

53. LF 47, 187v. The measure passed 146–54, the highest number of nays for any proposal voted that day.

54. PR 92, 323r (Mar. 13, 1403/1404); see LF 47, 188r, for its summary in the voting register of the Council of the Commune. It is unclear whether the proposal was altered after its approval by the Council of the Popolo or whether the first summary grossly misrendered its sense. While there is no evidence the Officers of Decency were granted specific jurisdiction over sodomy, a number of sodomy laws appear in the compilation of laws pertinent to this office (see UO 1). And apparently they did prosecute sodomy, though rarely, if it involved prostitutes who worked in the public brothels. For an early case in which a pimp was convicted—but only after repeated warnings by the Onestà—of sodomizing several brothel whores, see GAN 74, 237r (Feb. 1, 1415/1416). Gene Brucker kindly passed on this reference. For later cases, see Trexler, "La Prostitution," 995–96, and Table VII.

55. "Nec metu veritatis crimen prefatum impunitum relinquent"; *Statuti* 23, 86v. The 1408/1409 statutes, which would have reinforced authoritarian tendencies within the regime, were successfully blocked, and only after further changes were the definitive statutes approved in 1415. The measures on sodomy in the early version were carried over in the later with slightly more concise language; *Statuta*

1415, 1:320–23. These measures probably originated with the 1408/1409 statutes, though this cannot be determined with certainty. A review of all legislation from 1365 to 1408 failed to turn up any law on sodomy that might have been incorporated in the statutes. On the code of 1408/1409 and its reception see R. Fubini, "La rivendicazione di Firenze della sovranità statale e il contributo delle 'Historiae' del Bruni," in *Leonardo Bruni cancelliere della Repubblica di Firenze*, ed. P. Viti (Florence, 1990), 46–50; Zorzi, *L'amministrazione*, 13–17.

56. *Statuti* 23, 86v; cf. *Statuta 1415*, 1:321.

57. The third of Za's poems, "Lo studio d'Atene," also alludes to sodomy but less clearly so. See D. Guerri, *La corrente popolare nel rinascimento: Berte, burle e baie nella Firenze del Brunellesco e del Burchiello* (Florence, 1931), 33–48; A. Lanza, *Polemiche e berte letterarie nella Firenze del primo Rinascimento (1375–1449)*, 2d ed. (Rome, 1989), 271–97, 312–19. Lanza's edition of the poems appears only in the first edition (Rome, 1972), 309–25, 348–57. Lanza suggests only that Za's satires grew out of the climate of jubilation after the death of Giangaleazzo Visconti in 1402 and the defeat of Pisa in 1406 (pp. 223, 272). This may be, but the growing concern over sodomy in this decade also had a decisive and more direct influence.

58. J. Toscan, *Le Carnaval du langage: Le lexique érotique des poètes de l'équivoque de Burchiello à Marino (XVe–XVIIe siècles)* (Lille, 1981), 4:1671, 1705, 1720; he suggests (1720) that Monte Morello is once used as a metaphor for the female sexual organs, but in Za's poem the allusion is plainly to sodomy. The poems should be read with Toscan's work to grasp their rich sexual content. In Florentine slang today, *buco* is a derogatory term for homosexual, but it does not seem to have had this sense in the late Middle Ages. Another possible allusion comes from the so-called *compagnie delle buche* or *di notte*, names given to penitential confraternities that practiced especially strict forms of discipline; see J. Henderson, "Le confraternite religiose nella Firenze del tardo medioevo: Patroni spirituali e anche politici?" *Ricerche storiche* 15 (1985): 90–91. In general on Florentine confraternities, see R. Weissman, *Ritual Brotherhood in Renaissance Florence* (New York, 1982); J. Henderson, *Piety and Charity in Late Medieval Florence* (Oxford, 1994).

59. Guardi was one of the organizers of the events recounted in the poem. As Za wrote, "he was the companion of a member of the Fracassini family, and they committed a lot of sodomy together"; Lanza, *Polemiche e berte*, 284. On the Buco later in the century, see chapter 5.

60. An annotated list of many of the people named in Za's poems is found in *La buca di Monteferrato, Lo studio d'Atene, Il gagno*, ed. L. Frati (Bologna, 1884), 187–255. For the most obvious depictions of sodomites, see Lanza, *Polemiche e berte*, 284–85.

61. Lanza, *Polemiche e berte*, 300–1.

62. In Lanza, ed., *Lirici toscani del '400*, 1:570–71.

63. Guerri published this poem in *La corrente popolare*, 149–71, and suggested it was roughly contemporary with the poems of Za. Lanza offers the 1417 to 1425 date and attributes the poem to the herald Antonio di Matteo di Meglio, who was responsible for entertaining the priors while they dined; *Polemiche e berte*, 321–35.

64. Guerri, *La corrente popolare*, 153. A similar appeal to lawmakers follows this one.

65. Ibid., 171.

66. CP 43, 76v.

67. Ibid.; excerpts in Brucker, *Society*, 201.

68. CP 43, 77r (Dec. 8). Following the minutes of the speaker Vieri Rondinelli's remarks is the list of citizens he represented; their names appear in M. Rocke, "Male Homosexuality and its Regulation in Late-Medieval Florence" (Ph.D. diss., State University of New York at Binghamton, 1990), 69n.84. They included a number of the leading men of the regime. Within the spectrum of the governing class this group had a decidedly conservative cast, yet it is unclear whether their interests in intensifying repression of sodomy had a more articulated political purpose. Significantly, however, the list does not include the Medici, who were on the threshold of their rise to power and were sometimes accused of being "soft" on sodomy, nor any of their partisans (see later).

69. PR 105, 236r (Dec. 13, 1415). I am grateful to Andrea Zorzi for bringing this to my attention.

70. PR 106, 164v (Oct. 23, 1416).

71. CP 43, 185r (Mar. 31). The speaker was Felice Brancacci. I thank Gene Brucker for this reference.

72. PR 108, 2v–3v (Apr. 15, 1418); excerpts in Brucker, *Society*, 202–203.

73. PR 108, 245rv (Feb. 24, 1418/1419).

74. Ibid., 3rv. Bernardino of Siena warned Florentines who voted for sodomites after taking an oath not to that they committed a mortal sin; *Prediche* (Florence, 1425), 2:157.

75. PR 108, 245r.

76. See the remarks of Bernardino of Siena, later, and chapter 5.

77. PR 108, 3v.

78. Ibid., 245v. According to the same law, at the end of the commission's one-year term their duties were to pass to the Ufficiali dell'onestà. This perhaps strengthens the implicit association between the state's encouragement of prostitution and the control of sodomy.

79. The sermons on sodomy are in *Prediche* (Florence, 1424), 2:30–36, 37–56, 57–71; (Florence, 1425), 2:270–90; (Siena, 1425), 2:98–112; (Siena, 1427), 893–919; and "De horrendo peccato contra naturam," in *Opera omnia*, 3:267–84. The social content of Bernardino's commentary on sodomy is reviewed in M. Rocke, "Sodomites in Fifteenth-Century Tuscany: The Views of Bernardino of Siena," in *Pursuit of Sodomy*, ed. Gerard and Hekma, 7–31. See also Trexler, *Public Life*, 380–82.

80. Revised under Bernardino's direction, the statutes of 1425 in Perugia and Siena set harsh penalties for sodomy. But in both places his reforms were soon weakened or revoked; I. Origo, *The World of San Bernardino* (London, 1963), 152–53.

81. *Prediche* (Florence, 1424), 1:34.

82. Ibid., 2:20.

83. *Prediche* (Siena, 1425), 2:107.

84. Ibid., 106, 107; *Prediche* (Siena, 1427), 906, 908.

85. Bernardino of Siena, *Opera omnia*, 3:275.

86. *Prediche* (Siena, 1427), 906–907. Bernardino's stress on the link between demography and sodomy contrasts sharply with Savonarola's silence on this issue at the end of the century, when population growth had strongly recovered.

87. *Prediche* (Florence, 1424), 1:35; *Prediche* (Siena, 1425), 2:103, 104. On the reputation of Italy in general, *Prediche* (Siena, 1427), 899, 901, 902, 905.

88. *Prediche* (Siena, 1427), 898.

89. *Prediche* (Florence, 1424), 2:41; *Prediche* (Florence, 1425), 3:42.

90. *Prediche* (Florence, 1424), 2:40–41.

91. Ibid., 44; on gifts and flattery, ibid., 40, 47; *Prediche* (Siena, 1427), 903.

92. *Prediche* (Siena, 1425), 2:100.

93. *Prediche* (Florence, 1425), 3:42.

94. See chapter 5.

95. *Prediche* (Florence, 1425), 3:42–43. On parents "sprucing up" their sons until they became sodomites, ibid., 2:184.

96. *Prediche* (Siena, 1427), 908.

97. *Prediche* (Florence, 1424), 2:40, 35.

98. *Prediche* (Siena, 1427), 904. For other passages in which he singled out mothers, *Prediche* (Florence, 1425), 2:275 and 3:42; *Prediche* (Siena, 1425), 2: 102; *Prediche* (Siena, 1427), 904. On mothers who make their sons "effeminate" by feeding them "superfluous delights," Bernardino of Siena, *Opera omnia*, 3:269. For other allusions to "males making themselves females" through sodomy, see *Prediche* (Florence, 1424), 2:45, 141; *Prediche* (Florence, 1425), 3:33; *Prediche* (Siena, 1425), 2:106. David Herlihy argues that moralists' complaints about mothers' effeminizing effects on sons might have reflected what he depicts as the considerable influence women often had in Florentine families. Since husbands were on average thirteen years older than their wives, fathers were often aged and distant models or dead by the time their sons reached adolescence, and this ostensibly gave mothers a decisive role in passing on cultural values to them; Herlihy, "Vieillir," 1341–45; Herlihy and Klapisch-Zuber, *Les Toscans*, 394–400, 435–37, 603–6. Yet as Bernardino's remarks here show, he reproached fathers for the same influence Herlihy ascribes exclusively to mothers. Lauro Martines rightly cautions that moralists' fears about mothers' pernicious effects on sons were a "caricature" with ancient roots; "A Way of Looking at Women in Renaissance Florence," *Journal of Medieval and Renaissance Studies* 4 (1974): 23.

99. A *travestito* does appear in a case in 1497, but with an uncertain meaning and in a context quite unlike that suggested by Bernardino; see chapter 5. Guido Ruggiero discusses a case of male transvestism in fourteenth-century Venice (*Boundaries*, 136), but his conclusions are questioned by Trumbach in "Gender and the Homosexual Role," 162–63.

100. See chapter 3.

101. *Prediche* (Siena, 1425), 100.

102. *Prediche* (Florence, 1424), 2:40, 41.

103. Patronage has increasingly come to be seen as a key to understanding social and political relations in late medieval Florence and Italy. For an interpretation of sodomy in this light, and relevant bibliography, see chapter 5.

104. *Prediche* (Florence, 1424), 2:47.

105. For example, *Prediche* (Florence, 1425), 2:270–87.

106. Ibid., 3:44. On attitudes toward youths see Trexler, *Public Life*, 387–99 and passim; D. Herlihy, "Some Psychological and Social Roots of Violence in the Tuscan Cities," in *Violence and Civil Disorder in Italian Cities, 1200–1500*, ed. L. Martines (Berkeley, 1972), 135–37.

107. *Prediche* (Florence, 1424), 2:49–51.

108. See chapters 4 and 5.

109. *Prediche* (Florence, 1424), 2:35.

110. *Prediche* (Siena, 1425), 2:109.

111. His source was apparently a remark by Jerome in the Decretals; *Prediche* (Siena, 1427), 916.

112. *Prediche* (Florence, 1424), 1:416.

113. See chapter 4.

114. *Prediche* (Florence, 1425), 2:276; *Prediche* (Siena, 1427), 917, 910–11.

115. *Prediche* (Siena, 1425), 2:105.

116. *Prediche* (Siena, 1427), 410.

117. On relations between sodomites and women see also Rocke, "Sodomites," 20–22, and this work, chapter 4.

118. *Prediche* (Florence, 1425), 2:276.

119. *Prediche* (Florence, 1425), 2:184, 273; *Prediche* (Siena, 1427), 434–36, 897; *Prediche* (Florence, 1424), 1:387.

120. *Prediche* (Siena, 1427), 436, 853, 897; *Prediche* (Florence, 1424), 2:141. According to Jean Toscan, in Carnival songs and burlesque poems women's menstrual period was the justification most often given for practicing heterosexual anal intercourse; *Le Carnaval*, 258–63.

121. Bernardino of Siena, *Opera omnia*, 2:83.

122. *Prediche* (Florence, 1424), 2:47.

123. *Prediche* (Florence, 1424), 2:35; *Prediche* (Florence, 1425), 3:104.

124. For example, *Prediche* (Florence, 1425), 2:273; *Prediche* (Siena, 1425), 2: 103; see also chapter 4, 135.

125. *Prediche* (Florence, 1424), 2:51. Bernardino used the phrase "sono di quella arte," which reappears in other remarks (e.g., "Qui se ne fa arte! Annole posto nome l'arte gentile della seta!" ibid., 35) and in some denunciations for sodomy (e.g., UN 20, 40v and 57v). According to Toscan, in burlesque literature the word *arte*, which means "art, skill, or guild," indicated the anus, sodomy, or sexual activity in general; *Le Carnaval*, 4:1663. In its sense as a form of association, the term strengthens the notion that sodomites were thought to constitute a special interest group.

126. *Prediche* (Florence, 1425), 2:116.

127. See D. V. Kent, *The Rise of the Medici: Faction in Florence (1426–1434)* (Oxford, 1978); Brucker, *Civic World*, 472–507.

128. *Prediche* (Florence, 1425), 2:118; the editor, Cannarozzi, noted Bernardino's possible allusion to the Medici family. See also Trexler, *Public Life*, 381.

129. CP 43, 185r (Mar. 31).

130. Modern editions and Italian translations include *L'Ermafrodito*, ed. R. Gagliardi (Milan, 1980); *L'Ermafrodito*, ed. J. Tognelli (Rome 1968). On Beccadelli, the work, and its reception, with additional bibliography, see these editions, and G. Resta, "Antonio Beccadelli," in *Dizionario biografico degli italiani* (Rome, 1965), 7:400–406.

131. For unknown reasons, Cosimo declined to sponsor him. However, the legend that he burned the book (see *L'Ermafrodito*, ed. Tognelli, 23) is apparently belied by the presence in his son Piero's library of a manuscript of the work bearing the inscription "COSMI CODEX HIC EST.VALE," and its appearance in an inventory of 1456 (before Cosimo's death in 1464); see F. Ames-Lewis, *The Library and Manuscripts of Piero di Cosimo de' Medici* (New York, 1984), 249.

132. Mediceo avanti il principato 3n.125 (Mar. 13, 1431/1432); excerpts are

in C. Guasti, ed., *Commissioni di Rinaldo degli Albizzi per il Comune di Firenze dal MCCCXCIX al MCCCCXXXIII* (Florence, 1867–1873), 3:523n.1. The meaning of Tinucci's "man or woman" is not clear; the phrase possibly referred to Micheletto's preferred sexual role or, more plausibly, to his sexual ambiguity.

133. *Prediche* (Florence, 1424), 2:35, 42.

134. *Prediche* (Florence, 1425), 3:27; *Prediche* (Siena, 1425), 2:101.

135. *Prediche* (Florence, 1424), 2:66.

136. *Prediche* (Florence, 1425), 2:275.

137. *Prediche* (Florence, 1424), 2:48.

138. Sermons of April 5 to 8, ibid., 2:30–36, 37–56, 57–71; scribe's remark, 48; "burning of the vanities," 87.

Chapter 2

1. UN 5, 47r.

2. UN 31, 35r.

3. PR 123, 31v–36v. Votes were 189–39 in the Council of the Popolo and 199–25 in the Council of the Commune. Translated excerpts are in G. Brucker, *The Society of Renaissance Florence: A Documentary Study* (New York, 1971), 203–204.

4. PR 123, 31v–32r.

5. P. Labalme, "Sodomy and Venetian Justice in the Renaissance," *Legal History Review* 52 (1984): 224 and passim; G. Ruggiero, *The Boundaries of Eros: Sex Crime and Sexuality in Renaissance Venice* (New York, 1985), 134; E. Pavan, "Police des moeurs, société et politique à Venise à la fin du Moyen Age," *Revue historique* 264 (1980): 268.

6. Archivio di Stato di Lucca, Consiglio generale 16, 796v (Mar. 8); the magistracy operated until 1649. No specific studies exist of this office or of sodomy in Lucca. Useful if limited information can be found in L. Marcello, "Società maschile e sodomia: Dal declino della 'polis' al Principato," *Archivio storico italiano* 150 (1992):115–38; R. Canosa and I. Colonnello, *Storia della prostituzione in Italia dal Quattrocento alla fine del Settecento* (Rome, 1989), 57–73.

7. G. N. Zazzu, "Prostituzione e moralità pubblica nella Genova del '400," *Studi genuensi*, n.s., 5 (1987):60.

8. See chapter 6.

9. Earlier laws on sodomy referred explicitly to both males and females; e.g., *Statuti 1325*, 218, and *Statuta 1415*, 1:320–21. Mention of women returns to the laws only in the mid-1490s.

10. I have found only four convictions by the Night Officers for heterosexual sodomy before 1478. See also chapter 6.

11. PR 124, 148r (Aug. 5): hence the officials' new title, Ufficiali di notte e conservatori dell'onestà dei monasteri. The founding law of the original magistracy is PR 111, 45r (June 25, 1421). In 1436 Pope Eugenius IV attempted to have this function of the Office of the Night abolished as an infringement of ecclesiastical privilege; G. Brucker, *Renaissance Florence* (New York, 1969), 192.

12. PR 145, 2v (Apr. 10).

13. The first number is from Ruggiero (*Boundaries*, 128, Table 6), the second from Pavan ("Police," 276).

14. W. L. Gundersheimer, "Crime and Punishment in Ferrara, 1440–1500," in *Violence and Civil Disorder in Italian Cities, 1200–1500*, ed. L. Martines (Berkeley, 1972), 115; Canosa and Colonnello, *Storia della prostituzione*, 67, n. 25.

15. E. W. Monter, "Sodomy and Heresy in Early Modern Switzerland," in *Historical Perspectives on Homosexuality*, ed. S. J. Licata and R. P. Peterson (New York, 1981), 54–55.

16. W. Monter, *Frontiers of Heresy: The Spanish Inquisition from the Basque Lands to Sicily* (Cambridge, 1990), 289.

17. Ibid., 288–89. Total conviction figures from 1566 to 1620 for Barcelona, Valencia, and Saragossa, respectively, are 86, 107, and 178; R. Carrasco, *Inquisición y represión sexual en Valencia: Historia de los sodomitos (1565–1785)* (Barcelona, 1985), 76. For Seville see also M. E. Perry, "The 'Nefarious Sin' in Early Modern Seville," in *The Pursuit of Sodomy: Male Homosexuality in Renaissance and Enlightenment Europe*, ed. K. Gerard and G. Hekma (New York, 1989), 67. In Portugal the Inquisition tried 408 men for sodomy between 1587 and 1744, and convicted only about 30; L. Mott and A. Assunçao, "Love's Labors Lost: Five Letters from a Seventeenth-Century Portuguese Sodomite," in *Pursuit of Sodomy*, ed. Gerard and Hekma, 99.

18. Conviction estimates for the Night Officers are based on a count of all condemnations in extant records. Convictions are preserved both in the incomplete registers of the Ufficiali di notte and, for many of the missing years, in GAN 77–88 (*Condanne profferite dagli Ufiziali intrinseci*). Together these sources account for roughly fifty-six of the seventy years from 1432 to 1502 and document 1,953 convictions. Based on average numbers of convictions for different periods, it can be estimated that the Night Officers levied a total of approximately 2,416 convictions for homosexual sodomy.

The estimate of individuals incriminated for sodomy to the Night Officers derives from an analysis of their proceedings from 1478 to 1502 (UN 19–35). In the seventeen years for which registers are extant, 4,062 different persons were implicated and 582 convicted, some more than once for a total of 638 convictions (see later for more details on this survey). Assuming that the ratio of 6.4 persons implicated to every one conviction also held in earlier years, it can be estimated that nearly 15,500 individuals came to the Night Officer's attention for homosexual sodomy from 1432 to 1502.

Convictions by other magistracies over the same period amounted to several hundred, although a complete survey is impossible. From 1455 to 1466 the podestà and capitano condemned nine men for sodomy; S. Cohn, Jr., *The Laboring Classes in Renaissance Florence* (New York, 1980), 279–80, Appendix H.3. From 1478 through 1502 the Eight of Watch levied at least 247 convictions for homosexual sodomy and an estimated 800 up to 1532 (see further later).

19. Electoral procedures are described in PR 123, 32r, 35v–36r.

20. PR 137, 257rv (Dec. 30).

21. Officeholding qualifications are in PR 123, 32r. Their notaries also had to be at least forty years old and married; ibid., 143v (July 5, 1432).

22. PR 123, 34v.

23. PR 134, 253v (April 8). According to account books, by the 1490s their salaries had declined to three florins; UN 37–45.

24. UN 36, 98v, 104v, 114v, 121v, 128v, 133v, 137v.

25. PR 145, 75v (June 7, 1454).

26. On ritual see R. Trexler, *Public Life in Renaissance Florence* (New York, 1980); on the feast of St. John, 240–70.

27. PR 123, 32v.

28. A. Zorzi, *L'amministrazione della giustizia penale nella Repubblica fiorentina: Aspetti e problemi* (Florence, 1988), 79–82.

29. PR 123, 34rv.

30. For *tamburi* in Florence (1480), UN 19 (3), 5r; in Prato and Pistoia (1454), UN 36, 101r; Pisa and Prato (1481), UN 20, 9v; Arezzo and Empoli (1492), UN 27, 7r. Notaries sometimes translated accusations into Latin rather than transcribing the Italian.

31. UN 3 and 9 contain brief summaries of denunciations from 1452 to 1502 (procedural registers normally conserve the full accusations). The figure of 4,750 derives from a rough count of the summaries, ignoring repetition of names and other inaccuracies.

32. A retainer employed from at least 1480 to 1494 was identified both as a *secretus explorator* and as a *famiglio*, implying the two roles were the same; UN 19 (3), 7r; UN 20, 10r; UN 29, 5r. Officials in 1481 authorized themselves to hire their own spies, one for each; UN 20, 10r. This may suggest that they used their personal spies to pursue alleged sodomites, a practice that could easily have led to abuses.

33. Account books sometimes record payments or gifts to lawyers; e.g., UN 36, 121v; UN 37, 19v. For examples of legal advice, UN 1, 5r–8r; UN 30, 5r, 52r.

34. PR 123, 32v. Occasionally the officials agreed that fewer of them could authorize arrests, citations, or interrogations; e.g., UN 27, 7r; UN 29, 2r, 4v.

35. The law did not authorize use of torture and it was rarely recorded (but notaries may not have been required to do so). Only in the Savonarolan period is there ample proof that suspects were tortured. A graphic account is in UN 30, 48r; see also UN 30, 58r, 84v; UN 31, 16v, 20v.

36. PR 123, 33v.

37. Ibid., 33v; passage quoted, 34v.

38. See chapter 1, 32.

39. See R. Goldthwaite, *The Building of Renaissance Florence: An Economic and Social History* (Baltimore, 1980), 317–50, for wage rates and standard of living; also 429–30 on the value of the florin, and 435–42 on workers' wages. Goldthwaite estimates the minimum yearly cost of maintaining a single adult in fifteenth-century Florence at roughly 55 to 75 lire, around 14 to 19 florins (348). The steady appreciation of the gold florin with respect to the lira, the money of account tied to the local market, in the long run raised the value of fines paid in florins and made them weigh more heavily on working men.

40. PR 123, 32v–33r. While new to Florence, graduated penalties for sodomy had precedents in Tuscany and central Italy. In fourteenth-century Siena penalties were scaled by age, and in Perugia according to the number of convictions, as in Florence; see C. Falletti-Fossati, *Costumi senesi nella seconda metà del secolo XIV* (Siena, 1881), 159–60; on Perugia, M. Goodich, "Sodomy in Medieval Secular Law," *Journal of Homosexuality* 1 (1976): 300.

41. PR 123, 33rv.

42. *Statuta 1415*, 1:249. It should be observed that even though the founding law of the Office of the Night and other sodomy laws specified that the upper limit of minor status was eighteen years completed (that is, the eighteenth birthday),

officials commonly treated this boundary with a good deal of latitude. In effect, they extended it to include those whose age was indicated as eighteen and who were thus probably in their nineteenth year. In all discussions of age groups and minor status throughout this book, I have followed this practice, categorizing those whose given age was eighteen as minors.

43. See chapters 3 and 4.

44. In this regard, the contrast with Venetian practice is striking. First and foremost, the age of legal majority in Venice was fourteen years, compared with eighteen in Florence (at least regarding sodomy). Adolescents in Venice between the ages of fourteen and eighteen, whatever their role in sodomy, could thus be punished severely as adults, while their counterparts in Florence usually suffered no penalty whatsoever. Moreover, after 1424 Venetian authorities ordered some form of punishment even for boys over the age of ten. See Ruggiero, *Boundaries*, 123; Labalme, "Sodomy," 236; M. Rocke, "Il fanciullo e il sodomita: Pederastia, cultura maschile e vita civile nella Firenze del Quattrocento," in *Infanzie: Funzioni di un gruppo liminale dal mondo classico all'Età moderna*, Laboratorio di Storia, vol. 6, ed. O. Niccoli (Florence, 1993), 214–15.

45. See R. Trexler, "Ritual in Florence: Adolescence and Salvation in the Renaissance," in *The Pursuit of Holiness in Late Medieval and Renaissance Religion*, ed. C. Trinkaus and H. Oberman (Leiden, 1974): 200–264; Trexler, *Public Life*, 368–87. Ruggiero also suggests that increased attention to homosexual behavior might have helped refine notions of age categories; *Boundaries*, 160.

46. PR 123, 35r.

47. PR 140, 5v (Apr. 3).

48. PR 123, 34v–35r.

49. Andrea Zorzi endorsed this impression in a personal communication. Already in 1365, passives or their relatives for them were allowed to denounce themselves in return for immunity; see chapter 1, 22.

50. See Labalme, "Sodomy," 225. People derided the law also because it implicated mature men as passive partners.

51. See further later.

52. As Zorzi notes, all the citizen magistracies were limited to levying mainly monetary sanctions (*L'amministrazione*, 81). At least at their inception, none could apply sentences of corporal or capital punishments, reserved to the foreign judges. Still, the form of the new penalties for sodomy was unusual and reflected concerns specific to its control.

53. See Ruggiero, *Boundaries*, 121–26; Pavan, "Police," 276–78; Labalme, "Sodomy," 241–47. A systematic survey of penalties for sodomy in Italy is lacking, so it is hard to broaden the comparison.

54. Similarly, in Lucca a law of 1462 allowed the sodomy officials to commute corporal and capital penalties to fines to avoid scandals that might occur if the laws were enforced too strictly; Archivio di Stato di Lucca, Consiglio Generale 18, 528v (Aug. 25).

55. As suggested also by Zorzi, *L'amministrazione*, 56–57.

56. See A. Molho, *Florentine Public Finances in the Early Renaissance, 1400–1433* (Cambridge, Mass., 1971), esp. 153–82.

57. See, for example, UN 37, 3r.

58. The total amount of money the Night Officers took in cannot be determined, but their account books for a few years have survived. During the term

1453/1454 they collected some 767 florins; UN 36, 110r. From March 1495 to November 1502, they took in roughly 3,200 gold florins and 300 silver florins; UN 37–45. These were sizable sums, but most went to pay salaries, expenses, informants, and their obligations to the Convertite (see later); little remained for the municipal coffers. The problem of collecting fines is discussed further later.

59. PR 126, 264rv (Oct. 25); PR 131, 155v (Aug. 23).

60. PR 137, 318r (Mar. 11, 1446/1447); PR 138, 23v (Apr. 24, 1447); gifts in UN 36, 96v. See also later.

61. UN 37, 4r.

62. PR 123, 35r.

63. PR 131, 11v (Apr. 9).

64. PR 140, 5v (Apr. 3). However, see 66 and n. 123.

65. On Jews, see G. Antonelli, "La magistratura degli Otto di guardia a Firenze," *Archivio storico italiano* 92 (1954): 22. In a 1492 ruling that indirectly defines the limits of the Night Officers' competence, the Eight licensed their retainers to assist these officials with arrests "except in cases of anal injury and of crimes committed in churches"; OGBR 91, 56r (Apr. 28). See also 66.

66. PR 123, 143r.

67. See A. Zorzi, "I fiorentini e gli uffici pubblici nel primo Quattrocento: Concorrenza, abusi, illegalità," *Quaderni storici* 66 (1987): 725–51.

68. PR 123, 143r. Unlike later, these accusations were unfortunately not recorded.

69. Ibid., 34r; the justification comes from the July 5 law, 143r.

70. Ibid., 143r.

71. On the composition of the factions and the events of these years, see especially D. V. Kent, *The Rise of the Medici: Faction in Florence (1426–1434)* (Oxford, 1978); see also G. Brucker, *The Civic World of Early Renaissance Florence* (Princeton, 1977), 472–507.

72. UN 1, unfol. (May 22); 30r (July 12).

73. Biblioteca Riccardiana, Florence, Fondo Moreniano, ms. 301, 53r. Unsurprisingly, Spini failed to mention his conviction in his own *ricordanze*; Carte strozziane, 2d ser., 13.

74. UN 1, unfol. (May 22); 31v (July 12).

75. Ibid., 3r (July 23).

76. Ibid., 2v (Aug. 7, 1432).

77. Roberto's defense, ibid., 4v–5r (Aug. 8); the legal opinion, 5r–8r (Aug. 8); Antonio's absolution, 32v (Sept. 5). Goro di Giusto da Carmignano's arrest on the charge of harboring sodomites, 3v (July 28); Roberto's guarantee for him, 4r (Aug. 7).

78. GAN 77, 558r.

79. Balìe 25, 72rv (Nov. 25), 117v (Dec. 28). The same applied to men charged with entering convents.

80. Kent, *Rise*, 180–85.

81. On the Spini family, ibid. 163–64, 295. For Spini's rental arrangement with Strozzi, Catasto 75, 418r.

82. Kent, *Rise*, 74n, 165.

83. See chapter 5.

84. The only certain ally of the Medici who appeared in these years was Bernardo di Cristofano Carnesecchi, but he only put up the surety for Salvestro di ser Baldo,

accused but not convicted of hosting sodomites in his house; UN 1, 4r; see Kent, *Rise.* Also Piero di Giovacchino Ricci, aged between fourteen and eighteen, who was implicated as the passive partner of a convicted sodomite in 1432 but absolved, might have been the Medici partisan of this name identified by Dale Kent; UN 1, 36rv; *Rise*, Appendix I.

85. Kent, *Rise*, 290n.

86. Several officials were friends or partisans of the Medici, including Nerone Dietisalvi and Niccolò d'Arrigo di Corso in 1432/1433 (see Kent, *Rise*, 131–32, 260), and Giovanni Corbinelli, Luca degli Albizzi, and Bartolomeo Corsi in 1433/1434 (ibid., 52, 59, 60, 127). Officers in 1434/1435 included Piero Bonciani, an occasional confidant of the Medici, and Lorenzo Lenzi, an enemy of the Albizzi faction (ibid., 104, 282n, 320). The weak representation of the "aristocratic" party makes a sharp contrast. Lionardo Strozzi (ibid., 176, 182) and Tedice degli Albizzi, officers in 1432/1433, both had kin exiled in 1434, but they were not punished. Later even this tenuous conservative presence disappeared.

87. Figures derived from GAN 77, 79 (1 and 2), 80.

88. GAN 79 (2), 57r; see similar remarks in other sentences in the same volume.

89. PR 131, 11v (Apr. 9).

90. GAN 79 (2), 44rv (Jan. 13, 1435/1436).

91. These figures come from a survey of convictions in GAN 77–84 (records missing for 1448 to 1450 and 1453 to 1456). The Night Officers' own registers survive for only two years before 1459.

92. For how these estimates were derived, see n. 18. The Night Officers' procedural registers are extant for thirty of the forty-three years from 1459 to 1502 (volumes 4–35), and convictions for some missing years to 1477 are in GAN 85–88.

93. PR 137, 257rv (Dec. 30).

94. Ibid., 257r.

95. PR 149, 40r.

96. GAN 82, 132r. Earlier (44rv) they had fined him 200 florins, instead of the 100 prescribed. I have not located his remaining case.

97. GAN 84, 234rv, 284r.

98. UN 3, at dates.

99. PR 149, 40v.

100. GAN 84, 286r; their next sentence is ibid., 401r (June 27, 1459).

101. Balìe 29, 78v.

102. See S. Cohen, "Convertite e Malmaritate: Donne 'irregolari' e ordini religiosi nella Firenze rinascimentale," *Memoria: Rivista di storia delle donne* 5 (November 1982), 46–63; Cohen, *The Evolution of Women's Asylums Since 1500: From Refuges for Ex-Prostitutes to Shelters for Battered Women* (New York, 1992); M. S. Mazzi, *Prostitute e lenoni nella Firenze del Quattrocento* (Milan, 1991), 393–403.

103. PR 137, 318r (Mar. 11, 1446/1447); PR 138, 23r (Apr. 24, 1447). By the late fifteenth century, this quota had declined to one-fourth.

104. PR 146, 301r (Dec. 24). Related laws reinforcing the provisions of this first law followed; PR 146, 377r (Feb. 28, 1455/1456) and PR 147, 12v (Apr. 15, 1456).

105. PR 148, 441v (Feb. 21, 1457/1458).

106. Balìe 29, 78v.

107. After the suppression of the Office of the Night in 1502, the Convertite

petitioned the government to maintain the subsidy from fines in sodomy and convent cases, which they claimed was being withheld by the magistracies that took over the Night Officers' duties; PR 195, 4v (Mar. 31, 1504).

108. Balìe 29, 79r.

109. PR 150, 119v. Only four convictions are recorded in the ten months between this and the previous law; GAN 84.

110. Guido Ruggiero tends to blur this distinction in explaining why passives in Venice were usually given lighter penalties than their partners. Although he notes that most passives were under fourteen or in any case young, and admits that their age qualified their sentence, he draws the improbable conclusion that since the active partner was more culpable, Venetians "uniquely" reversed traditional Western prejudices against male sexual passivity; *Boundaries*, 121. On the vicious slurs Florentine informers used against passives, see chapter 3.

111. PR 165, 94v (July 22). For examples, see UN 16 and 17 (1472–1474); similar arrangements also appear later.

112. PR 181, 18v (June 11).

113. From UN 4, 8, and 16.

114. See N. Rubinstein, *The Government of Florence Under the Medici, 1434–1494* (Oxford, 1966), 88–135.

115. Trexler, *Public Life*, 387–418. On lower-class youths' support of the Medici during the Pazzi conspiracy see F. W. Kent, "Lorenzo de' Medici and the 'Lads from the Canto della Macina,' " *Rinascimento*, 2d ser., 23 (1983): 252–60.

116. See chapter 6, 206.

117. See the Epilogue.

118. Notaries' indexes of the magistracy's registers all begin with 1459, suggesting that by then earlier volumes were already scattered.

119. UN 19–35, for the years (from November to November) 1478 to 1483, 1485 to 1487, 1489 to 1494, 1495 to 1497, 1498 to 1499, 1500 to 1502. The results of the analysis discussed here slightly revise figures in M. Rocke, "Il controllo dell'omosessualità a Firenze nel XV secolo: Gli Ufficiali di Notte," *Quaderni storici* 66 (1987): 701–23. Imprecise or incomplete recording of names and other information sometimes makes it hard to identify as the same person individuals who appear repeatedly. The number of individuals given here is thus inevitably approximate.

120. The Eight received full jurisdiction over sodomy in 1494 (chapter 6), but prosecuted cases from at least 1460; see Antonelli, "La magistratura," 22. By this time the podestà's role in policing sodomy was negligible, reflecting this institution's decline; see Zorzi, *L'amministrazione*, 72–76. The Conservatori di legge gained competence over sodomy in 1495 (chapter 6), and may have tried some cases earlier, but its records for this period no longer survive.

121. OGBR 49–124 (sixty-three extant volumes). The difficulty of identifying individuals is compounded in these records since the Eight, unlike the Night Officers, often suppressed the passive partner's name. Between 1478 and 1502, at least ten persons were convicted by both magistracies.

122. On heterosexual sodomy, see chapter 6.

123. See 54. The Night Officers' observance of this ordinance was inconsistent. In the 1478–1502 survey, twenty-one cases involving anal injury were reported to them, and they delivered eleven convictions. Convictions in such cases are also found in the 1460s and 1470s. Fulfilling the spirit, if not the letter, of the

law, they sometimes convicted men who had injured their partners, and then informed one of the foreign judges so that his court could also prosecute them; e.g., UN 13, 15rv. At other times, they admitted their incompetence and notified one of the main courts or the Eight; e.g., UN 13, 23v; UN 27, 95r.

124. Antonelli, "La magistratura," 22.

125. See 54. For examples, see chapter 5, 156.

126. This number includes 187 passive partners (about 15 percent of the total and 40 percent of those questioned) who were interrogated but for whom no denunciation can be found. The absence of accusations is due mainly to the organization of the records: each volume corresponds to the one-year term of notaries, who began their office roughly halfway into the term of the officials. Thus in any given isolated volume or sequence of volumes, the first half-year of the first group of officials is missing, probably including accusations against boys later interrogated. Since for the same reason the second half-year of the last group of officials is also missing, the interrogations of some passive partners whose denunciations are preserved are also probably lacking.

127. UN 24, 43r; UN 29, 66r, 102r.

128. For claims that charges were made out of "enmity," UN 11, 3v; UN 30, 86r. Salvi Panuzzi claimed that a man falsely accused him of sodomy to avenge an affront Panuzzi had allegedly given him when the former was one of the Eight of Watch; UN 30, 88v. One boy said that a man who was madly in love with him had denounced him only because the boy refused to yield to him; UN 35, 37v.

129. See chapter 6, 219.

130. UN 19, 25v, 32r; UN 20, 49v, 53r, 58r; UN 21, 30r.

131. UN 19 (3), 73r.

132. UN 20, 42v–46v, 49v, 50r, 51r, 58v.

133. UN 22, 38r, 44r.

134. PR 181, 18v (June 11).

135. PR 186, 190r (Feb. 9, 1495/1496). On both these laws, see also chapter 6, 202, 208.

136. The difference between these figures and the total derives from the fact that four persons, as boys, were named as passive partners of self-accusers and later also denounced themselves for sodomizing someone else, and one man denounced himself for sodomizing someone and was also named by another passive self-accuser.

137. UN 23, 33r.

138. See chapter 4, 143.

139. UN 15, 5v.

140. UN 14, 36rv. See also 75.

141. UN 15, 5r; UN 18, 43v, where his age in 1474 is indicated as twenty-four; UN 18 (2), 38r, 84r. Jacopo may have been somewhat older than his recorded age, as he, or at any rate someone of this name, was convicted for active sodomy in 1460 and was said to be a minor aged eighteen or under; UN 5, 64r.

142. UN 22, 30r, 31r.

143. UN 20, 36v, 37v. By law, a person who denounced himself won immunity only if he had not already been incriminated for the same relationship. But in several cases in which men self-confessed after their partners had named them under interrogation, officials ignored regulations and accepted the self-accusation; e.g., UN 20, 45v, 46r.

144. For examples, see chapter 5, 188.

145. UN 16, 55r. For unknown reasons, Folchi's reversal and explanation were crossed out. I found only one similar case, UN 34, 32v, 35r.

146. They clearly expected boys named by self-accusers to confess when they were questioned. In four cases in which boys disclosed by self-denouncers denied, when questioned, that anyone had sodomized them, or seemed to withhold the names of some partners, the officers recorded their disbelief and punished each severely for his "obstinance"; UN 14, 69v, 80rv, 44v; UN 18 (2), 9v, 90v.

147. UN 20, 46r; UN 22, 37v; UN 23, 33r; UN 24, 42r.

148. UN 17, 27v, 54r; UN 18 (1), 45r; UN 18 (2), 42r; UN 19 (3), 28v. Further on Jacopo later and in chapter 4.

149. UN 16, 56r.

150. UN 18 (1), 57v; UN 21, 49v; UN 24, 37v.

151. OGBR 80, 130v.

152. This refers to the number of partners named, not to the individuals involved, many of whom were implicated various times by different boys.

153. UN 30, 63v; UN 32, 28r; UN 35, 42r.

154. OGBR 134, 87v; OGBR 141, 20v.

155. UN 30, 79r; and a complex case in UN 30, 65r, 67v, 68v–69v, 70r, 71rv.

156. UN 30, 79r.

157. UN 30, 91v-92r. For a gift to him, from an alleged lover, of hose that fit this description, see 37v.

158. UN 30, 63v.

159. UN 31, 46r. Pitti was convicted; 103v.

160. UN 31, 48rv. Bonsi was convicted and fined the large sum of 200 florins; 107r. Domenico also recounted a similar attempt to persuade him to change his testimony against a man of the Martini family, a priest; 46v.

161. This figure excludes several others who confessed but, as minors or clergymen, for example, were practically or legally immune from punishment.

162. For proportions of minors and clergymen, see chapter 4.

163. Of some 3,881 cases (usually relationships but sometimes an individual accused alone) in the 1478–1502 survey, 3,263 (84 percent) ended in absolution.

164. See more on this point in chapter 6, 214–15.

165. UN 14, 63rv; UN 16, 69v; UN 18, 82v; GAN 88, 472rv, 541r, 581rv; UN 20, 72v; UN 21, 70v, 77v, 80v; UN 22, 70r; UN 24, 61r. In 1481 the Eight convicted him for an unspecified crime, but it was probably sodomy since they ordered him to pay his fine to the Night Officers' treasurer; OGBR 59, 65r, 74r. Jacopo was also accused several other times but absolved from 1470 to 1487 (see chapter 4).

166. UN 17, 30r, 62v; UN 18 (1), 49v, 81r; UN 18 (2), 44r; UN 19, 31v, 73r; UN 21, 31v, 73r; UN 24, 39v, 40v, 41r; UN 25, 47v, 60v.

167. See also chapter 5, 174.

168. UN 12, 12r.

169. From 1478 to 1502, 143 family clans were represented among the Night Officers and their treasurers, and 92 had at least one incriminated member. Of the 203 officers or treasurers, 40 probably had close family members implicated.

170. See later, and chapter 4, 129.

171. See chapter 5, 181.

172. UN 28, 25rv; UN 29, 62v. Only the payment record survives for his con-

viction; UN 37, 1v. Implicated again in 1497 with the same boy he allegedly sodomized in 1494, he was again absolved; UN 31, 51rv. In 1480 Lenzoni was aged fifty with a wife and nine children; Catasto 1010, 312r.

173. UN 30, 44r, 184r, 185rv and 121r. Taddeo implored the officials to act as quickly and discreetly as possible, "especially so that [Bernardo] is not damaged even further and these things do not become common knowledge . . . and for Bernardo's peace and quiet, and in conformity with his honor and decorum" (185r). They fined him 100 florins, or 50 florins if paid that day; he settled immediately. He was accused again around this time with another boy, who denied the charge; UN 30, 47r, 56v. His earlier cases are in UN 18 (2), 42v, 44r; UN 24, 36v. In 1480 Lorini was aged forty-nine with a wife and seven children; Catasto 1018, 191r.

174. UN 31, 42r. The accuser perhaps misjudged this provincial man's influence, for his son was questioned; 65r.

175. For one of several examples, see UN 30, 63r.

176. UN 12, 17r. As it turned out, Zanobi was absolved without interrogation; 85r.

177. UN 14, 36r.

178. The case against Del Bianco is in UN 34, 67v, 70v; UN 35, 33v, 110rv. Notice of the Conservatori's conviction of the three officials is in UN 35, 110r, and of their expulsion from the office in Tratte 905, 52r. For other examples of corruption in sodomy cases, see OGBR 87, 111r, in which the Night Officers' notary falsified testimony so that three innocent men were condemned; OGBR 136, 86rv, in which a retainer of the Eight extorted money from a man whose son, he falsely claimed, risked being convicted for sodomy.

179. UN 34, 4r.

180. OGBR 109, 51rv.

181. GAN 88, 396r. Eight days later, this sum was canceled after he made certain unrecorded payments; 397r.

182. See R. Trexler, "De la ville à la Cour: La déraison à Florence durant la République et la Grand Duché," in *Le Charivari*, ed. J. Le Goff and J.-C. Schmitt (Paris, 1981), 170–71.

183. For miters painted with the word *sodomita*, UN 30, 129v; and with the letter *B*, UN 30, 115r, 118v, 122r.

184. Biblioteca Nazionale Centrale, Florence, Conventi Soppressi C.7.2630, T. 1, unfol., at the year 1703. I thank Riccardo Spinelli for this reference.

185. OGBR 58, 79r; OGBR 69, 94r.

186. OGBR 68, 14v. Typically, the Eight agreed to revoke their shamings if the passive paid 150 florins and 900 lire and the active paid 200 florins and 1,500 lire. Jews were not always fined so heavily; some got off with unusually light fines of a few florins.

187. OGBR 79, 12v.

188. Simone Filipepi, *Cronaca*, in *Scelta di prediche e scritte di fra Girolamo Savonarola*, ed. P. Villari and E. Casanova (Florence, 1898), 501–02. A few scholars have commented on Filipepi's account, but until now no one has dated the case correctly or identified Pacchierotto; see R. Ridolfi, *Vita di Girolamo Savonarola* (Rome, 1952), 2:223, n. 35; Trexler, "De la ville à la Cour," 171. The man was Lorenzo di Zanobi del Magno, alias il Pacchierotto; his sentence, identical to Fili-

pepi's description except for the prison scene, is in OGBR 74, 20r (July 17), 120v (Oct. 27). Later linked to the anti-Savonarolan brigade known as the Compagnacci, Paccheriotto had quite a reputation in Florence. Luigi Pulci composed a satirical epitaph dedicated to him; S. Carra, "Due inediti e un raro di Luigi Pulci," *Interpres* 3 (1980): 164–66. And in a letter to Niccolò Machiavelli some twenty years after Pacchierotto's death, Francesco Guicciardini joked that the wool guild's request to Machiavelli to procure a preacher was as preposterous as seeking Pacchierotto's aid, while he was still alive, to find a wife for a friend; Niccolò Machiavelli, letter of May 17, 1521, *Tutte le opere*, ed. M. Martelli (Florence, 1971), 1202. A contemporary, Francesco Gerini, also depicted him as a sodomite in his poem, "Fiore di verità"; C. Foligno, "Un poema d'imitazione dantesca sul Savonarola," *Giornale storico della letteratura italiana* 87 (1926), 16.

189. On the last point, see chapter 5, 154.

190. Filipepi's description suggests there was a ward within the Stinche reserved in part for sodomites, as in some other early modern cities. For fifteenth-century Siena, see Allegretto Allegretti, *Diario senese*, in *Rerum italicarum scriptores* (Milan, 1723–1751), 23:824; sixteenth-century Seville, Perry, " 'Nefarious Sin,' " 70–71; and seventeenth-century Lima, Peru, Antonio de la Calancha, *Crónica moralizada del orden de san Agustín en el Perú* ([Lima], 1974–1982), 3:821. I wish to thank Richard Trexler for the last reference. Randolph Trumbach has suggested that the singling out of sodomites from other men in the London prison around 1800 was one sign of a new conceptualization of the sodomite as a distinct type of person defined by his desire for other males, often adults, as opposed to the traditional notion that all men could have such desires, usually, however, for boys; "Sodomitical Subcultures, Sodomitical Roles, and the Gender Revolution of the Eighteenth Century: The Recent Historiography," *Eighteenth Century Life* 9, n.s., 3 (1985): 118–19. If the same argument can be applied to this evidence on earlier similar arrangements, then the distinction he notes would have to be moved considerably backward in time, at least for these "Latin" cultures.

191. Biblioteca Nazionale Centrale, Florence, Fondo nazionale II.I.138, 71r–143v. For an analysis of the numbers of persons executed between 1420 and 1574 and the manners of their deaths, based on this source, see S. Y. Edgerton, Jr., *Pictures and Punishment: Art and Criminal Prosecution During the Florentine Renaissance* (Ithaca, 1985), 231–38. Of the three men in my survey whose death sentences seem to have been carried out, none was identified as a sodomite in the confraternity's list.

192. Salvi's father declared a patrimony of 2,542 florins in his 1457 tax return; Catasto 823, 191r.

193. Tratte 606, 190v; Tratte 607, 3v, 38r; Tratte 904, 26r, 152v; Tratte 986, 33r, 34r, 35r, 81r.

194. UN 11, 41r; UN 18 (2), 55r; UN 19, 25r; UN 27, 86v, 108r; UN 9, unfol. (June 10, 1495); OGBR 91, 35v, 44v. On the latter case from 1492, see also chapter 6, 202. For an indication of Panuzzi's notoriety as a sodomite, from an offhand comment about him in an accusation in 1497 against another man, see UN 31, 58v.

195. See chapter 3.

196. UN 30, 87r–89v, 130v–132v. On notions about categorizing dedicated sodomites as insane, see also chapter 6, n. 138.

197. His payment, UN 38, 1v. Afterward the officers revoked not only his death sentence but also that of life imprisonment; UN 30, 133r. See further on Panuzzi in following chapters.

198. UN 37–46.

199. The total amount the Night Officers collected from 1495 to 1502, including fines from a few passive partners and from cases of heterosexual sodomy and the violation of convents, came to slightly more than 3,200 gold florins and roughly 300 silver florins.

200. See G. Papanti, ed., *Facezie e motti dei secoli XV e XVI* (Bologna, 1874), 85, 137.

201. UN 27, 81v. On gifts, see chapter 5, 166. For another example of a father attempting to discipline a wayward son, see UN 27, 59v.

202. UN 5, unfol. (Feb. 15, 1460/1461).

203. UN 8, unfol. (July 15, 1461), a charge the doctor confirmed (chapter 5, 163). Recomposition of disputes out of court was an expedient encouraged for many crimes, but not sodomy, at least not officially; see M. Becker, "Changing Patterns of Violence and Justice in Fourteenth- and Fifteenth-Century Florence," *Comparative Studies in Society and History* 18 (1976): 282–83. Related to this, when men convicted of sodomy petitioned the government for clemency, they had to show they had come to terms formally, through a notarized peace agreement, with the father or relatives of the boy they had sodomized. This pact assuaged the offended honor of the boy and his family and insured the offender against vendetta; it possibly also involved a monetary settlement. Examples are in PR 131, 88rv, 91rv, 92v–93r, 93v–94r (June 22, 1440). For a similar arrangement imposed by the Night Officers in a sentence, see UN 23, 42r.

204. UN 11, 3v, 6v. Rinaldo denied the charge, claiming it was made out of "enmity" and to "vituperate" him and Simone, and the two were absolved; 3v. Both were accused separately but absolved at least one other time as well: Rinaldo, UN 4, 20r; Simone, UN 11, 34r.

205. UN 16, 26r (two cases); UN 22, 41v; UN 26, 32r.

206. UN 31, 60v.

207. UN 30, 36r.

208. Christiane Klapisch-Zuber kindly informed me of Tribaldo de' Rossi's singular description of Guerrieri's case in his *ricordanze*. Parts of the *ricordanze* are published in *Delizie degli eruditi toscani*, ed. I. da San Luigi (Florence, 1770–1786), 23:236–303. The editor excluded the section that describes Guerrieri's arrest for sodomy and its aftermath. The account that follows is from the manuscript, Biblioteca Nazionale Centrale, Florence, Fondo nazionale II.II.357, 158r-159v. On the boy's adolescence and scholastic career, see C. Klapisch-Zuber, "Le chiavi fiorentine di Barbablu: L'apprendimento della lettura a Firenze nel XV secolo," *Quaderni storici* 57 (1984): 766–69.

209. In 1501 a boy confessed that Della Rena had sodomized him; UN 34, 37v. Described as a *puer* (boy), he was absolved because of his age; 8r.

210. Only a brief summary of the denunciation survives; UN 9, unfol. (May 5, 1500).

211. The diary broke off December 8, 1501. Guerrieri died in 1504 before reaching the age of nineteen; Klapisch-Zuber, "Le chiavi fiorentine," 785, nn. 5, 24.

212. See J. R. Farr, "Crimine nel vicinato: Ingiurie, matrimonio e onore nella

Digione del XVI e del XVII secolo," *Quaderni storici* 66 (1987): 839–54. On neighborhood control of homosexual activity in eighteenth-century Paris, see M. Rey, "Parisian Homosexuals Create a Lifestyle, 1700–1750: The Police Archives," *Eighteenth Century Life* 9, n.s., 3 (1985): 182–83.

213. UN 30, 60v. See also the testimony (64v) of a man who was among the crowd of vigilantes.

214. UN 27, 81v; UN 31, 31r. In the same years neighbors were also banding together to expel prostitutes from their districts; R. Trexler, "La Prostitution florentine au XVe siècle: Patronages et clientèles," *Annales, E.S.C.* 36 (1981): 1004.

215. "The neighbors have made this accusation"; UN 5, 36r; see also UN 8, unfol. (July 15, 1461). On the rare occasions informers identified themselves, they were often neighbors of the persons they accused; e.g., UN 12, 11v, 14r.

216. UN 12, 28v.

217. Antonio and his partners were absolved, officially for lack of proof. He and Zanobi were denounced again, but the charge was not pursued; UN 13, 3v. For an example from another neighborhood context of collective ridicule against a sodomite, see the mock-birthing ritual in D. Rollinson, "Property, Ideology and Popular Culture in a Gloucestershire Village, 1660–1740," *Past & Present* 93 (1981): 70–97.

218. UN 12, 17r.

219. GAN 79 (2), 44rv (Jan. 13, 1435/1436).

Chapter 3

1. Sabadino degli Arienti, *Le porretane*, ed. B. Basile (Rome, 1981), 106.

2. *Prediche* (Florence, 1425), 3:33.

3. UN 12, 11v.

4. For an overview of the organization of homosexual behavior from the ancient world to the present, drawing on historical and anthropological literature, see D. Greenberg, *The Construction of Homosexuality* (Chicago, 1988). An important analysis of the problems of representing different typologies of homoerotic interactions is G. W. Herdt, "Representations of Homosexuality: An Essay on Cultural Ontology and Historical Comparison," *Journal of the History of Sexuality* 1 (1991): 481–504, 603–32.

5. The best general expositions of the differences in the organization of homosexuality before and after 1700 are several studies by R. Trumbach, especially "Sodomitical Subcultures, Sodomitical Roles, and the Gender Revolution of the Eighteenth Century: The Recent Historiography," *Eighteenth Century Life* 9, n.s., 3 (1985): 109–21; "Gender and the Homosexual Role in Modern Western Culture: The 18th and 19th Centuries Compared," in *Homosexuality, Which Homosexuality?* (Amsterdam and London, 1989), 149–69; and "The Birth of the Queen: Sodomy and the Emergence of Gender Equality in Modern Culture, 1660–1750," in *Hidden from History: Reclaiming the Gay and Lesbian Past*, ed. M. B. Duberman, M. Vicinus, and G. Chauncey, Jr. (New York, 1989), 129–40. For England see also A. Bray, *Homosexuality in Renaissance England* (London, 1982), esp. 81–114; Bray curiously fails, however, to emphasize the predominance in Renaissance England of the adult-boy model, even though a great deal of evidence he presents points in this direction. On eighteenth-century Paris see M. Rey, "Police et sodomie à Paris au XVIIIe siècle: Du péché au désordre," *Revue d'histoire moderne et con-*

temporaine 29 (1982): 113–24; and "Parisian Homosexuals Create a Lifestyle, 1700–1750: The Police Archives," *Eighteenth Century Life* 9, n.s., 3 (1985): 179–91. Among the growing literature on the Netherlands, see T. van der Meer, "The Persecutions of Sodomites in Eighteenth-Century Amsterdam: Changing Perceptions of Sodomy," in *The Pursuit of Sodomy: Male Homosexuality in Renaissance and Enlightenment Europe*, ed. K. Gerard and G. Hekma (New York, 1989), 263–307. Comparative research on homosexuality in southern Europe after 1700 is badly needed to determine when and under what conditions a similar transformation occurred; it is likely that the older tradition persisted in the south much later than in northern countries, even well into our own century.

6. See Trumbach's critique of scholars who depend too heavily on modern analogies, in "Gender and the Homosexual Role," 161–64.

7. The humanist Antonio Beccadelli did use a form of this term in the *Hermaphroditus*, for example, but to my knowledge it does not occur in popular Florentine poetry or literature of this period, much less other sources.

8. Among the now numerous studies on the conventions and cultural contexts of homosexuality in ancient Greece, see K. J. Dover, *Greek Homosexuality* (Cambridge, Mass., 1978; New York, 1980); F. Buffière, *Eros adolescent: La pédérastie dans la Grèce antique* (Paris, 1980); P. Cartledge, "The Politics of Spartan Pederasty," *Cambridge Philological Society, Proceedings* 207 (1981): 17–36; M. Foucault, *Histoire de la sexualité* (Paris, 1976–1984) 2:205–48, and 3:219–66; D. Cohen, "Law, Society and Homosexuality in Classical Athens," *Past & Present* 117 (1987): 3–21; Greenberg, *Construction*, 106–10, 141–51; D. Halperin, *One Hundred Years of Homosexuality and Other Essays on Greek Love* (New York, 1990); J. Winkler, *The Constraints of Desire: The Anthropology of Sex and Gender in Ancient Greece* (New York, 1990), esp. 17–70; E. Cantarella, *Secondo natura: La bisessualità nel mondo antico*, 2d ed. (Rome, 1992). On Rome, see J. Boswell, *Christianity, Social Tolerance, and Homosexuality: Gay People in Western Europe from the Beginning of the Christian Era to the Fourteenth Century* (Chicago, 1980), 61–87; P. Veyne, "L'Homosexualité à Rome," *Communications* 35 (1982): 26–33; R. Macmullen, "Roman Attitudes to Greek Love," *Historia* 31 (1982): 484–502; S. Lilja, *Homosexuality in Republican and Augustan Rome* (Helsinki, 1983); Greenberg, *Construction*, 152–60; A. Richlin, "Not Before Homosexuality: The Materiality of the *Cinaedus* and the Roman Law Against Love Between Men," *Journal of the History of Sexuality* 3 (1993): 523–73; I have not seen the Ph.D. dissertation by C. Williams, "Homosexuality and the Roman Man: A Study of the Cultural Construction of Sexuality" (Yale University, 1992). Greenberg documents the persistence of pederasty in the Islamic countries of the Mediterranean in *Construction*, 174–80.

9. In addition to the works cited in the preceding note, studies of the values of masculinity, honor, and sexual virility in Mediterranean cultures, though with no specific focus on homosexuality, include J. Pitt-Rivers, *The Fate of Shechem* (Cambridge, 1977); S. Brandes, *Metaphors of Masculinity: Sex and Status in Andalusian Folklore* (Philadelphia, 1980); Brandes, "Like Wounded Stags: Male Sexual Ideology in an Andalusian Town," in *Sexual Meanings: The Cultural Construction of Gender and Sexuality*, ed. S. B. Ortner and H. Whitehead (Cambridge, 1981), 216–39; A. Blok, "Rams and Billy-Goats: A Key to the Mediterranean Code of Honour," in *Religion, Power and Protest in Local Communities: The Northern Shore of the Mediterranean*, ed. E. R. Wolf (Berlin, 1984), 51–70; M. Herzfeld, *The Poetics of Manhood: Contest and Identity in a Cretan Mountain Village* (Princeton, 1985);

D. Gilmore, *Manhood in the Making: Cultural Concepts of Masculinity* (New Haven, 1990), 30–55.

10. *Statuti 1325*, 218.

11. PR 52, 128rv (Apr. 3).

12. *Statuta 1415*, 1:321, which closely follows the wording of the 1408/1409 statutes, *Statuti* 23, 86v. The term "passive" had appeared in some trial summaries even in the fourteenth century. According to Guido Ruggiero, the active–passive distinction began to appear regularly in Venetian cases in the 1440s, though the two roles had, as in Florence, long been distinguished in judiciary practice; *The Boundaries of Eros: Sex Crime and Sexuality in Renaissance Venice* (New York, 1985), 121. What caused this semantic shift in the early fifteenth century is unclear.

13. UN 30, 43v.

14. Ibid.

15. *Statuta 1415*, 1:321–22, based on a law of 1365, PR 52, 128r (Apr. 3).

16. OGBR 70, 7v, fined 12 florins; 29v, fined 5 florins and forbidden to come within 200 *braccia* (ca. 117 meters) of the boy's house for three years; OGBR 71, 11v, twelve lashes; OGBR 94, 4r, two men each fined 2 florins. See also the case of Jacopo Panuzzi, chapter 5, 154.

17. OGBR 56, 69v, fined 8 and 4 florins; OGBR 115, 120r, both fined 60 lire.

18. OGBR 141, 45r.

19. An assumption that sodomy meant only anal copulation has led some to argue that males sometimes engaged in other sexual acts together to avoid being labeled "sodomites" (G. Dall'Orto, " 'Socratic Love' as a Disguise for Same-Sex Love in the Italian Renaissance," in *Pursuit of Sodomy*, ed. Gerard and Hekma, 35) or to escape the harsher punishment under the Inquisition that canon law prescribed for sodomy (L. Mott and A. Assunçao, "Love's Labors Lost: Five Letters from a Seventeenth-Century Portuguese Sodomite," in *Pursuit of Sodomy*, ed. Gerard and Hekma, 93). Yet no evidence is presented to support this imputation of motive. The evidence for both Florence and Venice (see Ruggiero, *Boundaries*, 114–17), where practically all same-sex sexual acts were penalized equally as sodomy, shows that this ostensible ruse made no sense. The Inquisition in Valencia also punished homoerotic acts other than anal penetration; R. Carrasco, *Inquisición y represión sexual en Valencia: Historia de los sodomitos (1565–1785)* (Barcelona, 1985), 47.

20. See Halperin, *One Hundred Years*, esp. 29–38; Veyne, "L'Homosexualité."

21. UN 30, 50r, 51v-52r, 53rv, 57r, 115r. Likewise, a woman reported she had been raped "a parte ante in the proper vessel" and sodomized "ex parte retro in the anus"; UN 30, 55v.

22. GAN 82, 280r. Similar expressions sometimes occur in Latin—for example, "ex parte post in ano" (UN 12, 31v) or "in foramine."

23. UN 19 (3), 33v. Nobili was absolved; 65v. His age is derived from MC Catasto 54, 11r (1480). Without being so explicit, another notary also implied that this phrase referred to oral sex. He recorded that since a boy, aged sixteen or seventeen, did not want to "service" his twenty-four-year-old partner a parte post (that is, in anal sodomy) the youth sodomized him instead a parte ante; UN 29, 102r, abs. 66r.

24. UN 18, 62r. Antonio was convicted; 90rv. On Lionardo, son of the painter Giovanni di ser Giovanni, known as Scheggia, see chapter 5, 187, 189.

25. UN 22, 30r, 34r, abs. 71r. The age of the boy, Niccolò di Francesco Bandini, is derived from MC Catasto 102, 64r (1480).

26. A graphic description of a man fellating a boy while masturbating himself is

in GAN 80, 417r. Other examples of "active" fellators of boys are UN 17, 51v; UN 20, 44v; UN 21, 33v; UN 25, 44v, 48r; UN 26, 33r; UN 30, 148v, 149v; UN 33, 54v. Once a notary distinguished sodomy, intended as anal intercourse, from fellatio: in the case of a forty-year-old man who "sucked the member" (*poppò la natura*) of a seventeen-year-old, the scribe wrote that the man "did not sodomize him" because the boy had an anal venereal disease; UN 31, 87v.

27. See also chapter 4, 129.

28. UN 30, 169r. He was sentenced to two hours in the pillory; 134r.

29. OGBR 146 bis, 341v. A denunciation alleging that a nineteen-year-old both let men sodomize him anally and fellated his partners is in UN 25, 48r. He was convicted, but his confession was not recorded. For an unusual case of mutual fellatio between a man aged eighty-three and a youth of eighteen, see later.

30. On classical Greek and Roman attitudes see Boswell, *Christianity*, 145, 162; Dover, *Greek Homosexuality*, 99, 101; Veyne, "L'Homosexualité," 29–30; Halperin, *One Hundred Years*, 96n.73; Richlin, "Not Before Homosexuality," 550. Fellatio is not mentioned in any Venetian studies, and Carrasco found few examples in Valencia; *Inquisición*, 126.

31. This unpublished dialogue is probably an apocryphal addition to a manuscript copy, in the Vatican library, of the Sienese Antonio Vignali's *La cazzaria*, ed. P. Stoppelli (Rome, 1984), written probably in 1525 or 1526. According to the editor, the added text dates from the sixteenth century and its author was not Sienese (156); the spellings and dialect suggest that he was not even Tuscan. The dialogue in question is in Biblioteca Vaticana, Rome, Codici Capponiani 140, fols. 78–109; the passage discussed here is on 86rv. I am currently preparing an edition of this text.

32. See Halperin, *One Hundred Years*, 31, 129–37; Foucault, *L'Histoire de la sexualité*, 2:245–47. In "Not Before Homosexuality," Richlin argues contrary to Halperin, Winkler, and the followers of Foucault, that in classical Rome and probably Greece there was a category of passive adult homosexuals, the *cinaedi*, to whom this representational ideal probably would not have applied.

33. For a few examples, UN 17, 47r; UN 27, 94r; UN 31, 79rv, 83v-84r.

34. Antonio Beccadelli, *L'Ermafrodito*, ed. R. Gagliardi (Milan, 1980), 37.

35. Antonio Rocco, *L'Alcibiade fanciullo a scola*, ed. L. Coci (Rome, [1988]), 80–83.

36. As the terms *fanciullo* in Italian and *puer* in Latin are sometimes thought to refer in this period only to boys up to the age of fourteen or so, I should stress that in Florentine legal and judiciary sources both terms are widely used to indicate adolescents up to at least eighteen years of age and sometimes older.

37. John Boswell argues, I suspect wrongly, that the apparent commonness of sexual relations between adults and boys in premodern societies was, in most cases, "an idealized cultural convention" that probably did not match reality; *Christianity*, 28. In *Homosexuality in Renaissance England*, Alan Bray also probably understates the prevalence of man-boy relations.

38. Ruggiero, *Boundaries*, 118, 121–25.

39. E. Pavan, "Police des moeurs, société et politique à Venise à la fin du Moyen Age," *Revue historique* 264 (1980): 284. P. Labalme does not address the problem of the age of either partner; "Sodomy and Venetian Justice in the Renaissance," *Legal History Review* 52 (1984): 217–54.

40. On the prevalence of relations between adults and boys in Valencia, see Carrasco, *Inquisición*, 111, 124, 220–25. Regrettably, Carrasco's more specific in-

formation is of little comparative value, since his table on sexual roles (123, Table 7) does not indicate ages, while his table on ages (221, Table 10) does not distinguish by sexual role. According to Gabriele Martini, *Il "vitio nefando" nella Venezia del Seicento: Aspetti sociali e repressione di giustizia* (Rome, 1988), 112–24 and Table 2, roughly three of four cases of homosexual sodomy prosecuted in seventeenth-century Venice involved either the prostitution of minors or violent pederasty; he does not specify the boys' ages but indicates that he included in these categories boys up to age sixteen or seventeen (118n.102). Yet even among the other nonviolent or nonexploitative cases, which Martini assumes involved what he dubiously calls an "existential choice" of homosexuality, the majority he discusses in fact featured a marked age difference between the two companions, with the junior partner often quite young (112–15).

41. This literature is discussed later and in chapter 4 with citations.

42. Rocco, *L'Alcibiade*, 75.

43. Ibid., 76.

44. The figure of 475 includes 362 individuals whose precise ages were recorded plus 41 identified only as *puer* (placed in the 18-and-under category), eight identified as aged eighteen or under, and one designated a *giovane* (placed in the 19-and-older category). Several with precise ages indicated appear in more than one year, and in these cases I computed their age for each appearance as if they were distinct individuals. The 362 passive partners with precise ages represent roughly 30 percent of all those implicated and over 66 percent of those interrogated.

45. The figure of 777 includes 657 individuals with precise ages recorded plus 49 who were absolved as minors (placed in the 18-and-under category). Again, when persons whose ages were noted appeared in more than one year, I computed their ages each time as if they were distinct individuals. Those with specific ages represent roughly 23 percent of all active partners implicated and about 33 percent of those who either were named in interrogations or denounced themselves.

46. On possible reasons for this discrepancy, see chapter 4, n. 11.

47. D. Herlihy and C. Klapisch-Zuber, *Les Toscans et leur familles: Une étude du catasto florentin de 1427* (Paris, 1978), 394–400.

48. The single exception regards eighty-three-year-old maestro Dino, a barber, and eighteen-year-old Matteo di Giovanni, a cook, who, as the latter confessed, had fellated each other more than fifty times during the past year; UN 26, 26r. Having confirmed this, Dino was convicted and fined 25 florins; 71r. Another possible exception is the somewhat suspect case of Simone Grazzini, discussed later.

49. UN 28, 19rv.

50. UN 28, 22r–23r.

51. UN 29, 50v.

52. UN 28, 66r. The relatively light sentences of the other four boys Antonio implicated and of Bramanti's friends are respectively in ibid., 67r, and UN 29, 126v, 129v.

53. The accusations against Piero and his several confessions in 1492 are in UN 27, 38v, 39rv, 59v, 60r, 61r, 62r, 65v, 67rv, 70r, 71v. He was absolved in both cases in 1502; UN 35, 39v, 42v. His conviction by the Eight is in OGBR 130, 275r.

54. UN 24, 37v; UN 30, 34v, 75r, 128r; OGBR 130, 19r. The latter sentence (1504) mentions that he was also convicted in 1495 and 1496, but these sentences are no longer extant. Bartolomeo was aged five in 1480; MC Catasto 13, 130r.

55. UN 19 (2), 2rv; UN 19 (3), 26r, 27v; his self-accusations, UN 20, 40r, UN

22, 31v, UN 22, 35r. He was repeatedly incriminated but absolved in 1491 and 1492: accusations, UN 26, 33r, UN 27, 33v, 37r, 38v, 41v, 48v, 52r, 54v; sentences, UN 27, 97r, 97v, 98v, 99r, 99v, 100v, 101v and 102r; UN 28, 17v; UN 29, 30v, 81r; UN 29, 54r, 128v. Berto was ten years old in 1469; Catasto 905, 672r.

56. Niccolò Machiavelli, *La vita di Castruccio Castracani da Lucca*, in *Tutte le Opere*, ed. M. Martelli (Florence, 1971), 628. I thank Dennis Romano for this reference.

57. *Quattro novelle di Francesco Maria Molza da una stampa rarissima del secolo XVI* (Lucca, 1869), 40–47.

58. Ibid., 41.

59. Biblioteca Vaticana, Rome, Codici Capponiani 140, 93r.

60. On Dante's and other traditional notions of life stages see D. Herlihy, "Vieillir à Florence au Quattrocento," *Annales, E.S.C.* 24 (1969): 1339; Herlihy and Klapisch-Zuber, *Les Toscans*, 202, with bibliography; see also R. Trexler, "Ritual in Florence: Adolescence and Salvation in the Renaissance," in *The Pursuit of Holiness in Late Medieval and Renaissance Religion*, ed. C. Trinkaus and H. Oberman (Leiden, 1974), 201n.2; P. Ariès, *Centuries of Childhood: A Social History of Family Life* (New York, 1962), 15–32.

61. Matteo Palmieri, *Vita civile*, ed. G. Belloni (Florence, 1982), 30; Bernardino of Siena, *Prediche* (Florence, 1425), 3:44.

62. See chapter 2, 51, and for the 1542 law, Epilogue, 233.

63. Trexler, *Public Life*, 370–71 and n. 11. Similarly, speaking of adolescence (roughly age 14 to 28), Matteo Palmieri advised against allowing "recently grown *fanciulli*" to frequent "already grown youths" in this same age category in order to avoid "disgraceful iniquities"; Palmieri, *Vita civile*, 34.

64. UN 31, 61r. On this case, see also chapter 5, 179.

65. OGBR 147, 56rv.

66. UN 30, 63r. Unfortunately, the youth's age is unknown. His alleged lover, Piero di Jacopo Morcelli, was questioned but denied the charge; ibid.

67. UN 35, 35r.

68. Ibid.

69. The joke appears among the anecdotes of the Piovano Arlotto (Mainardi), most of which were compiled after his death (1484); *Motti e facezie del Piovano Arlotto*, ed. G. Folena (Milan and Naples, [1953]), 182–3. A shorter version appears in a poem by Antonio di Jacopo Alamanni (b. 1464), in *Le più belle pagine del Burchiello e dei burchielleschi*, ed. E. Giovanetti (Milan, 1923), 285. Directed at the old man, the tale also gently pokes fun at the Night Officers.

70. UN 30, 46v. The officials took this charge seriously, as their repeated interrogations of Valore show, but there were probably political motives behind it that make the whole affair suspect. Grazzini was one of numerous creatures of the Medici on the Chancery staff, and held a key position as notary of the Tratte from 1484 to 1494. Suspected of having manipulated the electoral pouches, he fell into disgrace after the fall of the Medici, and his house was burned in the popular uprising after Piero de' Medici's flight; D. Marzi, *La cancelleria della Repubblica fiorentina* (Florence, 1910; reprint, 1987), 254–56, 263, 270. Valore confessed under torture that during the twelve years he had worked for Grazzini, his master sodomized him thirty times ex parte ante and he sodomized Simone twelve times ex parte post. But he claimed they had not had sexual relations for the past seven

or eight years, that is, well outside the office's one-year statute of limitations; UN 30, 45v. Tortured twice more, Valore maintained his story (47v–49r). Informed of his "obstinacy," the same accuser denounced them again and named other witnesses (49rv), but the officials declined to pursue the case further and absolved both men that same day (93r).

71. Cf. Toscan's dubious reading of the theme of old men as passives in Tuscan burlesque literature, suggesting that being sodomized was approved as a cure for older men's impotence; *Le Carnaval du langage: Le lexique érotique des poètes de l'équivoque de Burchiello à Marino (XVe–XVIIe siècles)* (Lille, 1981), 1:240–44. Given the source, such claims were probably ironical.

72. UN 29, 107r. The informer named five males who allegedly sodomized Villani; all involved were absolved. The writer might have mistakenly referred to Tedice di Lodovico (instead of Giovanni) Villani, who was denounced in 1465 and again in 1481; UN 11, 11v; UN 20, 65v. A wealthy citizen, he was aged sixty-seven in 1480, which would have made him eighty-one years old at the time of this accusation; MC Catasto 84, 596r.

73. See Trexler, *Public Life*, 12–30, 518–47.

74. Quoted in Labalme, "Sodomy," 251n.160.

75. Ibid.

76. Ibid., 234n.73.

77. OGBR 106, 39v.

78. OGBR 106, 40r. On this case see also chapter 5, 172.

79. OGBR 136, 236v. Other examples in UN 16, 51v; UN 31, 167v.

80. UN 11, 31r.

81. UN 11, 16v.

82. UN 30, 87r–89v. For Salvi's complete record, see chapter 2, 79.

83. UN 30, 130v–132r; passage quoted, 131r. For his public service record, see chapter 2, 79; further on him in chapters 4 and 6.

84. UN 28, 67r.

85. L. Cantini, ed., *Legislazione toscana raccolta e illustrata* (Florence, 1800–1808), 1:211–13. See Epilogue, 234.

86. The use of feminine imagery or metaphors to refer to boys who were sodomized occurs in roughly one-third of the denunciations to the Night Officers in the 1478–1502 survey.

87. See p. 88, with bibliographical citations.

88. Associations between taking the anally receptive role and "womanly" submission persist in modern Mediterranean and "Latin" cultures; see, for just a few examples, A. Dundes and A. Falassi, *La Terra in Piazza: An Interpretation of the Palio of Siena* (Berkeley, 1975), 189–93; Brandes, "Like Wounded Stags," 232–34; J. M. Carrier, "Cultural Factors Affecting Urban Mexican Male Homosexual Behavior," *Archives of Sexual Behavior* 5, no. 2 (1976): 110–17; Carrier, "Homosexual Behavior in Cross-Cultural Perspective," in *Homosexual Behavior: A Modern Reappraisal*, ed. J. Marmor (New York, 1980), 109–12.

89. These words occur in some 28 percent of the accusations that feature feminine imagery.

90. UN 19, 26r.

91. UN 20, 49r.

92. UN 21, 39v.

93. Rocco, *L'Alcibiade*, 63–4.

94. A. Lanza, ed., *Lirici toscani del '400* (Rome, 1973–1975), 2:639.

95. On what the Spaniards called *bardaje* in the New World, see R. Trexler, *Sex and Conquest: Gendered Violence, Political Order, and the European Conquest of the Americas* (Cambridge, 1995; Ithaca, 1995). Recent studies of the *berdache* in North America include W. Williams, *The Spirit and the Flesh: Sexual Diversity in American Indian Culture* (Boston, 1986); H. Whitehead, "The Bow and the Burden Strap: A New Look at Institutionalized Homosexuality in Native North America," in *Sexual Meanings*, ed. Ortner and Whitehead, 80–115; and on the North American *berdache* and related phenomena outside the Americas, Greenberg, *Construction*, 40–65. See also the critique by Herdt, "Representations," 481–504.

96. There is not a single reference in denunciations or trial protocols that boys who were sodomized dressed in female clothing. For an active partner who was described ambiguously as a *travestito*, however, see chapter 5, 153. Female prostitutes in Florence, though, did cross-dress as young men, perhaps to attract male clients; R. Trexler, "La Prostitution florentine au XVe siècle: Patronages et clientèles," *Annales, E.S.C.* 36 (1981): 995–96. According to the 1355 statutes, cross-dressers of either sex were subject to public whipping through the streets of the city; *Statuti* 19, 244v.

97. The Scottish traveler William Lithgow mentioned in 1609 that "bardassi, buggerd boyes," were common in villages and cities throughout Italy, while in Malta in 1616, he recorded the flight to Sicily of "above a hundred bardassos, whorish boys," after a Spanish soldier and a Maltese boy were burned to death there for sodomy; *The Totall Discourse of the Rare Adventures and Painful Peregrinations of Long Nineteene Years Travayles* (Glasgow, 1906), 38, 335. On the term *bardaje* or *bardajo* in early modern Valencia, see Carrasco, *Inquisición*, 103. Flaubert observed "bardashes" in Cairo as late as 1850; Greenberg, *Construction*, 179.

98. UN 18 (2), 36v.

99. UN 35, 43r. Comparisons of boys to prostitutes occurs in about 7 percent of accusations that employ feminine imagery.

100. On "bordellos" of boys, see chapter 5, 157–59. For the term *ghiotto*, which was used only in reference to passive partners, see UN 30, 72v; UN 35, 35r; and cf. Toscan, *Le Carnaval*, 4:1701.

101. These terms occur in roughly 16 percent of the denunciations that used feminine imagery.

102. UN 20, 49r.

103. UN 30, 35r.

104. OGBR 152 bis, 94r.

105. See *Prediche* (Siena, 1427), 897.

106. Metaphors of boys as women occur in half of the accusations that employ feminine imagery.

107. See chapter 1, 38. Interestingly, another early-fifteenth-century moralist, Giovanni Dominici, inverted this gender equation when he warned wives not to submit to spouses who wanted to sodomize them, "transforming you into a beast or into a male"; cited in Herlihy and Klapisch-Zuber, *Les Toscans*, 602n.106.

108. EOG 1520, 23r (Mar. 22, 1403/1404).

109. These or similar expressions occur in roughly 31 percent of the accusations featuring feminine imagery.

110. GAN 79 (2), 239r. Antonio, said to be over forty years old, was fined 50 florins, while Francesco, a minor under eighteen, was fined 10 florins.

111. UN 30, 43v.

112. UN 30, 149r. Taking the phrase *si tiene come donna* out of context, J. M. Saslow distorts its meaning by translating it as "he regards himself as a woman"; "Homosexuality in the Renaissance: Behavior, Identity, and Artistic Expression," in *Hidden from History: Reclaiming the Gay and Lesbian Past*, ed. M. B. Duberman, M. Vicinus, and G. Chauncey, Jr. (New York, 1989), 99. He then uses this to buttress his argument that, in the Renaissance, passive partners in homosexual relations were thought to have (and presumably thought of themselves as having) a "distinct psychological nature" and to constitute "a psychic hybrid amounting to a third gender." Taking the receptive role was indeed seen as a violation of gender norms. But the Florentine evidence offers no support for Saslow's "third gender" hypothesis, part of his effort to find elements of "modern [homosexual] consciousness" in this period (97). The problem of self-identification is a thorny one, given the nature of the records, but there is no indication that adolescents who were sodomized considered themselves women (quite different from being likened to women by hostile informers) or of an ambiguous gender. Moreover, no Florentine source intimated that the sexual passivity of boys or of the rare adult man was a sign of a constitutional defect or of a distinctive psychosexual type.

113. See chapter 5, 167. The same term was also used to describe relations men maintained with female prostitutes; e.g., UN 34, 57v.

114. This characterization occurs in 18 percent of the denunciations that employ feminine imagery.

115. UN 30, 80v; UN 31, 35v.

116. UN 27, 59v; UN 29, 53v.

117. UN 31, 40v. On the "gufo," see Toscan, *Le Carnaval*, 4:1704.

118. See chapter 5, 170–72.

119. For one example of such advice, see Palmieri, *Vita civile*, 37–38.

120. The range of ideal body types for adolescents might be exemplified in two famed Florentine sculptures of the young David (without suggesting anything about their possible homoerotic content): the one by Donatello (1430–1440), a slight, boyish figure with delicate features, and the other by Michelangelo (1504), powerful and athletic with well-muscled thighs, arms, and chest. On the representation of the beautiful male adolescent in Florentine art of the fifteenth century, see A. Chastel, *Art et humanisme à Florence au temps de Laurent le Magnifique: Études sur la Renaissance et l'humanisme platonicien* (Paris, 1961), 289–98.

121. UN 32, 37r.

122. UN 27, 88v; UN 30, 66v.

123. The word "sodomite" does appear in reference to the passive partner in a couple of trial summaries (out of thousands reviewed), but this usage was clearly exceptional and was foreign to common language.

124. In a number of other Mediterranean and Latin cultures that place high value on manliness, the active, sexually agressive and dominant role in homosexual relations commonly does not imply a particular social stigma. As Dundes, Leach, and Ozkok note in a study of Turkish boys' verbal insults, "In this context there is nothing insulting about being the active homosexual. In a homosexual relationship, the active phallic aggressor gains status; the passive victim of such aggression

loses status. It is important to play the active role in a homosexual relationship; it is shameful and demeaning to be forced to take the passive role"; quoted in Carrier, "Homosexual Behavior," 111. See also Dundes and Falassi, *La Terra in Piazza*, 188–93; Carrier, "Cultural Factors," 116–17; Brandes, "Like Wounded Stags," 232–34.

125. There is one example (a denunciation reportedly made by the boy involved, UN 16, 31r) in which a man, after much insistent courting, finally convinced a boy to yield to him, and then, when he finished sodomizing him, derided him. He did so, however, not by calling him names with feminine connotations (at least according to the boy) but by referring to him as a *poltrone*, a generic and not very forceful insult meaning sluggard or coward. The term possibly had some sexual or gendered allusions—its feminine form, *poltrona*, could mean female prostitute—but they were not explicit.

126. Carrasco, *Inquisición*, 107–10.

127. The effeminizing slurs used by Florentine accusers against passive boys strikingly resemble the language of homosexual relations in modern American prisons. Often such relationships are predicated on rape and are intended to establish dominance and submission; S. Brownmiller, *Against Our Will: Men, Women, and Rape* (Toronto, 1975), 285–97; and the stunning memoir of Jack Abbott cited in Halperin, *One Hundred Years*, 38–39.

Chapter 4

1. C. Singleton, ed., *Canti carnascialeschi del Rinascimento* (Bari, 1936), 431.

2. PR 150, 119v.

3. See D. Herlihy, "Vieillir à Florence au Quattrocento," *Annales, E.S.C.* 24 (1969): 1346–49; Herlihy, "Some Psychological and Social Roots of Violence in the Tuscan Cities," in *Violence and Civil Disorder in Italian Cities, 1200–1500*, ed. L. Martines (Berkeley, 1972), 145–47; D. Herlihy and C. Klapisch-Zuber, *Les Toscans et leurs families: Une étude du catasto florentin de 1427* (Paris, 1978), 414, 583–84.

4. On the former, see chapter 2, 63; and on the latter, Epilogue, 229–32.

5. *Prediche* (Florence, 1425), 3:44.

6. Leon Battista Alberti, *I libri della famiglia*, ed. R. Romano and A. Tenenti (Turin, 1972), 78; for similar opinions see Herlihy, "Some Psychological and Social Roots," 135–37.

7. See Introduction, 14.

8. *Opere politiche e letterarie di Donato Giannotti*, ed. F. Polidori (Florence, 1850), 1:230, quoted in R. Trexler's translation, *Public Life in Renaissance Florence* (New York, 1980), 387. In practice some underage youths were admitted to office; generally on youths see ibid., 387–99. On youth and politics in Venice, see S. Chojnacki, "Political Adulthood in Fifteenth-Century Venice," *American Historical Review* 91 (1986): 791–810.

9. Niccolò Machiavelli, letter of Apr. 17, 1523, *Tutte le opere*, ed. M. Martelli (Florence, 1971), 1210–11. On Vettori, see R. Devonshire Jones, *Francesco Vettori: Florentine Citizen and Medici Servant* (London, 1972).

10. These figures are based on 1,019 individuals with precise ages recorded (25 percent of the total 4,062 implicated). See chapter 3, notes 44 and 45, for a detailed account of my calculations.

11. Categories of persons who tended to be older seem to be overrepresented in this sample, skewing the figures on age upward. For reasons related to the matching of names from judiciary records with those in the *catasto*, the sample may contain an exaggerated proportion of household heads, usually relatively older men, and possibly of older bachelors who filed claims independently of other family members. The sample also has a high percentage of recidivists (36 percent as compared with 15 percent in the overall survey), whose mean age was considerably higher than others (see chapter 5, 174). Finally, the prominence of older men in this sample might reflect a real difference in age over time. The mean age of active partners from 1478 to 1492 (including the *catasto* group from 1478 to 1483) was five years higher than that from 1493 to 1502. This shift is hard to interpret, however; it is discussed further in chapter 6, 214.

12. The 1480 figures are derived from A. Molho, *Marriage Alliance in Late Medieval Florence* (Cambridge, Mass., 1994), Appendix 4, 413–15.

13. GAN 79 (2), 239r.

14. The prevalence of pederastic relations up through the early seventeenth century in Florence is deducible in L. Marcello, "Società maschile e sodomia: Dal declino della 'polis' al Principato," *Archivio storico italiano* 150 (1992): 134–38.

15. This statute distinguished between boys in the passive role aged fourteen to eighteen, who were to be fined 100 lire, and boys under fourteen, who were to be fined 50 lire or driven nude through the streets and flogged; *Statuti 1325*, 218.

16. This information is based on cases reviewed between 1348 and 1432 (see chapter 1, 23). A few summaries called the passive partner a *iuvenis*, which, like its Italian equivalent *giovane*, in Florence usually indicated youths aged roughly twenty-five to forty; R. Trexler, "Ritual in Florence: Adolescence and Salvation in the Renaissance," in *The Pursuit of Holiness in Late Medieval and Renaissance Religion*, ed. C. Trinkhaus and H. Oberman (Leiden, 1974), 201n. But in the one example (1365) in which the age of a *iuvenis* was given, he was fifteen; Pod. 1656, 8v, 45r. *Iuvenis* was also used in early protocols of the Night Officers to refer to minors aged eighteen or under; e.g., GAN 79 (1), 32v, 33v; GAN 79 (2), 44v, 69v; and others in these years. The term *iuvenis* thus seems to have been interchangeable with *puer* in these documents. Perhaps it referred to postpubescent boys, or had a juridical meaning different from its commonly accepted sense.

17. This information comes from cases found in UN 1 and GAN 77, 79, and 80. They include only cases in which at least the active partner was convicted; for these years, records of cases ending in the absolution of active partners have not survived.

18. One ten- or twelve-year-old, for example, confessed he was sodomized by two *pueri*, two boys aged twelve, one aged fourteen, and another aged seventeen; UN 29, 55rv.

19. See the cases cited in chapter 2, 81.

20. Just a few examples: a man in 1496 abused and injured his eight-year-old servant girl, mentioned in chapter 3, 92; another in 1501 raped an eight- or nine-year-old girl with her mistress's permission, OGBR 119, 131r; yet another in 1488 picked up several young beggar girls in the Mercato Nuovo and sodomized them, including one ten-year-old whom he also prostituted to other men in his home, OGBR 79, 9v.

21. *Prediche* (Florence, 1424), 2:50. See chapter 1, 39.

22. The ages of only 13 of 243 self-denouncers between 1478 and 1502 (5

percent) are indicated in the court records, while 36 of 159 men (23 percent) who accused themselves between 1478 and 1483 appear in the *catasto* sample.

23. See chapter 5, 174, on the relationship among number of sexual partners, self-denunciation, and conviction.

24. PR 134, 267v (Apr. 8).

25. PR 111, 83r (July 15, 1421).

26. *Prediche* (Florence, 1424), 1:416. See also chapter 1, 40–41.

27. See J. Schnitzer, *Savonarola* (Milan, 1931), 1:107.

28. The *catasto* does not directly indicate marital status, which must be inferred for males by the presence of a wife or legitimate children. Men of indeterminate marital status are generally taken to be men not previously married, but it is likely that some, especially older men, were widowers. See Herlihy and Klapisch-Zuber, *Les Toscans*, 402.

29. Proportions of married men in the population at large are derived from Anthony Molho's analysis of the 1480 *catasto* in *Marriage Alliance*, Appendix 4, 413–15.

30. On marriage as part of alliance strategies, see Molho, *Marriage Alliance*; see also F. W. Kent, *Household and Lineage in Renaissance Florence: The Family Life of the Capponi, Ginori, and Rucellai* (Princeton, 1977), 91–99; Herlihy and Klapisch-Zuber, *Les Toscans*, 543–51; H. Gregory, "Daughters, Dowries and the Family in Fifteenth-Century Florence," *Rinascimento* 27 (1987): 215–37; L. Fabbri, *Alleanza matrimoniale e patriziato nella Firenze del '400: Studio sulla famiglia Strozzi* (Florence, 1991).

31. Machiavelli, letter of Apr. 17, 1523, *Tutte le opere*, 1212.

32. Guido Ruggiero offers a similar but more speculative argument in *The Boundaries of Eros: Sex Crime and Sexuality in Renaissance Venice* (New York, 1985), 159–61.

33. UN 11, 24r; UN 12, 13r, 14v; UN 14, 29r, 61r. MC Catasto 34, 184r.

34. Alberti, *I libri della famiglia*, 57.

35. On the gendered space of the late medieval Italian city, see D. Romano, "Gender and the Urban Geography of Renaissance Venice," *Journal of Social History* 23 (1989): 339–53.

36. For a trenchant critique of this general interpretation, see G. W. Herdt, "Representations of Homosexuality: An Essay on Cultural Ontology and Historical Comparison," *Journal of the History of Sexuality* 1 (1991): 619–21.

37. R. Trexler, "La Prostitution florentine au XVe siècle: Patronages et clientèles," *Annales, E.S.C.* 36 (1981): 987–88. Mazzi reduces this number to around eighty in the early 1500s; *Prostitute e lenoni nella Firenze del Quattrocento* (Milan, 1991), 296. See also chapter 1, 30–31.

38. Trexler, "La Prostitution," 1003–6; Mazzi, *Prostitute*, 285–92.

39. Philip Gavitt calculates that 60 percent of the children abandoned to the Innocenti, some 200 a year by the mid-1460s, were offspring of masters and their slave or servant women; *Charity and Children in Renaissance Florence: The Ospedale degli Innocenti, 1410–1536* (Ann Arbor, 1990), 207; see also R. Trexler, "The Foundlings of Florence, 1395–1495," *History of Childhood Quarterly* 1 (1973–1974): 270–71; A. Molho and J. Kirshner, "The Dowry Fund and the Marriage Market in Early *Quattrocento* Florence," *Journal of Modern History* 50 (1978): 428–29; C. Klapisch-Zuber, "Women Servants in Florence during the Fourteenth and Fifteenth Centuries," in *Women and Work in Preindustrial Europe*, ed. B. A.

Hanawalt (Bloomington, Ind., 1986), 69–70. In a good example of the sexual use of slave women in patrician families, the young bachelor Paolo Niccolini fathered three children by a domestic slave, who continued to live with her children in the Niccolini house even after Paolo married and brought his wife into the household; see C. Klapisch-Zuber, " 'Parenti, amici, vicini': Il territorio urbano d'una famiglia mercantile nel XV secolo," *Quaderni storici* 33 (1976): 975n.24.

40. These gang rapes, numerous in the records of the Eight of Watch, closely resemble those in southern France studied by Jacques Rossiaud in *La prostituzione nel medioevo* (Bari, 1984).

41. See Herdt, "Representations," Part II, 620.

42. See chapter 1, 24–25; *L'Ermafrodito*, ed. R. Gagliardi (Milan, 1980), 39.

43. UN 30, 148v. For another possible example, UN 8, unfol. (Oct. 7, 1461).

44. Giovanni Boccaccio, *Decameron*, ed. V. Branca (Turin, 1980), 692–705; the point about Pietro's antifeminine nature is on 695.

45. *Quattro novelle di Francesco Maria Molza da una stampa rarissima del secolo XVI* (Lucca, 1869), 40–47.

46. Giovanni Cavalcanti, *Istorie fiorentine* (Florence, 1838), 2:288.

47. *Prediche* (Siena, 1427), 410. See also chapter 1, 40.

48. "In lode della pederastia," contrasted with the following poem, "Contro la pederastia," in F. Coppetta and G. Guidiccioni, *Rime*, ed. E. Chiorboli (Bari, 1912), 283–86. Sodomy is also linked to misogyny in A. Cornazzano, *Il Manganello: La reprensione del Cornazano contra Manganello*, ed. D. Zancani (Exeter, 1982).

49. *Novelle di Pietro Fortini*, ed. T. Rughi (Milan, 1923), 64. Recall that Lucca also had a special magistracy for sodomy, indicating that the practice was probably widespread there as well.

50. Sabadino degli Arienti, *Le porretane*, ed. B. Basile (Rome, 1981), 106. The reputedly Florentine "proverb" cited in an epigraph to chapter 3 is from this man's defense.

51. The latter was the case of Filippo di Domenico del Cavaliere, convicted in 1499 for repeatedly sodomizing his wife and in 1502 for sodomizing four women, including his wife again; UN 33, 53v, 131v; UN 35, 57r, 58r, 123r, 124v. He was called an "inveterate sodomite" in UN 33, 133r.

52. For the latter, see J. M. Saslow, "Homosexuality in the Renaissance: Behavior, Identity, and Artistic Expression," in *Hidden from History: Reclaiming the Gay and Lesbian Past*, ed. M. B. Duberman, M. Vicinus, and G. Chauncey, Jr. (New York, 1989), 90–105.

53. See Herdt, "Representations."

54. Toscan, *Le Carnaval du langage: Le lexique érotique des poètes de l'équivoque de Burchiello à Marino (XVe–XVIIe siècles)* (Lille, 1981), 1:187–346.

55. Gentile Sermini, *Novelle*, ed. A. Colini (Lanciano, 1911), 100–109, "Ruberto da Camerino"; see also 120–30, "Messer Agapito da Perugia," which has a similar outcome.

56. Biblioteca Vaticana, Rome, Codici Capponiani 140, 92v.

57. One man reportedly paid a boy he sodomized for his sexual "labors" by letting him sleep with his sister; UN 12, 17r. The boyfriend of another was said to have "carnally known" the man's wife; UN 19 (2), 4r. The young friend of Francesco Pandolfini reputedly maintained a prostitute in the brothel; UN 31, 41rv.

58. Messer Pierlodovico d'Antonio de' Saraceni, a lawyer and former judge of

the Commune of Florence, was convicted in 1508 of having sodomized two of his servants, one male and the other female, and of having raped a second girl; OGBR 141, 132r; on this case, see also Luca Landucci, *Diario fiorentino dal 1450 al 1516, continuato da un Anonimo fino al 1542*, ed. I. Del Badia (Florence, 1889), 286 and n. 3. Goro di Giovanni di Goro, a shoemaker, was convicted for sodomy in 1497 with a boy and in 1502 with a woman; UN 31, 138v; UN 35, 125v. Francesco di Nofri Del Forese was convicted in 1497 for taking part in the sodomitical gang-rape of a woman, and again later that year for sodomizing a boy; UN 31, 119v; UN 32, 33v. There are numerous other examples.

59. From 1478 to 1502, at least 12 of the more than 200 men convicted by the Officers of Decency were also implicated in sodomy with boys; from a rough comparison of names in UO 2 (*Libro di condanne, 1441–1523*), and UN 19–35.

60. OGBR 152 bis, 122r.

61. OGBR 147, 39rv.

62. Machiavelli, letter of Jan. 5, 1514, *Tutte le opere*, 1164–65. On the letters between Vettori and Machiavelli in these years, see J. M. Najemy, *Between Friends: Discourse of Power and Desire in the Machiavelli–Vettori Letters of 1513–1515* (Princeton, 1993).

63. For a more detailed breakdown of reported sexual relations, see chapter 5, 173.

64. These figures refer to only active partners aged nineteen or over. I have included five youths who according to the *catasto* were aged seventeen or eighteen in 1480, but who were nineteen when they were incriminated for sodomy.

65. For his self-denunciations and convictions, see chapter 2, 70, 72. His other cases are in UN 18, 49r; UN 19 (3) 37r, 67r; UN 23, 37v, 62v; UN 24, 40v, 41r. His tax return is in MC Catasto 83, 390r. Jacopo's death may have had some connection to his sexual proclivities, but since the young *garzone* fled, his motives for murdering his master—conceivably a violent reaction to his sexual advances or a fit of jealousy—remained unknown; OGBR 78, 50v, 99r.

66. MC Catasto 74, 17r. UN 22, 30v, 31v; UN 25, 41v, 43r.

67. MC Catasto 82, 677r. UN 17, 30r, 62v; UN 18 (1), 49v, 81r; UN 18 (2), 44r; UN 19, 31v, 73r; UN 21, 31v, 73r; UN 24, 39v, 40v, 41r; UN 25, 47v, 60v. Despite these many charges, which begin to have a ring of truth, Francesco was never convicted, probably out of deference to Lorenzo.

68. Recall the experience of Ridolfo, protagonist of Molza's novella, who purposely married a slim, mannish young girl to ease his transition from loving boys to married life.

69. MC Catasto 67, 238r. UN 16, 61r, 66v; UN 17, 47r; UN 19 (2), 4r, and an identical denunciation, UN 19 (3), 20v, abs. 60r; self-denunciation, UN 22, 42v. In 1489 the Eight convicted him for unnamed crimes, possibly sodomy considering the large fine they imposed of 800 lire; OGBR 82, 107r.

70. MC Catasto 67, 25r. Jacopo was still unmarried in 1457 and 1469, according to the family's tax declarations; Catasto 816, 277r, and 920, 516r.

71. GAN 85, 387r, 435r; UN 11, 34v; UN 17, 43v, 68r, where the summary notes he had been convicted at least once before in 1473; UN 18 (2), 53v, 93rv, 13r, 13v.

72. UN 20, 56r, 57v, 99v; UN 9, unfol. (Feb. 1, 1484/1485); UN 24, 43v; UN 32, 10r; OGBR 110, 184v. Giuliano Cerbini, a thirty-three-year-old bachelor in 1480 (MC Catasto 66, 407r), also had interests in boys similar to his older

brothers. He was convicted of sodomy in 1472 and again in 1473, implicated but absolved in 1474, condemned in 1479, and convicted a fourth time by the Eight in 1488; UN 16, 28r, 78v; UN 17, 38r, 64v; UN 19 (2), 2v, 4v; OGBR 78, 89r.

73. MC Catasto 84, 500r. For his record see chapter 2, 79, and chapter 3, 105.

74. In 1469 Jacopo had a wife and two children, but in 1480 his only dependent was a fifteen-year-old son; Catasto 924, 257r; MC Catasto 83, 372r. His sodomy cases are in UN 9, 7v; UN 12, 31v; UN 13, 12r; UN 14, 33v; UN 19 (3), 23v, 61r; UN 20, 30v, 71v; UN 20, 44v, 80rv; UN 20, 51v, 96r; UN 20, 58r, 106r; UN 22, 36v, 72r; UN 24, 45v. See also chapter 5, 154.

75. UN 20, 33r, 71v; UN 27, 33rv, 97r; UN 29, 35r, 63r; MC Catasto 54, 573r.

76. MC Catasto 103, 71r; GAN 85, 122v; GAN 86, 147r; UN 18 (1), 60r, 91r; UN 18 (1), 61v; UN 18 (2), 48r; UN 20, 55r; GAN 88, 472rv.

77. Antonio de' Nobili, aged sixty-four, fellated both Lorenzo Ubertini and sixteen-year-old Paolo da Lamole; UN 19 (3), 33v; UN 20, 35r. Jacopo Panuzzi, aged fifty-one, and Tommaso Fioravanti, aged sixty-six, both did the same with seventeen-year-old Andrea Bonsi; UN 20, 44v. And sixty-one-year-old Adimari Spini fellated eighteen-year-old Bartolomeo Cresci; UN 26, 33r. See chapter 3, 92ff.

78. UN 30, 87rv, 88r.

79. Gentile Sermini's story "Ruberto da Camerino" has a similar and even more durable happy ending; *Novelle*, 107. In "De ceco amore," a tale by Giovanni Sercambi, a sodomite compensated the youths he had sex with—and also pacified his spouse—by allowing them to sleep with his wife, an arrangement that contented everyone involved; *Novelle*, ed. G. Sinicropi (Bari, 1972), 1:417–20. The committed boy-lover Cavichiolo proposes the same arrangement to his unsatisfied wife in the anonymous Latin tale, "Quid, si non fueram Cavichiolo digna marito," in *Teatro goliardico dell'Umanesimo*, ed. V. Pandolfi and E. Artese (Milan, 1965), 31–45; my thanks for bringing this story to my attention go to Ralph Hexter.

80. UN 27, 49r, 101r. Another informer charged that a man kept a boyfriend "under the very eyes of his wife," a "great disgrace"; UN 29, 108v.

81. UN 5, unfol. (Oct. 11, 1460). Despite his confession, Marco was absolved (Nov. 10). An informer later claimed that Marco was boasting about his absolution, and had promised his boyfriend presents because he had not confessed, but he was absolved again; ibid. (Nov. 12 and Dec. 11).

82. UN 12, 17r. In a letter of 1542 Lodovico Dini told a similar story to Vincenzio Rinuccini: when Alessandro Fiorelli's wife discovered him in bed with a boy, she and her mother raised the roof with their anguished cries, and the angry wife beat the boy on the head with her slipper; Archivio Contemporaneo Gabinetto G. P. Vieusseux, Florence, Ginori Conti B.R. 195, letter no. 18 (June 4). I am indebted to Maria Romagnoli for this reference and her transcription.

83. UN 20, 50v.

84. UN 18, 28v. Despite the incriminating testimony of several witnesses, Lanfranchi was apparently absolved; at any rate no sentence against him is preserved.

85. UN 21, 39v.

86. UN 31, 31r. The informer claimed Sapiti had been driven out of Santa Maria Novella in Florence, the hospital of Pisa, and other places where he had been caught in the act, and that he had recently been excommunicated for sodomy.

87. UN 31, 40v, no sentence. Francesco was also denounced in 1482, but absolved; UN 22, 30r, 69v.

88. UN 12, 6v.

89. *Statuti 1325*, 219–20.

90. PR 52, 128rv; *Statuta 1415*, 1:321.

91. Toscan, *Le Carnaval*, 1:191.

92. Names of provenance (e.g., Ambrogio from Milan) have ambiguous meanings, above all because the date of immigration cannot be determined. Individuals identified by place name could have been recent immigrants or residents for generations, and among the upper classes the place of origin was often adopted as the family name. On these problems, see Herlihy and Klapisch-Zuber, *Les Toscans*, 303. In determining residence, wherever possible I depended on an individual's given residence or place of occupation, and only secondarily on toponymics. I have included individuals with place names that were also familiar family names among the presumed natives. When no such information was given I have assumed the person was a resident of Florence.

93. See Herlihy and Klapisch-Zuber, *Les Toscans*, 310, Table 39. By the later fifteenth century, the proportion of foreign immigrants in Florence had probably increased, making the contrast with persons implicated in sodomy even sharper; see S. Cohn, Jr., *The Laboring Classes in Renaissance Florence* (New York, 1980), 96 ff.

94. E. Pavan, "Police des moeurs, société et politique à Venise à la fin du Moyen Age," *Revue historique* 264 (1980): 286; R. Carrasco, *Inquisición y represión sexual en Valencia: Historia de los sodomitos (1565–1785)* (Barcelona, 1985), 171–73, 218–19.

95. Trexler, "La Prostitution," 985–88, 993–94. These findings may suggest that Florentine men tended to frequent boys rather than the brothel prostitutes. But it would be hazardous to draw general conclusions from them about males' preferred sexual activities. One purpose of municipalized prostitution was to encourage local men to satisfy their sexual desires with public women, so officials might have been inclined to be indulgent with Florentines who frequented the brothels.

96. See, for example, a case from 1496 in which the town of San Miniato al Tedesco, on the basis of ancient treaties, defended its judiciary autonomy against the Night Officers; UN 30, 60r, 66r, 18rv, 110v, 70v-71r, 73r. William Connell kindly brought to my attention a 1454 law according to which residents of Pistoia and its *contado* were also immune from prosecution by the Night Officers, among other Florentine courts; Statuti dei comuni soggetti 598, 28rv (Dec. 19). Earlier that same year (in May) these officials had paid for a new *tamburo* for Pistoia; UN 36, 101r.

97. For citations, see chapter 2, note 30. There were probably more than one *tamburo* in Prato by 1481 (see the following note).

98. According to a note from the Night Officers to the podestà of Prato, one of the boxes they placed in the local *pieve* in April 1481 was destroyed in November; UN 21, 2v. Whether it was replaced immediately is unknown, but a new box affixed in May 1492 was also demolished within days, as letters to the podestà from both the Night Officers and the Eight attest; UN 27, 15v; OGBR 91, 110v; OGBR 92, 17v. In 1500 both of the Night Officers' boxes in Prato were destroyed; UN 34, 2r. Florentine sources do not indicate whether the "vandals" in any of these cases were apprehended.

99. The proportions for parishes from my survey correspond fairly closely to those Cohn presents for a few parishes based on baptismal records from 1450 to 1530; *Laboring Classes*, 36, Table 1.6.

100. Ibid., 115–28.

101. Dante Alighieri, *Inferno*, ed. C. Singleton (Princeton, 1973), 1:*Text*, 159; 2:*Commentary*, 255–57, 269–71, 279–80.

102. *Prediche* (Florence, 1424), 2:46.

103. Ibid., 51.

104. Agnolo Firenzuola, *Opere*, ed. A. Seroni (Florence, [1971]), 995–97. On this theme in burlesque poetry, see Toscan, *Le Carnaval*, 1:195–201.

105. Benvenuto Cellini, *La vita*, ed. G. Davico Bonino (Turin, 1973), 416–17 (the year was 1546). On Cellini's interest in sodomy, see more later. In a more sober context, the Brescian priest Francesco Calcagno, tried in 1550 for sodomy by the Inquisition, reportedly said that even with female prostitutes he used only sodomy, for "to use women according to nature was for the rabble and the beasts"; cited in P. Labalme, "Sodomy and Venetian Justice in the Renaissance," *Legal History Review* 52 (1984): 241.

106. Biblioteca Vaticana, Rome, Codici Capponiani 140, 109rv.

107. Ibid., 82r–89r, 91r–93r, 96r–106r. For other examples see Toscan, *Le Carnaval*, 1:210–13, and the poem "L'Aquettino" in D. Guerri, *La corrente popolare nel rinascimento: Berte, burle e baie nella Firenze del Brunellesco e del Burchiello* (Florence, 1931), 149–71.

108. PR 150, 119v (Oct. 23). See chapter 2, 63.

109. Balìe 29, 78v, 79r (Dec. 9); PR 150, 119v (Oct. 23).

110. PR 181, 18v (June 11).

111. The most comprehensive information on occupations comes from analyses of the 1427 *catasto*, but figures regard only household heads and not individual workers. Further, different scholars have employed various criteria for grouping occupations, rendering systematic comparison even more difficult. Nonetheless one can make some limited and rough comparisons. Following the categories used by Giovanni Fanelli (*Firenze*, 3d ed. [Bari, 1985], 70–71), based on figures derived from Herlihy and Klapisch-Zuber's study of the *catasto*, it appears that textile workers, professionals (doctors, notaries, and apothecaries), and government employees were implicated in sodomy less often than expected given their proportion among household heads in 1427 (respectively, 24 as opposed to 30.5 percent, 3 as opposed to 8 percent, and 3.7 as opposed to 6.5 percent). Categories implicated in sodomy in larger-than-expected proportions include persons involved in making clothing (15.7 as opposed to 10.3 percent), and in food provisioning and sale (10 as opposed to 5.2 percent).

112. Cohn, *Laboring Classes*, 65–73.

113. On Venice, Ruggiero, *Boundaries*, 141–44; Pavan, "Police," 279–81; Labalme, "Sodomy," 237–41. On Valencia, Carrasco, *Inquisición*, 172, Table IX, 174–87.

114. Examples of referrals are UN 17, 62r; UN 30, 102v.

115. The active partners were mainly priests (26), monks (24), chaplains of churches (12), or clerics (*chierici*) (9), but also included a papal nuntio. Of the nineteen passive partners in this category, eighteen were clerics.

116. UN 14, 9v. The letter goes on to mention cases of sexual relations between laymen and nuns. In a similar letter in 1492, officials diplomatically reminded the bishop of Pistoia that he had ignored their previous letters: "Having received no

notice from your reverend lord, we wonder whether you have not received the said letters" (UN 27, 19v.).

117. I have not examined these records, but it is unlikely they would reveal a much different picture of Florentine sodomy than that offered by the civic judiciary records. For a 1507 case involving the archiepiscopal vicar of Pistoia, who confessed he had sodomized numerous clerics in his service, see chapter 5, 163. Some of the constitutions of archbishop Antoninus were directed against clergymen's sodomy; R. Trexler, "The Episcopal Constitutions of Antoninus of Florence," *Quellen und Forschungen aus italienischen Archiven und Bibliotheken* 59 (1979): 267–68, 271.

118. On the influence of the "Socratic eros" in the arts, see A. Chastel, *Art et humanisme à Florence au temps de Laurent le Magnifique: Études sur la Renaissance et l'humanisme platonicien* (Paris, 1961), 289–98.

119. The evidence on Donatello comes mainly from anecdotes by Agnolo Poliziano in *Detti piacevoli*, ed. T. Zanato (Rome, 1983), 83, 84, 99; see H. W. Janson, *The Sculpture of Donatello* (Princeton, 1957), 2:84–5. For a debate in part around the question of Donatello's presumed homoerotic interests, see L. Schneider, "Donatello's Bronze *David*," *Art Bulletin* 55 (1973): 213–16; J. Dixon, "The Drama of Donatello's *David*: Re-examination of an Enigma," *Gazzette des Beaux-Arts*, 6th ser., 93 (1979): 9–11; L. Schneider, "More on Donatello's Bronze *David*," *Gazzette des Beaux-Arts*, 6th ser., 94 (1979): 48. Curiously, John Pope-Hennessy dismisses the discussion of Donatello's alleged homosexual inclinations as so much "aberrant nonsense," lamenting that with regard to the David it has "left a little trail of slime on a great work of art"; "Donatello's Bronze *David*," in *Scritti di storia dell'arte in onore di Federico Zeri* (Milan, 1984), 1:125.

120. As is well known, in 1476 twenty-four-year-old Leonardo was denounced to the Night Officers for having sodomized seventeen-year-old Jacopo d'Andrea Salterelli, but was not convicted; UN 18 (2), 46v. If Leonardo's participation remains unproven, it is likely that Salterelli was sexually involved with men, since earlier a man denounced himself for having sodomized him; UN 18 (2), 138v. And as Gian Paolo Lomazzo's dialogue in *Il libro dei sogni* suggests (see epigraph of chapter 5), Leonardo's attraction to boys was well known even in the sixteenth century; *Scritti sulle arti*, ed. R. P. Ciardi (Florence 1973), 1:104–6. The classic but dated study of Leonardo's sexuality is Sigmund Freud's *Eine Kindheitserinnerung des Leonardo da Vinci* (Vienna, 1910). For a recent reevalution and bibliography, see S. L. Gilman, "Leonardo Sees Him-Self: Reading Leonardo's First Representation of Human Sexuality," *Social Research* 54, no. 1 (1987): 149–71.

121. Botticelli was also denounced to the Night Officers, in 1502. A summary of the lost accusation reads "Sandro di Botticello si tiene un garzone"; UN 9, unfol. (Nov. 16); see J. Mesnil, *Botticelli* (Paris, 1938), 98, 204.

122. On Michelangelo's relationship with the young Tommaso dei Cavalieri, see C. L. Frommel, *Michelangelo und Tommaso dei Cavalieri* (Amsterdam, 1979); generally, see J. M. Saslow, *Ganymede in the Renaissance: Homosexuality in Art and Society* (New Haven, 1986), 17–62.

123. Cellini was convicted twice in Florence for homosexual sodomy (1523 and 1557), and was prosecuted but absolved for heterosexual sodomy in France. The relevant Florentine documents are in L. Greci, *Benvenuto Cellini nei delitti e nei processi fiorentini ricostruiti attraverso le leggi del tempo* (Turin, 1930), though this work contains several errors about sixteenth-century sodomy legislation. For recent studies of Cellini's sexuality see Saslow, *Ganymede*, 142–74; I. Arnaldi, *La vita*

violenta di Benvenuto Cellini (Bari, 1986), 129–43. The latter, while perceptive about the nature of early modern sodomy, is confused about Florentine institutional realities. Although Cellini does not mention his sodomy convictions in his autobiography, his attraction and attachment to young men, often his apprentices, appear clearly here; see *La vita*, 44, 61–66, 69–71, 139, 236, 311.

124. Among the small number of boys located in the *catasto* of 1480, for instance, seven were indicated as attending a school or "learning to read."

125. UN 17, 46v-47v. Ser Francesco, a preacher or cleric in the cathedral, sodomized him many times in his school at the canto a Monteloro, "during the time in which he taught Filippo to read"; ser Piero di ser Bramante also sodomized him many times when "he taught Filippo" as a live-in student in his house; and ser Piero del Comandatore, also a cathedral priest, repeatedly sodomized him "when he taught grammar to Filippo" in his school at San Remigio.

126. *Prediche* (Siena, 1425), 2:103. On pedants, see Toscan, *Le Carnaval*, 1: 217–18; for jokes about teachers' interests in boys, see Antonio Doni, *I marmi*, ed. P. Fanfani (Florence, 1863), 104.

127. See chapters 5, 158, and 6, 203.

128. There are three doctors in the 1478–1502 survey (all active partners); fifty-four apothecaries (32 actives and 22 passives); eighteen notaries (all actives); twenty-one furriers (15 actives and six passives). Since the words *lanaiolo*, *setaiolo*, and *linaiolo* could refer to wool, silk, and linen manufacturers or dealers and to lowly textile workers, it is impossible to make accurate distinctions. In any case, individuals with eminent family names appear among all three groups. There are seventeen *lanaioli* (14 actives and three passives) and twenty-eight *setaioli* (19 actives and nine passives). *Linaioli* were in a minor guild, but were often fairly wealthy; there are forty-two (29 actives and 13 passives).

129. Herlihy and Klapisch-Zuber, *Les Toscans*, 286–90.

130. On surnames, see ibid., 537–43, and Molho, *Marriage Alliance*, 212–13. According to the latter, in 1480 slightly less than half of all Florentine households listed in that year's *catasto* bore surnames.

131. Molho, *Marriage Alliance*, 193–214; Appendix 3, 365–375.

132. Naturally, all these figures and proportions would be higher still if the missing volumes of the Night Officers' proceedings, for seven of the twenty-four years of the 1478–1502 survey, were extant. Similar analyses of two other groups of political elites—the citizens appointed in 1480 to the newly formed Council of Seventy, dominated by Medici partisans, and the major guild families who sat on the Great Council in 1508—reveal more or less the same patterns of participation in or incrimination for sodomy. On the Council of Seventy, see N. Rubinstein, *The Government of Florence under the Medici, 1434–1494* (Oxford, 1966), 197–202; members for 1480 appear on 309–10, 316–17. R. Pesman Cooper analyzes the membership of the Great Council in "The Florentine Ruling Group Under the '*Governo Popolare*,' 1494–1512," *Studies in Medieval and Renaissance History* 7 (1985): 71–181. For the family composition of the Council in 1508, see Appendix I, 130–48.

133. The figures here and in the following paragraphs represent the total taxable wealth before allowable deductions. They have been rounded to the lower florin. For the different categories of wealth, I follow Molho, *Marriage Alliance*, 215, Table 5.2.

134. UN 22, 43v, 77r; UN 29, 100r, no sentence; MC Catasto 110, 282r.

135. His brother Antonio complained about Tommaso, "We do not know what has become of him, nor where he is, nor whether he is alive or dead, since he never comes home, and he is very corrupt with evil behaviors" (MC Catasto 92, 98r). His sodomy cases are in UN 14, 43r; UN 22, 45r, 77v; UN 29, 33v, 61r; UN 30, 39v, 52r, 95r. Despite his self-righteous remark, Antonio was also later denounced twice for homosexual relations, but was also absolved; UN 29, 100r, no sent.; UN 31, 41v, 60r, 95v. A third brother, Giovanni, was accused and absolved in 1467; UN 12, 12v, 82v.

136. UN 21, 47r, 49r, 49rv; MC Catasto 110, 38r.

137. Domenico: UN 19 (2), 29v-31v. Paolo: UN 20, 32v-35r. The ages of both come from MC Catasto 5, 88r.

138. UN 20, 42v; MC Catasto 28, 187r. A boy also named him in his confession, but he was absolved; UN 21, 44r, 79v.

139. Catasto and judiciary references cited earlier, n. 69.

140. UN 19 (1), 2r; MC Catasto 92, 243r.

141. UN 22, 31r; MC Catasto 54, 187r.

142. See chapter 1, 35.

143. See chapter 2, 51.

144. On the whole, allegations of sodomy seem not to have damaged political careers. For instance, Mario di Niccolò di messer Guccio de' Nobili, member of an illustrious family, was implicated in sodomy—though never convicted—no less than eight times from 1467 to 1494 (see chapter 5, 181). Despite this he was one of the Twelve Buonuomini in 1494 when Piero de' Medici was expelled; G. Guidi, *Ciò che accadde al tempo della signoria di novembre dicembre in Firenze l'anno 1494* (Florence, 1988), 22, 177. As noted in chapter 2, the well-known sodomite Salvi Panuzzi's reputation and record did not keep him from holding several important positions, both in criminal offices and in the city's highest magistracies.

145. The three Rucellai were Giovanbatista di Mariotto (UN 34, 115v); Cosimo di Giovanni, called ser Zani (UN 34, 132r); and Giuliano di Girolamo (UN 35, 118v).

146. UN 23, 34r.

147. UN 16, 24v.

148. UN 29, 98r; UN 5, 53v. See other remarks in chapter 2, 73, and chapter 6, 323n.94.

149. UN 14, 33v, 64v.

150. UN 31, 31rv. He was denounced again (50v), and though he was interrogated twice he not surprisingly denied the charges (57r, 59r), and was absolved (95rv).

151. UN 16, 58r.

152. Machiavelli, letter of Jan. 5, 1514, *Tutte le opere*, 1164–65.

Chapter 5

1. "Sappi che l'amore masculino è opera sollamente di virtù che, congiungendo insieme gli uomini, con diverse affezioni di amicizia, acciò che da una età tenera vengano nella virile più fortificati amici" (Gian Paolo Lomazzo, *Il libro dei sogni*, in *Scritti sulle arti*, ed. R. P. Ciardi [Florence, 1973], 1:104). The speaker here is Leonardo da Vinci; his point refers explicitly to sexual relations between males (presumably pederastic in nature: "out of a tender age . . ."), not to sanitized,

neo-Platonic "friendship." For an analysis of the term "masculine love" as used by four European writers of the late sixteenth and seventeenth centuries (but not Lomazzo), see J. Cady, " 'Masculine Love,' Renaissance Writing, and the 'New Invention' of Homosexuality," *Journal of Homosexuality* 23 (1992): 9–40. Cady argues, unconvincingly, that this term constituted a European-wide "language" for representing a distinctive male homosexual orientation.

2. "Questo fece per grande amore et buona fratellanza, perché sono d'una compagnia insieme, et fece come fanno e buoni vicini"; UN 18 (2), 35r–36r.

3. See C. Klapisch-Zuber, " 'Parenti, amici, vicini': Il territorio urbano d'una famiglia mercantile nel XV secolo," *Quaderni storici* 33 (1976): 953–82; D. V. Kent, *The Rise of the Medici: Faction in Florence (1426–1434)* (Oxford, 1978); D. V. Kent and F. W. Kent, *Neighbours and Neighbourhood in Renaissance Florence: The District of the Red Lion in the Fifteenth Century* (Locust Valley, N.Y., 1982); F. W. Kent, *Bartolommeo Cederni and his Friends: Letters to an Obscure Florentine* (Florence, [1991]); S. Cohn, Jr., *The Laboring Classes in Renaissance Florence* (New York, 1980); R. Weissman, *Ritual Brotherhood in Renaissance Florence* (New York, 1982); N. Eckstein, *The District of the Green Dragon: Neighbourhood Life and Social Change in Renaissance Florence* (Florence, 1995).

4. Many studies of homosexuality in medieval and early modern Europe deal, to varying degrees and within different interpretive frameworks, with issues related to "subcultures" (whether qualified as sodomitical, homosexual, or even gay). See especially the historiographical review by R. Trumbach, "Sodomitical Subcultures, Sodomitical Roles, and the Gender Revolution of the Eighteenth Century: The Recent Historiography," *Eighteenth Century Life* 9, n.s., 3 (1985): 109–21, and his "Gender and the Homosexual Role in Modern Western Culture: The 18th and 19th Centuries Compared," in *Homosexuality, Which Homosexuality?* (Amsterdam and London, 1989), 149–169; D. Greenberg, *The Construction of Homosexuality* (Chicago, 1988), esp. 301–46; K. Gerard and G. Hekma, eds., *The Pursuit of Sodomy: Male Homosexuality in Renaissance and Enlightenment Europe* (New York, 1989). The rambling survey of evidence of sodomy across Europe by S. O. Murray and K. Gerard, "Renaissance Sodomite Subcultures?" in *Cultural Diversity and Homosexualities*, ed. S. O. Murray (New York, 1987), 65–94, does little to promote a better understanding of what constituted a "subculture." Some scholars, it should be noted, are justifiably cautious even about employing the term; for example, A. Bray, *Homosexuality in Renaissance England* (London, 1982), 56; M. Rey, "Parisian Homosexuals Create a Lifestyle, 1700–1750: The Police Archives," *Eighteenth Century Life* 9, n.s., 3 (1985): 179–91.

5. See chapter 3, 88; and G. Chauncey, *Gay New York: Gender, Urban Culture, and the Making of the Gay Male World, 1890–1940* (New York, 1994).

6. On the basis of more frequent prosecution of nobles and of what seem to be extended groups of sodomites, together with new evidence of known sodomitical meeting places, Guido Ruggiero argues that in Venice during the fifteenth century a distinctive "homosexual subculture" developed, or at least grew more visible; *The Boundaries of Eros: Sex Crime and Sexuality in Renaissance Venice* (New York, 1985), 135–40. Also in contemporary Florence, as will be seen, there were notorious haunts, and even more reliable evidence exists of sodomitical networks. These and other common features of same-sex sodomy, such as organized prostitution, are documented from the beginning of the fourteenth century (though on a much smaller scale, probably only because the courts seldom prosecuted sodomy and

focused narrowly on certain types of cases). For Florence, moreover, apparently in contrast to Venice, records permit detailed reconstructions of the anatomy of networks of sodomites, which is critical for defining and comprehending their social and sexual character.

7. The important distinction between networks of shared activities and subculture as a source of collective and personal identity is proposed by W. Dynes and W. Johansson, "London's Medieval Sodomites," *Cabirion and Gay Books Bulletin* 10 (1984): 34, and emphasized by Trumbach, "Sodomitical Subcultures," 116.

8. On the term *arte*, see the discussion in chapter 1, n. 125. For a group of sodomite friends who were called a "sect," see later, this chapter.

9. Niccolò Machiavelli, letter of Feb. 25, 1513/1514, *Tutte le opere*, ed. M. Martelli (Florence, 1971), 1170–71. On the charge against Machiavelli, see R. Trexler, "La Prostitution florentine au XVe siècle: Patronages et clientèles," *Annales, E.S.C.* 36 (1981): 995 and n. 79.

10. J. Toscan, *Le Carnaval du langage: Le lexique érotique des poètes de l'équivoque de Burchiello à Marino (XVe–XVIIe siècles)* (Lille, 1981), 4:1762.

11. Rey reports similar patterns for early eighteenth-century Paris in "Parisian Homosexuals," 180.

12. Toscan, *Le Carnaval*, 4:1722. Some indication of time was given for one of five confessed relations from 1478 to 1502, and 82 percent of these occurred after nightfall.

13. An analysis of reported relations from 1478 to 1483 produces this breakdown: January, 42; February, 37; March, 38; April, 35; May, 52; June, 76; July, 58; August, 44; September, 50; October, 61; November, 41; December, 25. These figures cannot be considered an accurate record—they are based on partners' recollections and were usually rounded ("6 months ago," "10 months ago," etc.)—but they are more or less indicative.

14. UN 27, 72v; see also UN 20, 44r, 55v; UN 24, 38r; UN 27, 60r; UN 35, 48r. On the social and cultural aspects of Carnival in Florence, see G. Ciappelli, "Carnevale e quaresima: Rituale e spazio urbano a Firenze (secc. XIII–XVI)," in *Riti e rituali nelle società medievali*, ed. J. Chiffoleau, L. Martines, and A. Paravicini Bagliani (Spoleto, 1994), 159–74; "Tempo di festa, tempo di penitenza: Carnevale e Quaresima a Firenze nel Quattrocento," in *Il tempo libero: Economia e società (Loisirs, Tiempo Libre, Freizeit), secc. XIII–XVIII*, Atti della "Ventiseiesima Settimana di Studi" [dell'Istituto Internazionale di Storia Economica "F. Datini," Prato], April 18–23, 1994, ed. S. Cavaciocchi (Florence, 1995), 233–43.

15. UN 30, 73r; OGBR 147, 9r.

16. OGBR 72, 68v.

17. Cited in R. Trexler, "Ritual in Florence: Adolescence and Salvation in the Renaissance," in *The Pursuit of Holiness in Late Medieval and Renaissance Religion*, ed. C. Trinkaus and H. Oberman (Leiden, 1974), 209.

18. UN 30, 167v.

19. UN 30, 147v.

20. UN 31, 51v; see chapter 2, 74. Zanobi Falchi also reportedly took his seventeen- or eighteen-year-old friend to his villa "every feast day"; UN 5, 35v.

21. UN 22, 40v; UN 20, 52v; UN 19 (1), 28v.

22. For examples of sodomy connected to the fair of Prato, see UN 8, unfol. (June 21 and 22, 1462); UN 7, unfol. (June 30, 1462); UN 22, 30r, 40r; UN 27, 33v; UN 29, 37v. On the joust, UN 16, 59r.

23. Despite their title, the Night Officers had no patrols to apprehend men found sodomizing in public after dark. Sometimes they licensed the guards of the Eight of Watch to do so; e.g. UN 19 (3), 7r. The Eight's night patrols did arrest some sodomites caught in flagrante delicto; e.g., OGBR 55, 73v; OGBR 58, 79r; OGBR 94, 70v.

24. UN 31, 153r. Nothing in the report suggests the *travestito* was wearing women's clothes, and the word commonly referred to a person in disguise. If he was dressed as a woman, neither Carlo, his friends, nor others he encountered seem to have made much of it, not to mention the officials, who did not pursue the issue. Carlo confessed in 1494 that he had been sodomized by twelve men, and in 1497 by seventeen others; UN 29, 50r, 54r, 55r, 96rv, 99v; UN 31, 85r-88v, 152rv. He was accused but not questioned in 1495; UN 30, 42v.

25. The officials absolved Buondelmonti in this case, but in 1495 they had convicted him for sodomy; UN 37, 2r.

26. On the brothels and other prostitution zones, see Trexler, "La Prostitution," 988–93, 1003–4; M. S. Mazzi, *Prostitute e lenoni nella Firenze del Quattrocento* (Milan, 1991), 249–92.

27. OGBR 61, 12r.

28. On Pacchierotto see chapter 2, 78. A couple of boys specified that this street was the locus of much of their sodomitical activity; UN 11, 13v; UN 25, 48r. See also UN 11, 34r.

29. The same was true in fifteenth-century Venice; Ruggiero, *Boundaries*, 139. On Paris, see Rey, "Parisian Homosexuals," 179–82, and "Police et sodomie à Paris au XVIIIe siècle: du péché au desordre," *Revue d'histoire moderne et contemporaine* 29 (1982): 114.

30. Trexler, "La Prostitution," 996; Mazzi, *Prostitute*, 356.

31. GAN 80, 285rv. Alessandro ended up spending eight nights with Antonio over one month, and Antonio sodomized him "several times."

32. UN 14, 30r.

33. UN 32, 2v.

34. OGBR 152 bis, 17r.

35. On the Eight's jurisdiction, see chapter 2, 54.

36. OGBR 91, 35v, 52v. Del Campana's crime is unspecified here, but is identified later in OGBR 93, 32v.

37. OGBR 94, 41r. For other examples see OGBR 123, 14rv, and OGBR 152, 244r.

38. UN 17, 27v. On "il Fornaino," see chapter 2, 70, 72, and chapter 4, 127.

39. UN 21, 35v, 76r.

40. "Usorono molte disonestà, col baciarsi et darsi la lingua l'uno al'altro"; Tratte 1086, 2:603r, from a report by Giovanni Conti dated March 11, 1552. I am grateful to Candice Adelson for this reference.

41. Of the 118 active partners in the *catasto* sample, twenty-six claimed either no dependents or only an aged mother or a female servant in their tax declaration. This refers only to the composition of their household for tax purposes, and does not necessarily mean they lived alone; some stated they resided with a brother who made a separate declaration, etc. Nonetheless, some probably lived alone, including a number of the unmarried, "inveterate" sodomites mentioned in chapter 4, 129: Salvi Panuzzi, Vieri Altoviti, Matteo Gherucci, and others.

42. See 176, 179.

43. For example, seventeen-year-old Piero di Piero del Ciulla confessed in 1497 that he was sleeping overnight in the same bed with four friends around his age, one of whom wanted to sodomize him. He refused and moved to the other end of the bed, but later when he woke up he found his thighs covered with the semen of one of his bedfellows who had sodomized him between the legs, he ingenuously claimed, while he slept undisturbed; UN 32, 29r. For a similar case of five boys sleeping together in the same bed, two of whom sodomized a third, who reciprocated with one of them, see UN 35, 50v.

44. Machiavelli, letter of Jan. 16, 1514/1515, *Tutte le opere*, 1190.

45. See chapter 2, 54.

46. Both men were flogged and levied enormous fines (the capitano wanted to execute Giovanni, as the ordinances decreed, but the Signoria forbade him to do so). After they spent several years in prison, the government granted both a reprieve. CPDA 3767, 8r–10r (June 18, 1455); Pod. 5027, unfol. (Dec. 9, 1458); PR 152, 93rv, 94v (June 20, 1461).

47. UN 12, 17r, absolved 85r. Cf. chapter 2, 74.

48. UN 12, 16v, absolved 85r.

49. OGBR 152 bis, 158r.

50. OGBR 130, 275r. For denunciations linking clandestine gambling parlors and sodomy, see OGBR 147, 33r, against a woman; and OGBR 152 bis, 158r.

51. UN 18 (2), 39r.

52. UN 12, 14v, 13r. For additional case references, see chapter 4, 121. On the Benintendi family, artisans famed for their wax votive statues for the church of Santissima Annunziata, see G. Masi, "La ceroplastica in Firenze nei secoli XV–XVI, e la famiglia Benintendi," *Rivista d'arte* 9 (1916): 124–142; A. Warburg, *Bildniskunst und florentinisches Bürgertum*, vol. 1: *Domenico Ghirlandaio in Santa Trinita: Die Bildnisse des Lorenzo de' Medici und seiner Angehörigen* (Leipzig, [1901]), 28–32. See also 179.

53. The accuser claimed to speak with authority, since Gerino had allegedly corrupted his son; UN 12, 12v, 16r; abs. 84v. I have been unable to locate his prior convictions mentioned by the informer. He was subsequently convicted at least twice (1470 and 1474), and denounced but absolved at least twice more; UN 15, 33v; UN 17, 46v, 75r; UN 18 (2), 30r, 80v; UN 19 (3), 20r, 60r. His age and other biographical data come from Catasto 818, 459r (1457) and MC Catasto 73, 459r (1480).

54. UN 35, 40v, 42v, conv. 114v; UN 35, 47v, conv. 120v. For other indications of *casini* used for sexual encounters, see UN 30, 34r; UN 32, 27v; UN 35, 47r, 48r.

55. OGBR 97, 7r (Mar. 4, 1493/1494). This measure accompanied others explicitly against sodomy, indicating that this was also the motive for closing the schools. On the context, see chapter 6, 201–4.

56. OGBR 222, 16r (Jan. 12, 1501/1502). On similar controls in Venice, see Ruggiero, *Boundaries*, 138.

57. By the seventeenth century, dancing classes were held in brothels, so lower-class women or prostitutes were probably involved; Trexler, "La Prostitution," 1003–4, n. 118. Whether they were in the fifteenth century is unclear. In any case, all the references to dancing schools in my sources indicate they were not located in brothels.

58. Only six boys said they had been sodomized in any school—none in fencing schools and four in dancing schools.

59. UN 5, 82v–86v. For another example of a boy who was sodomized by a fencing master "many times in his school"; UN 18 (1), 44r, conv. 78r.

60. UN 30, 35rv, 47r. The accuser named two sons of Luca degli Albizzi, Brancaccio Rucellai, Agostino Capponi, and boys of the Tosinghi and Adimari families.

61. UN 34, 62v.

62. Details on these men are in M. Rocke, "Male Homosexuality and its Regulation in Late-Medieval Florence" (Ph.D. diss., State University of New York at Binghamton, 1990), 372, ns. 51 and 54.

63. For a lively depiction of taverns, see Mazzi, *Prostitute*, 269–71.

64. *Statuti 1322*, 243–44. Similar injunctions do not appear in fifteenth-century legislation. The foods mentioned are "tortelli, liverwort, spleen, roasted meats, ravioli, fish, meat in aspic, chicken or any other kind of bird, or anything else related to delicacies or gluttony."

65. *Prediche* (Florence, 1424), 2:45.

66. *Giobbe*, 2:44 (Mar. 28, 1495); *Salmi*, 2:219 (Oct. 18, 1495).

67. See chapter 6, 203.

68. *Istorie di Giovanni Cambi cittadino fiorentino*, in *Delizie degli eruditi toscani*, ed. I. da San Luigi (Florence, 1770–1786), 23:17.

69. For names and locations of taverns and inns, see Mazzi, *Prostitute*, 271, n. 49; Biblioteca Nazionale Centrale, Florence, Fondo Nazionale II.IV.344; MR 110, 76v–77r (the latter reference kindly passed on by Anthony Molho). On the public baths as places for sexual encounters, Mazzi, ibid., 276–80.

70. See also Mazzi, *Prostitute*, 278–79.

71. Each was fined 5 florins; UN 27, 88r, 142rv, 143v.

72. UN 19, 37r; UN 20, 66r; UN 21, 37v; UN 33, 38v; UN 35, 33r.

73. Morello di Taddeo from Empoli, aged thirteen or fourteen, named fifty-seven men who had sodomized him (another self-confessed), fifteen of whom worked in or frequented the brothel taverns, including several "gamblers" and "card dealers"; UN 27, 41r, 50r; UN 28, 21v, 25r. For similar cases see UN 20, 30r; UN 20, 51r, 58r; UN 29, 39r, 40r. Two examples, among others, of pimps who sodomized boys are in UN 17, 39rv.

74. UN 13, 14v; UN 27, 34v.

75. The dancing school, run by a man implicated many times in sodomy, is mentioned in UN 23, 34v.

76. UN 21, 46r, 80v; OGBR 94, 14v. This was probably Francesco di Bartolomeo Gelli, whose license to sell wine at Sant'Andrea was renewed on October 2, 1492; PR 183, 44r.

77. See chapter 1, 33.

78. UN 29, 110r. The man denounced was Damiano di Taddeo, a butcher; on him and his brothers, see later. At least two other prominent sodomites who have been discussed elsewhere, il Fornaino and Berto Salvolini, were also said to keep rooms in the brothels; UN 24, 38r; UN 28, 17v.

79. His convictions and self-accusations: UN 15, 31r, 63r; UN 16, 44v, 74v; UN 18 (2), 42v, 86r; UN 20, 42v; UN 28, 17r, 65v; UN 29, 39r. Galeotto's younger brother Giuliano was also convicted of sodomy in 1478 and again in 1495, when he was identified as the "host at the Frascato"; UN 19, 70r; UN 37, 2r. See

also Catasto 820, 321r (1457), and 924, 406rv (1469); MC Catasto 83, 37r (1480).

80. UN 28, 17r; UN 29, 30v, 81v. On the men who operated the brothel-taverns, see Trexler, "La Prostitution," 991–92; Mazzi, *Prostitute*, 249–92.

81. Violence was also common in Venetian sodomy cases, though it declined over the fifteenth century; E. Pavan, "Police des moeurs, société et politique à Venise à la fin du Moyen Age," *Revue historique* 264 (1980): 284.

82. UN 30, 75r; fined 50 florins, 128r. In 1504 the Eight sentenced him to life in prison; OGBR 130, 19r. On Segni, see also chapter 3, 99.

83. OGBR 146 bis, 87v. The man was fined 50 florins and exiled for ten years to 100 miles from Florence.

84. On Venice see Ruggiero, *Boundaries*, 117–18.

85. UN 35, 52r. All three were exiled, two for two years and the third for two-and-a-half years; 119v, 121r.

86. Two, Francesco di Giovanni Baroncelli and the cutler Matteo di Domenico, were sentenced to be beheaded (the sentence of the third is unknown) as "public and notorious sodomites [who] corrupted and sodomized with violence and by force many, many boys and women in the *contado*." As for the other gang members, Baroncelli's brother Filippo was exiled for life to Naples for other crimes including sodomy, while Filippo di Giovanbattista Bartoli was exiled for life from Italy; OGBR 117, 84v, 143r-146r.

87. For the 1521 case, in which the one rapist who was captured was hanged from a window of the Bargello, see Cambi, *Istorie*, 22:183. The 1524 case is reported by Tedaldo Della Casa in a letter to Giansimone Buonarroti; P. Barocchi, K. Loach Bramanti, and R. Ristori, eds., *Il carteggio indiretto di Michelangelo* (Florence, 1988–), 1:218–19. The one person captured, a notary's son, was sentenced to be beheaded. I thank Bill Kent for this reference.

88. UN 8, unfol. (July 15, 1461). On sexual relations between masters and dependents or apprentices, see also L. Marcello, "Società maschile e sodomia: Dal declino della 'polis' al Principato," *Archivio storico italiano* 150 (1992): 128–31.

89. UN 16, 105r.

90. UN 26, 27v, 70v. On Girolami, see R. Pesman Cooper, "The Florentine Ruling Group under the '*Governo Popolare*,' 1494–1512," *Studies in Medieval and Renaissance History* 7 (1985): 158, 181.

91. Bochi named thirteen boys he had sodomized, mostly clerics, but also said that while he was vicar he had sodomized virtually all the clerics who came to clean his room, plus many others whose names he could no longer remember. Transcripts of the court proceedings (twenty-nine folios in all) are in Notarile antecosimiano G57, no. 4 (1504–1509), unfol. (March and April 1507). I am indebted to Gene Brucker for this reference.

92. UN 31, 56v–57r. Bruscoli was sentenced to stand mitered in the pillory for one hour (118rv). Similarly, in a self-accusation in 1480, thirty-one-year-old ser Francesco di ser Bramante Martini said he took a sixteen-year-old servant with him when he went to military service and sodomized him many times over four months; UN 19 (3), 24r. See also UN 30, 183v.

93. UN 30, 40r, 41v, 58r. One of the four, Michele di Bartolomeo Becchi, was absolved as a minor, but had to make certain payments of grain and money to be distributed to the poor; 92v, 96r. The other three were convicted, two of them twice; 109r, 112r, 118v, 120r. In a similar example, Niccolò di Bartolo di Do-

menico confessed in 1497 that six young soldiers sodomized him at various times in the fortress of Pontedera; UN 32, 34r, 36r, 37r.

94. PR 131, 93v–94r (June 22). The man's sentence, a fine of 50 florins, is in GAN 79 (2), 52r. Also one of the reasons officials absolved Michele Becchi (see note 93) was "in consideration of the place, occasion, and other inducements." For other allegations of soldiers' involvement in sodomy, see UN 5, unfol. (Jan. 5, 1460/1461); UN 32, 26v, 33v.

95. *Prediche* (Florence, 1425), 3:42.

96. Here I have eliminated one boy who confessed, since the notary wrote merely that he named "several" partners.

97. This information might well have been distorted by boys who minimized their sexual contacts with men to protect their own reputations. For example, a man denounced himself for having sodomized a boy "many many times" and "up to the present day," but when the boy was questioned he said that they had had sex only once; UN 19 (3), 28v, 38v.

98. The four were Morello di Taddeo del Sordo, Lorenzo di Piero Cattani, with the allusive "upside-down" nickname Carnasciale (Carnival), Filippo di Jacopo Canacci, and Francesco di Girolamo della Rosa. Their cases extend from 1492 to 1494, and are found in UN 27, 28, and 29.

99. See chapter 1, 21. In Venice there were laws from 1470 on against pimps for sodomy; Pavan, "Police," 284–85.

100. UN 5, 70r; UN 11, 3r; UN 19 (3), 35r; UN 29, 42r; UN 30, 36v.

101. OGBR 67, 19r; for the latter see 160.

102. UN 4, 3v; UN 16, 53v; UN 19, 31v, 32r.

103. On the mediating role of gifts or services in Florence, see R. Trexler, *Public Life in Renaissance Florence* (New York, 1980), 131–58; C. Klapisch-Zuber, "Le Complexe de Griselda: Dot et dons de mariage au Quattrocento," *Mélanges de l'École Française de Rome* 94, no. 1 (1982): 7–43. The practice of male suitors giving gifts to boys was unlikely limited to Florence, but it is not reported in the literature on sodomy in Venice.

104. UN 20, 43r–44r. On Bonsi, see chapter 2, 68. For a rough idea of the value of these sums, in 1481 10 soldi was the average daily wage of an unskilled laborer and about three-quarters of a skilled worker's daily wage; R. Goldthwaite, *The Building of Renaissance Florence: An Economic and Social History* (Baltimore, 1980), Appendix 3. A grosso equaled 5.5 soldi.

105. UN 35, 52r.

106. For example, UN 16, 47r; UN 17, 48r, 48v; see also the example later of the mercer Bonifacio di Giovanni.

107. UN 20, 30v. So as not to overburden the notes with lists of archival references to gifts, in this paragraph I shall cite only the most illustrative examples.

108. UN 30, 61v.

109. UN 19 (3), 36r.

110. UN 31, 53v.

111. UN 31, 41v. Lorenzo denied the charge; 61v. On Antonio Landi and his brother Tommaso, see chapter 4, 142.

112. UN 13, 28r. See also chapter 4, 130.

113. UN 17, 45r. Neither was interrogated.

114. UN 30, 87v.

115. On family involvement, see later. Few historians have seriously considered

that homosexual relations might have been one link in the patronage system. Generally see F. W. Kent and P. Simons, eds., with J. C. Eade, *Patronage, Art, and Society in Renaissance Italy* (Oxford, 1987), esp. the editors' introduction, 1–21; R. Weissman, "Taking Patronage Seriously: Mediterranean Values and Renaissance Society," in ibid., 25–45; G. Fitch Lytle, "Friendship and Patronage in Renaissance Europe," in ibid., 47–61, with an acknowledgment of possible homoerotic elements (p. 52); Kent, *Rise*; Kent and Kent, *Neighbours*; A. Molho, "Cosimo de' Medici: *Pater patriae* or *padrino*?" *Stanford Italian Review* 1 (1979): 5–33; Molho, "Il patronato a Firenze nella storiografia anglofona," *Ricerche storiche* 15 (1985): 5–16; Trexler, *Public Life*, 131–58; J. Henderson, "Le confraternite religiose nella Firenze del tardo medioevo: Patroni spirituali e anche politici?" *Ricerche storiche* 15 (1985): 77–94; C. Klapisch-Zuber, "Compèrage et clientèlisme à Florence (1360–1520)," *Ricerche storiche* 15 (1985): 61–76; F. W. Kent, "Patron–Client Networks in Renaissance Florence and the Emergence of Lorenzo as 'Maestro della Bottega,' " in *Lorenzo de' Medici: New Perspectives*, ed. B. Toscani (New York, 1993), 279–313. On patronage in Venice, see D. Romano, "Aspects of Patronage in Fifteenth- and Sixteenth-Century Venice," *Renaissance Quarterly* 46 (1993): 712–33. For an analysis of intersections between images of the sodomite and of the male friend (the latter understood as a patron-client relationship) in Renaissance England, see A. Bray, "Homosexuality and Signs of Male Friendship in Elizabethan England," *History Workshop* 29 (1990): 1–19.

116. UN 20, 38r. The man was absolved; 75v.

117. UN 29, 48r. The boy confessed, and Ciapero was convicted; 88v.

118. UN 30, 43v. The boy denied the accusation; 45r. Gerini was later convicted on another charge; UN 34, 60r, 127v. On Piero's uncle Gerino, see 158, 189–90.

119. "Several years," according to a man who denounced himself; UN 22, 31v. From confessions: three years, UN 27, 34v; four years, UN 35, 59v; five years, OGBR 94, 48r, 92v; six years, UN 35, 41r. Denunciations: three years, UN 27, 69v; UN 28, 16r; UN 29, 35r, 42v; six years, UN 16, 28v.

120. UN 17, 48v, 51v.

121. UN 29, 47v.

122. Not unlike what happens in modern prisons, where entering into a homosexual relationship is reportedly one way of gaining protection from gang rape; S. Brownmiller, *Against Our Will: Men, Women, and Rape* (Toronto, 1975), 293.

123. UN 18 (2), 39r; UN 31, 61rv, 64r.

124. UN 18 (2), 45r; UN 31, 40v; UN 5, 70r. Giovanni Cambi also reported that "on account of sodomy" youths caused brawls and even murdered one another; *Istorie*, 21:252.

125. UN 27, 73r.

126. "Ser Giovanni di Currado, a sodomite and man of evil condition and reputation, keeps for use as a woman ser Jacopo . . . who is no more nor less than a bitch in heat, and he takes him with him day and night, and does it to him, and has him do it with many a master" (UN 11, 25r [neither was interrogated]). See also UN 12, 30v.

127. UN 30, 44r.

128. See chapter 1, 24–25.

129. UN 13, 3v (maestro Sansonetto); UN 30, 30r, 31r (Catozzo and Roberto Corbizzi). The officials acknowledged Roberto's guilt but absolved him, with cer-

tain conditions, as a minor; 94v. At the time, his father Filippo was Gonfalonier of Justice, the Republic's highest office, and this no doubt helped ensure that he and Piero were absolved. Piero was implicated with two boys in 1492, another in 1501, and was convicted twice in 1502 for having sodomized two others; his convictions are in UN 35, 120v. For other examples of men who were *guasti* over boys, see UN 8, unfol. (Apr. 28, 1462); UN 12, 28v–29v; UN 13, 28r; UN 18 (2), 41v; UN 27, 81v; UN 29, 54r; UN 30, 34r, 47r. As a noun, *guasto* was roughly equivalent to "lover"; e.g., UN 21, 38r; UN 29, 103v; UN 30, 35r; UN 31, 40v.

130. UN 15, 29r, 34r.

131. UN 15, 34v; UN 16, 40rv, 41v. Mea was fined 10 florins and exiled from the state for five years; 71v. From 1469 to 1492, Mea was named by twelve boys and implicated with two others, denounced himself once, and was convicted five more times. His other convictions are UN 13, 81r; UN 14, 65r, 67r; UN 16, 74v; UN 18 (1), 112r. For other examples of boys who said the men who sodomized them were in love with them, UN 24, 46r; UN 35, 37v.

132. UN 8, unfol. (Sept. 11 and Oct. 7, 1461); UN 29, 98r. See also chapter 3, 108–9.

133. UN 30, 43r and 50v. The officials declined to investigate.

134. Among the precolonial Azande, young unmarried warriors who were denied relations with women by strict adultery laws "married" boys between the ages of twelve and twenty, with full societal approval, before later taking female wives; E. E. Evans-Pritchard, "Sexual Inversion Among the Azande," *American Anthropologist* 72 (1970): 1428–34. It was also common for migrant mineworkers in South Africa, isolated from their homes and families, to take a junior male partner up to his midtwenties as their "wife"; T. D. Moodie, with V. Ndatshe and B. Subuyi, "Migrancy and Male Sexuality on the South African Gold Mines," in *Hidden from History: Reclaiming the Gay and Lesbian Past*, ed. M. B. Duberman, M. Vicinus, and G. Chauncey, Jr. (New York, 1989), 411–25. See also G. W. Herdt, *Guardians of the Flutes: Idioms of Masculinity* (New York, 1981); Herdt, "Representations of Homosexuality: An Essay on Cultural Ontology and Historical Comparison," *Journal of the History of Sexuality* 1 (1991): 603–32.

135. UN 16, 103v.

136. J. Boswell, *Same-Sex Unions in Premodern Europe* (New York, 1994).

137. Giovanni Battista Petrucci, *Poema anepigrafico su S. Giacomo della Marca*, ed. L. De Luca and G. Mascia (Naples, 1975), 116–19. I thank Marc Deramaix for this reference.

138. Michel Montaigne, *Journal de voyage en Italie par la Suisse et l'Allemagne en 1580 et 1581*, ed. M. Rat (Paris, 1956), 120.

139. OGBR 106, 42r.

140. OGBR 106, 40rv. Carlo was fined 50 florins, jailed until he paid the full fine, and then was to be exiled for two years. Michele was fined 150 florins, reduced to 75 florins plus twenty-four bushels of grain if he paid within fifteen days.

141. See R. Trexler, "Ritual Behavior in Renaissance Florence: The Setting," *Medievalia et Humanistica*, n.s., 4 (1973), 126–27; Trexler, *Public Life*, 112, 115–16.

142. On contemporary Tuscan marriage rites see C. Klapisch-Zuber, "Zacharie ou le père évincé: Les rituels nuptiaux toscans entre Giotto et le Concile de Trente," *Annales, E.S.C.* 34 (1979): 1216–17.

143. See chapter 3, 99.

144. This figure was derived by averaging individuals' ages at the chronological limits of their recorded activity.

145. See chapter 4, 128–29.

146. UN 33, 133r. The remark was made in regard to Filippo di Domenico del Cavaliere, who repeatedly sodomized his wife and other women.

147. *Prediche del beato fra Giordano da Rivalto dell'Ordine dei predicatori, recitate in Firenze dal MCCCIII al MCCCVI*, ed. D. Moreni (Florence, 1831), 1: 230.

148. *Statuti 1325*, 218–19.

149. *Prediche* (Siena, 1425), 2:100.

150. UN 20, 46v, 50r. Neither charge was investigated.

151. UN 31, 40v. The Night Officers ignored the accusation, but the Eight pursued it with an unknown outcome; OGBR 106, 49r. The man involved, Francesco di ser Alberto, called il Gufo, had been denounced but absolved in 1482; UN 22, 30r, 69v. One of the two sons, Piero di Benastro, in 1486 confessed that he had been sodomized by five men, was denounced again, and was also named by a self-accuser; UN 23, 36v, 41v, 42r. For other examples, see UN 30, 72r, 86r.

152. A boy claimed that Andrea, who "works for Domenico del Ghirlandaio," had sodomized him and that Andrea was kept in turn by "Guidetto, who sings"; UN 27, 72v. His name is given in his absolution as "Andreino del Ghirlandaio"; 106r.

153. UN 29, 47r, abs. 62v.

154. UN 9, unfol. (June 10, 1495).

155. UN 30, 54r. Evidently the boy was not questioned.

156. In the 1480s in Venice, parents were also said to prostitute their sons; Pavan, "Police," 285. Parents in Libya are reported as late as the 1930s to have regularly prostituted their sons; Greenberg, *Construction*, 118, 178. For convictions of parents for prostituting daughters, see, for example, OGBR 54, 73v; OGBR 146, 88r.

157. UN 30, 72v. Both Boscoli and the young soldier he allegedly kept were interrogated and denied the charge; 23v, 166v. They were denounced again in 1497, but evidently were not questioned; UN 32, 26v.

158. UN 14, 34v.

159. UN 16, 50r.

160. For Bernardo's *catasto* returns of 1469 and 1480, filed jointly with Niccolò, see MC Catasto 18, 216r, and 20, 222r. In 1469 the two bachelors, aged twenty-four and nineteen, valued their combined patrimony at roughly 485 florins, and in 1480, when both were married with several children, at 857 florins.

161. UN 27, 59r. In a rare display of conscience, however, the informer retracted his charge, claiming he had only heard the story secondhand; ibid. Raffaello was absolved without interrogation; 103r.

162. UN 27, 59v, 67r, 81r. He was not interrogated, and was absolved each time; 103r, 104v, 107v.

163. UN 30, 186v, 66v. Jacopo was interrogated after the second accusation (67r), denied, and was absolved (103v).

164. Lorenzo: UN 30, 75v. Giovanni denied the charge, but admitted that he had been sodomized two years earlier by the famed Angelo Poliziano (78v; see chapter 6). In 1499 the Eight banished Giovanni for four years for having sodomized Luigi di Jacopo de' Bardi; OGBR 115, 124r. The accusations naming Raffaello

are in UN 30, 165r. He was arrested (166v), but no sign remains of his interrogation or his sentence. Francesco Cavalcanti, whom he allegedly sodomized, had also been denounced earlier as the passive partner of two other men (79v). He was interrogated but denied the charge (82v), and despite reservations the officials absolved him (106v). He evidently was not questioned about Raffaello.

165. UN 30, 71r.

166. ". . . non siene cura, sa ssì e portamenti loro e di loro chasa perchè è ne utile di chasa" (ibid., emphasis added).

167. In 1459 Piero di Tommaso di Paolo, from the Lorenzi's neighboring ward of the Green Dragon in Santo Spirito, was said to "keep and use [Bernardo] as his wife" [*retinet et utitur . . . ut eius uxor*]; UN 4, 8v (a second similar accusation 25v, abs. 38v). Neither was interrogated.

168. The first three families named appear as ruling-class lineages in A. Molho, *Marriage Alliance in Late Medieval Florence* (Cambridge, Mass., 1994), Appendix 3, 365–75. The Strinati appear among the major guild families in the Great Council in 1508; Pesman Cooper, "Florentine Ruling Group," Appendix 1, 144. The Lorenzi are absent from both lists of leading families.

169. See Catasto 814, 165r (1457), declaration of Marco Fei; MC Catasto 66, 293r (1480), declaration of his son Francesco, then a thirty-three-year-old bachelor and a poor silkworker ("I earn almost nothing").

170. UN 5, 31r.

171. See Trexler, *Public Life*, 224–40 and passim. In Florence, documented *feste* like the one over which Francesco Fei ruled as *messere* were normally aristocratic affairs with feudal trappings, featuring ephemeral brigades of youths and staged by the city's wealthy and powerful clans. It is unusual, then, that the otherwise undistinguished Fei boy and his family would have organized such a feast, which may suggest it was indeed sponsored by some influential patron.

172. The Night Officers convicted Bugnolo in 1465; GAN 86, 72r. In 1467 Alessandro di Guglielmo Cortigiani confessed that Bugnolo had sodomized him "many, many times," but he was absolved; UN 12, 8r, 80v.

173. The Night Officers convicted Santi for sodomy at least four times, in 1465, 1466, 1468, and 1476; GAN 86, 64r, 373v; UN 12, 88v; UN 18 (2), 97v. He was named by three other boys in 1468, 1475, and 1476, and denounced in 1470, but was absolved each time. In 1487 the Eight banished him for two years for unspecified "crimes and errors," possibly sodomy again; OGBR 77, 110r. In 1469 Santi was aged thirty-eight, married, and had five children; Catasto 926, 342r (1469).

174. See MC Catasto 45, 1r (1480).

175. There is no record that Francesco was interrogated after this charge, and all four men were absolved for "lack of proof"; UN 5, 31r. A second similar accusation does not mention Piero Bocchi; UN 5, 36r. Later Francesco was arrested and held for some ten days, but the records contain no notice of his testimony; ibid.

176. UN 5, 57v.

177. UN 31, 61rv.

178. UN 27, 39r, 99r; UN 29, 97v, 131r.

179. Francesco's cases are in UN 11, 24r; UN 12, 13r, 14v; UN 14, 29r, 61r. Matteo's conviction and self-accusation are in UN 18 (2), 62r, 95r; UN 19, 32r. Attaviano's and Matteo's ages come from MC Catasto 34, 267r (1480), and that

of Francesco from ibid., 184r. On the Benintendi family, see Masi, "La ceroplastica in Firenze"; Warburg, *Bildniskunt und florentinisches Bürgertum*, 28–32.

180. UN 31, 70r, 95v.

181. UN 31, 78v.

182. UN 32, 10v, 12r, 12v.

183. UN 31, 166rv. His penalty was reduced to 50 florins on condition he would pay within one month.

184. The denunciation is recorded in UN 33, 32r (Nov. 16?, 1498), but was copied from the preceding notary's records, probably dating between April and November 1498.

185. In 1483, sixty-four-year-old Lorenzo di Maffeo Schiattesi denounced himself for having sodomized sixteen-year-old Annibale di Luigi Schiattesi and his eleven-year-old brother Alessandro, possibly Lorenzo's nephews; UN 22, 41r; MC Catasto 40, 73r, and ibid. 84, 503r. In 1520 a man who was convicted of having sodomized his own son was paraded through the city, had his flesh torn with pincers, and was then burned to death. After this gruesome spectacle, according to Giovanni Cambi, "that sin was never again heard of in the city" (*Istorie*, 22:178). Modern experience suggests that the sexual abuse of children by family members seldom reaches the courts, so also in Florence it might have been more common than it appears from judiciary records.

186. Most of these family groups were identified by their names and other biographical information; in some cases two or more men who sodomized the same boy were identified by the boy himself as brothers.

187. *Prediche* (Siena, 1427), 898.

188. For Jacopo's record, see chapter 2, 69; his son Domenico, UN 30, 51rv. For a similar but not so well confirmed example involving Gentile Altoviti and his son Niccolò, see UN 17, 43r, 69r; UN 19 (3), 31v, 65r; UN 30, 33v, 42v, 50v, 51r.

189. Lorenzo was absolved; UN 27, 36r, 98v. On his son Piero, see chapter 3, 99, and this chapter, 157. Among several other examples, see those of the Del Massaio and Del Mazzante families cited later.

190. Zanobi: UN 18, 125rv, 132r; UN 18 (2), 60r, 61v, 63v, 66r. Giovanbattista: UN 18 (2), 47r, 61rv, 62v, 64r, 66r. Similar examples include Domenico and Paolo di ser Manno da Lamole (chapter 4, 142–43); Bartolomeo, Francesco, and Lodovico, sons of Bencivenni dello Scarfa (in UN 14, 15, and 16); and Tommaso and Matteo, sons of Giovanni Lucalberti (in UN 16, 18, and 18 [2]).

191. UN 13, 14v, 70r; UN 16, 102r; UN 18, 133r; UN 20, 35v, 38r, 74r, 75v; UN 20, 58v; UN 32, 35r, 38r. See also MC Catasto 54, 204r.

192. On the Panuzzi see chapter 2, 79, and chapter 4, 129; on the Cerbini, chapter 4, 128.

193. Mario, sixty-six years old with a wife and six children in 1480, was named by five boys between 1467 and 1476, and denounced twice in 1494, but he was always absolved; UN 12, 3v, 4v; UN 14, 21r, 55r; UN 16, 28r, 66r; UN 18, 62r, 92r; UN 18 (2), 38r, 83v; UN 29, 98v, 65v, 104v; MC Catasto 54, 394r. Paolo, a sixty-five-year-old bachelor in 1480, was named by three boys from 1459 to 1477, when he was finally condemned; UN 4, 16v; UN 18, 65v, 94v; GAN 88, 541r–542r; MC Catasto 54, 486r. Antonio, a sixty-four-year-old bachelor in 1480, was named by three boys in 1480 (always absolved) and denounced himself in 1481

for having sodomized another; UN 19 (2), 27v, 33v, 62r, 65v; UN 20, 35r, 42v, 73r; MC Catasto 54, 11r.

194. UN 29, 110v.

195. Giuliano (one self-accusation, three convictions): UN 18 (2), 35v, 83r; UN 20, 63v, 71r; UN 23, 40r; UN 25, 42v; UN 34, 56v; OGBR 128, 126r. Cosimo (one self-accusation, one conviction): UN 18, 50v, 53v, 126v, 116v. Damiano: UN 23, 40r; UN 27, 45v, 53v, 100r, 101v; UN 29, 110v. Mariotto (one self-accusation, five convictions): UN 21, 43r, 79v; UN 22, 39r; UN 24, 41v; OGBR 77, 122r; UN 26, 33v; UN 27, 34r, 97v; UN 27, 60v, 135v; UN 34, 47r, 119v; UN 34, 56v, 126v; OGBR 128, 154v. For their 1480 tax return, MC Catasto 67, 386r.

196. Lorenzo: UN 16, 84v. Giovanni: UN 18 (2), 84v. Jacopo: UN 18 (2), 94v; GAN 88, 172r; UN 19, 76r; UN 23, 33v. Bastiano: UN 18, 125v; UN 18 (2), 84v, 61r, 94r, 95r; UN 19, 76r; UN 20, 32v. Bartolomeo: UN 37, 2r (payment record only); OGBR 121, 93v. The family was variously identified in the records as Del Mazzante, Mazzanti, Del Mazzante de' Cagnacci, or Cagnacci.

197. UN 29, 55rv (May 23, 1494).

198. For one example—of many possible—regarding only the brothers mentioned earlier, Niccolò di Francesco Cambini confessed that Giuliano, Damiano, and Mariotto di Taddeo "Capretta" each had sodomized him, but all three were absolved; UN 23, 39v-40r, 62v.

199. R. B. Litchfield, "Demographic Characteristics of Florentine Patrician Families, Sixteenth to Nineteenth Centuries," *Journal of Economic History* 29 (1969): 197–98.

200. *Salmi*, 1:164 (May 3, 1495). Savonarola referred to boys who took the receptive role in sex, but his comment also applies to men who did not want to sire children.

201. *Ricordanze* di Andrea di messer Tommaso Minerbetti, Biblioteca Medicea Laurenziana, Florence, Acquisti 229, 82v-83r. For this reference I am indebted to Christiane Klapisch-Zuber, who discusses this dispute and the Minerbetti family further in "Famille, religion et sexualité à Florence au Moyen Age," *Revue de l'histoire des religions* 219 (1992): 381–92. See also Molho, *Marriage Alliance*, 172–77.

202. In his confession in 1496, Salvi Panuzzi admitted that it was partly at the instigation of his brother (presumably referring to the notorious sodomite Jacopo) that he had solicited a youth to sodomize him; UN 30, 87r.

203. On the importance of interpersonal networks for sodomy in early modern Europe, see Trumbach, "Sodomitical Subcultures," 115–16. On the fundamental nature of male bonding in human and primate societies, with suggestive but undeveloped insights on the relationships between homoeroticism and general bonding patterns among men, see L. Tiger, *Men in Groups*, 2d ed. (New York, 1984), 216–17 and passim. Tiger's suggestion of the utility of seeing homoeroticism as a special feature of male bonding seems particularly apt in the Florentine context.

204. UN 14, 21v. Several, if not all, of the eight men were part of a circle of friends around Giovanni Maringhi, called Mea, a notorious sodomite (see this chapter, 170, 189. Several denunciations also alleged that groups of six, eight, or even ten men together sodomized a boy; e.g., UN 27, 59r, 65r; UN 35, 59r.

205. See 164–65.

206. UN 29, 47v–48v.

207. The testimony of the five boys who were eventually questioned is in UN 29, 48v, 50v, 55rv, 103r, 107v.

208. All five whose residence is known lived within this area.

209. One of the boys, Carlo di Pasquino, who lived on via Maggio near San Felice, had no partners identified as neighbors, but all five of the eight men he named whose workplace was recorded worked in the same area, in Por Santa Maria, near the Parte Guelfa, or in the Mercato Nuovo. Another, Filippo d'Antonio, worked for the tailor Francesco di Gregorio, "el Danese," near the Medici bank; one partner, also a tailor, worked behind his shop, and another in the nearby Mercato Vecchio, but he was also sodomized by three fellow employees, all near his age.

210. On this point see also Ruggiero, *Boundaries*, 159.

211. This case reinforces the importance scholars have attributed to the strength of neighborhood associative life in Florence; see, for example, Kent and Kent, *Neighbours*; F. W. Kent, "Ties of Neighbourhood and Patronage in Quattrocento Florence," in *Patronage, Art, and Society*, ed. Kent and Simons, 79–98; Eckstein, *District of the Green Dragon*. On the importance of neighborhood to the organization of rebellious workers in the fourteenth century and to festive life in the fifteenth, see R. Trexler, "Neighbors and Comrades: The Revolutionaries of Florence, 1378," *Social Analysis* 14 (1983): 53–106; Trexler, *Public Life*, 399–418.

212. Niccolò di Benozzo, who lived in via Pentolina (the present via de' Macci in Sant'Ambrogio), in 1494 named ten partners; all six whose ages are known were between eighteen and twenty-four, and six of the eight whose residences are known lived in these two parishes; UN 29, 36r. Bartolomeo di Lionardo, called Falsina, who lived in the same street, named a total of sixteen partners in 1494 and 1495; all fifteen whose ages are known were between eighteen and twenty-two, and ten of the fourteen whose residences are known lived in the two parishes; UN 29, 52v; UN 30, 40r, 42r. He and his friend Raffaello di Niccolò, called el Pianella, who also lived in via Pentolina, sodomized each other many times, and the other three partners Raffaello named were youths who also sodomized Bartolomeo; UN 30, 58r. Lorenzo di Stagio Dalle Pozze da Dicomano, who lived a block away in Borgo Allegri, named seventeen partners in 1496; of the fifteen whose ages are known, nine were aged eighteen to thirty and thirteen aged eighteen to thirty-five, and nine of the eleven whose residences are known lived in these two parishes; UN 30, 183r.

213. UN 35, 54v.

214. See 163, and the example just cited of Filippo d'Antonio, sodomized by three co-workers. In 1472 a twenty-year-old stationer self-confessed that he had sodomized a boy for more than two years, many, many times, "and this [was] because they worked together in the shop of the stationer Agnolo di Giovanni"; UN 16, 46r.

215. On the family members see earlier. Two employees, the habitual sodomite Giuliano di Taddeo "Caprettino" and a certain Piero, were both condemned for having sodomized a twelve-year-old boy many times in this butcher shop; UN 20, 63rv and 71rv. Another, Francesco, was named by a boy but absolved; UN 23, 34r, 62r. In 1490 the same Giuliano, who now worked in his family's shop in the square of San Sisto, denounced himself for having sodomized a fourth Del Mazzante employee, Michele; UN 25, 42v. Another often-implicated sodomite whose family had a butcher shop on the bridge, where several employees worked who were also incriminated, was Bernardino di Matteo del Gaburro, between the ages

of twenty and thirty-one; his cases are in UN 23, 33r; OGBR 91, 36v (convicted); UN 30, 43r; UN 31, 78v; see MC Catasto 13 (1480), 77r.

216. Antonio was convicted in 1465; GAN 86, 70r. For his two sons, Tommaso (Massaino) and Jacopo (Finochio), see UN 18 (2), 37r, 83v; UN 19, 34v, 74r; UN 20, 31r, 62r, 63r, 71v. In 1480 Antonio was aged fifty with a wife and six children, Tommaso was twenty-two, and Jacopo was nineteen; MC Catasto 54, 38r. Andrea di Orsino, called Lanfredino, who worked for Antonio del Massaio before opening his own grocery on the Ponte Vecchio by 1480, was implicated at least eight times between the ages of seventeen and thirty, denounced himself once, and was convicted at least three times; UN 12, 19v, 86v; UN 16, 54r; UN 18 (1), 44r, 79r; UN 18 (1), 70v, 96r; UN 19 (1), 35r, 74v; UN 19 (3), 30r, 65r, and 36r, 44v; UN 20, 33r, 73r. In 1480 he was aged thirty; MC Catasto 12, 17r.

217. UN 19 (1), 36r; UN 19 (3), 29v; UN 20, 62r, 63r. For examples of men who sodomized in a friend's shop on the bridge, UN 19 (1), 36v; UN 19 (3), 31r.

218. For concentrations of individuals who worked in the same street or area: 37 in Borgo San Lorenzo; 16 in via tra' Pellicciai; 23 in via Porta Rossa; 29 around the church of Orsanmichele; 105 in the Mercato Vecchio. In the 1478–1502 survey some fifty shops can be identified in which two or more employees were implicated in sodomy (involving over one-quarter of the roughly 440 individuals whose employer was noted); a good example, in which four co-workers sodomized the same boy, is UN 33, 34v, 123r, 126r. Moreover, in addition to the fifty-four employers who reportedly sodomized their own servants or apprentices, another fifty employers of alleged sodomites or passive boys were implicated in sodomy with boys who were not their employees.

219. Ronald Weissman emphasizes the sociability of Florentine confraternities in *Ritual Brotherhood.* Mary Ann Clawson examines various forms of fraternalism, including confraternities, and their importance for male bonding in "Early Modern Fraternalism and the Patriarchal Family," *Feminist Studies* 6 (1980): 368–91.

220. Simone Filipepi, *Cronaca*, in *Scelta di prediche e scritte di fra Girolamo Savonarola*, ed. P. Villari and E. Casanova (Florence, 1898), 492. Filipepi aimed to point out the miserable end of Scheggia, who had derided Savonarola after his death: during his lesson he began to vomit, was carried home in a drunken stupor, and died soon after without absolution. Scheggia, a mercer, was undoubtedly Lionardo, son of the painter Giovanni di ser Giovanni called lo Scheggia. He died in 1500 at the age of around forty-one. See U. Procacci, "Le portate al catasto di Giovanni di ser Giovanni detto lo Scheggia," *Rivista d'arte* 37, 4th ser., 1 (1984): 250, 256, 267. Lionardo confessed in 1475, at the age of fifteen or sixteen, that he had been sodomized (see chapter 3, 93), and he was named ("Lionardo detto lo Scheggia") in a boy's confession in 1492 but absolved; UN 27, 36r, 98v. In 1492 he also employed Piero di Lorenzo "Broda," who admitted that many men had sodomized him and later was a notorious sodomite himself (see chapter 3, 99, and this chapter, 157). It is worth noting that Scheggia, the infamous sodomite, was also convicted twice in the 1490s by the Officers of Decency for criminal acts involving female prostitutes; see Trexler, "Prostitution," 1011n.68. I thank Margaret Haines for her help in identifying Scheggia.

221. UN 18 (2), 34r. The informer accused Antonio Baronci, but in the men's absolution (see note 222) his name appears as Giuliano. On the membership of this company see Weissman, *Ritual Brotherhood*, 58–80.

222. Sacchetti: GAN 85, 443r; UN 11, 41r. Giuliano d'Antonio Baronci: UN

18 (2), 45v, 88r. The three men named in the 1475 denunciation were absolved, UN 18 (2), 82v.

223. See, for example, Biblioteca Riccardiana, Florence, Fondo Riccardiano, ms. 1748, fol. 17 (Sant'Antonio, 1501); Weissman, *Ritual Brotherhood*, 88.

224. Compagnie religiose soppresse da Pietro Leopoldo 1594, 33r (March 25, 1469); Weissman, *Ritual Brotherhood*, 128. The same company expelled another man for sodomy in 1475 (above volume, 34v). For another example, brought to my attention by Jonathan Nelson, see Compagnie religiose soppresse da Pietro Leopoldo 119, 162r (Sant'Antonio Abate).

225. Giovanni's confession is in UN 13, 17v. The three men, two of whom also confessed, were convicted, 73r.

226. UN 18 (2), 35r–36r.

227. UN 19, 25r; UN 22, 31r. For similar examples, see UN 19 (2), 2r; UN 20, 32v; UN 20, 42v, 45v–46r; UN 20, 51r.

228. UN 19, 32r. Similarly, two men self-confessed together in 1473, naming four boys they had sodomized; UN 17, 25v. Other examples in UN 20, 47rv; UN 22, 31v and 34v.

229. UN 18 (1), 125r–132r.

230. UN 8, unfol. (Apr. 27). Fruosino was convicted after his young partner's confession; ibid. (May 6), UN 7, unfol. (May 19).

231. UN 15, 34r. Chief among Mea's friends, with whom he was often implicated in relations with the same boys, were another painter, once Mea's employer, named Filippo di Marco, called la Pippa, who denounced himself once and was convicted at least five times; and Marco di Domenico (or del Crocetta), convicted at least six times. Filippo: UN 13, 24v, 81r; UN 14, 29v; UN 15, 65v; UN 16, 37r; UN 17, 28r, 61r; UN 18 (1), 114v. Marco: UN 14, 31r, 33v, 61v, 65r, 66v; UN 16, 71v, 74v.

232. Filipepi, *Cronaca*, 491–92.

233. UN 12, 12v. On Gerino, see 158, and on Santi, 178.

234. See Santi's *catasto* declarations of 1469 and 1480 (Catasto 926, 342r; MC Catasto 93, 378r), and the Gerini brothers' declaration of 1480 (MC Catasto 73, 459r).

235. UN 19 (3), 2v; UN 41, 1r. For other examples of sureties given by sodomites, see UN 20, 16r (Bernardo Lorini, the later Night Officer), and 18v (again Bastiano del Mazzante).

236. UN 12, 29r; see chapter 2, 83. For similar warnings, see the remark cited in chapter 2, 74–75; UN 18 (2), 39r.

237. See chapter 1, 41–42.

238. See chapter 1, 35, and chapter 2, 55.

239. Giovanni Cavalcanti, *Istorie fiorentine* (Florence, 1838), 1:623–26. This event occurred in 1435. In that year, Bordoni was aged thirty-three, Baldesi was thirty-eight, and Mangioni, the object of their "affectionate desires," was twenty-four; see, respectively, Catasto 77, 319v, 398r, 102r.

Chapter 6

1. Girolamo Savonarola, *Ruth*, 1:28 (May 8, 1496).

2. Simone Filipepi, *Cronaca*, in *Scelta di prediche e scritte di fra Girolamo Savonarola*, ed. P. Villari and E. Casanova (Florence, 1898), 507; see 221.

3. For a review of the literature on Savonarola, see D. Weinstein, "Hagiography, Demonology, Biography: Savonarola Studies Today," *Journal of Modern History* 63 (1991): 483–503. Also see later, n. 38.

4. PR 185, 17r.

5. P. Villari, *La storia di Girolamo Savonarola e de' suoi tempi* (Florence, 1859, 1861), 1:47; R. Ridolfi, *Vita di Girolamo Savonarola* (Rome, 1952), 1:20. On the New-Piagnoni historians, see D. Weinstein, *Savonarola and Florence: Prophecy and Patriotism in the Renaissance* (Princeton, 1970), 3–12, and "Hagiography, Demonology, Biography." A number of recent works, several of which are the products of scholarly conferences held in conjunction with the fifth centenary of Lorenzo de' Medici's death in 1492, have helped bring the figure and significance of "the Magnificent" into sharper historical focus. These include G. C. Garfagnini, ed., *Lorenzo de' Medici: Studi* (Florence, 1992); P. Viti, ed., "Studi su Lorenzo dei Medici e il secolo XV" [special issue], *Archivio storico italiano* 150 (1992); G. C. Garfagnini, ed., *Lorenzo il Magnifico e il suo tempo* (Florence, 1993); B. Toscani, ed., *Lorenzo de' Medici: New Perspectives* (New York, 1993); M. M. Bullard, *Lorenzo il Magnifico: Image and Anxiety, Politics and Finance* (Florence, 1994); N. Mann, ed., *Lorenzo the Magnificent: Culture and Politics in Medicean Florence* (London, forthcoming).

6. See chapter 1, 42–43, and chapter 2, 64–65.

7. See especially A. Chastel, *Art et humanisme à Florence au temps de Laurent le Magnifique: Études sur la Renaissance et l'humanisme platonicien* (Paris, 1961), 289–98; V. Bullough, *Sexual Variance in Society and History* (New York, 1976), 414–20; G. Dall'Orto, " 'Socratic Love' as a Disguise for Same-Sex Love in the Italian Renaissance," in *The Pursuit of Sodomy: Male Homosexuality in Renaissance and Enlightenment Europe*, ed. K. Gerard and G. Hekma (New York, 1989), 33–65; J. M. Saslow, *Ganymede in the Renaissance: Homosexuality in Art and Society* (New Haven, 1986).

8. UN 17, 30r, 62v; UN 17, 43r, 73v; UN 19, 32r, 73r. For his vitriolic polemic with Franco, see Luigi Pulci and Matteo Franco, *Il "Libro dei sonetti,"* ed. G. Dolci (Milan, 1933).

9. See chapter 2, 73, and chapter 4, 128.

10. UN 19, 31v–32r; all the men he named were absolved, 73r. In addition to Martelli, the boy reported that Piero di Filippo Cacciabrani, Francesco de' Medici, a servant of Agnolo Della Stufa (whose son was a member of the Lorenzan circle), Alessandro Stagnesi, and two men who were identified only by their given names, all sodomized him in Martelli's house or stable during the previous five to eight months. On Lorenzo's friends in these years (the late 1470s), see A. Rochon, *La Jeunesse de Laurent de Médicis (1449–1478)* (Paris, 1963), 88–91. Alessandro Stagnesi was implicated by another boy in 1476 but absolved; UN 18 (2), 51r, 10r. He was also convicted twice for heterosexual sodomy, by the Eight in 1491 and by the Night Officers in 1497, at the age of seventy; OGBR 87, 113rv; UN 31, 137v (fined 300 florins).

11. The latter boy was Giovanni di Bernardo Bellacci, aged seventeen: "Dixit quod dominus Angelus de Monte Politiano, preceptor Pieri de Medicis, ad presens mortus, una vice tamen ante quam decedetur sodomitavit ex parte post dictum Johannem"; UN 30, 78v (July 23, 1496). On his incrimination in 1492, see 202. A number of Poliziano's anecdotes on sodomy are in *Detti piacevoli*, ed. T. Zanato (Rome, 1983), nos. 33, 99, 136, 184, 228, 242, 251, 260, 302, 303, 306, 371,

396, 404, 408. On his letters to youths (in *Epigrammi greci*, ed. and trans. A. Adizzoni [Florence, 1961]) and the passage from *Orfeo*, see Saslow, *Ganymede*, 29–31. For a critical study of the sources on Poliziano's death that gives credit to the thesis linking it to his homoeroticism, see C. Dionisotti, "Considerazioni sulla morte di Poliziano," in *Culture et société en Italie du Moyen-Age à la Renaissance: Hommage à André Rochon* (Paris, 1985), 145–56.

12. UN 14, 15, 16; GAN 86; UN 17. Yearly totals are 101, 93, 93, 161, and 87. In this magistracy's extant records, convictions reached these levels in only one other year, 1493/1494, with 100.

13. U. Dorini, *Lorenzo il Magnifico* (Florence, 1949), 57–58, 62–65; G. Pampaloni, "Fermenti di riforme democratiche nella Firenze medicea del Quattrocento," *Archivio storico italiano* 119 (1961): 11–62; N. Rubinstein, *The Government of Florence under the Medici, 1434–1494* (Oxford, 1966), 155–64.

14. Rubinstein, *Government*, 181–86.

15. R. Trexler, *Public Life in Renaissance Florence* (New York, 1980), 438–42.

16. UN 20. This surge of convictions apparently had little to do with the Pazzi conspiracy in 1478 and the subsequent war with Pope Sixtus IV. After the plot, in fact, condemnations for sodomy declined sharply, from seventy-nine in 1476/1477 to thirty-three in 1478/1479 and only twelve in 1479/1480; UN 18 (2), 19.

17. For the Pazzi conspiracy and its consequences, see Dorini, *Lorenzo il Magnifico*, 67–103; H. Acton, *The Pazzi Conspiracy: The Plot Against the Medici* (London, 1979). On the reforms of 1480, see Rubinstein, *Government*, 197–202.

18. On the return of Carnival and other festive activities, Trexler, *Public Life*, 450–51. In *Trionfi e canti carnascialeschi toscani del Rinascimento* (Rome, 1986), R. Bruscagli attributes a Carnival song (dated 1490) that has allusions to sodomy to Lorenzo de' Medici (23–24). On the erotic content of Carnival songs and other burlesque poetry, the best study is by J. Toscan, *Le Carnaval du langage: Le lexique érotique des poètes de l'équivoque de Burchiello à Marino (XVe–XVIIe siècles)* (Lille, 1981); see also G. Ferroni, "Il doppio senso erotico nei canti carnascialeschi fiorentini," *Sigma* 11 (1978): 233–50.

19. Excerpts from the letter are in R. Ridolfi, *Studi savonaroliani* (Florence, 1935), 262–63. Guicciardini's age is derived from the *catasto* of 1480; MC Catasto 13, 126.

20. PR 181, 18v (June 11), passed after some eight months in which not a single denunciation was recorded (UN 25); see chapter 2, 64, 68.

21. On the latter point see A. Zorzi, *L'amministrazione della giustizia penale nella Repubblica fiorentina: Aspetti e problemi* (Florence, 1988), esp. 72–78, 100–104.

22. "E fra gli altri uno garzone che si chiama Duccio Mancino ne squittinò assai, e fra gli altri messer Agnolo da Montepulciano, che chome e' nominò lui intendo non ne volle più" (Archivio Guicciardini, Florence, Legazioni e Commissarie 1, 111 [Apr. 7, 1492]). Ridolfi did not publish this part of the letter. I wish to thank Bill Kent for bringing the original to my attention, and Gino Corti for his assistance in gaining access to the Guicciardini archive and in deciphering Niccolò's difficult hand. The records of the Eight preserve no information on the events that Guicciardini described, with the exception of the sentences of the two men mentioned immediately following in the text.

23. Ibid. For his conviction, OGBR 91, 36v. His other cases: UN 23, 33r; UN 30, 43r; UN 31, 78v.

24. OGBR 91, 35v.

25. Archivio Guicciardini, Florence, Legazioni e Commissarie 1, 111. On April 14, the Eight exiled Panuzzi from the city for three years and deprived him of office; he was not to be allowed back or reinstated to political privileges without the unanimous vote of the Eight in office; OGBR 91, 44v.

26. OGBR 91, 36r.

27. OGBR 91, 41r.

28. OGBR 94, 7r (Mar. 2, 1492/1493); OGBR 97, 7r (Mar. 4, 1493/1494).

29. OGBR 91–96.

30. UN 27, 6v (Apr. 23). This admonition appeared regularly throughout the following decade.

31. UN 27, 7r (Apr. 30, 1492). *Tamburi* of the Night Officers are documented in Pisa in 1481 and in Prato in 1454 and 1481 (UN 20, 9v; UN 36, 101r), but after the box in Prato was vandalized in 1481 (chapter 4, 133) they are not mentioned again in either place until the deliberation of 1492. Subsequent letters to the capitano of Pisa and to the podestà of Prato commanded them to affix the new boxes sent from Florence; UN 27, 11r (May 18, 1492), 12v (May 29).

32. See chapter 4, 133.

33. UN 25 and 26.

34. UN 26 and 27. The number of persons denounced refers to those who were first named in either *tamburagioni* or other secret accusations, that is, not divulged first in boys' interrogations and later, after their absolution, denounced again, as commonly happened in this period.

35. UN 27 and 28.

36. UN 28 and 29.

37. On this crisis period see Ridolfi, *Vita*, 1:116–26.

38. The historical literature on Savonarola is vast. The older standard works, partisan to Savonarola, include Villari, *Storia*; J. Schnitzer, *Savonarola* (Milan, 1931); Ridolfi, *Vita*. More recent, judicious studies include Weinstein, *Savonarola and Florence*; Trexler, *Public Life*, esp. 462–90; G. Brucker, "Florence and Savonarola: The Intolerable Burden," in *Studies in the Italian Renaissance*, ed. G. P. Biasin, A. Mancini, and N. Perella (Naples, 1985), 119–33; L. Polizzotto, *The Elect Nation: The Savonarolan Movement in Florence, 1494–1545* (Oxford, 1994). For a historiographical review, see Weinstein, "Hagiography, Demonology, Biography."

39. *Istorie di Giovanni Cambi cittadino fiorentino*, in *Delizie degli eruditi toscani*, ed. I. da San Luigi (Florence, 1770–1786), 21:128 (see the text quoted later, 221); F. Guicciardini, *Storie fiorentine* [and] *Ricordi* (Novara, 1977), 113.

40. Lorenzo Violi, *Le giornate*, ed. G. C. Garfagnini (Florence, 1986), 62; J. Nardi, *Istorie della città di Firenze*, ed. L. Arbib (Florence, 1842), 1:121.

41. For a discussion of the sodomy laws and limited aspects of prosecution during the Savonarolan period, see U. Mazzone, *"El buon governo": Un progetto di riforma generale nella Firenze savonaroliana* (Florence, 1978), 96–111.

42. Savonarola's followers were scornfully dubbed Frateschi (monkish) or Piagnoni (whiners); the other factions were the Bigi (grays), partisans and relatives of the Medici who favored their return, and the Arrabbiati (rabids), who opposed both Savonarola and the Medici and favored a "narrow" oligarchic regime. On the factions as rudimentary political parties, see S. Bertelli, "Embrioni di partiti politici alle soglie dell'età moderna," in *Per Federico Chabod (1901–1960)*, vol. 1: *Lo stato e il potere nel rinascimento*, ed. S. Bertelli (Perugia, [1981]), 17–35.

43. The most extensive study of the Savonarolan boys' movement is R. Trexler, "Ritual in Florence: Adolescence and Salvation in the Renaissance," in *The Pursuit of Holiness in Late Medieval and Renaissance Religion*, ed. C. Trinkaus and H. Oberman (Leiden, 1974), 250–63; see also Trexler, *Public Life*, 474–82; O. Niccoli, "Compagnie di bambini nell'Italia del Rinascimento," *Rivista storica italiana* 101 (1989): 366–70; Polizzotto, *Elect Nation*, 38–40, 119–27.

44. On the reforms see N. Rubinstein, "Politics and Constitution in Florence at the End of the Fifteenth Century," in *Italian Renaissance Studies*, ed. E. F. Jacob (London, 1960), 148–83; S. Bertelli, "Constitutional Reforms in Renaissance Florence," *Journal of Medieval and Renaissance Studies* 3 (1973): 139–64; G. Guidi, *Ciò che accadde al tempo della signoria di novembre dicembre in Firenze l'anno 1494* (Florence, 1988).

45. On the Great Council see N. Rubinstein, "I primi anni del Consiglio Maggiore di Firenze (1494–1499)," *Archivio storico italiano* 112 (1954): 151–94, 321–47; R. Pesman Cooper, "The Florentine Ruling Group Under the '*Governo Popolare*,' 1494–1512," *Studies in Medieval and Renaissance History* 7 (1985): 71–181. On Savonarola's role, see Rubinstein, "Politics," 155–62.

46. Savonarola, *Aggeo*, 220. Savonarola forbade women to attend this sermon; Luca Landucci, *Diario fiorentino dal 1450 al 1516, continuato da un Anonimo fino al 1542*, ed. I. Del Badia (Florence, 1889), 92. The friar appears here to question the ubiquity of sodomy in Florence, a point stressed by R. Trexler ("La Prostitution florentine au XVe siècle: Patronages et clientèles," *Annales, E.S.C.* 36 [1981]: 1006), and J. Rossiaud (*La prostituzione nel medioevo* [Bari, 1984], 148n). Yet his many claims to the contrary, plus the evidence presented here on the extent of sodomy, suggest his comment was more rhetoric than substance, and should not be exaggerated.

47. PR 185, 17r. Votes were 201–4 and 170–10.

48. Landucci, *Diario*, 94.

49. Piero Parenti, *Istorie fiorentine*, in *Quellen und Forschungen zur Geschichte Savonarolas*, ed. J. Schnitzer (Munich, 1902–1904; Leipzig, 1910), 4:28–29. Rubinstein discusses Parenti's interpretation in "Politics," 158–59, but he focuses only on the political reforms. Guidi also stresses the political trade-off; *Ciò che accadde*, 88.

50. While noting their obvious severity, others who have discussed the Savonarolan-period sodomy laws failed fully to recognize their radical content since they were unaware of the preceding low fines; see Mazzone, *"El buon governo,"* 99–100; Toscan, *Le Carnaval*, 1:187–93.

51. UN 30, 59v. The two institutions' penalties are compared in Mazzone, *"El buon governo,"* 105–8, and more extensively in this work, chapter 2 and Appendix A.

52. UN 30, 53v, 149v, 186r. In the case of ser Simone Grazzini, discussed in chapter 3, 103, the informer warned that he had made copies of his accusation as a precaution. One he gave to one of the officials; fearing this man would conceal it, he dropped another in their *tamburo*; the third he would give to the Eight if the Night Officers failed to carry out the law against Grazzini; and the fourth he would then submit to the Guardians of the Law to proceed against them for obstructing justice; UN 30, 46v.

53. See 224–26.

54. *Giobbe*, 2:44 (Mar. 28, 1495), 77 (Mar. 30), 130 (Apr. 3); *Salmi*, 1:156–57 (May 1), 167 (May 3), 285 (June 3).

55. In the first six months of 1495 the Night Officers received only twenty accusations, ten in February alone (UN 9, at dates). This refers to single denunuciations found in their *tamburi*, not to individuals named.

56. UN 30, 49r. See chapter 3, 103.

57. *Salmi*, 2:168–69 (July 28, 1495); *Amos*, 3:97 (Mar. 24, 1496).

58. PR 186, 61r (June 25). The abolition of fines had also posed practical problems for the Night Officers, as their salaries and expenses came out of fines collected. The council votes suggest there was substantial opposition to this change: 51–25 in the Council of Eighty, and 512–199 in the Great Council.

59. They received eighty-eight denunciations in the second half of 1495, compared with twenty during the first six months of the year. See Figure 6.2.

60. "Make a pretty fire, or two or three, there in the square, of these sodomites . . ." (*Salmi*, 2:124 [July 5, 1495]). "Don't punish with money or secretly, but make a fire that can be smelled in all of Italy" (ibid., 168 [July 28, 1495]). See also *Ruth*, 1:361 (June 26, 1496).

61. Respectively, PR 186, 159rv, 190r. At the time, Savonarola was observing Pope Alexander VI's order, imposed on him in September, to abstain from preaching. The Signoria for November and December 1495 pressed the pope to allow him to resume his sermons, while the priors for January and February commissioned him to preach the Lenten cycle, papal ban notwithstanding. It was also under the latter Signoria that Savonarola's reformed boys made their public debut in disciplinary actions and in the first of their great Carnival processions (Feb. 16). See Schnitzer, *Savonarola*, 1:365–78; Villari, *Storia*, 1:402–20.

62. UN 30, 122v.

63. One of these men was Salvi Panuzzi, discussed in chapter 2, 79. The Eight allowed a man they sentenced to death for heterosexual sodomy to pay only 50 florins; OGBR 105, 24r. The third death sentence, apparently carried out, was imposed probably because the man was also said to be an infamous thief and bandit, for which the penalty was normally death; OGBR 106, 118r; S. Cohn, Jr., *The Laboring Classes in Renaissance Florence* (New York, 1980), 275n.

64. PR 186, 190r (Feb. 9, 1495/1496).

65. PR 187, 129rv (Feb. 1, 1496/1497). See 219–20.

66. Parenti, *Istorie fiorentine*, 68. In the same context he mentions the suppression of the horse race for the feast of San Giovanni on June 24, 1495, so presumably this is the period of the transformation to which he refers.

67. Nardi, *Istorie*, 1:96. Guicciardini also reported that no one gambled in public and only with fear in private, taverns were closed, "sodomy was largely extinguished and subdued," women dressed with modesty, and boys gave up "many indecencies" (Guicciardini, *Storie fiorentine*, 138).

68. On the reputation and activities of Florentine *fanciulli*, see Trexler, *Public Life*, 368–87; A. Zorzi, "Rituali di violenza giovanile nelle società urbane del tardo Medioevo," in *Infanzie: Funzioni di un gruppo liminale dal mondo classico all'Età moderna*, Laboratorio di Storia, vol. 6, ed. O. Niccoli (Florence, 1993), 185–209; G. Ciappelli, "Carnevale e quaresima: Rituale e spazio urbano a Firenze (secc. XIII–XVI)," in *Riti e rituali nelle società medievali*, ed. J. Chiffoleau, L. Martines, and A. Paravicini Bagliani (Spoleto, 1994), 159–74; Niccoli, "Compagnie di bambini";

Niccoli, *Il seme della violenza: Putti, fanciulli e mammoli nell'Italia tra Cinque e Seicento* (Rome and Bari, 1995). On the ages of the boys in the movement, see Trexler, "Adolescence," 250–52, and *Public Life*, 480–81, who characterizes them as between five or six and twenty. Observers gave varying accounts of the boys' ages, which are important for specifying the nature and organization of the reform. Though very young boys took part in the processions Savonarola staged, the movement's core was probably composed of adolescents aged eleven to twenty, that is, those whom he allowed to take communion and to occupy the grandstands erected for them to hear sermons in the cathedral; see Trexler, "Adolescence," 251n.1, 252. Some diarists reduced this range even further. Jacopo Nardi, himself part of the friar's troops, later recorded that boys under twelve were excluded from the stands, and elsewhere that 1,300 boys aged eighteen and under took communion in the cathedral on Christmas Day, 1496; *Istorie*, 1:95, 111. Lorenzo Violi said he once saw 600 to 800 boys aged fourteen to sixteen take communion in the cathedral; *Le giornate*, 28.

69. According to one Piagnone biographer, these boys became the "mirror, norm, and example of decent living" to their elders; Pseudo-Burlamacchi, *La vita del beato Ieronimo Savonarola, scritta da un Anonimo del secolo XVI e già attribuita a fra Pacifico Burlamacchi*, ed. P. Ginori Conti (Florence, 1937), 119. On the impression the boys made on adults, see Trexler, *Public Life*, 477–80.

70. Placido Cinozzi, *Epistola de vita et moribus Ieronimi Savonarolae fratri Jacobo Siculo*, in *Scelta di prediche e scritti di fra Girolamo Savonarola*, ed. P. Villari and E. Casanova (Florence, 1898), 7. Similarly, Pseudo-Burlamacchi, *Vita*, 119.

71. Boys are so dressed up they seem like women, *Salmi*, 2:170 (July 28, 1495); boys are like prostitutes, *Amos*, 1:200 (Feb. 23, 1496); and like cows, ibid., 324 (Feb. 28, 1496); no distinction between sexes, ibid., 194 (Feb. 23, 1496).

72. Pseudo-Burlamacchi, *Vita*, 121, with a description of the "rule" the boys and their instructors devised for them, 121–22. For other depictions see also Violi, *Le giornate*, 27–28; Guicciardini, *Storie fiorentine*, 138.

73. Based on 110 passive partners whose ages are known out of 278 implicated in this role between November 1495 and November 1497 (UN 30, 31).

74. See Trexler, *Public Life*, 475–76; Bertelli, "Embrioni," 27–28.

75. *Amos*, 1:91 (Feb. 19, 1496). The term *ribaldo* that Savonarola uses here and elsewhere to refer to sodomites had precise sexual and insulting connotations. See R. Trexler, "*Correre la terra*: Collective Insults in the Late Middle Ages," *Mélanges de l'École française de Rome* 96 (1984): 848–72.

76. Landucci, *Diario*, 127. On bands of twenty-five to thirty boys, see Cinozzi, *Epistola*, 7–8. Various chroniclers said the boys' actions struck terror in their enemies; Cinozzi, *Epistola*; Pseudo-Burlamacchi, *Vita*, 124; Filipepi, *Cronaca*, 477; Parenti, *Istorie fiorentine*, 93.

77. Pseudo-Burlamacchi, *Vita*, 124.

78. Landucci, *Diario*, 124.

79. On the boys' march on the government palace and their petition to the Signoria, see Pseudo-Burlamacchi, *Vita*, 125–27. Another *Piagnone* chronicler claimed the boys "had the favor of the Eight and the priors, who greatly encouraged them"; Cinozzi, *Epistola*, 8.

80. For the post-Medicean Savonarolan period (November 1494 through May 1498), procedural records of the Night Officers survive for only two years, from November 1495 to November 1497 (UN 30, 31). Sentences only of the Eight of

Watch are extant for September to December 1495 (OGBR 102), September 1496 to April 1497 (OGBR 105–106), November 1497 to August 1498 (OGBR 108–110). In addition, a summary list of the denunciations found in the Night Officers' *tamburi* (but not those that were hand-delivered) for the entire period is in UN 9. The records of the Conservatori di legge, who were authorized to prosecute sodomy in 1495, unfortunately no longer survive. This lacuna renders any quantitative analysis merely indicative.

81. Only U. Mazzone has systematically explored the policing of sodomy in these years, but his study is limited to the first four months of 1497; *"El buon governo,"* 103–8.

82. The date taken as the dividing mark between the two periods is April 23, 1492, when the first group of Night Officers after Lorenzo's death took office.

83. The Eight convicted thirty-five men for homosexual sodomy in the twenty months for which their activities are documented.

84. These figures refer only to active partners convicted.

85. UN 29, 80r.

86. UN 30, 121v; UN 31, 167v. The latter sentence against Bartolomeo, son of the barber Lorenzo di Pasquino, might have been so harsh because of the boy's connections, however indirect: one of the companions he named was a servant of Giovanni di Pierfrancesco de' Medici, thought to be the financial and political power behind the Compagnacci, the anti-Savonarolan youth group. Several other men he named were also associated with this youth brigade (see later).

87. OGBR 106, 39v and 40r.

88. The issue of heterosexual sodomy, to which I devote only a few remarks here, will be the subject of a separate article. On heterosexual sodomy in Venice, where cases also increased noticeably toward the end of the century, see G. Ruggiero, *The Boundaries of Eros: Sex Crime and Sexuality in Renaissance Venice* (New York, 1985), 118–20; E. Pavan, "Police des moeurs, société et politique à Venise à la fin du Moyen Age," *Revue historique* 264 (1980): 285.

89. Trexler, "La Prostitution," 989 and n. 35; see also 998, Table VII.

90. For examples, see UN 33, 42v–43r, 43v; UN 34, 67v–69r.

91. UN 31, 157r; UN 35, 58r. In the latter case the man sodomized both his serving woman and her daughter.

92. In 1497, a woman was anally raped by fourteen men, only two of whom were convicted; UN 31, 65r–66v, 119v. Another woman was reportedly sodomized by a gang of thirty men; UN 34, 56r. For another case involving five men who sodomized two women, OGBR 147, 76r and 78r.

93. UN 31, 45rv; UN 35, 1v, 45r, 55r; MR 117, 57r (n.d., 1513).

94. The author of the following denunciation, for example, expressed views about the equality of justice for all, rich or poor, that probably locate him among the friar's followers: "I would like to see the rich punished like the poor, because divine justice does not want anyone to be held in special regard, and if you contradict this you will have to render an explanation before God" (UN 30, 80r). Similarly, another informer who denounced a Machiavelli threatened to take his charge to Savonarola if the magistrates failed to act, "so that not only butchers are punished" (UN 30, 36r).

95. See the example cited later, 219.

96. Of the men convicted for sodomy who can be identified in the Savonarolan literature (including, for the friar's followers, the famous 1497 petition on his behalf

to the pope), none was directly involved in the partisan struggles of these years. Filippo di Giovanbatista Bartoli, whose father frequented San Marco, was convicted by the Night Officers in 1496; UN 30, 113v; see Villari, *Storia*, 2:ccxxviii. The family of Attaviano di Giuliano Benintendi, whose conviction in 1497 was discussed in chapter 5, 179, was linked to the Medici but played no known political role during the Savonarolan years. Studies of the signers of the petition in favor of Savonarola include G. Pampaloni, "Il movimento piagnone secondo la lista del 1497," in *Studies on Machiavelli*, ed. M. Gilmore (Florence, 1972), 337–47; G. Guidi, "La corrente savonaroliana e la petizione al papa del 1497," *Archivio storico italiano* 142 (1984), 31–46.

97. On the laws, see earlier; for the boys' activities, see Trexler, *Public Life*, 475–80.

98. UN 30, 35v. See also ibid., 47r, 36r, 186r, 66v.

99. UN 30, 7v; UN 37, 21v.

100. UN 30, 147v–148v. A total of twenty-two denunciations were found in the *tamburo*, eighteen of which were against persons with recognizable surnames. Several days later, Alamanno de' Medici, one of the officials, handed over another accusation against his son Bivigliano that was originally among this group. He had pocketed it to protect his son when the *tamburo* was opened (149r).

101. Rucellai, Capponi, and Nerli are all identified by Guicciardini as leaders of the faction opposed to Savanarola; *Storie fiorentine*, 113. See also Guidi, *Ciò che accadde*, 165–66 (Capponi), 176 (Nerli), 183 (Rucellai); Villari, *Storia*, 1:233, 2: ci (Nerli), 2:cxlv, cclvi (Strozzi); Ridolfi, *Vita*, 1:365 (Nerli), 1:296, 297 (Strozzi).

102. Villari, *Storia*, 2:clvii, clix (dello Scarfa); ibid., 2:162, ciii, clvii (Albizzi).

103. On this competition, which the Eight banned for security reasons, see Schnitzer, *Savonarola*, 1:447. Parenti identifies the "king" only as Bernardo Nasi's son (*Istorie fiorentine*, 160), while Filippo Nerli identifies him as Roberto di Benedetto Nasi; *Commentari dei fatti civili occorsi dentro la città di Firenze dall'anno 1215 al 1537* (Trieste, 1859), 1:82. The youth was probably Roberto di Bernardo, who was eighteen; see MC Catasto 5, 115. Roberto was also named this year in a boy's confession but was absolved as a minor, even though the officials admitted that "he might have committed the said vice"; UN 31, 98v; UN 32, 8r. Parenti identifies the "duke" of the opposing squad of youths only as the son of Girolamo Martelli; *Storie fiorentine*, 160.

104. On Pandolfini, see Ridolfi, *Vita*, 1:58, 136. On Tornabuoni and the conspiracy, see Villari, *Storia*, 2:44–62; Ridolfi, *Vita*, 1:315; and 221.

105. UN 30, 96v.

106. Piero Guiducci, named in two accusations, had self-confessed two months previously to sodomizing Raffaello, a cleric called ser Stella; UN 30, 51r. Giovanbatista di Mariotto Rucellai, also denounced earlier, was convicted of sodomy in 1501; UN 30, 34r; UN 34, 40r. Others were implicated on other occasions but were absolved.

107. On the city's problems and on popular sentiment in late 1496, see Villari, *Storia*, 1:473–500. For Savonarola's criticisms of magistrates for not punishing sodomy, and his calls for "justice," see *Ezechiele*, 1:16 (Nov. 30, 1496), 52 (Dec. 8), 101 (Dec. 13).

108. On Valori's tenure, see Villari, *Storia*, 1:500–06. The law on boys' dress is in PR 187, 111r (Jan. 25, 1496/1497).

109. Parenti, *Istorie fiorentine*, 154.

110. Ibid., 157.

111. Nardi, *Istorie*, 1:119–20. On the entrance of youths into the Great Council, see Rubinstein, "I primi anni," 186ff.; Trexler, "Adolescence," 258–59.

112. I plan to study the Compagnacci in a future article. For now, see the remarks on them later and in Trexler, *Public Life*, 515; Bertelli, "Embrioni," 33–34. Basic information is in Villari, *Storia*, 1:501, 2:31, 139–42, 151, 154, 163–74, 181; and Schnitzer, *Savonarola*, 1:296–97, 376, 437, 457, 2:58–61, 71, 74, 83–85, 109–110, 125, 428.

113. Sources disagree on the attribution and timing of this remark, yet its wide reportage gives it credit. Pseudo-Burlamacchi simply noted it was said by "the wicked" after the Ascension Day riot; *Vita*, 109. Bartolomeo Redditi agreed on the timing but attributed it to a member "of the highest magistracy of the city," presumably the Signoria; "Breve compendio e somario della verità predicata et profetata dal R. P. fra Girolamo da Ferrara," in *Quellen und Forschungen zur Geschichte Savonarolas*, ed. Schnitzer, 1:49–50. Finally, Filipepi assigned the remark to Benvenuto del Bianco, according to him one of the Ten, who uttered it to a colleague during Savonarola's execution; *Cronaca*, 507. Del Bianco was not one of the Ten elected after Savonarola's arrest (see Villari, *Storia*, 2:c), but he was indeed a prior for May and June 1497, when the riot occurred (Cambi, *Istorie*, 21:104). On the May 4 tumult, see Villari, *Storia*, 2:19–22; on the resurgence of "vice" after the riot, see also Cambi, *Istorie*, 104–5; Landucci, *Diario*, 149.

114. Villari, *Storia*, 2:25–31; see also Nardi, *Istorie*, 1:126–27.

115. See Villari, *Storia*, 2:44–62.

116. The first figure includes both *tamburagioni* and hand-delivered accusations, while the second refers only to the accusation boxes, the sole evidence on denunciations after November 1497; see UN 32 and UN 9 at these dates.

117. Cambi, *Istorie*, 21:128; see also Guicciardini, *Storie fiorentine*, 113.

118. A description of their most famous feast is in Bartolomeo Cerretani, *Storia fiorentina*, ed. G. Berti (Florence, 1994), 241–43. For other activities, see Filipepi, *Cronaca*, 467, 481–89.

119. UN 29, 112r; UN 30, 43r. Spini was not questioned or sentenced in either case. In 1499, the Arrabbiati came to Spini's defense and managed to suppress the charge; Parenti, *Istorie fiorentine*, 291.

120. On ser Francesco, see G. O. Corazzini, "Ser Ceccone di ser Barone," *Miscellanea fiorentina di erudizione e storia* 2 (1899): 129–37; G. Ristori, "Ceccone di ser Barone," in *Dizionario biografico degli italiani* (Rome, 1969), 23:287–90; Ristori, "Ser Francesco di ser Barone Baroni e il suo servizio nella cancelleria della Repubblica fiorentina (1480–1494)," *Archivio storico italiano* 134 (1976): 231–80. On his arrest at age fourteen for sodomy in Siena, see Ristori, "Ceccone," 287, and "Ser Francesco," 233–34. Francesco was freed after the intervention of the Signoria of Florence and the Milanese ambassador to Florence, probably on the recommendation of the Medici, with whom the Baroni family had close ties. For his incrimination in 1494, UN 29, 100r.

121. Adimari was named in a boy's confession, but absolved after the boy withdrew the charge; UN 32, 11v, 23r, 99r; see Villari, *Storia*, 2:lxxxii. Nerli was named by a boy who confessed (UN 23, 34r), and he and Strozzi were both denounced in the group of "political" accusations discussed earlier. On their role in the attack on San Marco, see Villari, *Storia*, 2:ci; Ridolfi, *Vita*, 1:365.

122. Filipepi, *Cronaca*, 501–2, 492.

123. Ibid., 493. After the work was circulated, he claimed, certain "giovanetti," probably from the boys' companies, threateningly "persuaded" the priest to stop preaching.

124. Ibid., 495. A boy claimed that da Verrazzano fondled him and offered him money, but he refused his advances and fled; UN 30, 166r.

125. Nardi, *Istorie*, 1:161. Several elements in this account suggest this man was a sodomite, though Nardi never identified him as such. "Ribald" had sexual connotations, as noted earlier, but Nardi also called the man a *vile cartaro*, perhaps meaning Cathar, the heretical sect among whom sodomy was allegedly common. He also said that the man had previously been exiled, a penalty often imposed on sodomites in the Savonarolan years. Finally, the man's words and actions probably referred to Savonarola's calls to burn sodomites, a fate he urged for no others, to my knowledge.

126. Filipepi, *Cronaca*, 495.

127. Toscan, *Le Carnaval*, 4:1704.

128. Filipepi, *Cronaca*, 491–92.

129. "Pareva aperto l'inferno," Landucci, *Diario*, 181; also Nardi, *Istorie*, 1: 162–3; Filipepi, *Cronaca*, 490–98; Cambi, *Istorie*, 21:128.

130. PR 193, 87v. On the broader institutional reform, see Zorzi, *L'amministrazione*, 101–4.

131. See chapter 2, 75, and chapter 4, 133.

132. UN 34 and 35; OGBR 119–124.

133. See R. Pesman Cooper, "L'elezione di Pier Soderini a gonfaloniere a vita," *Archivio storico italiano* 125 (1967): 145–85; S. Bertelli, "La crisi del 1501: Firenze e Cesare Borgia," in *Essays Presented to Myron P. Gilmore*, ed. S. Bertelli and G. Ramakus (Florence, 1978), 1:1–19.

134. Parenti, *Istorie fiorentine*, 300.

135. PR 193, 87v (Dec. 29, 1502).

136. Mazzone studies Cecchi's reform project in *"El buon governo."* On his proposal about sodomy and its context, 97–111; the text of his "Nota de' soddomiti" is on 194–97.

137. Ibid., 195.

138. Ibid., 109–10, 195–96. Cecchi's proposal to confine habitual sodomites among the insane parallels the sentence levied, but not applied, against the infamous Salvi Panuzzi in 1496 (chapter 2, 79). Both perhaps reveal a precocious sense in Florence that something was inherently deviant in the personality of men who engaged repeatedly in sodomy, a still quite limited view that became canonical only in the late nineteenth century.

139. "Levò l'ufficio di notte per la vergogna della terra, el quale riconosceva sopra i sogdomiti"; *Istorie fiorentine*, Biblioteca Nazionale Centrale, Florence, Fondo nazionale, II.II.153, unfol., at December 1502. Landucci also noted the law of December 29, but only said discreetly that "certain holy laws against the unmentionable vice and against blasphemy were reformed"; *Diario*, 251.

140. Based on convictions in 1503 and then even-numbered years through 1514; OGBR 125–160.

Epilogue

1. See R. Trexler, *Public Life in Renaissance Florence* (New York, 1980), 515–16.

2. OGBR 147, 33rv.

3. Ibid., 60r.

4. Ibid., 62r.

5. OGBR 152 bis, 158r.

6. *Istorie di Giovanni Cambi cittadino fiorentino*, in *Delizie degli eruditi toscani*, ed. I. da San Luigi (Florence, 1770–1786), 21:252.

7. Ibid., 23:17.

8. Ibid., 21:308–9. Cambi identified youths of the Albizzi, Rucellai, Tornabuoni, Pitti, Corbinelli, Bartoli, and Buondelmonti families, among others. Jacopo Nardi, who mentioned only the youths' demand that Soderini step down, also included young men of the Capponi and Vespucci families among the group, which he said numbered thirty youths; *Istorie della città di Firenze*, ed. L. Arbib (Florence, 1842), 1:496–97. See also Francesco Vettori, *Sommario della istoria dell'Italia (1511–1527)*, in *Scritti storici e politici*, ed. E. Niccolini (Bari, 1972), 143.

9. Cambi, *Istorie*, 21:332. This episode certainly implies that the Soderini regime intensified repression of sodomy, but a review of the Libri fabarum from 1502 to 1512 failed to uncover the laws against the practice that Trexler asserts were passed under Soderini; *Public Life*, 516.

It is symptomatic of most historians' disregard for the relevance of sodomy in Florentine political and social life that the scholars who have devoted most attention to this conspiracy nearly all ignore Cambi's account of the youths' specific demand about sodomy; see R. Devonshire Jones, *Francesco Vettori: Florentine Citizen and Medici Servant* (London, 1972), 56–61; R. Pesman Cooper, "La caduta di Pier Soderini e il 'Governo popolare': Pressioni esterne e dissenso interno," *Archivio storico italiano* 153 (1985): 252–53; H. Butters, *Governors and Government in Early Sixteenth-Century Florence, 1502–1519* (Oxford, 1985), 163–64, and on the youths involved in Giuliano de' Medici's palace coup, 183–84; J. Stephens, *The Fall of the Florentine Republic, 1512–1530* (Oxford, 1983), 58. The one exception to this regrettable neglect is Trexler, *Public Life*, 516.

10. Two men allegedly assaulted and raped Giovanni di Salvestro Neretti in the garden of the Medici house, where twelve- or thirteen-year-old Giovanni de' Medici had asked the boy to spend the night. Both were sentenced to six years in prison, while the young Medici, whose role is unclear from the documents, was exiled for two years to beyond twenty miles of the city; Signori e collegi, deliberazioni, ordinaria autorità 113, 57r-66r (June 6–18, 1511). On Giovanni de' Medici, see C. Mini, *La vita e le gesta di Giovanni de' Medici, o storia delle Bande Nere e dei celebri capitani che vi militarono* (Florence, 1851); P. Gauthier, *Giovanni delle Bande Nere* (Milan, 1937); E. Grassellini and A. Fracassini, *Profili Medicei* (Florence, 1982), 53–55. Typically, none of these sources report this case, but claim instead that Giovanni was exiled for accidently killing a youngster around his own age.

11. MR 66, 361rv (Jan. 24, 1513/1514); LF 72, 151r.

12. The specific provisions of this law, which did not distinguish sexual roles or set penalties for minors, are as follows: for youths aged eighteen to twenty-five who were eligible for office, the law set a fine of 30 florins for a first conviction, 60 florins for a second, and 100 florins plus lifelong loss of officeholding privileges for a third. Penalties for older citizens were considerably harsher. For a first conviction, men over twenty-five were to be fined 60 florins and prohibited from holding office for life; for a second, fined 120 florins and jailed for five years; for a third, fined 200 florins and condemned to death by burning.

In contrast, penalties for the majority of Florentine males who were ineligible for office were more severe and the graduated scale was more limited. Youths aged eighteen to twenty-five were to be fined 30 florins for a first conviction, commutable to corporal punishment if they were unable to pay the fine; a second brought a fine of 60 florins or corporal punishment, plus life exile. Men over twenty-five were to be fined 60 florins and exiled for life for a single conviction.

13. PR 205, 12r (May 23, 1520).

14. This law retained the penalties set in the previous law for citizen youths aged eighteen to twenty-five. It reduced the first two penalties for citizens over twenty-five, keeping the original fines but stipulating privation from office only for a second conviction and, as before, death for a third. For sodomites ineligible for office, the scale of penalties was extended up to three convictions. Youths aged eighteen to twenty-five were to be fined progressively 30 florins, 60 florins, and 100 florins, and for a third conviction they were also to be jailed or exiled for life. Penalties for older men were a fine of 60 florins for a first offense, 60 florins plus either life imprisonment or exile for a second, and death by burning for a third.

15. Pesman Cooper argues that the republican Great Council (1494–1512) had already represented a closing of the local political class; "The Florentine Ruling Group Under the *'Governo Popolare,'* 1494–1512," *Studies in Medieval and Renaissance History* 7 (1985): 71–181. Aristocratic tendencies only increased with the return of the Medici and the abolition of the Council. On the transition from the Republic to the principate, see R. von Albertini, *Das florentinische Staatsbewußtsein im Übergang von der Republik zum Prinzipat* (Bern, 1955); Butters, *Governors and Government*; Stephens, *Fall of the Florentine Republic.*

16. On the importance of youth during the Medicean restoration, see Trexler, *Public Life*, 515–21. As Trexler notes, however, youths were becoming a political force in their own right, and neither the Medici nor anyone else could take their allegiance for granted. In the Last Republic youths supported the anti-Medicean, republican cause (521–47).

17. *Le vite de' più eccellenti pittori scultori ed architettori scritte da Giorgio Vasari pittore aretino*, in *Le opere di Giorgio Vasari*, ed. G. Milanesi (Florence, 1906; reprint, Florence, 1973), 6:389, 390n (life of Sodoma).

18. A hint of generational conflict over sodomy also appears in a denunciation in 1502 against certain youths in the provincial town of Figline, written by "6 men all aged 50 years or more"; UN 35, 37r.

19. Cambi, *Istorie*, 23:178, 183. See also the 1524 case reported in chapter 5, 163.

20. G. Busini, *Lettere di Giovambattista Busini a Benedetto Varchi sopra l'assedio di Firenze* (Florence, 1860), 35–36.

21. PR 206, 17r. On the Republic of 1527 to 1530, see C. Roth, *The Last Florentine Republic* (London, 1925).

22. Like earlier sixteenth-century laws, this measure was aimed at adults aged eighteen or over with no mention of minors, though it did now refer specifically to both active and passive roles. For citizen youths aged eighteen to twenty-five the law set a fine of 30 florins for a first conviction, and 60 florins for a second plus privation of office for life; eligible twenty-five-to thirty-year-olds were to be fined 60 florins, then 80 florins and disqualified from office for life. Men aged eighteen to thirty who were ineligible for office were penalized first with a fine of 30 florins, then 60 florins and four *tratti di fune*. Apart from the extension of the age categories, the greatest innovation of this law was that all youths aged thirty or

under, regardless of their political status, who were convicted a third time for sodomy were to be sentenced to death by burning.

Penalties for older men, especially citizens, were much harsher. For a first conviction men over thirty who were eligible for office were to be fined 100 florins and stripped of office for ten years; others over thirty were to be fined 60 florins. For men in both categories the law now prescribed the death sentence for a second offense. Magistrates were also given maximum liberty to substitute corporal punishments for fines or to levy even heavier penalties if they saw fit.

23. On youth in the Last Republic, see Trexler, *Public Life*, 521–44.

24. In 1529 a man preaching Lutheran doctrines in the city was reported to have boasted of a large following among youths; Carte strozziane, 1st ser., 67 (letter of Ottaviano Ciai, May 29, 1529).

25. A pertinent example of libertine sexual culture in Tuscany is Antonio Vignali's *La cazzaria* (ed. P. Stoppelli [Rome, 1984]), written in Siena around 1525 or 1526.

26. PR 206, 18v.

27. L. Cantini, ed., *Legislazione toscana raccolta e illustrata* (Florence, 1800–1808), 1:211–13.

28. Bernardo Segni, *Storie fiorentine di messer Bernardo Segni gentiluomo fiorentino dall'anno MDXXVII al MDLV, colla vita di Niccolò Capponi descritta dal medesimo Segni suo nipote* (Florence, 1835), 2:298.

29. On the reorganization of the judiciary system under Cosimo I and the consolidation of the ducal state, see E. Fasano Guarini, "Considerazioni su giustizia stato e società nel ducato di Toscana del Cinquecento," in *Florence and Venice: Comparisons and Relations,* I Tatti Studies, vol. 5 (Florence, 1979–1980), 2:135–68; J. Brackett, *Criminal Justice and Crime in Late Renaissance Florence, 1537–1609* (Cambridge, 1992); F. Diaz, *Il Granducato di Toscana—i Medici* (Turin, 1987), 85–109. On the reign of Cosimo I, see also E. Cochrane, *Florence in the Forgotten Centuries, 1527–1800: A History of Florence and Florentines in the Age of the Grand Dukes* (Chicago, 1973), 13–92.

30. Cantini, ed., *Legislazione toscana*, 1:211–12.

31. *Memorie di Antonio da San Gallo dall'anno 1536 [fino al 1555]*, Biblioteca Nazionale Centrale, Florence, Manoscritti Capponi 91, 21v–23v (Oct. 12–15, 1543). I thank Leatrice Mendelsohn for bringing this source to my attention.

32. See Trexler, *Public Life*, 521–44.

33. For a first conviction, minors aged twenty or under who took the active role were to be fined 50 scudi (a scudo was roughly the equivalent of the old florin); in addition, citizens were to be jailed for one year, while *artefici*—craftsmen and other mere subjects—were to be pilloried for one hour with a sign around their necks labeling them sodomites. Passives aged twenty or under were to receive fifty lashes, citizens inside the Bargello or other courts, *artefici* in public. For men over twenty convicted a first time, whatever their sexual role, the law prescribed a fine of 50 scudi plus, for citizens, four years in prison and privation from office for life, or, for *artefici*, two years of labor on the galleys; Cantini, ed., *Legislazione toscana*, 1:211–13.

34. Ibid.

35. Ibid.

36. See chapter 5, 174.

37. Segni, *Storie fiorentine*, 2:298, 300. See also *Memorie di Antonio da San Gallo*, Biblioteca Nazionale Centrale, Florence, Manoscritti Capponi 91, 21v–23v.

38. William Thomas, *The History of Italy (1549)* (Ithaca, 1963), 97.

39. Segni, *Storie fiorentine*, 2:298.

40. I am grateful to Donald Weinstein for this information.

41. L. Marcello, "Società maschile e sodomia: Dal declino della 'polis' al Principato," *Archivio storico italiano* 150 (1992): 134–38, on the prosecution of sodomy around the turn of the sixteenth century. Unfortunately, the imprecision and unsystematic nature of the information presented here makes any significant comparison impossible. See also Brackett, *Criminal Justice*, 68, 112, 131–32.

42. R. Galluzzi, *Storia del Granducato di Toscana* (Florence, 1781, 1822), 1: 112.

Bibliography

Manuscript Sources

Archivio Contemporaneo Gabinetto G. P. Vieusseux, Florence
Ginori Conti

Archivio di Stato, Florence
Balìe
Capitano del popolo e difensore delle arti
Carte Strozziane
Catasto
Compagnie religiose soppresse da Pietro Leopoldo
Consulte e pratiche
Esecutore degli ordinamenti di giustizia
Giudice degli appelli e nullità
Libri fabarum
Mediceo avanti il principato
Miscellanea repubblicana
Monte comune o delle graticole. Copie del Catasto dell'archivio del Monte
Notarile antecosimiano
Otto di guardia, Principato, Suppliche
Otto di guardia e balìa, Repubblica
Podestà
Provvisioni, Registri
Signori e collegi, deliberazioni, ordinaria autorità
Statuti dei comuni soggetti
Statuti del Comune di Firenze
Tratte poi Segreteria delle tratte
Ufficiali dell'onestà
Ufficiali di notte e conservatori dell'onestà dei monasteri

Archivio di Stato, Lucca
Consiglio generale
Offizio sopra l'onestà

Archivio Guicciardini, Florence
Legazioni e Commissarie

Biblioteca Medicea Laurenziana, Florence
Acquisti

Biblioteca Nazionale Centrale, Florence
Conventi soppressi
Fondo nazionale
Manoscritti Capponi

Biblioteca Riccardiana, Florence
Fondo Riccardiano
Fondo Moreniano

Biblioteca Vaticana, Rome
Codici Capponiani

Printed Sources

Alberti, Leon Battista. *I libri della famiglia.* Ed. R. Romano and A. Tenenti. Turin, 1972.

Alighieri, Dante. *Inferno.* Ed. C. Singleton. 2 vols. Princeton, 1973.

Allegretti, Allegretto. *Diario senese.* In *Rerum italicarum scriptores,* 23:765–860. 25 vols. Milan, 1723–1751.

Arienti, Sabadino degli. *Le porretane.* Ed. B. Basile. Rome, 1981.

Barocchi, P., K. Loach Bramanti, and R. Ristori, eds. *Il carteggio indiretto di Michelangelo.* Vols. 1– . Florence, 1988– .

Beccadelli, Antonio (Panormita). *L'Ermafrodito.* Ed. J. Tognelli. Rome, 1968.

———. *L'Ermafrodito.* Ed. R. Gagliardi. Milan, 1980.

Beccuti, Francesco (Coppetta), and G. Guidiccioni. *Rime.* Ed. E. Chiorboli. Bari, 1912.

Bernardino da Siena. *Le prediche volgari.* Ed. C. Cannarozzi. 2 vols. Pistoia, 1934.

———. *Le prediche volgari.* Ed. C. Cannarozzi. 3 vols. Florence, 1940.

———. *Le prediche volgari.* Ed. C. Cannarozzi. 2 vols. Florence, 1958.

———. *Le prediche volgari.* Ed. P. Bargellini. Milan, 1936.

———. *S. Bernardini Senensis ordinis fratrum minorum opera omnia.* 9 vols. Florence, 1950–1965.

Boccaccio, Giovanni. *Decameron.* Ed. V. Branca. Turin, 1980.

Bruscagli, R., ed. *Trionfi e canti carnascialeschi toscani del Rinascimento.* Rome, 1986.

Burlamacchi, Pseudo-. *La vita del beato Ieronimo Savonarola. scritta da un Anonimo del secolo XVI e già attribuita a fra Pacifico Burlamacchi.* Ed. P. Ginori Conti. Florence, 1937.

Busini, Giovambattista. *Lettere di Giovambattista Busini a Benedetto Varchi sopra l'assedio di Firenze.* Florence, 1860.

Caggese, R., ed. *Statuti della repubblica fiorentina.* Vol. 1, *Statuto del capitano del popolo degli anni 1322–1325*; vol. 2, *Statuto del podestà dell'anno 1325.* Florence, 1910, 1921.

Calancha, Antonio de la. *Crónica moralizada del orden de san Agustín en el Perú.* 6 vols. [Lima], 1974–1982.

Cambi, Giovanni. *Istorie di Giovanni Cambi cittadino fiorentino.* In *Delizie degli eruditi toscani.* Ed. I. da San Luigi, vols. 20–23. 24 vols. Florence, 1770–1786.

Cantini, L., ed. *Legislazione toscana raccolta e illustrata.* 32 vols. Florence, 1800–1808.

Cavalcanti, Giovanni. *Istorie fiorentine.* 2 vols. Florence, 1838.

Cellini, Benvenuto. *La vita.* Ed. G. Davico Bonino. Turin, 1973.

Cerretani, Bartolomeo. *Storia fiorentina.* Ed. G. Berti. Florence, 1994.

Cinozzi, Placido. *Epistola de vita et moribus Ieronimi Savonarolae fratri Jacobo Siculo.* In *Scelta di prediche e scritti di fra Girolamo Savonarola.* Ed. P. Villari and E. Casanova, 3–28. Florence, 1898.

Cornazzano, A. *Il Manganello. La reprensione del Cornazano contra Manganello.* Ed. D. Zancani. Exeter, 1982.

Doni, Antonio. *I marmi.* Ed. P. Fanfani. 2 vols. Florence, 1863.

Filipepi, Simone. *Cronaca.* In *Scelta di prediche e scritte di fra Girolamo Savonarola.* Ed. P. Villari and E. Casanova, 453–518. Florence, 1898.

Finiguerri, Stefano di Tommaso. *La buca di Monteferrato, Lo studio d'Atene, Il gagno.* Ed. L. Frati. Bologna, 1884.

Firenzuola, Agnolo. *Opere.* Ed. A. Seroni. Florence, [1971].

Fortini, Pietro. *Novelle di Pietro Fortini.* Ed. T. Rughi. Milan, 1923.

Giannotti, Donato. *Opere politiche e letterarie di Donato Giannotti.* Ed. F. Polidori. 2 vols. Florence, 1850.

Giordano da Rivalto (Pisa). *Prediche del beato fra Giordano da Rivalto dell'Ordine dei predicatori, recitate in Firenze dal MCCCIII al MCCCVI.* Ed. D. Moreni. 2 vols. Florence, 1831.

———. *Prediche inedite del beato Giordano da Rivalto dell'Ordine de' predicatori, recitate in Firenze dal 1302 al 1305.* Ed. E. Narducci. Bologna, 1867.

———. *Quaresimale fiorentino 1305–1306.* Ed. Carlo del Corno. Florence, 1974.

Giovanetti, E., ed. *Le più belle pagine del Burchiello e dei burchielleschi.* Milan, 1923.

Guasti, C., ed. *Commissioni di Rinaldo degli Albizzi per il Comune di Firenze dal MCCCXCIX al MCCCCXXXIII.* 3 vols. Florence, 1867–1873.

Guicciardini, Francesco. *Storie fiorentine* [and] *Ricordi.* Novara, 1977.

Landucci, Luca. *Diario fiorentino dal 1450 al 1516, continuato da un Anonimo fino al 1542.* Ed. I. Del Badia. Florence, 1889.

Lanza, A., ed. *Lirici toscani del '400.* 2 vols. Rome, 1973–1975.

Lithgow, William. *The Totall Discourse of the Rare Adventures and Painful Peregrinations of Long Nineteene Years Travayles.* Glasgow, 1906.

Lomazzo, Gian Paolo. *Scritti sulle arti.* Ed. R. P. Ciardi. 2 vols. Florence, 1973.

Machiavelli, Niccolò. *Tutte le opere.* Ed. M. Martelli. Florence, 1971.

Mainardi, Arlotto. *Motti e facezie del Piovano Arlotto.* Ed. G. Folena. Milan and Naples, [1953].

Molza, Francesco Maria. *Quattro novelle di Francesco Maria Molza da una stampa rarissima del secolo XVI.* Lucca, 1869.

Montaigne, Michel. *Journal de voyage en Italie par la Suisse et l'Allemagne en 1580 et 1581.* Ed. M. Rat. Paris, 1956.

Nardi, Jacopo. *Istorie della città di Firenze.* Ed. L. Arbib. 2 vols. Florence, 1842.

Nerli, Filippo. *Commentari dei fatti civili occorsi dentro la città di Firenze dall'anno 1215 al 1537.* 2 vols. Trieste, 1859.

Palmieri, Matteo. *Vita civile.* Ed. G. Belloni. Florence, 1982.

Pandolfi, V., and E. Artese, eds. *Teatro goliardico dell'Umanesimo.* Milan, 1965.

Papanti, G., ed. *Facezie e motti dei secoli XV e XVI.* Bologna, 1874.

Parenti, Piero. *Istorie fiorentine.* In *Quellen und Forschungen zur Geschichte Savonarolas.* Ed. J. Schnitzer, vol. 4. 4 vols. Munich, 1902–1904; Leipzig, 1910.

Petrucci, Giovanni Battista. *Poema anepigrafico su S. Giacomo della Marca.* Ed. L. De Luca and G. Mascia. Naples, 1975.

Pierozzi, Antonino. *Sancti Antonini summa theologica.* 4 vols. Graz, 1959.

Poliziano, Angelo. *Detti piacevoli.* Ed. T. Zanato. Rome, 1983.

———. *Epigrammi greci.* Ed. and trans. A. Adizzoni. Florence, 1961.

Pulci, Luigi, and Matteo Franco. *Il "Libro dei sonetti."* Ed. G. Dolci. Milan, 1933.

Redditi, Bartolomeo. "Breve compendio e somario della verità predicata et profetata dal R. P. fra Girolamo da Ferrara." in *Quellen und Forschungen zur Geschichte Savonarolas.* Ed. J. Schnitzer, vol. 1. 4 vols. Munich, 1902–1904; Leipzig, 1910.

Rocco, Antonio. *L'Alcibiade fanciullo a scola.* Ed. L. Coci. Rome, [1988].

Rondini, G., ed. *I più antichi frammenti del costituto fiorentino.* Florence, 1882.

Rossi, Tribaldo de'. *Ricordanze.* In *Delizie degli eruditi toscani.* Ed. I. da San Luigi, 23:236–303. 24 vols. Florence, 1770–1786.

Savonarola, Girolamo. *Prediche sopra Aggeo, con il Trattato circa il reggimento e governo della città di Firenze.* Ed. L. Firpo. Rome, 1965.

———. *Prediche sopra Amos e Zaccaria.* Ed. P. Ghiglieri. 3 vols. Rome, 1971–1972.

———. *Prediche sopra Ezechiele.* Ed. R. Ridolfi. 2 vols. Rome, 1955.

———. *Prediche sopra Giobbe.* Ed. R. Ridolfi. 2 vols. Rome, 1957.

———. *Prediche sopra i Salmi.* Ed. V. Romano. 2 vols. Rome, 1969.

———. *Prediche sopra Ruth e Michea.* Ed. V. Romano. 2 vols. Rome, 1962.

Segni, Bernardo. *Storie fiorentine di messer Bernardo Segni gentiluomo fiorentino dall'anno MDXXVII al MDLV, colla vita di Niccolò Capponi descritta dal medesimo Segni suo nipote.* 2 vols. Florence, 1835.

Segre, A. "I dispacci di Cristoforo da Piacenza, procuratore mantovano alla corte pontificale." *Archivio storico italiano,* 5th ser., 43 (1909): 27–95; 44 (1910): 253–326.

Sercambi, Giovanni. *Novelle.* Ed. G. Sinicropi. 2 vols. Bari, 1972.

Sermini, Gentile. *Novelle.* Ed. A. Colini. Lanciano, 1911.

Singleton, C., ed. *Canti carnascialeschi del Rinascimento.* Bari, 1936.

Statuta populi et communis florentiae publica auctoritate collecta castigata et praeposita anno salutis MCCCCXV. 3 vols. Fribourg, 1778–1783.

Thomas, William. *The History of Italy (1549).* Ithaca, 1963.

Vasari, Giorgio. *Le vite de' più eccellenti pittori scultori ed architettori scritte da Giorgio Vasari pittore aretino.* In *Le opere di Giorgio Vasari.* Ed. G. Milanesi. 9 vols. Florence, 1906. Reprint. Florence, 1973.

Vettori, Francesco. *Sommario della istoria dell'Italia (1511–1527).* In *Scritti storici e politici.* Ed. E. Niccolini, 133–246. Bari, 1972.

Vignali, Antonio. *La cazzaria.* Ed. P. Stoppelli. Rome, 1984.

Violi, Lorenzo. *Le giornate.* Ed. G. C. Garfagnini. Florence, 1986.

Secondary Works

Acton, H. *The Pazzi Conspiracy: The Plot Against the Medici.* London, 1979.

Albertini, R. von. *Das florentinische Staatsbewußtsein im Übergang von der Republik zum Prinzipat.* Bern, 1955.

Ames-Lewis, F. *The Library and Manuscripts of Piero di Cosimo de' Medici.* New York, 1984.

Antonelli, G. "La magistratura degli Otto di guardia a Firenze." *Archivio storico italiano* 92 (1954): 3–39.

Ariès, P. *Centuries of Childhood: A Social History of Family Life.* New York, 1962.

Arnaldi, I. *La vita violenta di Benvenuto Cellini.* Bari, 1986.

Becker, M. "Changing Patterns of Violence and Justice in Fourteenth- and Fifteenth-Century Florence." *Comparative Studies in Society and History* 18 (1976): 281–296.

———. *Florence in Transition.* 2 vols. Baltimore, 1967, 1968.

Bertelli, S. "Constitutional Reforms in Renaissance Florence." *Journal of Medieval and Renaissance Studies* 3 (1973): 139–164.

———. "La crisi del 1501: Firenze e Cesare Borgia." In *Essays Presented to Myron P. Gilmore,* ed. S. Bertelli and G. Ramakus, 1:1–19. Florence, 1978.

———. "Embrioni di partiti politici alle soglie dell'età moderna." In *Per Federico Chabod (1901–1960).* Vol. 1: *Lo stato e il potere nel rinascimento.* Ed. S. Bertelli, 17–35. Perugia, [1981].

Blackwood, E., ed. *The Many Faces of Homosexuality: Anthropological Approaches to Homosexual Behavior.* New York, 1986.

Blok, A. "Rams and Billy-Goats: A Key to the Mediterranean Code of Honour." In *Religion, Power and Protest in Local Communities: The Northern Shore of the Mediterranean.* Ed. E. R. Wolf, 51–70. Berlin, 1984.

Bongi, S., ed. *Inventario del R. Archivio di Stato di Lucca.* 4 vols. Lucca, 1872–1888.

Boswell, J. *Christianity, Social Tolerance, and Homosexuality: Gay People in Western Europe from the Beginning of the Christian Era to the Fourteenth Century.* Chicago, 1980.

———. *Same-Sex Unions in Premodern Europe.* New York, 1994.

Brackett, J. *Criminal Justice and Crime in Late Renaissance Florence, 1537–1609.* Cambridge, 1992.

Brandes, S. "Like Wounded Stags: Male Sexual Ideology in an Andalusian Town." In *Sexual Meanings: The Cultural Construction of Gender and Sexuality,* ed. S. B. Ortner and H. Whitehead, 216–39. Cambridge, 1981.

———. *Metaphors of Masculinity: Sex and Status in Andalusian Folklore.* Philadelphia, 1980.

Bray, A. "Homosexuality and Signs of Male Friendship in Elizabethan England." *History Workshop* 29 (1990): 1–19.

———. *Homosexuality in Renaissance England.* London, 1982.

———. Review of *The Boundaries of Eros: Sex Crime and Sexuality in Renaissance Venice,* by G. Ruggiero. In *The Pursuit of Sodomy: Male Homosexuality in Renaissance and Enlightenment Europe,* ed. K. Gerard and G. Hekma, 499–505. New York, 1989.

Brown, J. *Immodest Acts: The Life of a Lesbian Nun in Renaissance Italy.* New York, 1986.

Brownmiller, S. *Against Our Will: Men, Women, and Rape.* Toronto, 1975.

Brucker, G. "Florence and Savonarola: The Intolerable Burden." In *Studies in the Italian Renaissance,* ed. G. P. Biasin, A. Mancini, and N. Perella, 119–33. Naples, 1985.

———. *The Civic World of Early Renaissance Florence.* Princeton, 1977.

———. *Renaissance Florence.* New York, 1969.

———. *The Society of Renaissance Florence: A Documentary Study.* New York, 1971.

Buffière, F. *Eros adolescent: La pédérastie dans la Grèce antique.* Paris, 1980.

Bullard, M. M. *Lorenzo il Magnifico: Image and Anxiety, Politics and Finance.* Florence, 1994.

Bullough, V. *Sexual Variance in Society and History.* New York, 1976.

Butters, H. *Governors and Government in Early Sixteenth-Century Florence, 1502–1519.* Oxford, 1985.

Cady, J. " 'Masculine Love,' Renaissance Writing, and the 'New Invention' of Homosexuality." *Journal of Homosexuality* 23 (1992): 9–40.

Canosa, R. *Storia di una grande paura: La sodomia a Firenze e a Venezia nel Quattrocento.* Milan, 1991.

Canosa, R., and I. Colonnello. *Storia della prostituzione in Italia dal Quattrocento alla fine del Settecento.* Rome, 1989.

Cantarella, E. *Secondo natura: La bisessualità nel mondo antico.* 2d ed. Rome, 1992.

Carmichael, A. *Plague and the Poor in Renaissance Florence.* Cambridge, 1986.

Carra, S. "Due inediti e un raro di Luigi Pulci." *Interpres* 3 (1980): 158–92.

Carrasco, R. *Inquisición y represión sexual en Valencia: Historia de los sodomitos (1565–1785).* Barcelona, 1985.

Carrier, J. M. "Cultural Factors Affecting Urban Mexican Male Homosexual Behavior." *Archives of Sexual Behavior* 5, no. 2 (1976): 103–24.

———. "Homosexual Behavior in Cross-Cultural Perspective." In *Homosexual Behavior: A Modern Reappraisal,* ed. J. Marmor, 100–22. New York, 1980.

Cartledge, P. "The Politics of Spartan Pederasty." *Cambridge Philological Society, Proceedings* 207 (1981): 17–36.

Chastel, A. *Art et humanisme à Florence au temps de Laurent le Magnifique: Études sur la Renaissance et l'humanisme platonicien.* Paris, 1961.

Chauncey, G. *Gay New York: Gender, Urban Culture, and the Making of the Gay Male World, 1890–1940.* New York, 1994.

Chojnacki, S. "Political Adulthood in Fifteenth-Century Venice." *American Historical Review* 91 (1986): 791–810.

Ciappelli, G. "Carnevale e quaresima: Rituale e spazio urbano a Firenze (sec. XIII–XVI)." In *Riti e rituali nelle società medievali,* ed. J. Chiffoleau, L. Martines, and A. Paravicini Bagliani, 159–74. Spoleto, 1994.

———. "Tempo di festa, tempo di penitenza: Carnevale e Quaresima a Firenze nel Quattrocento." In *Il tempo libero: Economia e società (Loisirs, Tiempo Libre, Freizeit), secc. XIII–XVIII.* Atti della "Ventiseiesima Settimana di Studi" [dell'Istituto Internazionale di Storia Economica "F. Datini," Prato], April 18–23, 1994, ed. S. Cavaciocchi, 233–43. Florence, 1995.

Clawson, M. A. "Early Modern Fraternalism and the Patriarchal Family." *Feminist Studies* 6 (1980): 368–91.

Cochrane, E. *Florence in the Forgotten Centuries, 1527–1800: A History of Florence and Florentines in the Age of the Grand Dukes.* Chicago, 1973.

Cohen, D. "Law, Society and Homosexuality in Classical Athens." *Past & Present* 117 (1987): 3–21.

Cohen, S. "Convertite e Malmaritate: Donne 'irregolari' e ordini religiosi nella Firenze rinascimentale." *Memoria: Rivista di storia delle donne* 5 (November 1982): 46–63.

———. *The Evolution of Women's Asylums Since 1500: From Refuges for Ex-Prostitutes to Shelters for Battered Women*. New York, 1992.

Cohn, S., Jr. "Criminality and the State in Renaissance Florence, 1344–1466." *Journal of Social History* 14 (1981): 211–33.

———. *The Laboring Classes in Renaissance Florence*. New York, 1980.

Compton, T. "Sodomy and Civic Doom." *Vector* 11, no. 11 (1975): 23–27, 57–58.

Corazzini, G. O. "Ser Ceccone di ser Barone." *Miscellanea fiorentina di erudizione e storia* 2 (1899): 129–37.

Dahm, G. *Das Strafrecht Italiens im ausgehenden Mittelalter*. Berlin and Leipzig, 1931.

Dall'Orto, G. " 'Socratic Love' as a Disguise for Same-Sex Love in the Italian Renaissance." In *The Pursuit of Sodomy: Male Homosexuality in Renaissance and Enlightenment Europe*, ed. K. Gerard and G. Hekma, 33–65. New York, 1989.

Davidsohn, R. *Storia di Firenze*. 8 vols. Berlin, 1896–1927; Florence, 1956–1968.

Devonshire Jones, R. *Francesco Vettori: Florentine Citizen and Medici Servant*. London, 1972.

Diaz, F. *Il Granducato di Toscana—i Medici*. Turin, 1987.

Dionisotti, C. "Considerazioni sulla morte di Poliziano." In *Culture et société en Italie du Moyen-Age à la Renaissance: Hommage à André Rochon*, 145–56. Paris, 1985.

Dixon, J. "The Drama of Donatello's *David*: Re-examination of an Enigma." *Gazzette des Beaux-Arts*, 6th ser., 93 (1979): 7–12.

Dorini, U. *Il diritto penale e la delinquenza a Firenze nel secolo XIV*. Lucca, [1923].

———. *Lorenzo il Magnifico*. Florence, 1949.

Dover, K. J. *Greek Homosexuality*. Cambridge, Mass., 1978; New York, 1980.

Dundes, A., and A. Falassi. *La Terra in Piazza: An Interpretation of the Palio of Siena*. Berkeley, 1975.

Dynes, W., and W. Johansson. "London's Medieval Sodomites." *Cabirion and Gay Books Bulletin* 10 (1984): 6–34.

Eckstein, N. *The District of the Green Dragon: Neighbourhood Life and Social Change in Renaissance Florence*. Florence, 1995.

Edgerton, S. Y., Jr. *Pictures and Punishment: Art and Criminal Prosecution During the Florentine Renaissance*. Ithaca, 1985.

Evans-Pritchard, E. E. "Sexual Inversion Among the Azande." *American Anthropologist* 72 (1970): 1428–34.

Fabbri, L. *Alleanza matrimoniale e patriziato nella Firenze del '400: Studio sulla famiglia Strozzi*. Florence, 1991.

Falletti-Fossati, C. *Costumi senesi nella seconda metà del secolo XIV*. Siena, 1881.

Fanelli, G. *Firenze*. 3d. ed. Bari, 1985.

Farr, J. R. "Crimine nel vicinato: Ingiurie, matrimonio e onore nella Digione del XVI e del XVII secolo." *Quaderni storici* 66 (1987): 839–54.

Fasano Guarini, E. "Considerazioni su giustizia stato e società nel ducato di Toscana del Cinquecento." In *Florence and Venice: Comparisons and Relations*. I Tatti Studies. vol. 5, 2:135–68. 2 vols. Florence, 1979–1980.

Ferroni, G. "Il doppio senso erotico nei canti carnascialeschi fiorentini." *Sigma* 11 (1978): 233–50.

Fitch Lytle, G. "Friendship and Patronage in Renaissance Europe." In *Patronage, Art, and Society in Renaissance Italy*, ed. F. W. Kent and P. Simons, with J. C. Eade, 47–61. Oxford, 1987.

Flandrin, J.-L. "Mariage tardif et vie sexuelle: Discussions et hypothèses de recherche." *Annales, E.S.C.* 27 (1972): 1351–78.

Foligno, C. "Un poema d'imitazione dantesca sul Savonarola." *Giornale storico della letteratura italiana* 87 (1926): 1–35.

Foucault, M. *Histoire de la sexualité*. 3 vols. Paris, 1976–1984.

Freud, S. *Eine Kindheitserinnerung des Leonardo da Vinci*. Vienna, 1910.

Frommel, C. L. *Michelangelo und Tommaso dei Cavalieri*. Amsterdam, 1979.

Fubini, R. "La rivendicazione di Firenze della sovranità statale e il contributo delle 'Historiae' del Bruni." In *Leonardo Bruni cancelliere della Repubblica di Firenze*, ed. P. Viti, 29–62. Florence, 1990.

Galluzzi, R. *Storia del Granducato di Toscana*. 11 vols. Florence, 1781, 1822.

Garfagnini, G. C., ed. *Lorenzo de' Medici: Studi*. Florence, 1992.

———, ed. *Lorenzo il Magnifico e il suo tempo*. Florence, 1993.

Gauthier, P. *Giovanni delle Bande Nere*. Milan, 1937.

Gavitt, P. *Charity and Children in Renaissance Florence: The Ospedale degli Innocenti, 1410–1536*. Ann Arbor, 1990.

Gerard, K., and G. Hekma, eds. *The Pursuit of Sodomy: Male Homosexuality in Renaissance and Enlightenment Europe*. New York, 1989. Published simultaneously in the *Journal of Homosexuality* 16, nos. 1, 2 (1988).

Gilman, S. L. "Leonardo Sees Him-Self: Reading Leonardo's First Representation of Human Sexuality." *Social Research* 54, no. 1 (1987): 149–71.

Gilmore, D. *Manhood in the Making: Cultural Concepts of Masculinity*. New Haven, 1990.

Goldthwaite, R. *The Building of Renaissance Florence: An Economic and Social History*. Baltimore, 1980.

———. "The Florentine Palace as Domestic Architecture." *American Historical Review* 77 (1972): 977–1012.

Goodich, M. "Sodomy in Medieval Secular Law." *Journal of Homosexuality* 1 (1976): 295–302.

———. *The Unmentionable Vice: Homosexuality in the Later Medieval Period*. Santa Barbara, Calif., 1979.

Grassellini, E., and A. Fracassini. *Profili Medicei*. Florence, 1982.

Greci, L. *Benvenuto Cellini nei delitti e nei processi fiorentini ricostruiti attraverso le leggi del tempo*. Turin, 1930.

Greenberg, D. *The Construction of Homosexuality*. Chicago, 1988.

Gregory, H. "Daughters, Dowries and the Family in Fifteenth-Century Florence." *Rinascimento* 27 (1987): 215–37.

Guerri, D. *La corrente popolare nel rinascimento: Berte, burle e baie nella Firenze del Brunellesco e del Burchiello*. Florence, 1931.

Guidi, G. *Ciò che accadde al tempo della signoria di novembre dicembre in Firenze l'anno 1494*. Florence, 1988.

———. "La corrente savonaroliana e la petizione al papa del 1497." *Archivio storico italiano* 142 (1984): 31–46.

———. *Il governo della città-repubblica di Firenze del primo Quattrocento*. 3 vols. Florence, 1981.

Gundersheimer, W. L. "Crime and Punishment in Ferrara, 1440–1500." In *Violence and Civil Disorder in Italian Cities, 1200–1500*, ed. L. Martines, 104–28. Berkeley, 1972

Halperin, D. *One Hundred Years of Homosexuality and Other Essays on Greek Love.* New York, 1990.

Henderson, J. "Le confraternite religiose nella Firenze del tardo medioevo: Patroni spirituali e anche politici?" *Ricerche storiche* 15 (1985): 77–94.

———. *Piety and Charity in Late Medieval Florence.* Oxford, 1994.

Herde, P. "Politische Verhaltensweisen der Florentiner Oligarchie, 1382–1402." In *Geschichte und Verfassungsgefüge: Frankfurter Festgabe für Walter Schlessinger*. Frankfurter Historische Abhandlungen, Vol. 5, 156–249. Wiesbaden, 1973.

Herdt, G. W. *Guardians of the Flutes: Idioms of Masculinity.* New York, 1981.

———. "Representations of Homosexuality: An Essay on Cultural Ontology and Historical Comparison." *Journal of the History of Sexuality* 1 (1991): 481–504, 603–32.

———, ed. *Ritualized Homosexuality in Melanesia.* Berkeley, 1984.

Herlihy, D. "Some Psychological and Social Roots of Violence in the Tuscan Cities." In *Violence and Civil Disorder In Italian Cities, 1200–1500*, ed. L. Martines, 129–54. Berkeley, 1972.

———. "Vieillir à Florence au Quattrocento." *Annales, E.S.C.* 24 (1969): 1338–52.

Herlihy, D. and C. Klapisch-Zuber. *Les Toscans et leurs familles: Une étude du catasto florentin de 1427.* Paris, 1978.

Herzfeld, M. *The Poetics of Manhood: Contest and Identity in a Cretan Mountain Village.* Princeton, 1985.

Heywood, W. *The "Ensamples" of Fra Filippo: A Study of Medieval Siena.* Siena, 1901.

"Istituzioni giudiziarie e aspetti della criminalità nella Firenze tardomedievale" [special issue], *Ricerche storiche* 18, no. 3 (1988).

Janson, H. W. *The Sculpture of Donatello.* 2 vols. Princeton, 1957.

Kent, D. V. *The Rise of the Medici: Faction in Florence (1426–1434).* Oxford, 1978.

Kent, D. V., and F. W. Kent. *Neighbours and Neighbourhood in Renaissance Florence: The District of the Red Lion in the Fifteenth Century.* Locust Valley, N.Y., 1982.

Kent, F. W. *Bartolommeo Cederni and his Friends: Letters to an Obscure Florentine.* Florence, [1991].

———. *Household and Lineage in Renaissance Florence: The Family Life of the Capponi, Ginori, and Rucellai.* Princeton, 1977.

———. "Lorenzo de' Medici and the 'Lads from the Canto della Macina.' " *Rinascimento*, 2d ser., 23 (1983): 252–60.

———. "Patron–Client Networks in Renaissance Florence and the Emergence of Lorenzo as 'Maestro della Bottega.' " In *Lorenzo de' Medici: New Perspectives*, ed. B. Toscani, 279–313. New York, 1993.

———. "Ties of Neighbourhood and Patronage in Quattrocento Florence." In *Patronage, Art, and Society in Renaissance Italy*, ed. F. W. Kent and P. Simons, with J. C. Eade, 79–98. Oxford, 1987.

Kent, F. W., and P. Simons, eds., with J. C. Eade. *Patronage, Art, and Society in Renaissance Italy.* Oxford, 1987.

Kirshner, J. "Pursuing Honor While Avoiding Sin: The *Monte delle doti* of Florence." *Studi senesi* 87 (1977): 175–256.

Klapisch-Zuber, C. "Le chiavi fiorentine di Barbablu: L'apprendimento della lettura a Firenze nel XV secolo." *Quaderni storici* 57 (1984): 765–92.

———. "Compèrage et clientèlisme à Florence (1360–1520)." *Ricerche storiche* 15 (1985): 61–76.

———. "Le Complexe de Griselda: Dot et dons de mariage au Quattrocento." *Mélanges de l'École Française de Rome* 94, no. 1 (1982): 7–43.

———. "L'Enfance en Toscane au dèbut du XVe siècle." *Annales de démographie historique* (1973): 99–122.

———. "Famille, religion et sexualité à Florence au Moyen Age." *Revue de l'histoire des religions* 219 (1992): 381–92.

———. " 'Parenti, amici, vicini': Il territorio urbano d'una famiglia mercantile nel XV secolo." *Quaderni storici* 33 (1976): 953–82.

———. "Women Servants in Florence During the Fourteenth and Fifteenth Centuries." In *Women and Work in Preindustrial Europe*, ed. B. A. Hanawalt, 56–80. Bloomington. Ind., 1986.

———. "Zacharie ou le père évincé: Les rituels nuptiaux toscans entre Giotto et le Concile de Trente." *Annales, E.S.C.* 34 (1979): 1216–43.

Kohler, J. *Das Strafrecht der Italienischen Statuten.* Mannheim, 1897.

Kohler, J. and G. degli Azzi. *Das florentiner Strafrecht des XIV Jahrhunderts.* Mannheim and Leipzig, 1909.

Krekić, B. "Abominandum Crimen: Punishment of Homosexuals in Renaissance Dubrovnik." *Viator: Medieval and Renaissance Studies* 18 (1987): 337–45.

Labalme, P. "Sodomy and Venetian Justice in the Renaissance." *Legal History Review* 52 (1984): 217–54.

Lanza, A. *Polemiche e berte letterarie nella Firenze del primo Rinascimento (1375–1449).* Rome, 1972, 1989.

Lilja, S. *Homosexuality in Republican and Augustan Rome.* Helsinki, 1983.

Litchfield, R. B. "Demographic Characteristics of Florentine Patrician Families, Sixteenth to Nineteenth Centuries." *Journal of Economic History* 29 (1969): 191–205.

Macmullen, R. "Roman Attitudes to Greek Love." *Historia* 31 (1982): 484–502.

Manikowska, H. "Polizia e servizi d'ordine a Firenze nella seconda metà del XIV secolo." *Ricerche storiche* 16 (1986): 17–38.

Mann, N., ed. *Lorenzo the Magnificent: Culture and Politics in Medicean Florence.* London, forthcoming.

Marcello, L. "Società maschile e sodomia: Dal declino della 'polis' al Principato." *Archivio storico italiano* 150 (1992): 115–38.

Martines, L. "A Way of Looking at Women in Renaissance Florence." *Journal of Medieval and Renaissance Studies* 4 (1974): 15–28.

———. *Lawyers and Statecraft in Renaissance Florence.* Princeton, 1968.

Martini, G. *Il "vitio nefando" nella Venezia del Seicento: Aspetti sociali e repressione di giustizia.* Rome, 1988.

Marzi, D. *La cancelleria della Repubblica fiorentina.* 2 vols. Florence, 1910. Reprint. Florence, 1987.

Masi, G. "La ceroplastica in Firenze nei secoli XV–XVI, e la famiglia Benintendi." *Rivista d'arte* 9 (1916): 124–42.

Mazzi, M. S. "Cronache di periferia dello Stato fiorentino: Reati contro la morale nel primo Quattrocento." *Studi storici* 27 (1986): 609–35.

———. "Il mondo della prostituzione nella Firenze tardo medievale." *Ricerche storiche* 14 (1984): 337–63.

———. *Prostitute e lenoni nella Firenze del Quattrocento.* Milan, 1991.

Mazzone, U. *"El buon governo": Un progetto di riforma generale nella Firenze savonaroliana.* Florence, 1978.

Mesnil, J. *Botticelli.* Paris, 1938.

Mini, C. *La vita e le gesta di Giovanni de' Medici, o storia delle Bande Nere e dei celebri capitani che vi militarono.* Florence, 1851.

Molho, A. "Cosimo de' Medici: *Pater patriae* or *padrino*?" *Stanford Italian Review* 1 (1979): 5–33.

———. *Florentine Public Finances in the Early Renaissance, 1400–1433.* Cambridge, Mass., 1971.

———. "Investimenti nel Monte delle doti di Firenze: Un'analisi sociale e geografica." *Quaderni storici* 61 (1986): 147–70.

———. "Il patronato a Firenze nella storiografia anglofona." *Ricerche storiche* 15 (1985): 5–16.

———. *Marriage Alliance in Late Medieval Florence.* Cambridge, Mass., 1994.

———. "Politics and the Ruling Class in Early Renaissance Florence." *Nuova rivista storica* 52 (1968): 401–20.

Molho, A., and J. Kirshner. "The Dowry Fund and the Marriage Market in Early *Quattrocento* Florence." *Journal of Modern History* 50 (1978): 403–38.

———. "Il monte delle doti a Firenze dalla sua fondazione nel 1425 alla metà del sedicesimo secolo: Abbozzo di una ricerca." *Ricerche storiche* 10 (1980): 21–47.

Monter, W. *Frontiers of Heresy: The Spanish Inquisition from the Basque Lands to Sicily.* Cambridge, 1990.

———. "Sodomy and Heresy in Early Modern Switzerland." In *Historical Perspectives on Homosexuality*, ed. S. J. Licata and R. P. Petersen, 41–55. New York, 1981.

Moodie, T. D., with V. Ndatshe and B. Subuyi. "Migrancy and Male Sexuality on the South African Gold Mines." In *Hidden from History: Reclaiming the Gay and Lesbian Past*, ed. M. B. Duberman, M. Vicinus, and G. Chauncey, Jr., 411–25. New York, 1989.

Mott, L., and A. Assunçao. "Love's Labors Lost: Five Letters from a Seventeenth-Century Portuguese Sodomite." In *The Pursuit of Sodomy: Male Homosexuality in Renaissance and Enlightenment Europe*, ed. K. Gerard and G. Hekma, 91–101. New York, 1989.

Murray, S. O., and K. Gerard. "Renaissance Sodomite Subcultures?" In *Cultural Diversity and Homosexualities*, ed. S. O. Murray, 65–94. New York, 1987.

Najemy, J. M. *Between Friends: Discourse of Power and Desire in the Machiavelli–Vettori Letters of 1513–1515.* Princeton, 1993.

———. *Corporatism and Consensus in Florentine Electoral Politics, 1280–1400.* Chapel Hill, 1982.

Niccoli, O. "Compagnie di bambini nell'Italia del Rinascimento." *Rivista storica italiana* 101 (1989): 346–74.

———. *Il seme della violenza: Putti, fanciulli e mammoli nell' Italia tra Cinque e Seicento.* Rome and Bari, 1995.

———, ed. *Infanzie: Funzioni di un gruppo liminale dal mondo classico all'Età moderno.* Vol. 6 of Laboratorio di storia. Florence, 1993.

Origo, I. *The World of San Bernardino.* London, 1963.

Otis, L. *Prostitution in Medieval Society: The History of an Urban Institution in Languedoc.* Chicago, 1985.

Pampaloni, G. "Fermenti di riforme democratiche nella Firenze medicea del Quattrocento." *Archivio storico italiano* 119 (1961): 11–62.

———. "Il movimento piagnone secondo la lista del 1497." In *Studies on Machiavelli*, ed. M. Gilmore, 337–47. Florence, 1972.

Pastor, L. *Geschichte der Päpste seit dem Ausgang des Mittelalters.* 22 vols. Freiburg im Breisgau, 1901–1933.

Pavan, E. "Police des moeurs, société et politique à Venise à la fin du Moyen Age." *Revue historique* 264 (1980): 241–88.

Pequigney, J. "Sodomy in Dante's *Inferno* and *Purgatorio.*" *Representations* 36 (1991): 22–42.

Perry, M. E. "The 'Nefarious Sin' in Early Modern Seville." In *The Pursuit of Sodomy: Male Homosexuality in Renaissance and Enlightenment Europe*, ed. K. Gerard and G. Hekma, 67–89. New York, 1989.

Pesman Cooper, R. "La caduta di Pier Soderini e il ''Governo popolare': Pressioni esterne e dissenso interno." *Archivio storico italiano* 153 (1985): 225–60.

———. "L'elezione di Pier Soderini a gonfaloniere a vita." *Archivio storico italiano* 125 (1967): 145–85.

———. "The Florentine Ruling Group Under the '*Governo Popolare*,' 1494–1512." *Studies in Medieval and Renaissance History* 7 (1985): 71–181.

Pitt-Rivers, J. *The Fate of Shechem.* Cambridge, 1977.

Plummer, K., ed. *The Making of the Modern Homosexual.* London, 1981.

Polizzotto, L. *The Elect Nation: The Savonarolan Movement in Florence, 1494–1545.* Oxford, 1994.

Pope-Hennessy, J. "Donatello's Bronze *David.*" In *Scritti di storia dell'arte in onore di Federico Zeri*, 1:122–27. Milan, 1984.

Procacci, U. "Le portate al catasto di Giovanni di ser Giovanni detto lo Scheggia." *Rivista d'arte* 37, 4th ser., 1 (1984): 235–68.

Resta, G. "Antonio Beccadelli." In *Dizionario biografico degli italiani*, 7:400–06. Rome, 1965.

Rey, M. "Parisian Homosexuals Create a Lifestyle, 1700–1750: The Police Archives." *Eighteenth Century Life* 9, n.s., 3 (1985): 179–91.

———. "Police et sodomie à Paris au XVIIIe siècle: Du péché au désordre." *Revue d'histoire moderne et contemporaine* 29 (1982): 113–24.

Richlin, A. "Not Before Homosexuality: The Materiality of the *Cinaedus* and the Roman Law against Love Between Men." *Journal of the History of Sexuality* 3 (1993): 523–73.

Ridolfi, R. *Studi savonaroliani.* Florence, 1935.

———. *Vita di Girolamo Savonarola.* 2 vols. Rome, 1952.

Ristori, G. "Ceccone di ser Barone." In *Dizionario biografico degli italiani*, 23: 287–90. Rome, 1969.

———. "Ser Francesco di ser Barone Baroni e il suo servizio nella cancelleria della Repubblica fiorentina (1480–1494)." *Archivio storico italiano* 134 (1976): 231–80.

Rochon, A. *La Jeunesse de Laurent de Médicis (1449–1478)*. Paris, 1963.

Rocke, M. "Il controllo dell'omosessualità a Firenze nel XV secolo: Gli Ufficiali di Notte." *Quaderni storici* 66 (1987): 701–23.

———. "Il fanciullo e il sodomita: Pederastia, cultura maschile e vita civile nella Firenze del Quattrocento." In *Infanzie: Funzioni di un gruppo liminale dal mondo classico all'Età moderna*. Laboratorio di storia, vol. 6, ed. O. Niccoli, 210–30. Florence, 1993.

———. "Male Homosexuality and Its Regulation in Late-Medieval Florence." Ph.D. diss., State University of New York at Binghamton. 1990.

———. "Sodomites in Fifteenth-Century Tuscany: The Views of Bernardino of Siena." In *The Pursuit of Sodomy: Male Homosexuality in Renaissance and Enlightenment Europe*, ed. K. Gerard and G. Hekma, 7–31. New York, 1989.

Rollinson, D. "Property, Ideology and Popular Culture in a Gloucestershire Village, 1660–1740." *Past & Present* 93 (1981): 70–97.

Romano, D. "Aspects of Patronage in Fifteenth- and Sixteenth-Century Venice." *Renaissance Quarterly* 46 (1993): 712–33.

———. "Gender and the Urban Geography of Renaissance Venice." *Journal of Social History* 23 (1989): 339–53.

Ross, J. B. "The Middle-Class Child in Urban Italy, Fourteenth to Early Sixteenth Century." In *The History of Childhood*, ed. L. de Mause, 183–228. New York, 1974.

Rossiaud, J. *La prostituzione nel medioevo*. Bari, 1984.

Roth, C. *The Last Florentine Republic*. London, 1925.

Rubinstein, N. *The Government of Florence Under the Medici, 1434–1494*. Oxford, 1966.

———. "Politics and Constitution in Florence at the End of the Fifteenth Century." In *Italian Renaissance Studies*, ed. E. F. Jacob, 148–83. London, 1960.

———. "I primi anni del Consiglio Maggiore di Firenze (1494–1499)." *Archivio storico italiano* 112 (1954): 151–94, 321–47.

Ruggiero, G. *The Boundaries of Eros: Sex Crime and Sexuality in Renaissance Venice*. New York, 1985.

———. "Sessualità e sacrilegio." *Studi storici* 22 (1981): 751–65.

Saslow, J. M. *Ganymede in the Renaissance: Homosexuality in Art and Society*. New Haven, 1986.

———. "Homosexuality in the Renaissance: Behavior, Identity, and Artistic Expression." In *Hidden from History: Reclaiming the Gay and Lesbian Past*, ed. M. B. Duberman, M. Vicinus, and G. Chauncey, Jr., 90–105. New York, 1989.

Scarabello, G. "Devianza sessuale ed interventi di giustizia a Venezia nella prima metà del XVI secolo." In *Tiziano e Venezia,* Atti del Convegno Internazionale di Studi, Venezia 1977, 75–84. Vicenza, 1980.

Schneider, L. "Donatello's Bronze *David*." *Art Bulletin* 55 (1973): 213–16.

———. "More on Donatello's Bronze *David*." *Gazzette des Beaux-Arts*, 6th ser., 94 (1979): 48.

Schnitzer. J. *Savonarola*. 2 vols. Milan, 1931.

Sherr, R. "A Canon, a Choirboy, and Homosexuality in Late Sixteenth-Century Italy: A Case Study." *Journal of Homosexuality* 21, no. 3 (1991): 1–22.

Smith, A. K. "Fraudomy: Reading Sexuality and Politics in Burchiello." In *Queering the Renaissance*, ed. J. Goldberg, 84–106. Durham, N.C., 1994.

Stephens. J. *The Fall of the Florentine Republic, 1512–1530*. Oxford, 1983.

Sterns, L. I. *The Criminal Law System of Medieval and Renaissance Florence*. Baltimore, 1994.

Symonds, J. A. *Renaissance in Italy*. 7 vols. London, 1875–1886, 1904–1908.

Tamassia, N. *La famiglia italiana nei secoli decimoquinto e decimosesto*. Naples, 1910. Reprint. Rome, 1971.

Tiger, L. *Men in Groups*. 2d. ed. New York, 1984.

Toscan, J. *Le Carnaval du langage: Le lexique érotique des poètes de l'équivoque de Burchiello à Marino (XVe–XVIIe siècles)*. 4 vols. Lille, 1981.

Toscani, B., ed. *Lorenzo de' Medici: New Perspectives*. New York, 1993.

Trexler, R. "Le Célibat à la fin du Moyen Age: Les religieuses à Florence." *Annales, E.S.C.* 27 (1972): 1329–50.

———. "*Correre la terra*: Collective Insults in the Late Middle Ages." *Mélanges de l'École française de Rome* 96 (1984): 848–72.

———. "De la ville à la Cour: La déraison à Florence durant la République et la Grand Duché." In *Le Charivari*, ed. J. Le Goff and J.-C. Schmitt, 165–76. Paris, 1981.

———. "The Episcopal Constitutions of Antoninus of Florence." *Quellen und Forschungen aus italienischen Archiven und Bibliotheken* 59 (1979): 244–72.

———. "The Foundlings of Florence, 1395–1495." *History of Childhood Quarterly* 1 (1973–1974): 259–84.

———. "Neighbors and Comrades: The Revolutionaries of Florence, 1378." *Social Analysis* 14 (1983): 53–106.

———. "La Prostitution florentine au XVe siècle: Patronages et clientèles." *Annales, E.S.C.* 36 (1981): 983–1015.

———. *Public Life in Renaissance Florence*. New York, 1980.

———. "Ritual Behavior in Renaissance Florence: The Setting." *Medievalia et Humanistica*, n.s., 4 (1973): 125–44.

———. "Ritual in Florence: Adolescence and Salvation in the Renaissance." In *The Pursuit of Holiness in Late Medieval and Renaissance Religion*, ed. C. Trinkaus and H. Oberman, 200–264. Leiden. 1974.

———. *Sex and Conquest: Gendered Violence, Political Order, and the European Conquest of the Americas*. Cambridge, 1995; Ithaca, 1995.

———. *The Spiritual Power: Republican Florence Under Interdict*. Leiden, 1974.

Trumbach, R. "The Birth of the Queen: Sodomy and the Emergence of Gender Equality in Modern Culture, 1660–1750." In *Hidden from History: Reclaiming the Gay and Lesbian Past*, ed. M. B. Duberman, M. Vicinus, and G. Chauncey, Jr., 129–40. New York, 1989.

———. "Gender and the Homosexual Role in Modern Western Culture: The 18th and 19th Centuries Compared." In *Homosexuality, Which Homosexuality?* 149–69. Amsterdam and London, 1989.

———. "London's Sodomites: Homosexual Behavior and Western Culture in the 18th Century." *Journal of Social History* 11 (1977): 1–33.

———. Review of *The Boundaries of Eros: Sex Crime and Sexuality in Renaissance Venice*, by G. Ruggiero. In *The Pursuit of Sodomy: Male Homosexuality in Renaissance and Enlightenment Europe*, ed. K. Gerard and G. Hekma, 506–10. New York, 1989.

———. "Sodomitical Subcultures, Sodomitical Roles, and the Gender Revolution of the Eighteenth Century: The Recent Historiography." *Eighteenth Century Life* 9, n.s., 3 (1985): 109–21.

Van der Meer, T. "The Persecutions of Sodomites in Eighteenth-Century Amsterdam: Changing Perceptions of Sodomy." In *The Pursuit of Sodomy: Male Homosexuality in Renaissance and Enlightenment Europe*, ed. K. Gerard and G. Hekma, 263–307. New York, 1989.

Veyne, P. "L'Homosexualité à Rome." *Communications* 35 (1982): 26–33.

Villari, P. *La storia di Girolamo Savonarola e de' suoi tempi.* 2 vols. Florence, 1859, 1861.

Viti, P., ed. "Studi su Lorenzo dei Medici e il secolo XV" [special issue]. *Archivio storico italiano* 150 (1992).

Warburg, A. *Bildniskunst und florentinisches Bürgertum.* Vol. 1: *Domenico Ghirlandaio in Santa Trinita: Die Bildnisse des Lorenzo de' Medici und seiner Angehörigen.* Leipzig, [1901].

Weeks, J. *Sex, Politics and Society: The Regulation of Sexuality Since 1800.* London and New York, 1981.

Weinstein, D. "Hagiography, Demonology, Biography: Savonarola Studies Today." *Journal of Modern History* 63 (1991): 483–503.

———. *Savonarola and Florence: Prophecy and Patriotism in the Renaissance.* Princeton, 1970.

Weissman, R. *Ritual Brotherhood in Renaissance Florence.* New York, 1982.

———. "Taking Patronage Seriously: Mediterranean Values and Renaissance Society." In *Patronage, Art, and Society in Renaissance Italy*, ed. F. W. Kent and P. Simons, with J. C. Eade, 25–45. Oxford, 1987.

Whitehead, H. "The Bow and the Burden Strap: A New Look at Institutionalized Homosexuality in Native North America." In *Sexual Meanings: The Cultural Construction of Gender and Sexuality*, ed. S. B. Ortner and H. Whitehead, 80–115. Cambridge, 1981.

Williams, C. "Homosexuality and the Roman Man: A Study of the Cultural Construction of Sexuality." Ph.D. diss., Yale University. 1992.

Williams, W. *The Spirit and the Flesh: Sexual Diversity in American Indian Culture.* Boston, 1986.

Winkler, J. *The Constraints of Desire: The Anthropology of Sex and Gender in Ancient Greece.* New York, 1990.

Witt, R. "Florentine Politics and the Ruling Class, 1382–1407." *Journal of Medieval and Renaissance Studies* 6 (1976): 243–67.

Zazzu, G. N. "Prostituzione e moralità pubblica nella Genova del '400." *Studi genuensi*, n.s., 5 (1987): 45–67.

Zorzi, A. *L'amministrazione della giustizia penale nella Repubblica fiorentina: Aspetti e problemi.* Florence, 1988.

———. "Contrôle social, ordre public et répression judiciaire à Florence à l'époque communale: Éléments et problèmes." *Annales, E.S.C.* 45 (1990): 1169–88.

———. "I fiorentini e gli uffici pubblici nel primo Quattrocento: Concorrenza, abusi, illegalità." *Quaderni storici* 66 (1987): 725–51.

———. "Rituali di violenza giovanile nelle società urbane del tardo Medioevo." In *Infanzie: Funzioni di un gruppo liminale dal mondo classico all'Età moderna.* Laboratorio di storia, vol. 6, ed. O. Niccoli, 185–209. Florence, 1993.

Index